Also by Reggie Marra

Enough with the…Talking Points:
Doing More Good than Harm in Conversation

Killing America: Our United States of Ignorance,
Fear, Bigotry, Violence and Greed (poetry)

And Now, Still: Grave & Goofy Poems (poetry)

Coaching and Healing:
Transcending the Illness Narrative (co-author)

This Open Eye: Seeing What We Do (poetry)

Living Poems, Writing Lives:
Spirit, Self and the Art of Poetry

Who Lives Better Than We Do? (poetry)

The Quality of Effort: Integrity in Sport and Life
for Student-Athletes, Parents and Coaches

"Having worked as a psychologist for more than 35 years, I have spent a great amount of time in the shadow of the human psyche. I can attest that in order to heal from the possession of the shadow we must do the archeological work of uncovering all aspects and integrating even the most demonic energies. Not a fun task, and as Grandpa Jung said, 'self-discovery is never a pleasant task.' Marra is doing the collective archeology in his book as he explores how Collective shadow multiplies the power of personal shadow exponentially. Not integrating shadow is not an option, as we stand at the edge of the abyss looking down at the reflection of the demonic that is us. Clergy has failed in leading us on this treacherous journey. The creators of the new path are the dreamers, poets, storytellers and all who follow an ancient path of relationship with our earth. Marra is giving us the diagnosis and some of the treatment plan we need if we are to survive even into the near future. Let this poet, Reggie Marra, clear a new path into a new way of being as we integrate and befriend our personal and collective shadow."

—Eduardo Duran (Tiospaye Ta Woapiye Wicasa), Ph.D.
Vietnam veteran, author of *Healing the Soul Wound:*
Trauma-Informed Counseling for Indigenous Communities

"*Healing America's Narratives* bears blunt, bold, eloquent witness to the hidden assumptions and attitudes that have shaped America's history and psychology. Reggie Marra achieves something extraordinary here: he clarifies difficult concepts and shines unfaltering light on painful truths, yet he never loses sight of the voices, ideals, and possibilities that have been, and continue to be, dedicated to healing and wholeness. Stunning, insightful, intelligent, and fearless, this book deserves a place among the great narratives of the American psyche."

—Trebbe Johnson, author of *Radical Joy for Hard Times: Finding*
Meaning and Making Beauty in Earth's Broken Places

"In *Healing America's Narratives,* Reggie Marra offers compelling and extensive historical research regarding the deep trauma and dysfunction of which our current social fabric is woven. In a conversational tone that expresses welcome, humor, courage, and a non-judgmental attitude, he invites the reader to 'wake up, grow up, clean up, show up' as an everyday practice of individual and collective listening, learning, and working for the good of all. This litany beckons us to commit our best efforts as we explore faultlines, deconstruct imposed barriers, and build more inclusive platforms of support.

"Marra writes, 'The process of uncovering, recognizing, owning, and integrating Shadow is discomfiting at best, horrifying at worst, and inevitably necessary for the health of any individual, organization, nation, or species.' He emphasizes that we stand to receive countless gifts in working to heal personal, collective, and ancestral Dis-ease. Aspects of Shadow into which Marra delves include violence against women, Native Americans, and people of African descent; destruction of the environment; and atrocities of war in Vietnam and Iraq.

"Acknowledging that many more civil rights challenges exist, the author presents connections and angles that have the potential to inspire any person – regardless of history, identity, and experience – to consider the larger picture in a new or shifted way.

"*Healing America's Narratives* posits that we are all composed of intertwining stories, that these stories are made of basic life energy, and that we have the ability to learn and apply healing skills in navigating and transforming the full range of human understanding. Marra invokes the spirit of John Lewis's 'Beloved Community' in affirming that we have something valuable to learn from those with whom we disagree. No matter where a conversation begins, Marra asserts, it is possible through active and empathetic listening to promote the next genuine connection.

"In the spirit of kindness, hope, and tenacity, Reggie Marra reminds us that regardless of the particular issues we face, each and every one of us needs and deserves the healing that arises from this essential work of becoming more fully human."

—Janet E. Aalfs, author of
What the Dead Want Me to Know

"In this courageous, compassionate, wise, and visionary wake-up call, Reggie Marra asks some very deep and challenging questions about who we are as a nation, questions that all Americans would be asking if we were brave enough to look in our collective mirror. His socially, politically, and psychologically sophisticated answers are both shocking and self-evident, both outrageous and kind, both arresting and liberating.

"An exceptionally well-written and readable book, *Healing America's Narratives* goes right to the heart and to the root of what ails our nation … and to what just might enable us to build a better world, a life-enhancing society. Brilliant. Thoroughly researched and referenced. A tour de force. Read it."

—Bill Plotkin, Ph.D.
author of *Soulcraft* and *The Journey of Soul Initiation*

"Throughout his eloquent and thorough exploration of America's collective Shadow, Reggie Marra embraces 'truth' both as evidence-based and as an ongoing conversation about things that matter. Deeply engaging both the political lens of our collective historical and current events, as well as the psychological lens of our individual inner terrain, the lingering effect of this book fosters hope and proactively embraces the possibility of a radical shift in how humans interrelate, even—and especially—while some of the worst traits of our humanity are so dismally on display."

—Bridgit Dengel Gaspard, author of
The Final 8th: Enlist Your Inner Selves to Accomplish Your Goals

"Outraged yet hopeful, sweeping in its conclusions…Marra's impassioned treatise calls for a national effort to face and 'integrate' the collective 'shadow' of the United States …. for Americans to face themselves and our past, acknowledging the darkness and daring to do better, in both personal and political spheres. To lay out a path, Marra offers pained, unstinting examinations of historical American failings (the ongoing subjugation of women and Black Americans; the betrayal of Native Americans; the last half century's worth of elective wars), all times and tendencies in which Shadow has prevailed…. In precise, inviting prose, Marra urges readers to look with clear eyes at ourselves. He makes clear throughout that he's one of us rather than some presumed authority, putting in the work to understand himself and his nation…. This call for Americans to face their 'collective shadow' will thrill readers eager for compassionate change."

—*Booklife*

"*Healing America's Narratives* is brilliant at so many levels. Reggie Marra takes the history of America—the good, the bad, and the in-between—and turns it into a guide for transforming the heart and mind, not just for Americans, but for anyone interested in the radical transformation of body, mind, and spirit. His prose, both inspiring and engaging, invites us to embrace a new narrative that discerns among cultural givens and other means that mold us. Reading this book feels like a rehearsal for new ways of being in the world. It is a manual on becoming fully human and embracing love as the universal language it is.

"Marra brings voices together, rightening history with unprecedented accuracy. In his voice we find a confluence of narratives from opposite, alienated, privileged, unprivileged, and marginalized perspectives—balanced with gender, race, ideological and social strata representations. This book is actually a summit about what we can hope is the end of an era. Reading it requires us to redefine history, healing, shadow, and love. In the author's hands, history is a living source of healing. Savvy readers will walk away feeling affirmed that from ill-told history, new vistas arise from which to tell whole new personal and collective stories that heal.

"The extensive research supports testimony that transcends simple abstractions about justice or rightness, and embraces the living flesh of spirit and the unambiguous language of universal love. The final two chapters both invite and gently coerce the reader to show up, elegantly pick up the scraps, and put the world back into a cohesive whole in which the masculine and feminine dance as they are meant to dance."

—Marianela Medrano, Ph.D.
author of *Rooting: Selected Bilingual Poems*

"An educator's vision for healing America's traumatic past and politically fractured present.... the book is optimistic in tone, emphasizing hope in the possibility of national healing....Marra is well versed in classical literature, philosophy and history.... a sophisticated presentation of critical theory, U.S. history and philosophy, the book carefully balances nuance with accessibility and practical application.... A convincing, if occasionally unwieldy, guidebook for a better future."

—*Kirkus Reviews*

Healing America's Narratives

The Feminine, the Masculine,
& Our Collective National Shadow

Becoming More Fully Human

REGGIE MARRA

From the Heart Press

2022 From the Heart Press First Edition
https://healingamericasnarratives.com/

Healing America's narratives: the feminine, the masculine, & our collective national shadow / Reggie Marra

ISBN: 979-8-9862690-2-3 (hardcover)
ISBN: 979-8-9862690-0-9 (trade paper)
ISBN: 979-8-9862690-1-6 (Kindle)

Library of Congress Control Number: 2022909654

The author gratefully acknowledges the following author for permission to reprint previously published material.

Doug Anderson, "The Mass Graves at Huè," "Letting Go," and "Same Old" from *Horse Medicine,* (New York: Barrow Street, 2015). Copyright © 2015 by Doug Anderson. "Free Fire Zone" and "Mine" from *The Moon Reflected Fire,* (Cambridge MA: Alice James, 1994). Copyright © 1994 by Doug Anderson. Reprinted with permission of the author.

For Christine Washington, the Eufemia and Luna
families that nurtured her, and the Washington
family that she and Caliph nurtured

And in memory of Black Kettle, Standing Bear,
John Lewis, Ruth Bader Ginsberg, and
Thich Nhat Hanh, who, despite diverse
cultural givens and chosen trajectories, met on the path
towards peace and equality for all

"I don't believe there is any problem of American politics and American public life which is more significant today than the pervasive civic ignorance of the Constitution of the United States and the structure of government....an ignorant people can never remain a free people. Democracy cannot survive too much ignorance.

....

"I don't worry about losing republican government in the United States because I'm afraid of a foreign invasion. I don't worry about it because I think there is going to be a coup by the military as has happened in some other places. What I worry about is that when problems are not addressed, people will not know who is responsible. And when the problems get bad enough, as they might do, for example, with another serious terrorist attack, as they might do with another financial meltdown, some one person will come forward and say, 'Give me total power and I will solve this problem.' That is how the Roman republic fell. Augustus became emperor not because he arrested the Roman senate. He became emperor because he promised he would solve problems that were not being solved.

"If we know who is responsible, I have enough faith in the American people to demand performance from those responsible. If we don't know, we will stay away from the polls. We will not demand it. And the day will come when somebody will come forward and we and the government will in effect say, 'take the ball and run with it. Do what you have to do.' That is the way democracy dies. And if something is not done to improve the level of civic knowledge, that is what you should worry about at night."

- David Souter, Retired U. S. Supreme Court Justice, from an interview
at the University of New Hampshire Law School, September 14, 2012[1]

CONTENTS

What better time than right now to encounter a book that both nudges and guides us out of the cynicism and denial that enshrouds the American body politic? *Healing America's Narratives: The Feminine, the Masculine, & Our Collective National Shadow* is such a book – a soulful encounter. From its beginning pages to the final footnotes, Reggie Marra offers the possibility that troubling truths may also be a healing balm. In so doing, he unravels the unbroken and interlaced threads of feral deceit and abusive power from the 17th century to the 21st century: savagery that belies cherished American creeds of innocence, equality, and exceptionalism. That said, this book is no brutish screed; it is instead an aching love story to an America capable of healing through an evolving imagination of human meaning and possibility.

From the outset, Marra insists on clarity—of standpoint, purpose, and language. He begins by situating himself in the "cultural givens" (some quite humorous) that shaped his becoming as a second-generation Italian-American male human. From that point, he grounds his thesis in a precise explanation of Shadow, removing it from the domain of esoteric jargon where it is little understood and from the muddled appropriations of popular culture. Hence, he reveals Shadow as lived experience manifest through interactions as mundane as short-lived interpersonal encounters, and as significant as presidential politics and US military operations. Using deep history, literary allusions, insights from psychological theory, and an occasional dose of good humor, Marra is unflinching in his insistence that truth counts. He chafes at the use of euphemisms to contaminate truth, as in: *"The arrival of Europeans in North America opened a new chapter in the history of Native peoples."* Similarly, he takes on the hypocrisy of academic scholars who, whether in a quest for tenure or media attention for a loudmouth, denounce critical and comprehensive analysis of history and culture as bad for marginalized citizens.

To read this book is to live the political as personal. Reggie Marra invites us into Shadow for our personal and collective evolution. And he does so as a co-journeyer, not a pedant. There may be moments when the searing revelations might elicit a *'say it ain't so'* reaction and cause you to step away, which is fine, but for God's sake come back. There are plenty of opportunities for reflective practice, but the book is not a workshop and won't be apprehended by cognitive intelligences alone. It unearths the history that lives in us; it invites us to open our bodies to edifying truths. Read the book; then read it again and again.

—Maureen Walker, Ph.D.
author of *When Getting Along Is Not Enough:*
Reconstructing Race in Our Lives and Relationships

*In what games are you attempting to limit the players in
order to win and end play, and in what games are you
attempting to invite players and keep the game going?*[1]

IN EARLY SEPTEMBER 2016, AFTER the Republican party had
chosen their presidential candidate, I wrote an online essay[2]
that explored his embodiment of the "collective American
Shadow." A week or so before the 2018 midterm elections, I
revisited and updated[3] the original piece with an abundance of
new evidence to support this embodiment. What you're
reading now contains the essence and integration of those
2016 and 2018 pieces along with a larger historical perspective
and updates that continue to emerge as this book goes to press.

Simply put, the words and actions of the 2016 Republican
candidate, who became the 45th President of the United States,
embody the collective Shadow of the United States of
America—those undesirable beliefs and traits that we, as a
nation, see "out there" in others and deny in ourselves. While
this writing focuses on his time as the Republican candidate
and president, it is clear that he has embodied and continues
to embody this Shadow throughout his public life. His access
to the bully pulpit and titular authority that the White House
provided enabled him to invite to the surface—into the
mainstream—these elements of our culture that we, as citizens

of the United States, prefer to deny and to see only in other countries, cultures, political parties or neighborhoods.

That said, this book concerns itself not with this one guy, but with our collective American Shadow—what it is, how it manifests, and what we might be able to do with and about it if we have the will, stomach, and heart to do the work. The 45th president's aberrant and often abhorrent behavior is simply a convenient, glaring symptom of our collective Shadow, which carries the disowned or repressed aspects or traits of an individual or group that the individual or group doesn't recognize in itself and unknowingly tends to project onto to others—whether or not the trait is considered positive or negative, and whether or not the others actually embody the projected trait. Sometimes they do; sometimes they don't.[4]

His embodiment of these Shadow elements invites them to surface and become increasingly visible, and we, the people, consequently are given the opportunity to choose to better recognize, own, and integrate them. Through such integration, we become more whole in our shared movement toward a more perfect union. The process of uncovering, recognizing, owning, and integrating Shadow is discomfiting at best, horrifying at worst, and inevitably necessary for the health of any individual, organization, nation, or species.

Said differently, the damage Donald Trump has done and continues to do through his self-centered ignorance, arrogance, manipulation, and dishonesty gives Americans and others the gift of a clear look into the worst of ourselves in one handy musculoskeletal frame. This gift, if we are to benefit from it, is one we must unwrap and own together. Our national Shadow, of course, remains even in his absence from the White House. He, those who tolerate, enable, or overtly support him, and those who oppose him while demonizing all of his supporters are all symptoms of the deeper, more insidious problems that are at the core of this book.

The more-or-less easily discernible elements of the collective Shadow of the United States include, but are not necessarily limited to, *ignorance, arrogance, fear, bigotry, violence, greed, excess, bullying,* and *untrustworthiness,* which often manifests as *betrayal.* Sometimes two or more of these elements overlap and feed on each other. In Chapter Two, we'll define how each of these words is used in this volume.

The following chapters will also present more detail about what Shadow is and is not. They will briefly reflect on five specific events and issues in American history and current events, and they will explore the words and behaviors of the 45th president—all in light of the Shadow elements mentioned above. The closing pages consider how we, as individuals, communities, states, and a nation, might increasingly recognize, own, and integrate our collective Shadow, and outline the benefits of so doing—should we be willing to do the work required.

PART I—ME, AND MY SHADOW—provides context and establishes tone by offering my perspective and by clarifying what the word *Shadow* means and doesn't mean as it's used in the book.

Chapter One, in the tradition of an *apologia,* acknowledges my point of view—the perspective through which the writing emerges, as far as I can tell. In presenting my "cultural givens"—those beliefs and values I received through the time, place and people of my birth—my education, my experiences, and my ongoing intentional development as an adult, I invite you, gentle reader, through my example, to explore your own "givens" and development. This chapter makes clear that the book does not randomly convey some general (or generic) "truth" but rather presents an argument that emerges through a very specific view of the world, as all arguments do.

Chapter Two provides an introduction to the basic elements of Shadow. As Jung used the term, Shadow refers to that which we do not recognize or own in ourselves, and which we often project onto others. This is differentiated from another use of the word shadow that often refers to the "dark" or negative aspects of ourselves that we do not like. Again, as used in this book, Shadow refers to that which I (or we) see in you (or them), but not in myself or ourselves. Shadow sees the evil "out there" but not "in here." Finally, although the book focuses on the negative aspects of American Shadow, Shadow, be it individual or collective, is not necessarily negative.

In Part II—The Evil Out There—we explore the presence of the collective American Shadow through five narratives: the fear of the feminine and the subjugation of women; the removal, betrayal, and slaughter of Native Americans; slavery, Reconstruction, Jim Crow, lynching, civil rights, and the African-American experience; the Vietnam War; and the invasions in 2001 of Afghanistan and in 2003 of Iraq. Each chapter explores the denial and projection of specific disowned traits onto various *others*.

Chapter Three recognizes women's experiences, roles (or lack thereof), and influence in the founding and unfolding of the United States (and in everything else in history). Though Mary Wollstonecraft did not make the Atlantic crossing, her 1792 *A Vindication of the Rights of Woman: with Strictures on Political and Moral Subjects* set the tone in Great Britain and in the new United States for a closer look at the then-current cultural givens concerning women's roles and expectations. In addition to the political, social, and private events and changes that follow—from Seneca Falls in 1848 to the 19th Amendment in 1920 to the ongoing resistance to passing an Equal Rights Amendment that could ensure educational, employment, and salary parity—we also explore and clarify what we mean by *woman, man, feminine* and *masculine,* and we provide evidence that *unhealthy* masculine tendencies, reinforced by fear of the *healthy* feminine, drive the negative aspects of the collective American Shadow

In Chapter Four we acknowledge the various European arrivals on what are now known as North, South, and Central America and the islands of the Caribbean. We focus on those arrivals on the portion of North America now known as the United States—beginning with the pre-1776 Dutch, English, and French competitions for various pieces of the northeast, and then turning to the post-American Revolution trajectory of skirmishes, wars, thefts, treaties, betrayals, removals, and attempts to assimilate that characterizes the relationships among diverse Native American Nations and the United States. This chapter's exploration of ignorance, arrogance, greed, excess, violence, and untrustworthiness takes a close look at the 1830s period of "Indian removal" and examines the ramifications of the Fort Laramie Treaties of 1851 and 1868. It also acknowledges and reflects upon the subsequent breaking of those agreements by the government and the people of the United States.

In Chapter Five, we again begin with the Europeans—first acknowledging the kidnapping of Africans who were shipped to the "New World" and then exploring pre- and post-American Revolution enslavement, the American Civil War, Reconstruction, Jim Crow, the U. S. civil rights movement and the backlash against it, ongoing attempts, primarily but not only in former slave states, to disenfranchise black voters, and the violence by some in law enforcement against unarmed people of color. Finally, this chapter acknowledges the cumulative impact of this history on twenty-first-century American society. We acknowledge here both the progress that has been made and the work that remains to be done. Included in this acknowledgment are the debates around critical race theory and antiracism.

Chapter Six begins with the end of World War II and the movement into the Cold War, which together provided rich soil for the cross-fertilization of ignorance, arrogance, fear, greed, and violence in the United States. Five presidential administrations, beginning with Truman in 1945 and ending with Nixon thirty years later, refused to acknowledge Ho Chi Minh's post-World War II plea for help, financed as much as 80% of France's failed military efforts to retain its colonial power in Vietnam, refused to sign the 1954 Geneva Agreements intended to end the violence, helped prevent the 1956 Vietnamese national elections, regularly lied to the American public, and eventually spent billions of dollars, thousands of American lives, and millions of Vietnamese lives in a failed attempt to prevent the Vietnamese people from engaging in self-determination—expenditures that tore at the hearts of America and Vietnam.

Chapter Seven explores the similarities and differences between the Vietnam conflict and the U. S. invasions of Afghanistan and Iraq. Despite claims from both political and military leaders concerning lessons learned from Vietnam, the Bush administration preemptively invaded Iraq in March 2003—first under the pretense of removing weapons of mass destruction and then under the pretense of removing Saddam Hussein, whom the U.S. had armed and financed in an earlier war against Iran. Removing Saddam ostensibly supported freedom for the Iraqi people. Six weeks after the 2003 invasion began, President Bush stood under a "Mission Accomplished" banner on an aircraft carrier and declared that the United States and its allies had prevailed. And yet, more than 4,000 U.S. military personnel would die in Iraq after that declaration. The war in Afghanistan went on for twenty years— including ten years beyond the killing of Osama bin Laden. Despite significant differences in some details, the invasions of Afghanistan and Iraq are characterized by similarities to

Vietnam, not the least of which are the lies told to the public, the lack of clear, justifiable reasons for being and/or staying there, and the loss of one human life, millions of times—while making billions in profits for defense contractors.

Chapter Eight moves beyond the specific narratives developed in chapters three through seven and identifies additional examples of our uniquely American collective Shadow's manifestation. These examples include care of the planet itself (which, if not addressed, renders the rest of the discussion moot), the prevalence of depression, anxiety, and suicide; unprecedented gun violence; access to affordable health care; biases and violence against American citizens perceived as "other," including those who appear to be from Asia, the Middle East, and Spanish-speaking Caribbean, Central or South American countries, as well as those whose sexual orientation or identity is perceived as other than cisgender and heterosexual. In each case, we see in various degrees the same foundational elements explored in detail regarding women, Native Americans, slavery and African Americans, Vietnam, Iraq, and Afghanistan—ignorance, arrogance, fear, bigotry, violence, greed, excess, untrustworthiness and bullying.

Chapter Nine proposes that bullying is the Shadow element most consistently manifested—both leading to and resulting from the other elements. Whether bullying physically, emotionally, intellectually, financially, politically, or in some combination of these, the bully is often ignorant, arrogant, violent, afraid, and untrustworthy, and sometimes motivated by greed or excess. This chapter further clarifies the underlying bullying perspective in the histories and current events that were explored in chapters three through eight. It also takes a close look at how the bully shows up on all sides of contemporary "woke" and "cancel culture" debates.

Chapter Ten presents the case that 1) the 2016 Republican presidential candidate who became the 45th President of the United States embodies all of the collective Shadow elements explored thus far; 2) his words and actions, before, during, and after his presidency invite, allow, and embolden those Americans who also embody these elements to become increasingly visible and outspoken; and 3) his so doing unwittingly provides a gift to those Americans who are authentically inclined to begin the work of recognizing, owning, and integrating their own individual Shadows and our collective national Shadow. The lasting gift of this integration is a movement toward healing our diverse American narratives.

In Part III—Prospects & Possibilities for Healing—we explore some strategies, tactics, practices, and ways of being in the world that can help us on the path of realizing the "promise" of this book's title and subtitle.

Chapter Eleven begins with the body and the breath as essential elements of the healing process. It then offers and explores individual, collective, contemporary, and ancient wisdom, practices, and resources for such healing. The offering and exploration arise through five questions and two statements: Who am I really? Everything is a story. What's my impact and what impacts me? What am I not seeing or not understanding? Who are my people? I am going to die. How am I in relationship with all of this?

The chapter implicates readers and encourages them to shine the light of awareness first on their own Shadow and then on their country's Shadow by exploring each question and statement.

Chapter Twelve, a complement to Chapter One, reflects briefly on my cultural givens, my ongoing development, and the integration of my "view from here," and invites readers to embrace their own integration toward an inevitable engagement with love.

Appendix I juxtaposes Dwight Eisenhower's post-World War II precepts with lessons learned and not learned from Robert McNamara's post-Vietnam War reflections and with ongoing reports from the office of the Special Inspector General for Afghanistan Reconstruction (SIGAR).

Appendix II depicts, through poetry, the normalization of violence in American society—both in terms of relentless military engagement and in unprecedented civilian violence, especially, but not only, with firearms.

Appendix III provides a synopsis of my 2020 volume, *Enough with the Talking Points,* with the aim of embodying the book's subtitle, *doing more good than harm in conversation.* The synopsis is followed by an excerpt of a step-by-step application of the book's recommendations to a "real-life" social media thread.

IF THIS INTRODUCTION LEADS YOU to feel uncomfortable or angry—perhaps because you imagine that the ideas herein might be "un-American" or "unpatriotic," or, as we'll explore below, conveniently "Marxist," "socialist," or "leftist," I admit that I share your discomfort and anger, but perhaps for different reasons. Making believe that our history and our current events are *not* characterized by these traits, along with many other good traits, is, in fact, un-American and un-patriotic, especially if we want to continue growing toward a more perfect union in which *every one of us* has access to equal protection of the laws. And while our founders spoke of law as a means toward the ends of life, liberty, and the pursuit of happiness, I, embracing the benefits of two-hundred-plus years of our unique experiment, would argue that care, compassion, empathy, community, mercy, and love, among other traits and qualities, are equally important ends.

That Donald Trump spent four years in the White House, and that most Republicans in Congress are afraid of him, while problematic, is not the essential problem. The essential problem, which is considerably more complex, is that more than seventy million Americans were willing to give him four more years, and some of them, at his beckoning, vandalized the U. S. Capitol and attempted to overturn the 2020 election and prevent the peaceful transfer of power that lies at the heart of our democracy. We'll say more about the complexities of this problem in the coming chapters.

Finally, the questions that appear at the beginning of this Introduction and of all subsequent chapters except Chapter Two were inspired by James P. Carse's 1986 book, *Finite and Infinite Games: A Vision of Life as Play and Possibility*. For Carse, a finite game is played with a limited number of players whose intentions are to win and bring the game to an end; an infinite game is played by an unlimited number of players whose intentions are to invite more players to play and to keep the game going.

The pages that follow beckon us to acknowledge the limitations of our finite wins and losses, and to embrace an infinite game that allows and invites all of us to continue to play.

PART I

ME, AND MY SHADOW

Cultural Givens & the View from Here

*What boundaries do the limits of your vision create,
and how might you expand what you see?*[1]

IT USED TO BE THAT authors, to the best of their abilities, would develop and identify their most accurate sense of their own views, positions, and identities as a self-reflective and honest prelude to their writing. In the best of times, this was done with integrity in an attempt to be transparent about themselves and the writing that would emerge from their perspectives. This process was not a form of self-aggrandizement, and it was not offered in an other-criticizing manner. I intend to honor that approach here.

As with any written statement, what follows is filtered through the author's worldview—in this case, mine. It is the result of my experiences, beliefs, values, relationships, aspirations, and ongoing development. It also includes those aspects of myself of which I'm not yet aware—my own individual Shadow. (More about this in Chapter Two). My current worldview, at its best, allows me to see every human being on the planet as an equal—not in terms of physiology, talents, particular aspirations, or what I'll refer to as "cultural givens," but in terms of our common humanity, in terms of each of us being a member of the human species, *Homo sapiens*. This view is referred to by some as "world-centric" or "global," in the most positive sense of those words. My view also embraces the importance of paradox for twenty-first-century adults. It allows me to recognize—in fact it *demands* that I recognize—apparently contradictory facts and opinions and to understand them as being simultaneously true.

At its worst, my worldview can be ego- or group-centric—in an unhealthy sense of being certain or "knowing" that I am, or my particular group is, good and right, and everyone else or all the other groups are bad and wrong. Perhaps this sounds familiar, since from birth and throughout our earliest years, each of us is provided with a set of "cultural givens"—direct experiences of and beliefs about the world that our family of origin holds to be true. These experiences and beliefs include everything from ethnicity to local community to religious belief (or lack thereof) to national citizenship to our parents' personalities to geography, climate, and year of birth.[2]

It is possible to embrace these cultural givens and live our lives without ever questioning them. It is also possible, and advisable, from the perspective of physical, emotional, mental, and spiritual health, to embrace these givens early on and then, most commonly in adolescence and beyond but sometimes earlier, to reflect on them, challenge them, and see how they hold up against our direct experience of life.

My current worldview is not the one I was given at birth and began to accept in early childhood. That worldview held that I was living in the greatest country in history and tended to favor being Italian-American, Catholic, and a New Yorker, among other characteristics. I'm not criticizing my own cultural givens or anyone else's. Criticizing our earliest views and ways of being in the world makes as much sense as criticizing an acorn for not yet being an oak or an infant for not being an adult. There is, however, a time to wake up, grow up, clean up, and show up. In waking up, we commit to seeing 'what is' through various states of consciousness. In growing up, we develop by seeking and taking increasingly inclusive, comprehensive, complex, and balanced perspectives. In cleaning up, we recognize, own, and integrate Shadow. And in showing up, we live authentically and help others. You get the idea. We'll touch on these "ups" along the way and say more about them in Chapter Eleven.

Simply put, a *world-centric* or *global* view, as used in the context of this writing, means that all humans deserve equal opportunity, freedom, and rights to the extent that their exercise of these does not infringe upon, sabotage, thwart, or in any other way negatively impact or limit these same rights for others. As used here, "all humans" should not need to be further clarified by "regardless of gender, skin pigmentation, race, ethnicity, sexual orientation" or any other quality. Yet, such clarification has been and still is necessary.

"All" is a pretty clear, simple and straightforward word in the twenty-first century, *and* it's important to note that the cultural givens of the former British colonists who wrote the seminal documents of our emerging nation carried meaning that, at the time, was different from current interpretations. When the writers of the Declaration of Independence wrote that "all men are created equal," their "all" did not include women or other men who were not both white and land-owners. It is equally important to note that one of the reasons that I am able to write this book now as I do, and that John Lewis, Ruth Bader Ginsburg, Barbara Lee, Alexandria Ocasio-Cortez, Barack Obama, Thurgood Marshall, Cory Booker, Clarence Thomas, and Kamala Harris, among many others, have served or are serving in the U.S. federal government is that cultural givens continue to evolve. Regardless of what I or anyone else thinks about the respective beliefs and worldviews of those named above, the people of the United States, through their elected officials, have seen fit since 1787 to expand on some of the limitations of the cultural givens of the British colonists who became our "founding fathers." Namely, we have translated the spirit, if not the letter, of "all men" and we continue to argue for the equality of "all humans." The expansion of these limitations is not complete, and is, and needs to be, ongoing.

The excerpted lines below, from my poem, "Broken Branches," capture a *world-centric* or *global* response that, in regard to the violent death of a human being, embraces this more inclusive, comprehensive understanding of "all":

> [Someone] who feels and speaks from
> exactly the same gut-wrenching heartache
> when the first-grader, the police officer, the
> black man, the soldier, yes,
> the human being
> dies a violent death
> in Bethesda or Baghdad,
> Singapore or Sandy Hook,
> San Bernardino or Saigon,
> Hiroshima or Harlem...[3]

More specifically, such a view celebrates and grieves human triumphs and disasters, regardless of the gender, race, skin pigmentation, orientation, age, ethnicity, or other characteristics of the individual or group being celebrated or grieved. It doesn't laugh at others' misfortunes, though it is able to laugh at itself and with others through the compassionate wisdom that comes from embracing the birth-to-death trajectory that we all share through our many extraordinarily unique stories and histories. This view captures both the conceptual simplicity and the complexity of manifesting what the late U.S. Congressman John Lewis (and others) referred to as the Beloved Community.[4]

In full transparency, I grew up in the greater New York City area, in Yonkers, and became aware of the man who would lose the 2020 U.S. presidential election when he was a young heir, purported millionaire, and real estate developer who began appearing in the New York tabloids and on local television stations. I learned that he was given millions of dollars as an inheritance, lived a privileged if not entirely happy life, and spoke with an heir's air of having accomplished something important each time he appeared in the news. His existence was, for the most part, irrelevant to my life at the time. Many Americans became aware of him decades later in his role as a reality television celebrity, roleplaying the fictional leader of fictional companies for entertainment purposes. Many of his television viewers, through these fictions, saw him as a successful, wealthy business executive and leader—a profile that he has repeatedly disproved throughout his life. In Chapter Ten, we'll explore his posturing as a presidential candidate, as president, and in his post-presidential attempts to remain relevant.[5]

Finally, I write this book aware that my intentional biases currently tend toward the strength that I find in *truth, truthfulness, clarity, courage, belonging, wisdom, compassion, justice, mercy, empathy, inclusiveness, balance, vulnerability,* and in the broadest sense of the word, *love.* I know that there are many worldviews besides my own—some narrower, some broader, some shallower, some deeper. The diversity available at the intersections of genetics, experience, ethnicity, ancestry, beliefs, values, development, interpretation, choice, and so on, is abundant. My desire is that leaders understand at least as much about the interiors and exteriors of the world—in the broadest, deepest sense of that word—as I do. Preferably more. Nothing in my experience of Donald Trump, except perhaps in the transactional areas of inheritance, real estate, tax strategies, personal branding, and projection, leads me to believe that he has such an understanding. I find no conclusive evidence that he understands the U.S. Constitution, any sacred scripture, the rule of law, other cultures, or any human being who was born into less privileged circumstances than his own.

For one concise, insightful commentary on leadership that sharply contrasts the behavior of the 45th president, consider retired General Stanley McChrystal's comments from October 1, 2020:

> I'm looking for a president that is humble enough to understand that they are a servant. I don't think we need a genius. I don't think we need a magician. We just need an honest person who's willing to listen. We need someone who will take in information, surround themselves with talented people, and lead the country as best they can.... If we pick for character, if we pick for values, we'll be best off....[6]

Chapter Ten provides evidence that the forty-fifth president's *exteriors*—his words and actions—informed by his *interiors*—his values, beliefs, and viewpoints—tend to be narrow, self-serving, and manipulative. They have nothing to do with "the greater good" or forming "a more perfect union." *Narrow, self-serving* and *manipulative* are not gratuitous labels, but rather are accurate, evidence-based descriptions of his words and behaviors, which we'll explore in some detail.

I ENCOURAGE YOU TO EXPLORE your own cultural givens as you read this book (and as you live the rest of your life). Toward that end, I'm providing below a selective summary of my own, along with some commentary. What's below is not the right or only way to make your way through this reflective process. It is a modeling of the type of information that may be helpful if you choose to explore your own cultural givens. The basic exploration would include the values, beliefs, and views that you were given; the behaviors that were required of you and/or that you observed; the nature of shared values in relationship with others; and the environments and systems, both natural and human-made, that were influential—including the time period and physical location(s) of your childhood years. My early years were generally "safe." I was cared for and sensed that I was loved, but it was clear that certain behavioral expectations accompanied the love and care. I grew up at a time during which teachers and parents often still hit kids for misbehaving, generic bullying by older, larger kids was common, air-raid sirens were tested on Saturdays, and air-raid drills were held in school so we would know where and how to sit in order to protect ourselves should the Soviet Union send nuclear bombs in our direction.

I was born on May 28, 1954 in Yonkers, N. Y. in the United States. Both of my parents were first-generation Italian-American Catholics whose parents came through Ellis Island between 1895 and 1906. My mom was 38 and my dad was 47 when I was born. Married in 1952 at 36 and 45 respectively, they brought my sister into the world almost nine months to the day after their wedding; I followed her eleven months later. A first-grade teacher, my mom was the first in her family to attend and graduate college (CUNY, Hunter College). My dad graduated high school, served in the Pacific in the Navy during World War II, and made his living as a plumber. As did many men of his generation, he spoke of having attended the "college of hard knocks." My parents' nine siblings gave me thirty-four cousins in nine families spread across Yonkers, the lower Hudson Valley, Staten Island, and Long Island, and we saw many of them with some regularity on weekends and holidays.

I grew up in suburban Yonkers with lots of chronological peers and several close friends on my block and on surrounding streets. Sports fields were adjacent to the elementary schools mentioned below, and ample wooded areas lay near and along the Saw Mill River. Most of our homes were built eight-to-an-acre on 50' x 100' plots.

I attended public school from kindergarten through second grade, and received religious instruction at the local parish once a week. For grades three through eight, I transferred across the street to the newly built Catholic school. Both schools were a ten-minute walk from home, so I usually ate lunch at home. I attended a co-ed Catholic high school about three miles away, and earned a bachelor's degree from St. John's University in Jamaica, New York, and a master's from Iona College in New Rochelle.

Beyond these educational basics, my early years included doctors who made house calls; black-and-white television with seven stations available and signals received through a roof antenna and/or "rabbit ears" atop the TV. During my early childhood, my dad, uncles, and older cousins handed down their New York biases toward the Yankees and the football Giants. In later childhood and adolescence, I gravitated toward a cousin's and an older neighbor's biases toward basketball. Along with my best friend, Paul, I discovered some competence in middle- and long-distance running, and I discovered the blessing of learning that when I did my work and studied, I performed well academically.

There is a lot more detailed information both within and beyond the above synopsis. I'll share several larger perspectives that informed what I was given:

The national, regional, state, local, religious, educational, media, and familial cultures into which I was born and in which I was raised early on 'gave' my childhood self a worldview that conveyed various beliefs as "truths." These included:

- I lived in the greatest country in the world because it was a democracy and it won the wars it fought.

- Other democracies were not as great as my country because they relied on us, especially in war.
- Japan and Germany were bad countries, and we were giving them a chance to redeem themselves after World War II. Various people, books, movies, and television shows made this clear.
- Cowboys were good guys; Indians were savages. There were some good Indians like Tonto, and movies and television shows backed up these facts.
- Slavery was bad, but Abraham Lincoln and the Civil War ended it.
- Catholicism was the one true religion, and we had a relationship with the Jews through the Judeo-Christian tradition. We called their writings the Old Testament, and we called the story of Jesus's life the New Testament. Jewish people messed up by not accepting Jesus as the Savior that God had promised them, but God still loved them.
- According to the Baltimore Catechism we studied as children, God was "the Supreme Being who made all things" and Jesus was his only Son. Together, with a magical, mystical bird known as the Holy Ghost or Holy Spirit, they formed the Holy Trinity and dwelt in heaven.
- If I said certain prayers a specified number of times, I could limit the time I might spend in Purgatory, where I'd go if I didn't get to Heaven right away but was good enough not to go to Hell.
- I was expected to be obedient and defer to all authority—which included the Ten Commandments and pretty much any adult. My parents, my sister, and I referred to many of my friends' parents as "aunt" and "uncle"—and all of them kept an eye on all of us when we were young.
- The Yankees were the greatest baseball team in history. No other team came close in terms of World Series championships.

- Reading books was a good thing to do.

The final two bullets are the only ones that actually hold up over time (☺). Smiley face aside, there are flaws and limitations in each of the bulleted givens that precede the final two. In terms of specific *events*, my childhood and adolescence also included, among much else:

> the assassinations of Medgar Evers, Denise McNair, Addie Mae Collins, Cynthia Wesley, Carole Robertson, John F. Kennedy, Malcolm X, Martin Luther King, Jr., and Robert F. Kennedy; the war in Vietnam; Woodstock; the Cold War; and the moon landing.
>
> More personally and locally, I often went to work with my father on weekends when he was called for plumbing "emergencies"—and I learned some cool lessons from and about him, about his trade, and about people in general. He always left his work area, whether bathroom, kitchen or basement, cleaner than he had found it.
>
> I got to experience the 1969-1970 New York Knicks NBA Championship (while getting cut from my high school and university basketball teams); and I was deeply moved, at the age of sixteen, by the emerging story of Kris Kristofferson's life as a college athlete, Golden Gloves boxer, award-winning fiction writer, Rhodes Scholar, U.S. Army Ranger Captain and helicopter pilot, singer-songwriter, and movie star—all by his mid-thirties—a trajectory that *my* givens would never have thought possible. Thanks again, Kris.

Upon reflection, still amid my ongoing work of waking up, growing up, cleaning up, and showing up,[7] the worldview I was given as a child was a blend of what I would today call mythic and rational. While science impacted my life and was an important subject in school, certain non-scientific "mythic truths" were given, and it was my childhood job to embrace and honor these "truths" about God and country as they were handed down to me. To do otherwise would be to lose my faith or be unpatriotic, either of which would carry unpleasant consequences. Being faithful and patriotic in the greatest country ever and worshipping according to the One True Church were safe ways to be a kid. They were also limited, limiting, and in some cases *wrong*—in terms of both what was known and not taught or shared, and what was not yet known, available to, or accessible by the majority of the adults with whom I had contact in the culture at the time.

What's above is an incomplete summary of what I was given at birth and during childhood. Its obvious (and easy to forget) importance, and the reason I'm sharing it here, is that *every person born anywhere and at any time since humans first appeared has his, her, or their own set of givens*—in every location on the planet, with or without religion, and in poverty and wealth (however those two concepts might have been experienced at the time and place of each birth). You get the idea, yes? Each of us has a *given* story—an initial set of givens—whether or not we are aware of it. Some of it is given in order to simplify a complex world for young children; some of it is given as literal truth by the adults who believe it; and each of us continues to be given more input through late childhood, adolescent, young adult, and adult experiences and observations.[8] What we choose to accept, embrace, revise, or reject is up to us.

The following statements directly address the impact of what culture gives us. Thomas Merton wrote the first circa 1967 without the benefit of adult developmental research. Ken Wilber wrote the second, with access to adult developmental research, almost forty years later:

> Reflect, sometimes, on the disquieting fact that most of your statements of opinions, tastes, deeds, desires, hopes and fears

are statements about someone who is not really present. When you say 'I think' it is often not you who think, but 'they'—it is the anonymous authority of the collectivity speaking through your mask. When you say 'I want', you are sometimes simply making an automatic gesture of accepting, and paying for, what has been forced upon you. That is to say, you reach out for what you have been made to want.[9]

You can be listening to someone coming from, say, the **multiplistic level** (orange altitude) and it is obvious that this person is not thinking of these ideas himself; almost everything he says is completely predictable.... He has no idea that he is the mouthpiece of this structure, a structure he doesn't even know is there. It almost seems as if it is not he who is speaking, but **the orange structure itself that is speaking through him**—this vast intersubjective network is speaking through him.[10] [bold in original]

Enough. I encourage you to explore your own cultural givens. Tune into what you still embrace and what you've revised or rejected. Ask yourself how your story and what you have chosen to accept of it influence your experience of this journey into America's collective Shadow. Finally, the qualities below inform what follows. I'll name them here and refer to them as appropriate in the coming chapters:

Skillful means: The surgeon's knowledge and feel allow him to make the incision at the right place, the right depth, and the right length (and on the right patient). The mechanic's knowledge and feel allow her to stop tightening the screw or bolt without stripping the threads. Loving parents and teachers (and other adults) interact with children in age-appropriate and developmentally appropriate ways. No matter what we're doing, how we do it matters as much as, if not more than, what we're doing. Skillful means are necessary in order to be both truthful *and* kind; demanding *and* caring.

Development: As used here, development refers not to more or deeper knowledge or technique (which are important and have their place), but to an increasingly inclusive, comprehensive, balanced and complex view of things. Development determines what and how we see and how we experience life amid all the finite, everyday ways we differ. It beckons us toward the infinite way we're the same. It can, but doesn't necessarily, continue through adulthood. We'll say more about this later. For now, some shorthand: what we see of the world and how we see what we see will be very different if our perspective is *me*-centric (it's about me); *us*-centric (it's about us); *all-of-us*-centric (it's about all of us); or *all-that-is*-centric (it's about all that is).

Paths to development may include healthy recovery from *trauma* (or even "just" a major challenge—in which our world is shaken and our worldview expands in response as we recover; *grace* (or serendipity), which is an insight or other positive experience that comes from nowhere, or seems to, and our worldview expands; and *intentional practice*, in which we aspire to expand our worldview and intentionally practice toward that end. My personal bias is not to seek trauma and not to wait around for grace. I'm biased toward intentional practice, about which I'll say more below.

Engaging development through skillful means: The intersection of development and skillful means is essential so that our critiques and reflections don't dismiss our ancestors or our contemporaries for what we (think we) know that they didn't or don't. We know much of what we know *because of* the dignities and disasters of those who preceded us—who they were, what they did and didn't do, and what they gave us—all of which each succeeding generation is free to embrace, revise or reject. We're not speaking about letting anyone off who deserves to be on the hook (so to speak). We're employing skillful means in order to avoid projecting later developmental worldviews onto those that emerged earlier (or onto folks who currently hold earlier views)—just as we hope our successors will understand our current foibles through their later views. A later, more inclusive developmental view may be unskillfully swung like a ball-peen hammer, or skillfully held up as a clarifying lens.

Intentional practice: Our repeated thoughts, moods, speech (both content and patterns), and behaviors, whether conscious or unconscious, are all forms of practice. Each repetition deepens a groove and further defines who and how we are. Intentional practice is a choice to engage repeated thoughts, moods, words, and behaviors that serve us—whether we are learning or improving a skill or technique, or if, as above, we are committing to our ongoing development. Every day, life gives us opportunities to practice understanding, patience, generosity, civility, compassion, mercy, and love. This is "life as practice." In chapters three through ten we'll look at conscious and unconscious practices of ignorance, arrogance, fear, bigotry, violence, bullying, greed, excess, and untrustworthiness in American history and current events. Chapters eleven and twelve will offer some prospective alternative paths. Consider these questions as you read: What have you practiced? What are you practicing? What would you like to practice? What's holding you back?

Seeking the most comprehensive, inclusive, and balanced view that is possible (or available) in the moment: One way to begin to do this is to check in with 1) your individual beliefs, values, and perspectives; 2) your individual body and behavior; 3) the perspectives, beliefs, values, and views you share with others; and 4) the systems, infrastructure, and environment, both natural and human-made, in which you (we all) live. More simply, worldview, behavior, relationship, and environment capture the interiors and exteriors of individuals and collectives. They "tetra-arise" and interrelate. If we change, privilege, or ignore one of them, each of them is impacted.[11]

Honoring the power and paradox of silence: In "The Transformation of Silence into Language and Action," Audre Lorde wrote that "I was going to die, if not sooner then later, whether or not I had ever spoken myself. My silences had not protected me. Your silence will not protect you."[12] Millions of voices have been silenced by America's narratives and collective Shadow. Yet, the mystical branch of every wisdom tradition and the deepening evidence of true science are increasingly clear that silence—becoming aware of, working with, and quieting our incessant mind chatter, and regularly retreating from the noise of our human-made infrastructure—is good for us and allows us to hear, see and feel more deeply. Each is true and necessary. Preventing the external silencing of any voice and encouraging and choosing the intentional silencing of our interior and exterior noise are necessary for individual and societal health.

Truth: When journalism, law, science, government, academia, and other systems are functioning in their highest, most authentic capacities, truth is sought through evidence that can be observed, validated, and refuted by competent communities of practice whose members agree to abide by accepted professional standards. Evidence and community. Truth invites the individual voice and also invites other voices that may validate and confirm that voice or refute it with different interpretations or additional evidence. As valid methods of investigation evolve and new methods emerge, previous evidence may be understood differently and new evidence may emerge.[13] Throughout this book, our working definition of truth comes from educator and activist Parker J. Palmer: "Truth is an eternal conversation about things that matter, conducted with passion and discipline."[14]

Love: Much has been written about love. Our working definition in this book emerges at the intersection of the views of Brother David Steindl-Rast, M. Scott Peck, and Marianne Williamson's reflections on *A Course in Miracles.* Love is "the joyful acceptance of belonging," and "the will to extend one's self for the purpose of nurturing one's own or another's spiritual growth," as if fear is absent. So, love embraces joy, acceptance, and belonging, the will to act for the benefit of self and others, and it embraces and wills even in the face of fear.[15]

SO, LET'S ENGAGE SKILLFUL MEANS; development; applying skillful means to how we navigate development; intentional practice; seeking comprehensive, inclusive, and balanced views; honoring the power and paradox of silence; truth; and love in our exploration of America's narratives and collective Shadow. What could go wrong? What has gone wrong? Let's buckle up and find out, with a focus on what could go right.

CHAPTER TWO

A Brief Overview of Shadow

"Deliberately to place something in the underland is almost always a strategy to shield it from view. Actively to retrieve something from the underland almost always requires effortful work. The underland's difficulty of access has long made it a means of symbolizing what cannot openly be said or seen..."

- Robert Macfarlane[1]

IN MID-MARCH, 2003 I SAT with Animas Valley Institute's Bill Plotkin and others at the Merritt Center in Payson, Arizona, for five days of an experience entitled "Sweet Darkness: The Initiatory Gifts of the Shadow, Projections, Subpersonalities, and the Sacred Wound." On the evening of our first day there, the United States, under orders from President George W. Bush, began bombing Iraq. So while we at the Merritt Center were exploring our respective individual Shadows and projections, our country's collective Shadow and projections—"the evil out there" that we tend to see in other nations, groups, cultures, genders, colors, orientations, and people—was on full display, providing us an opportunity for recognition, ownership, and integration at the national level as well. As many folks claimed in the months leading up to March 2003, and as we now know, the reasons for attacking Iraq were fabricated;

as each reason was discredited, the Bush administration added another one to the news cycle—something we'll take a closer look at in Chapter Seven.

Jungian analyst Robert Johnson refers to "persona" as "what we would like to be and how we wish to be seen by the world….our psychological clothing"—the mask we wear. He refers to "ego" as "what we are and know about consciously" and to "Shadow" as "that part of us we fail to see or know…. that which has not entered adequately into consciousness."[2]

In *A Little Book on the Human Shadow*, Robert Bly describes children as "living globe[s] of energy." Behind each of us in childhood, "we have an invisible bag, and the part of us our parents don't like, we, to keep our parents' love, put in the bag." In order to keep our elementary-school teachers happy, we continue to fill the bag, and by high school we throw more stuff into the bag in order to fit in with our peers. "We spend our life until we're twenty deciding what parts of ourself to put in the bag, and we spend the rest of our lives trying to get them out again. Sometimes retrieving them feels impossible, as if the bag were sealed."[3] To the point of our work here, Bly points out that "There is also a national bag, and ours is quite long…. we are noble; other nations have empires. Other nations endure stagnant leadership, treat minorities brutally, brainwash their youth, and break treaties."[4]

With the above as our foundation and as it is used throughout this book, Shadow refers to disowned or repressed aspects or traits of an individual or group that the individual or group doesn't recognize in itself and unknowingly tends to project onto others, whether or not the trait is considered positive or negative and whether or not the others actually embody the projected trait. Sometimes they do; sometimes they don't. For example, if I tend to have a *disproportionately* highly charged emotional response to someone I experience as angry, there's a very good chance that I've repressed or disowned my own anger—it's in my invisible bag.[5] Until I recognize this dynamic and work to integrate my anger, anger will follow me around and allow me to see all these angry people "out there" everywhere I go, while I remain oblivious to my being the one constant at every scene of all this anger. Everyone else is angry. I'm not. Oops.

So, the behavior or trait itself—in this case, anger, whether considered healthy or unhealthy, is *not* Shadow. The repression/denial of the trait in myself, and the projection of the trait or behavior onto others—again, whether or not they actually have or do it—*is* Shadow.

As mentioned above, the repressed, projected trait can be positive, although sadly and necessarily, we're not focusing on positive projections in this book. If I have a disproportionately intense admiration for or attraction to someone because of his, her, or their generosity, creativity, patience, intelligence, or trustworthiness, there's a good chance that I have not yet owned my own generosity, creativity, et cetera, and am projecting it onto the other, again, whether or not he, she, or they actually have the trait in the abundant way I perceive it. In each case, whether considered positive or negative, the key lies at the intersection of the "disproportionate" nature of my response, my denial of the trait in myself, and my projection of the trait onto the other(s).

People who know us, and especially people who know us well, can see our Shadow and projections much more easily than we can. For example, if I'm irresponsible in some particular way that I do not see, even if I'm generally a responsible person, and I'm constantly and passionately pointing to others' lack of responsibility, some of my friends and family will see this pretty clearly and perhaps attempt to bring it to my attention. If I'm not willing to do the work of recognizing, owning, and integrating the trait, I'll simply continue to deny it. If I am willing, and I do the work, I will grow into an increasingly integrated or whole(r) way of being in the world. In recognizing that I am capable of *acting irresponsibly* sometimes, and in understanding that that does not mean *I am irresponsible* all the time, I will become more fully human. I will have a more accurate and honest sense of myself. As we'll see, our cultural givens are a significant source of what we put in our individual and collective "invisible bags"—albeit often with very different content amid our diverse experiences and cultures.

Finally, the word *shadow* is sometimes used to refer to negative, undesired, or "dark" traits that we recognize in and don't like about ourselves. We might refer to these traits as our "dark side." These undesired traits that were never in or that we've already retrieved from our invisible bag are *not* what we mean by *Shadow* in this book.[6] We don't know our Shadow is there. Our repression and denial are not conscious choices. "Collective" Shadow as used here refers to elements that are common to individuals in the United States. A *nation* does not have a discrete psyche or Shadow. A nation's Shadow exists in the collective impact of individual Shadow elements that are common to many—not necessarily all—of its citizens.

BEGINNING SOME TWELVE YEARS after that mid-March "Sweet Darkness" gathering in Arizona and Iraq bombing, and continuing as this volume goes to press, we citizens[7] of the United States of America once again were and are still gifted with an opportunity to see our disowned, repressed, and projected traits. This opportunity arose in the presidential candidacy, expanded during the presidency, and now continues to beckon to us, in the post-presidency words and behaviors of one man.

This book explores selected chips from the tip of the very large national iceberg that floats in a vast ocean that covers most of the tiny planet that circles an average star within a solar system within a galaxy within the universe of context within which this exploration takes place. One of the most challenging aspects of this writing, perhaps captured in the preceding sentence, is tied directly to one of the traits that characterizes our national Shadow—that of excess. The evidence of Donald Trump's embodiment of our Shadow is itself excessive. The process of completing Chapter Ten has been one of deletion—what to leave out, how to bring the exploration to a close. The challenge has been to sort through the mire he continues to create, especially but not only amid his excessive denial of the 2020 election results and his remarkably excessive invisibility as a leader amid a global pandemic that killed more than 185,000 Americans—more than 2,300 every day—in the 79 days between November 3, 2020, when he lost the presidential election, and January 20, 2021, when Joe Biden was inaugurated as America's 46th president.[8]

Virtually every day that goes by, sometimes every hour of every day, he says or does something new, or repeats something old, that serves as evidence of the ignorance, arrogance, fear, bigotry, violence, greed, excess, bullying, and untrustworthiness he embodies.[9] If you disagree with him, you are "fake," "failing," or a "loser." If he wins, he claims he would have won by more if the system and media weren't against him. If he loses, he rages that the system is rigged and he'll use his wealth, or convince others to use theirs, to pay his lawyers to litigate. This behavior is evident not just in his two presidential runs; it is his *modus operandi* in life. And again, it is only in his public embodiment of our national Shadow that he is relevant to the core of this book. He is a useful symptom, and, as with many symptoms of underlying disease, we may discover and treat the cause if we pay attention to the symptom. Perhaps, then, we can begin the healing process.

The examples of our national Shadow that follow in chapters three through seven are selective and illustrative. They are not exhaustive. They do not and cannot capture the enormity of the suffering and loss of the ordinary men, women, and children—U. S. citizens and others—whose lives were ended or catastrophically changed by the perpetrators and perpetuators of the events depicted. Much has been written already about each. We return to them here specifically as evidence in our exploration of our American Shadow and the perception within and projection from the United States of the "evil out there." Our intention is to neither blame nor praise the United States unnecessarily. Part of our focus is on the opportunities that the 45th president's time in the White House and influence in the public sphere give us to recognize, work with, and integrate the Shadow of the "American experiment"—its underbelly, its less desirable traits. If we are truly committed to the ongoing effort required to form a more perfect union, we must recognize the need for infinite play, which may be unlike anything we have imagined in our past and current finite games.

Such reflection, recognition, and integration are necessary and need to be ongoing. Samuel Flagg Bemis, former president of the American Historical Association and Pulitzer Prize-winning historian, asked in 1961:

> Have not our social studies been tending overmuch to self-study—to what is the matter with us rather than to perils and strengths that test our liberty? Too much self-study, too much self-criticism is weakening to a people as it is to an individual. There is such a thing as a national neurosis.[10]

If we emphasize Bemis's "too much," then perhaps self-study and self-criticism, as with too much of almost anything, can be weakening. But too *little* self-study and self-criticism sustains ignorance, which weakens a people and an individual as well.

As Justice Souter reminded us in 2012, "an ignorant people can never remain a free people."[11] We'll proceed here with the hypothesis that too little self-study and self-criticism, and the quality of each, are at play.

Again, the Shadow characteristics we're concerned with include ignorance, arrogance, fear, bigotry, violence, greed, excess, bullying, and untrustworthiness, which often overlap and reinforce each other and are present in varying degrees in the examples we'll explore. They all do share, however, a common foundation, what we'll call the traits of the "unhealthy masculine." Underlying America's collective Shadow is a disproportionate and destructive focus on the individual, at the expense of community; freedom, at the expense of equality; rights, at the expense of caring and responsibility; and winning, at the expense of cooperation— each and all of which lead to a deepening disconnection. There is, of course, nothing inherently wrong with *healthy* manifestations of the individual, or of freedom, rights, or winning. We'll have more to say about the traits of the *healthy* and *unhealthy masculine* and *feminine* in Chapter Three. [12]

Here's how we'll be using the language of these Shadow elements in the pages that follow:

Ignorance refers to not knowing—which is, ironically, also the best place from which to learn. When we do not learn and when we make assumptions and take action informed by our ignorance, we can cause great harm, as we did and do through our ignorance of various "others." We have done great harm, for example, to the people, cultures and histories of hundreds of indigenous Nations; to multiple African, and later, African-American people, cultures and histories; to the Vietnamese people, culture, and history; to Iraqi people, culture, and history; to Afghan people, culture, and history; and to women, across cultures and histories.

Arrogance, in this volume, refers to the manifestation of a sense of superiority, which often, if not always, is based in ignorance. Historically, when the dominant white Christian male cultures in Europe and the United States engaged with others about whom they were ignorant, they assumed that their "difference from" these others indicated "better than" or "superior to" as well. This sense of superiority is often accompanied by a need to save face and avoid the humiliation of being wrong, especially in public—which leads to much of the bullying and lying we'll see in chapters three through ten. While they're not exact synonyms, we'll occasionally use *arrogance* and *hubris* synonymously.

Fear is a body-mind response to a perceived future threat, whether that future is five years or five seconds away. Once we have something, whether comfort, health, money, material goods, power, position, opinion, reputation, or perspective, we often develop an unhealthy attachment to what we have, which leads us to fear losing it, or to fear others who have, or may soon have, different versions of it—whether we perceive the difference to be better or worse. A combination of ignorance and arrogance can lead to and reinforce fear of these others and of a change to our current status. Healthy, rational fear, or caution, is necessary for survival; unhealthy, irrational fear leads us to harm others who are not a threat to us.

Bigotry refers to negative attitudes and actions we may take against those about whom we are ignorant, arrogant, or fearful. Once we have our ignorance, arrogance, and fear in place, it's easy—perhaps inevitable—to turn the energy of these three states of being into diminishing, ridiculing, and attacking others. To recognize, learn from, and celebrate difference is healthy; to recognize difference, resent it, refuse to tolerate it, and attack it is bigotry.

Bullying, which will be discussed in some detail in Chapter Nine, refers to the abuse of physical, emotional, financial, political, or intellectual power by those who appear, or may actually be, somehow stronger than their victims. We often choose to bully because of our own fear and/or sense of inadequacy. Bullying, therefore, is often informed by ignorance and insecurity.

Violence refers to the use of force or the threat to use force against another or oneself. (It also refers to the destructiveness of natural events like hurricanes, but our focus here is on intentional human violence). The force can be physical, emotional, and/or intellectual-psychological. Its tools can include the body, a physical object such as a gun or a pipe, or drugs, words, money, or the law. When the law is used to perpetrate or perpetuate violence, it is unethical, despite the costume of legality. Indian "removal" and Jim Crow laws, which we'll discuss in Chapter Four and Chapter Five, are examples of this kind of violence. Words that we disagree with or that bring up a sense of discomfort are not *necessarily* violent, but can be—especially when they deliver literal, personal threats. The ongoing debate between "words that wound" and "freedom of speech" is an essential one, and both relevant to and beyond the scope of this book.

Greed refers to an excessive desire for getting or having something. Often, that "something" refers to money and things. Greed, as we're using the term, can lead to excess.

Excess, related to and different from greed, refers to a behavior or a quantity of something that is more than what is necessary or usable. Excess, as we're using the term, can, but need not, result from greed.

Untrustworthiness refers to being undeserving of trust, usually because of past or current duplicity or dishonesty. Betrayal refers to the act of violating an agreement, trust, or one's word. The act of betrayal often results from the trait of being untrustworthy.

~

WHAT FOLLOWS IN PART II provides unsettling reminders of American history and current events. Each of us has his or her individual experience of the world. When we read in history books or in the daily news, stories of this war, that pandemic, this insurrection, that mass shooting, this hero, that victim, this natural disaster, and that election result, the unique birth, life, and death of each human being impacted by the larger stories is often minimized or lost entirely. Rabbi Marc Gellman eloquently made this minimization clear in his September 23, 2001 comments at Yankee Stadium. Just twelve days after the September 11 attacks, the estimated the number of people killed was around 6,000:

> On that day—on that day—6,000 people did not die. On that day, one person died 6,000 times…. We say 6,000 died, or we say six million died and the saying and the numbers explain nothing except how much death came in how short a time…. The real horror of that day lies not in its bigness, but in its smallness. In the small searing death of one person 6,000 times, and that one person was not a number. That person was our father or our mother or our son or our daughter or our grandpa or grandma or brother or sister or cousin or uncle or aunt or friend or lover, our neighbor, our co-worker, the woman who delivered our mail or the guy who put out our fires and arrested the bad guys in our town. And the death of each and every one of them alone would be worthy of such a gathering and such a grief…. The dimensions of last week's horror only become fully drawn when we enter each murdered world one world at a time….[13]

John Tarrant put it this way: "…counting the worth of people only as numbers, which the corporate and bureaucratic mind loves to do, is puritan because it ignores the necessary uniqueness of each person."[14] Ta-Nehisi Coates, railing against the death of Prince Jones, reminds us of "all the love poured into him"—from school tuitions to sleepovers, to "soccer balls, science kits…model trains" and "all the private jokes, customs, greetings, names, dreams…"[15] Gellman, Tarrant, and Coates remind us that the names we know and the stories we read do not capture the unique details of each human life and death.

We often think we understand events through the titles, headlines and slogans we create—*Slavery, Jim Crow, Operation Iraqi Freedom, Wounded Knee, Vietnam, #MeToo, the Trail of Tears, My Lai, 9/11, Sandy Hook, Women's Rights, Black Lives Matter, the Bill of Rights, January 6, 2021, the 13th, 14th, 15th and 19th Amendments.* We may think we understand all the more deeply if we are familiar with some of the more well-known names that history passes on to us—Sojourner Truth, Abraham Lincoln, Frederick Douglass, Robert McNamara, Elizabeth Cady Stanton, Teddy Roosevelt, Crazy Horse, George W. Bush, John Lewis, John Trudell, Audre Lorde, Robert Kennedy, Barbara Lee, Barack Obama, Gloria Steinem, Donald Trump, Kamala Harris, and so on. But what warrants remembrance and exploration is how each of us lives his or her life, the day-to-day, moment-to-moment experience of our breath-by-breath existence—that which poet Jack Gilbert, after his wife's death, lamented having lost in "two thousand habitual / breakfasts" and "that commonplace I can no longer remember."[16]

With an *all of us* or *all that is* view, we can then extend that remembrance and exploration—perhaps enhanced by imagination and love, one life at a time, one breath at a time—to the billions of individuals who live and lived through our current and historical events. Often unnamed and unknown, these are the very real human beings who were enslaved, displaced, oppressed, bombed, shot, lynched, subjugated, harassed, raped, lied to, and otherwise minimized by those who, lacking ethical awareness and moral authority, had the physical, and sometimes legal, power to so treat them. And if we want the fullest understanding, we need to extend that same remembrance and exploration to the individual enslavers, oppressors, bombers, shooters, rapists, and others who so abused their power(s).[17]

None of these explorations is easy. Remembering and attempting to understand the individual perpetrators of violence is exceptionally difficult, and the purpose of such attempts to understand is not to condone or justify abhorrent acts, but to understand them in a way that enables us to minimize or eliminate their ever happening again. This is essential work; if we do not do it, we risk repeating the same horrors, costumed for new generations by new perpetrators.

Toward this end, we are called to open our hearts and minds to the unnamed, unknown, real human beings who lived, died, "won," and "lost" on all sides of the conflicts depicted in chapters three through eight. We'll explore the historical and current aspects of our collective American Shadow that some of us would rather deny concerning women, Native Americans, African Americans, and the wars in Vietnam, Afghanistan and Iraq. The scope of each exploration is necessarily limited; volumes have been and continue to be spoken, written, and otherwise expressed about these issues and the ancillary issues that inform them. The examples of collective Shadow that are of deepest concern to you, as a reader, may not be included here—I ask for your understanding. Captured here are selected snapshots of what we would prefer to deny, ignore, or minimize as a nation—that which we have stuffed into the long, invisible bag we drag behind us. I have chosen these snapshots in order to point to where we are in the context of where we've been and with an increasingly deep, wise, clear, and loving interest in where we might go from here.

While these histories provide necessary context, their purpose is to inform the present—the moment-to-moment lives of Vietnamese, Afghan, and Iraqi survivors and American veterans of those wars and their families; of the lives of the individual members of the more than 560 Native American tribes, both on and off the reservation today; of the individual lives of twenty-first-century African Americans and other people of color; and the individual life of every girl and woman within and beyond these selected groups. As James Baldwin wrote, "…the great force of history comes from the fact that we carry it within us."[18]

Essential in this exploration is the need to recognize both the horrors of the past and the relative advantages of hindsight and new learning we humans have today in our understanding of that past and our attempts not to repeat those, or any new, horrors. Our critiques of the shortcomings of the men who wrote and ratified what we now call the U. S. Constitution and its Amendments would be more difficult to voice today without the still imperfectly realized rights, freedoms, and responsibilities that they handed down to us. Said differently, the framers did not have access, as we do, to the two-hundred-plus years of implementation and amendment of the documents they framed. Both our critiques of these men and our gratitude for their unique, imperfect invitation to play an infinite game are valid.

Homo erectus and *Homo habilis* were not stupid or wrongheaded *Homo sapiens;* they were earlier versions. The framers succeeded in doing something that had never been done before on earth—implementing a democratic republican form of government that was voted on and ratified by representatives of the people from the various states that would be governed.[19] This bears repeating. We can see the imperfections in what they gave us in large part *because of ongoing applications of and revisions to what they gave us*, not the least of which was the wisdom to remind us to keep working toward "a more perfect union." The evolution of humans' individual worldviews, behaviors, cultures and societies is real.[20] It is also not guaranteed, and it does not always manifest in healthy ways. As author of *Recapture the Rapture,* Jamie Wheal, put it in a 2021 interview:

> Somewhere in the midst of the articulation of capitalism, the articulation of nation states and democracy, and all the things that came out of the French Enlightenment, the American experiment, was this infinite game of all men and women are entitled to life, liberty and the pursuit of happiness, regardless of race, color or creed. Now there's all sorts of frustrated, pissed off and bitter folks that are saying '*that* was a lie.' But the question is, 'Was it a *lie* or was it a noble, fragile experiment that has never been fully attempted or satisfactorily executed, but the idea is still one of the best ideas we've ever had.[21]

We should neither withhold informed, thoughtful criticism of the past—whether of people or events—nor impose upon that past the wisdom and knowledge that we (think we) hold today and that was not yet available to our predecessors. It is our responsibility—if we choose to play with an expanding community of truth-seeking players in an infinite game, rather than with a limited team of win-seeking players in a variety of finite games—to explore with imagination, integrity, and due diligence that which is possible for us today in the context of that which was not yet available to them.

We are the people of today, and we will be looked upon and variously criticized and praised in an ongoing series of tomorrows—if our species is fortunate enough to survive. What is it, exactly, that we need to access, recover, recognize, and integrate in the United States of America (and elsewhere) in order to be increasingly whole as a people? Let's check that seatbelt buckle again and find out together.

PART II

THE EVIL OUT THERE

Fear of the Feminine & the Subjugation of Women: Getting Their Feet from off of Our Necks

*Would you prefer to be seen as powerful or as
someone who plays skillfully with strength?*[1]

AS IS TRUE FOR BOYS AS WELL, a girl born in 1774, 1862, 1917, 1963, 1971, 2001, 2017, 2022, or any other year received cultural givens and expectations that were unique to the time, place, and familial, ethnic, racial, and financial circumstances of her birth and childhood. That she was born a biological female provided an additional given that would impact what was expected of and available to her.

While the examples of our collective national Shadow that will follow in chapters four through seven disclose disturbing manifestations of what we refuse to see in ourselves, this first example, an exploration of fear of the feminine and the subjugation of women, is both a disturbing manifestation of Shadow and an underlying trait that is present in the next four chapters as well. More to the point, it is the persistent absence of the qualities of the healthy feminine, further undermined by the relentless presence of the qualities of the unhealthy masculine, that encourages and amplifies, and may very well be the primary cause of, America's collective Shadow.

Below is an overview of the specific language used in this chapter. These usages are neither the "right" nor the only ones available; they are appropriate and accurate in the context in which they are used in this book.

> The words *woman, women, man,* and *men* refer to individuals who manifest the traditional physiological/biological traits of females or males, and who identify themselves according to those traits. This chapter, in our exploration of collective Shadow in America, does not address the increasingly complex and relevant questions concerning how any bisexual, transexual, transgender, non-binary, gender-fluid, and other individual might relate to the words, "woman" and "man" other than to acknowledge that individuals of *any* orientation or identity do not necessarily relate to them in exactly the same way. To delve more deeply into this issue is beyond the scope and intention of this book.
>
> For our purposes, the words *masculine* and *feminine* refer to other-than-physiological traits or characteristics that any human being might have and can develop—that is, these traits are not specific only to someone who identifies as a biological man or woman, and they can be developed and embodied by anyone of any sexual orientation or identity or lack thereof. Historically, a majority of men have embodied more of the masculine traits and a majority of women have embodied more of the feminine. The reasons for this can be attributed to a variety of factors, including culture, biology, and means of production, among others.[2] It's becoming increasingly clear that any human being who embodies an integration of both healthy feminine and healthy masculine traits tends to be, well, healthier—in the sense of being more inclusive, balanced, comprehensive, and complex—and therefore more difficult to pigeonhole or stereotype and less likely to pigeonhole or stereotype others.
>
> More to the point, the *feminine,* as we'll use it here, tends more toward a concern with care, embrace, collaboration,

mercy, and compassion, among other traits; the *masculine* tends more toward a focus on rights, independence, individualism, justice, and wisdom. While this not an exhaustive list, notice that each tendency, whether it's considered feminine or masculine, can be beneficial in its healthy manifestation—whether at an *earlier/lower* or *later/higher* level,[3] and that all of them are descriptive, not prescriptive. We can observe them, but we're not suggesting that any woman or man is "supposed to" embody the respective feminine or masculine tendencies in a certain way.

Before birth, everyone who reads this sentence, and everyone who never will, was carried in and nurtured through the body of a woman, which is perhaps the most intimate human relationship we may have—albeit an involuntary one on the part of the one who is carried (beliefs in reincarnation or that we choose our parents notwithstanding).

And yet (or perhaps, *of course*) each example of collective American Shadow in the following chapters—the betrayal, slaughter, and "removal" of American Indians, the enslavement of Africans and subsequent oppression of their progeny, and the attacks and their consequences in Vietnam, Afghanistan, and Iraq, were perpetrated through the worldview, values, and energy of the earlier/lower me-centric and the later/medium us-centric levels of the unhealthy masculine—that is, through an *unhealthy* focus on rights, independence, individualism, justice, and wisdom just for *me* or for *me* and for others I perceive to be *like me—my group*. It's important to emphasize *unhealthy* here. A healthy view from any level transcends and includes all earlier levels: so, if I embody a healthy *all-of-us* perspective, I am still concerned with my various groups and myself. Said differently, at the later-emerging, higher levels, *I* am still concerned with myself and my group(s), but I hold these concerns in a larger, more inclusive, and balanced context, embracing *my*, and *our* places in the greater human family—or even in the family of all sentient beings and all matter. As we will see, there is nothing in the examples of collective American Shadow in chapters three through eight that indicates health, concern, or healthy concern for *all* humans.

While an unhealthy me-centric orientation can be dangerous, historically it's been the *unhealthy* group/us-centric orientation that designs and executes most human-made horrors at scale. Again, our group-centric tribes can be healthy. Each increasingly inclusive and embodied group identification leaves fewer beings out there to project upon and persecute—an embodied identification with all humans or all sentient beings essentially leaves no one to persecute. Believing this to be true is an important step, but it is not enough. Embodiment is key. We have to live it.

While the historical *subjugation of women* is visible for any honest person who is willing to look, the *fear of the feminine* manifests in less obvious ways. This chapter posits that those men who primarily manifest *unhealthy* versions of masculine traits like rights, independence, individualism, justice and wisdom—which historically have resulted in dominance over, violence against, and subjugation of women and others—often fear healthy feminine traits like responsibility, relationship, care, mercy, and compassion as emasculating rather than integrating. More specifically, cisgender, heterosexual males who historically have been conditioned to "be men" (i.e. stereotypically masculine) experience both a strong attraction to the power of the feminine in women and a fear-of-emasculation-based aversion to the feminine in themselves. They mistake healthy feminine-masculine integration as emasculation, which terrifies them, so they subjugate what they fear.

More men are integrating the healthy masculine and feminine in the third decade of the twenty-first century. Such integration was not popular for at least the first two-thirds of the twentieth century, and was rarely a cultural option before that. We still have a long way to go.

IN 1792, SIXTEEN YEARS AFTER the British colonists in what is now called the United States declared independence from their homeland, a thirty-three-year-old woman who had not made the Atlantic crossing published *A Vindication of the Rights of Woman: with Strictures on Political and Moral Subjects.* Mary Wollstonecraft's treatise is considered by many to be the first formal statement of women's rights—"the first great feminist manifesto."[4] Wollstonecraft criticized the system of education within British society that kept women in a state of "ignorance and slavish dependence," and she asserted that the "'tyranny of man'" caused many of the circumstances that limited women. Welcomed and praised by many, the publication was also ridiculed. Horace Walpole, embodying the unhealthy masculine traits of his culture at the time—the very traits that Wollstonecraft critiqued, called her "'a hyena in petticoats.'"[5] Her treatise has held up significantly better than his ridicule in the ensuing two-plus centuries.

More than half a century after Wollstonecraft's *Vindication,* back in the New World, Lucy Stone earned her baccalaureate at Ohio's Oberlin College in 1847. When she was asked to write the commencement address for her class, she refused upon learning that her words would have to be read by a man. In her later work against slavery and for equal rights for women and blacks, she became known as a powerful orator, and when she spoke publicly, audience members threw water and books at her. She married Harry Blackwell, kept her maiden name, and their shared vows omitted the traditional language that subordinated women to their husbands. "When she refused to pay taxes because she was not represented in the government, officials took all her household goods in payment, even her baby's cradle."[6]

Sarah Grimké was born the year that Wollstonecraft published *A Vindication of the Rights of Women,* and lived up to her predecessor's vision. Born into a slave-holding South Carolina family and later influenced by the Quakers, Sarah and her sister Angelina wrote and spoke forcefully about both abolition and equal rights for women. "I ask no favors for my sex," wrote Sarah. "I surrender not our claim to equality. All I ask of our brethren is that they will take their feet from off of our necks, and permit us to stand upright on the ground which God has designed us to occupy."[7] Some 180 years later Supreme Court Justice Ruth Bader Ginsberg would paraphrase Sarah Grimké's words in reference to both her fellow Supreme Court brethren and to her larger quest to provide equal protection of the law to all women and men.[8]

At the intersection of the fights for women's rights and abolition, "[c]ertain black women faced the triple hurdle—of being abolitionists in a slave society, of being black among white reformers, and of being women in a reform movement dominated by men."[9] Among the "triple hurdle" voices of the time, Isabella Bomfree was born into slavery in upstate New York in 1797, escaped in 1827, a year before New York banned slavery, and had her freedom purchased by an abolitionist family for $20.00. In 1843, declaring that she was called to preach the truth, she changed her name to Sojourner Truth and spent the rest of her life living up to that name—especially regarding abolition and women's rights.[10] Her "And ain't I a woman" speech at the 1851 Women's Rights Convention in Akron, Ohio is perhaps her most famous, but in her 1867 address to the American Equal Rights Association in New York, three years before the passage of the 15th Amendment, she expanded the view of slavery and intuited an early recognition of what would later be called *intersectionality* when she asserted that, "… if colored men get their rights, and not colored women theirs, you see the colored men will be masters over the women, and it will be just as bad as it was before."[11]

Among countless others who have continued this American struggle are Harriet Tubman, Elizabeth Cady Stanton, Susan B. Anthony, Rachel Carson, Fannie Lou Hamer, Shirley Chisholm, Geraldine Ferraro, Wilma Rudolph, Ruth Bader Ginsberg, Audre Lorde, Barbara Lee, Hillary Clinton, Joan Baez, Rosa Parks, Maxine Waters, Linda Ronstadt, Viola Davis, Billy Jean King, Adrienne Rich, Carol Gilligan, Jean Baker Miller, Joanna Macy, Carolyn Forché, Laura Divine, Linda Chavez-Thompson, Naomi Shihab Nye, Stacy Abrams, Sonia Sotomayor, C. Vivian Stringer, Joanne Hunt, Serena Williams, Brandi Carlile, Rosie Perez, Tarana Burke, Megan Rapinoe, Tracy K. Smith, Muriel Bowser, Allyson Felix, the women of the WNBA, Leslie Williams, bell hooks, Diane Musho Hamilton, Ketanji Brown Jackson, and Janet E. Aalfs. Of course, this list is incomplete. Beyond the names you recognize and those you don't, sit for a few minutes and imagine the lives of the millions of unnamed mothers, daughters, sisters, and spouses before and during the ongoing movement for equality.

FAST-FORWARD TO THE 1970s AND 1980s and Jean Baker Miller's *Toward a New Psychology of Women* and Carol Gilligan's *In a Different Voice: Psychological Theory and Women's Development.* Miller's early work, "toward a new psychology of women," called out the unhealthy masculine structures of dominance and subordination in mainstream American society, and called for a turn toward a more relational-centered—that is, healthy feminine—psychology. As she and her colleagues evolved their work, they recognized and challenged their own assumptions of a "norm that would define 'woman' as a white, economically privileged, able-bodied, and heterosexual female." They embraced the "essentiality of connection across difference," and thus joined *relational* and *cultural* to form Relational Cultural Theory (RCT). RCT is alive and well today through the International Center for Growth in Connection.[12]

In *Toward a New Psychology of Women*, written in response to the state of society, psychology, women, and men in the late 1960s and early 1970s, Dr. Miller acknowledges that women have often been deeply involved in the economic production of society, but that "they have rarely, if ever, had an equal role in the *direction* of the society." She further notes that "All social structures that male society has built so far have included within them the suppression of other men," and that "What a relatively few men in our advanced society have been able to build has been at the great expense of other men." Miller points out that within these exclusive male social structures that suppressed other men, women's roles (such as raising children and whatever men were too busy to do) were considered "less important" and apart from "real life" (which included making money, making war and making money making war). Said more simply, women were still expected to be subservient to men, regardless of what Elizabeth Cady Stanton, Sojourner Truth, and others had had to say. Miller then shares the connecting, generous, relational recognition that "men are capable of something altogether different" but "they will not move forward if women continue to subsidize the status quo."[13]

More than two decades after Miller so clearly connected men's and women's fates, Susan Faludi's *Stiffed* corroborated this connection. She began her multi-year exploration with "why do our male brethren so often and so vociferously resist women's struggles toward independence and a fuller life?" As she listened to men over the course of her research, she found that "the gender battle was only a surface manifestation of other struggles." She then chose to "put aside [her] prefigured map" and followed the threads of these other struggles, much as we'll see Andrew Bacevich subject his embrace of "conventional wisdom…to sustained and searching scrutiny" in Chapter Seven. Faludi and Bacevich each made moves toward a more comprehensive, balanced worldview. Researching, learning, and developing as she went, Faludi was surprised to find that:

> the journey men led me on ultimately led me back to feminism….[where] I was struck all the more by how tragic it is that women and men find themselves so far apart. If my travels taught me anything about the two sexes, it is that each of our struggles depends upon the success of the other's.[14]

Much has shifted since Miller and Faludi wrote their respective words, and much more needs to shift. The challenge to this status quo, from Wollstonecraft forward, continues. The integration of the healthy feminine and the healthy masculine within each of us provides more promise than pitting women and men against each other.

Particular aspects of Carol Gilligan's work also play a significant role in identifying the feminine and masculine tendencies referred to on pages 36-37. Gilligan brought the feminine voice and perspective to Lawrence Kohlberg's studies on moral reasoning and found an underlying bias in how the responses of Kohlberg's research subjects (both male and female) were interpreted. Put simply, Kohlberg's interpretation didn't take into consideration the different ways that males and females see, approach, and process moral dilemmas. While a moral concern that impacted just oneself, others, or all others was a road that both female and male respondents traversed, Gilligan began to see that *how* they navigated the process was quite different. It's important to note that this research concerns itself with moral *reasoning,* not moral decisions—*how each of us processes* a moral dilemma and makes a decision, not *which decision we make.*

In one specific classic example, Kohlberg's research presented a scenario in which a man, Heinz, can't afford a drug that would save his wife's life. Research subjects are asked, "Should Heinz steal the drug?" from the pharmacist, and then they are asked some follow-up questions. Two eleven-year-olds, a boy and a girl, respond. They are described by Gilligan as "both highly intelligent and perceptive about life, though in different ways." The boy formulates his responses through logic, deduction, and individual rights. The girl comes to her responses through caring about the relationships among the man, his wife, and the pharmacist. Gilligan characterizes these "two views of morality" as "complementary rather than sequential or opposed." She points out that neither view appears "as a precursor of the other's position," and asks, "what is the significance of this difference, and how do these two modes of thinking connect?"[15] Note that Gilligan's approach here itself integrates logic, curiosity, and connection.

Finally, Gilligan further contextualizes her work in the words of both Wollstonecraft and Stanton, with the former's challenging "'the mistaken notions that enslave my sex,'" and the latter's assertion that, "'The thing which most retards and militates against women's self-development is self-sacrifice.'"[16] The status quo (men in power) argued that keeping women in their subservient, 'less important,' and outside of 'real life' roles was for the better; women argued that equal opportunities for development for all was better for all— emphasis on *for all.*

In the 1993 edition of *In a Different Voice,* Gilligan included a "Letter to Readers" in which she reflected on a decade of responses to the book and on her own ongoing learning: "When I hear my work being cast in terms of whether women and men are really (essentially) different or who is better than whom, I know that I have lost my voice, because these are not my questions." Her questions are "about our perceptions of reality and truth: how we know, how we hear, how we see, how we speak," "about voice and relationship," and "about psychological processes and theory, particularly theories in which men's experience stands for all of human experience—theories which eclipse the lives of women and shut out women's voices."[17] The status quo's processes, views and theories that Gilligan was exploring "in a different voice," intentionally or just out of habit, insisted on misunderstanding and denying her voice and its intentions.

THE WHITE, BRITISH, CHRISTIAN, MALE founders and earliest leaders of the United States could not foresee Miller's, Gilligan's, and Faludi's perspectives. Their Bill of *Rights* did not explicitly demonstrate any *care* about or for women; their Declaration of *Independence* did not *embrace* women; their proclamations of freedom and *justice* for all included no *mercy* for women, and the significant *wisdom* inherent in the Constitution they framed lacked *compassion* for women as well. As we'll see in subsequent chapters, each of the above statements is equally true for the Africans they brought here and enslaved, for their enslaved descendants, and for the native peoples who were betrayed, expelled, and slaughtered. Whether it was their inherent, culturally-given lack of these traits, their intentionally excluding these traits from the foundations of the country they were forming, some combination of these, or something else entirely that led them to ignore their mothers, daughters, and wives—the very people who embodied the very traits they lacked—ignore them they did.

And again, yes, it is easy to look back from the third decade of the twenty-first century, with the benefit of much of what these founders gave us and invited us to subsequently discover, and point out where we think they came up short. *Their* cultural calling was to push back against and separate from monarchy. They had the benefit of neither the documents they created nor the learnings from subsequent fits and starts of implementing those documents, as we do, in the not-yet-300 years of this nation's history. This lack of care, embrace, mercy, and compassion impacted anyone who was not a white, male property owner. Care, embrace, mercy and compassion were completely denied to native peoples and slaves, and on a smaller, but no less real scale, to early immigrants from China, Japan, Germany, France, Italy, Poland and Ireland, among others, some of whom were partially protected by their skin pigmentation and facial features, but all of whom were exposed when they spoke out loud. Again, this is both a cautionary tale and a love letter: "We need to talk. I still love the things that originally attracted me, but we've got some serious issues that we need to address."

WITH THIS NECESSARILY BRIEF, INCOMPLETE accounting before us, and using the 1848 Seneca Falls Convention[18] as an American milestone, the 19th Amendment granted women the right to vote in 1920—seventy-two years after the convention and fifty years after the 15th Amendment granted that right to freed male slaves. Amendments and dates aside, it was not particularly easy in the years immediately following 1920 for all white women to register and vote, especially in states that voted against women's suffrage. And many black women and men, especially in the South, would wait until the passage of the Voting Rights Act of 1965 to actually *begin* to exercise what the amended Constitution declared to be true ninety-five years earlier. Attempts to make it more difficult for blacks to register and to vote continue in some states and precincts as this book goes to print. In 2022. Do the math. It is no mystery that the strongest voices for equality in America are black women.

As we move into the events of the twentieth and twenty-first centuries, the progress toward women's being considered equal to men in both public and private spheres continues across every aspect of American culture and society, as does resistance to that progress. Progress includes the passage of the Education Amendments of 1972, the most well-known piece of which is Title IX, an extension of the Civil Rights Act of 1964. Title IX provides that "No person in the United States shall, based on sex, be excluded from participation in, be denied the benefits of, or be subjected to discrimination under any education program or activity receiving Federal financial assistance." While its most socially visible effect has been around increasingly equal opportunities in interscholastic and intercollegiate sports for girls and women, its focus, when passed, was on civil rights. Equity in sports funding was just one of its impacts.[19] One example of resistance to such progress is the continuing failure since 1923 to ratify the Equal Rights Amendment. Seen through Rabbi Gellman's one-life-at-a-time lens, some 171 million individual females are still fighting for the same rights as some 163 million males in the United States of America (projected 2023 numbers).

A more current, specific, and concrete example exposed the equipment disparities in the training facilities provided for women in San Antonio and men in Indianapolis at the 2021 NCAA basketball tournaments. The University of Oregon's Sedona Prince took to social media with video and voice-over of the two facilities, and when the NCAA initially responded that the issue was space, not money, Prince returned with video proving that the women's facility had plenty of unused space.[20] The disparities in facilities and space ultimately can be traced back to dollars and cents (*greed*, in this volume). The women's and men's Division I NCAA basketball tournaments are admittedly exclusive, small-scale examples—only a small number of student-athletes compete, and that's not a disparagement of them, their families, their coaches or their schools. It is an instructive example for that very same reason—its exclusivity. If such disparity characterizes socially visible, televised, and corporate-sponsored multibillion-dollar events, what is happening where the rest of us live and play?[21]

This push and pull of progress and resistance continues in such varied endeavors as job qualifications (especially but not only where physical strength or capacity is involved); job evaluations; pay equity; childcare; parental leave; and, recently, pandemic support. Culturally and socially imposed norms and traditions limit women's (and men's) options when one spouse or partner chooses to step back professionally—whether partially or completely, temporarily or permanently—when stepping back is helpful to support the other's career. These same norms view the addition of professional engagement and success to a woman's expected roles of wife and mother as disruptions of traditional perspectives on both the workplace and the family. Again, each new move in healthy development, which equality for women is, leads to an increasingly inclusive, comprehensive, balanced, and complex view and experience. Emphasis here on *complex.*

A prohibitive number of areas to explore and examples to cite present themselves; we'll consider just a few. Apologies if your personal favorite is omitted. One measure of the country's view of women can be seen through the lens of its federally elected officials. Jeannette Rankin, from Montana, was the first woman to serve in the U.S. Congress, before she, herself, could vote. Elected to the House in the 65th Congress (1917-1919) as the only woman, she "was held to impossible standards and expectations."[22] When she was re-elected to the 77th Congress (1941-1943), she was one of ten women. That number doubled in the 87th Congress (1961-63), was back down to eleven in the 91st Congress (1969-1971), and fluctuated and continued to grow until the 117th Congress (2021-

2023), which seated 146 women—24 Senators, 118 Representatives, and 4 delegates,[23] a number reduced by one when Senator Kamala Harris became the Vice President and was replaced by Alex Padilla. In terms of trust in women's leadership, current Speaker of the House, Nancy Pelosi, now in that role for the fourth time, is the first and only woman to serve in that position. She has also served as the Minority Leader through six Congresses and the Democratic Whip once—leading in these roles consistently from the 108th through the 117th Congress.[24]

The salaries paid to men and women in the House and Senate are identical ($174,000 since 2009), with the Speaker and majority and minority leaders making more.[25] Contrasted with the uniformity of these elected federal positions and other federal, state, and local government jobs in the public sector (for example, in the military, law enforcement, and public education), the private sector offers no such uniformity. In the private sector, women are not always paid the same as men for the same position; the gender gap in pay is narrowing; and the volume of words written and spoken about this issue is significant. In many instances this volume of words would be served by the recommendations in *Enough with the... Talking Points* to avoid generalizations and stay on topic. That women historically were paid less than men is consistent with and a consequence of the mistaken perceptions that kept them out of higher education, the voting booth, and large areas of the work force to begin with. Once they were allowed to enter these arenas, not surprisingly, they were valued less than men and were harassed by some men who didn't understand or agree with the disruption of what they had been led to believe was the natural order of things.

Two schools of thought dominate discussions about the gender pay gap: one points to what is considered the median salary calculated according to the raw data of all the women and men who get paid for work. This calculation is called the "uncontrolled gender pay gap" and includes teachers, plumbers, nurses' aides, retail cashiers, attorneys, corporate officers and every employee in the corporation, software developers, arts administrators, nannies, hedge fund managers, delivery drivers, medical doctors, nurses, receptionists, professional athletes, restaurant wait staff, actors, and bakers, to name a few. When we add up the total number of women and men in all of these jobs, and the total amount they are paid respectively, and we divide the total that women make by the number of women, and do the same for the men, the median wage for men in 2020 was approximately 18% higher than that for women. Women were earning 82 cents for every dollar earned by a man—a shift from 2015 when the median wage for men was approximately 26% more than for women, who were making 74 cents for every dollar men earned. These calculations do not take into account that there are far fewer highly paid C-suite and VP-level executives and other highly paid professionals—a disproportionate number of whom have been and still are men—than there are primary grade teachers, nurses, secretaries, various "aides" and nannies—a dispropor-tionate number of whom have been and still are women. The lower numbers of women in high-level positions is another consequence of women having been denied full access to higher education, voting, athletics, and other endeavors for so long.

The second school of thought on the gender pay gap gets more specific regarding what is being compared and takes into consideration, among other things, the type of job, the industry, and the job-holder's experience and qualifications. With these factors considered, when we contrast the salaries of a man and a woman with similar experience and qualifi-cations in the same job and industry, we find that women are paid 99 cents for every dollar a man makes—1% less for no apparent reason. This is called the "controlled gender pay gap." It was at 97 cents per dollar in 2015, and it narrows by a fraction of one percent when it does shrink from year to year. Both the uncontrolled and controlled gender pay gaps are significantly larger for African-American, Native-American, Latina, and Asian-American women when each group is studied separately.[26]

Each of these measurements is valid and has meaning. The former "uncontrolled" 18% disparity allows gender-pay-equity "debunkers" to dismiss the gap as an "apples and oranges" fallacy—*of course there's a gap, you're comparing CEOs with first-grade teachers* (to cite just one example). This debunking chooses to ignore the historic lack of access women had to education, the voting booth, and the world of work beyond the home, the classroom, and limited places in the hospital—a lack of access that guaranteed men would dominate virtually every industry and discipline early on. The latter "controlled" 1% disparity allows those who want gender-pay-parity to point to these historical inequalities as causative and to demand an end to the gap: every woman and every woman's family can make good use of the average additional 1%, the $300.00, $500.00, $1,500.00 or $2,500.00 she is denied, and that a man makes, in an annual, pre-tax $30k, $50k, $150k or $250k job. If you think $300.00 in a year is no big deal, it's clear you're making more than $30k before taxes, or someone else is paying your way. If you think any of these amounts is negligible, send me a check for that amount this week. Include your address and I'll send you a thank-you note and tell you how I used the money.

The World Economic Forum's Global Gender Gap Report, released in March 2021 provides data that estimates when pay equity will be achieved in various parts of the globe. It includes the impact of the COVID-19 pandemic on the economy and its disproportionate impact on women around the world.[27]

ONCE EQUAL ACCESS TO EDUCATION and jobs is provided, and even if pay equity were achieved, other obstacles await women in the workplace—industry by industry, company by company, job by job, boss by boss, co-worker by co-worker. Among the many ways we might speak about these varied obstacles that women still face as they gain access to what Jean Baker Miller called the "real life" world of men, we'll pick one that many women feel gets to the heart of the matter—the tension between, the expectations about, and the ability to embody both *grit* and *grace* especially, but not only, in the workplace. *Grit*, a word traditionally and culturally most often ascribed to men, includes the abilities to assert, differentiate, step in, get it done, and go it alone if need be. *Grace,* traditionally and culturally most often ascribed to women, includes the abilities to accept, allow, unify, connect, and embrace.

Traditionally, men have been expected to be gritty in the workplace (and elsewhere). As women gained and gain increasing access to the world of men's workplaces, they were and are expected to engage the masculine workplace culture's version of grit while retaining their feminine grace.[28] Early on, and still now, many men and women in the workplace were and are unprepared for this dynamic. Those who truly see each other as equals recognize and work through the resentment and awkwardness that arise. Those who don't see each other as equals often behave poorly. The more comprehensive, inclusive perspective that women and men deserve equal treatment is also more complex and more balanced.

THE TRADITIONALLY HYPER-MASCULINE WORLD of the military provides a unique set of challenges for the acceptance of women in the workplace. Aggression and learning how to kill are necessary parts of the experience. Women who choose to serve in the military, especially, but not only, in combat roles, face a range of challenges beyond the formal, structural demands of their training. When they enlist, most of them and their male counterparts are in their late teens and early twenties. Their sudden transition from civilian to military culture is highly stressful. Women and men alike must engage their masculine aggression (fight and kill) in a group-centric (us vs. them) container of feminine connection (squad, unit, platoon) in the service of and with loyalty to God and country—when they're barely out of their teens.

Sexual harassment and assault anywhere are horrendous. The shame, stigma, and desire for privacy that victims need and desire lead to under-reporting of such crimes by both women and men. In the closed system of the United States armed forces, justice has been rare for the victims.

> Of the more than 6,200 sexual-assault reports made by United States service members in fiscal year 2020, only 50 — 0.8 percent — ended in sex-offense convictions under the Uniform Code of Military Justice, roughly one-third as many convictions as in 2019.[29]

Marine Pfc. Florence Schmorgoner was raped by a Marine friend on base in California. She didn't know the protocol for reporting the assault, she lived in the same building as her attacker, and she saw him regularly. She gradually fell into depression and tried to kill herself six times. A conversation with another female Marine who had been assaulted gave her the courage to file a report. N.C.I.S. began a rape investigation, which led to a recorded conversation between Schmorgoner and her attacker, who admitted to the assault and apologized. Eventually the Marine commander and N.C.I.S. recommended against a court-martial of the rapist, who completed his Marine contract and received an honorable discharge. Schmorgoner struggled with posttraumatic stress and fell more deeply into despair and disillusionment with the Corps.[30] That's one example. There are many more.

Prosecuting major military crimes, including sexual assault, has traditionally been within the purview of the commander under whose jurisdiction the crime took place. Since 2013 New York Senator Kirsten Gillibrand has annually introduced legislation designed to move that authority from the commander to an independent prosecutor.[31] By mid-2021 she had yet to succeed, but the tide seemed to be changing.

The Department of Defense's "Annual Report on Sexual Assault in the Military" found over 20,000 instances of "unwanted sexual contact" in 2018. In December 2020, fourteen "officials" at the Army's Fort Hood base in Texas were fired or suspended after "a series of violent deaths, suicides and complaints of sexual harassment." Senator Gillibrand's ongoing attempts to introduce this legislation have increasing support in the Senate, and are supported by the recommendations of a panel created by Secretary of Defense Lloyd Austin, III. What will actually become law is complicated by demands to address additional issues with other crimes committed and prosecuted within the military.[32]

IT'S WORTH NOTING THAT AS women demanded and took more seats at various tables in the private and public sectors, leadership capacities and approaches had been evolving historically from *autocratic* (do what I say or there will be consequences) to *authoritarian* (be loyal to us, the hierarchy, and the mission and we'll take care of you) to *strategic* (be the best, outperform others, and the sky's the limit) to *collaborative* (relationships and teamwork are key—take care of all stakeholders) to *integral* (the rare ability to embody and engage the appropriate leadership approach in a given context).[33] Those first three capacities, still the most prevalent in corporate America, are largely grounded in distinctly masculine tendencies. The collaborative and integral capacities introduce (and attempt to integrate) the connection and embrace of the feminine.

Again, we're not suggesting that *men = bad* and *women = good* (which would be an unhealthy masculine move). We're pointing out that an integration of the feminine and masculine in each of us makes for happier, "wholer," and more balanced women and men. We're saying that because of men's historical lack of understanding and fear of the feminine, which has manifested as a historical subjugation of women by men, this integration of the feminine and masculine is quite a bit behind schedule, so to speak. Individual men didn't *choose* this, although many were caught up in and helped perpetuate it.

The subtitle to Susan Faludi's 1999 *Stiffed* is "The Betrayal of the American Man." According to her research, when post-World War II, "Boomer" men found themselves feeling "boxed in" as adult men in a society that was not keeping the promises it had raised them on, they were chided, "Who are they to complain?" And they were "told that the box is of their own manufacture, designed to their specifications…. designed to showcase…not to confine" them.[34] Faludi's research explored one generation of men's experiences and found yet another pervasive, albeit subtle, example of othering—this time of the men who were supposed to be to blame for subjugating women, and who, themselves, felt boxed into social roles that limited who and how they could be. Folks who need an easy, generalized scapegoat for society's ills have been slow to acknowledge, much less accept this because it's too complex. As Jean Baker Miller observed, what a few men in our society have built has been at the expense of other men (see note 13). Intentionally doing the work to integrate healthy feminine and masculine tendencies in every human is a better idea than pitting men against women for some finite prize.

On June 24, 2022 the U. S. Supreme Court overturned *Roe v. Wade* and ruled that state governments can once again limit or remove a woman's authority over her body. More than 60% of Americans—Republican, Democrat, and Independent—oppose government control of women's bodies. Very rarely do those who disagree on this issue engage in thoughtful discourse beyond passionate slogans and talking points. While awareness of the struggles women face in America continues to expand, sexual harassment, sexual abuse, and legal, physical, and psychological assaults against women continue both in the military and in greater numbers among civilians.

Any sense of progress or regress, of course, resides in the hearts, minds, and perspectives of the beholders. Women's progress may be experienced by some men as regress, threat, or an opportunity for more subtle harassment. On December 11, 2020, a man wrote an opinion piece entitled, "Is There a Doctor in the White House? Not if You Need an M.D." Deemed worthy of publication by the *Wall Street Journal*, the subtitle reads "Jill Biden should think about dropping the honorific, which feels fraudulent, even comic." Here's the first paragraph:

> Madame First Lady—Mrs. Biden—Jill—kiddo: a bit of advice on what may seem like a small but I think is a not unimportant matter. Any chance you might drop the "Dr." before your name? "Dr. Jill Biden" sounds and feels fraudulent, not to say a touch comic. Your degree is, I believe, an Ed.D., a doctor of education, earned at the University of Delaware through a dissertation with the unpromising title "Student Retention at the Community College Level: Meeting Students' Needs." A wise man once said that no one should call himself "Dr." unless he has delivered a child. Think about it, Dr. Jill, and forthwith drop the doc.[35]

The opinion writer, Joseph Epstein, who has written some books, goes on to expose his undergraduate degree from the University of Chicago, his thirty years of teaching at Northwestern University "without a doctorate or any advanced degree," and his years as "editor of the American Scholar." He expresses his opinion about the declining value of doctoral degrees and his disdain for using the title "Dr." before one's name unless one happens to be a medical doctor. What he doesn't write speaks volumes.

He never mentions why he has not written similar pieces about or to male doctor-imposters like Dr. Henry Kissinger or Dr. Phil (McGraw), or about Dr. Scott Atlas, who *is* a medical doctor and who has chosen to speak outside his area of expertise, putting anyone who listens to him at risk amid a pandemic. Perhaps because it's outside his social circle and field of view, he makes no reference to the valuable role that retention plays in meeting students' needs in educational institutions generally and in community colleges more specifically, and to the essential role that community colleges play in the lives of millions of Americans. He ignores that Dr. Biden has indeed delivered a child, with a higher level of investment, commitment, and intimacy than any assistance offered by the medical doctor at her daughter's birth.

Each of these omissions supports the point of this chapter and this book. What Mr. Epstein—Joe—kiddo doesn't address, whether because he doesn't know they're there, or knowing their presence, doesn't care, is that his cultural givens are speaking through his mask. Merton's "anonymous authority of the collectivity,"[36] Wilber's "…vast intersubjective network,"[37] and the unhealthy masculine foundation of the collective American Shadow are speaking through him. He chooses to publicly target a woman he's never met, apparently because he can, and despite the availability of other public targets who are men. Epstein's writing echoes Walpole's desperate, failed attempt to demean Wollstonecraft. Despite having at his disposal his apparent erudition, intellect, acclaimed under-graduate education, and some 228 years of developmental progress since Walpole got it wrong, Epstein himself manifests the traits of the hyena, albeit sans petticoat.

What good did this particular bit of public writing do? Why not give Dr. Biden a call or write her a letter if he feels so strongly about her D and her r? Why choose this particular woman as his target? As the saying goes, cognitive development is necessary, but not sufficient, for moral development. Walpole's ignorance may have been invincible due to the cultural norms of his time; Epstein's ignorance was vincible in 2020. Northwestern University made a public statement on December 12, 2020, disavowing Epstein's "misogynistic views," noting that he had not taught there since 2003, and removing his presence from their website.[38]

Epstein's specific reason(s) for targeting Dr. Biden notwith-standing, his behavior is consistent with what Faludi, among others, referred to as the "backlash" against women's progress. Her 1991 book by that name was integrated enough to create its own backlash both from women and men who self-identified as supporters of the women's movement, *and* from men and women who believed the women's movement was effectively destroying the American family and social fabric. Faludi's reporting, rather than uncovering an organized conspiracy against women's progress, however, pointed to the embedded, interrelated influences of 1980s news and com-mentary, television, movies, fashion, beauty, and pop psy-chology, all simply accepted by many Americans as acceptable, true and/or desirable at the time. We now have an over-abundance of print, broadcast, and streaming sources of (mis/dis)information and content that we are free to ignore, engage, believe, and deem acceptable, true, and desirable—or not.[39] The Public Religion Research Institute's (PRRI) March

2021 survey, to take just one example, found that 15% of adult Americans believe that the "government, media, and financial worlds in the U.S. are controlled by a group of Satan-worshipping pedophiles who run a global sex trafficking operation."[40] In light of that remarkable belief—which, is, shall we say, evidence-light—it is both sad and surprising that substantial numbers of men and women still do not or cannot accept that women and men are different in some very real and obvious ways—*and equal.*

Faludi's work refuted diverse myths and partial truths about the alleged damage women's progress was doing to, well, women's progress, and by extension to American society, and it called out the ways those myths and partial truths were being perpetuated in the 1980s. More subtle, nuanced versions of those myths and partial truths regarding women's rights persist today, and while some Americans still want to qualify how women should live their lives, many have added new fantastic myths and outright lies to their repertoires. As noted above, Faludi published *Stiffed* after *Backlash.* Many men, it seems, were suffering as well, and they continue to suffer, because of America's cultural myths and partial truths about what it means to be a man. *Anonymous authority of the collectivity* and *vast intersubjective network,* indeed.

BEYOND WOMEN IN GOVERNMENT, CORPORATIONS, the military, elite athletic events, bestselling books, awkward missives to the First Lady-elect, and other more socially visible examples of gender-based discrimination and progress lie additional issues that are more personal and often invisible—even to other women. We'll briefly look at two. One is avoidable and resolvable; the other is new and still not fully understood. The first is *period poverty,* which is defined as "the inability to access menstrual hygiene products." This lack of access affected 20% of 13-19-year-olds in 2019 and 23% in 2021. Not surprisingly, period poverty particularly affects "lower-income and students of color." Among those affected, 51% admit to wearing period products for longer than recommended because of their lack of access; 65% "agree that society teaches people to be ashamed of their periods;" and 85% "agree that periods should be recognized as an indicator of good health rather than as something dirty or gross."[41]

Check in for a moment with how you feel as you read this— no judgment. Just notice what comes up for you around the topic of and statistics on the menstrual cycle, especially for the young, poor and uninformed (through no fault of their own). Good. Thanks. Dr. Shelby Davis, a pediatrician at the Children's Hospital of Philadelphia, is active in their Policy Lab, where she works primarily with adolescents. She notes two basic questions that we know are important and developmentally natural during adolescence: *Who am I?* and *Am I normal?* (We'll return to that first one in Chapter Eleven). Dr. Davis reminds us that as young women are living with and into these questions, the first period "is a huge developmental milestone" that in America is "still connected to so much shame and stigma," because "we do a poor job of normalizing" what is a perfectly normal experience. She asks us to imagine (or remember) what this experience is like for girls whose parents, doctor, or school has never taught them to expect a period and what it is. Davis reports that they:

> feel alone, scared, embarrassed, [and may] worry that there's something wrong with them, that they're dying, and even worse for this age group, they feel like they're not normal…but on top of that, imagine that this person doesn't have the means to afford menstrual products.[42]

In addition to the basic information not provided by some parents, doctors, and schools, as of May 2021 thirty states didn't consider menstrual products medical necessities and subjected them to sales tax—further burdening the young women most in need (and bringing income to the states). Some states exempt such health-related products as acne medication, aspirin, other pain relievers, lip balm, sunscreen, and dandruff shampoo from taxes, but tax menstrual products. You get the idea. It's a state-by-state issue. These are our daughters. In every state. In the United States. So to speak.

And yes, many kids can find any information they want online (a blessing and a curse, and part of the second issue we'll address), so some girls can learn about menstruation on their own. True, and in late elementary or middle school, they can also read up on those Satan-worshipping, sex-trafficking pedophiles who 15% of American adults believe are running the country. Are we to trust, then, that our early adolescent daughters, grounded in their slightly more than a decade of life, will be able to decide without competent adult support whether Satan-worshipping pedophiles are running the country and if unexpected bleeding for no apparent reason is okay, normal or dangerous? Dr. Davis describes her work in the Policy Lab as a multi-pronged approach that includes "advocating for medically accurate, age-appropriate, and comprehensive sex ed," and helping legislators make menstrual products more available in public restrooms, schools, and other appropriate locations.[43]

The current generation of girls who are impacted by period poverty (and those who aren't), along with the boys with whom they're growing up, have experienced an America amid ongoing war abroad, ongoing gun violence in schools and elsewhere, other kinds of violence, catastrophic hurricanes, floods, and fires, and a global pandemic. Some of those who might guide them through these events are adults—chronologically if not developmentally—who are unable or unwilling to engage respectfully when they disagree, and, in many cases, are immersed in a lifestyle that, at its best, endorses, and, at its worst, insists on and appears to reward speed, immediate gratification, relentless distraction, and the singular pursuit of material fulfillment. Every one of these children deserves and needs to have an honest, loving, and reasonably well-informed adult she or he can count on at home, in the medical office, and in school. And yes, that's not news. Which leads us to the second, issue, which is still emerging and not yet fully understood.

From 2011 through 2016, the percentage of adolescents (aged 12-17) who reported at least one major depressive episode went up—about 2% for boys (rounded, the increase went from 4% to 6%) and about 7% for girls (rounded, the increase went from 12% to 19%). Note that girls began that time period with a higher rate of reported depression than boys and increased at a higher rate as well. These increases, among other worrisome trends, were generally consistent across socio-economic status, region of the country, and type of location (rural, suburban, urban), among students who identified as "White," "Black," or "Hispanic." This group of adolescents, known as Generation Z or iGen ("internet generation") is "the first generation to grow up with the internet in their pockets."[44] Social psychologist Jean Twenge marks 1995 as the first birth year for iGen, which means the oldest members would have been between 11 and 16 years old when Facebook lowered its membership age requirement to 13, and Twitter, Tumblr, Instagram and Snapchat became available between 2006 and 2011. Though not the first smartphones, both the iPhone and Samsung's Galaxy, debuted in these years as well.[45]

We know that social media has changed and is changing our lives, and not just the lives of females, the young, or iGen. We are beginning to identify correlations and patterns, but we do not yet have evidence-based conclusions—we are still learning about the impacts social media and screen time have on our physiological, cognitive, emotional, and social lives. Twenge's research, however, shows that *two* activities correlate significantly with depression (and suicide-related outcomes): electronic device use and watching television. *Five* activities are inversely correlated with those two risks: sports and exercise; religious services; reading books and other print media; socializing in-person; and doing homework. Less screen time, especially when accompanied by these five activities, leads to lower incidences of depression and suicide.[46]

What we *do* know is that prior to 2011 adolescent girls reported higher rates of depression and anxiety than adolescent boys, and more female than male college students identified as having a psychological disorder. Since 2011 and at least through 2016, those rates have risen for both groups, and the rates for girls have risen significantly higher than for boys.[47] Again, we know some of the *what,* but have not yet validated the *why* behind what is happening to our daughters.[48]

To what extent do ignorance, arrogance, greed, bigotry and other components of our collective Shadow inform the particulars of period poverty and increasing depression and anxiety amid the larger American herstories and histories? How is it that a self-described exceptional, wealthy, powerful nation spends trillions of dollars on various elective wars and corporate and industrial special interests, but seems unable to provide or make affordable, basic, necessary healthcare products for its daughters and to create and steward a culture, a society, and a way of being that do not induce depression and anxiety? The question is directed at all of us—parents, politicians, educators, healthcare providers, and anyone else who is, has, or has had a mother, daughter or sister.

At least two related questions arise for which this book does not have evidence-based answers. To what extent do the narratives of women's subjugation and the fear of the feminine influence, play into, or account for the significantly higher rate of increase in depression and anxiety for iGen girls? And what will be the long-term impacts of social-media's influence on how we interact with our children and each other? Various hypotheses and intuitive responses suggest that (of course) centuries of bias against women does play a role in these changes. For now, accepting this as a given, how can we better prepare our own and each other's daughters for the world we have co-created for them?

One practical place we might put our attention is paid maternity leave. Remarkably, as of October 2021, the U. S. was one of eight countries on the planet without paid national maternity leave—which many developed countries simply call parental leave. Jody Heymann, founder and director of the World Policy Analysis Center at U.C.L.A., laments that "The rest of the world, including low-income countries, has found a way to do this." Our record is similarly abysmal when it comes to paid national paternity leave.[49] Voters and lawmakers who oppose women's rights to abortion also block national attempts to help new parents stay home during their newborns' earliest weeks and months.

Faced with inequity and contradiction, how might we best love our daughters and nurture their recognition and ownership of their authentic voices as we continue our practice in the community of truth?

TOWARD THAT END, WE'LL BRIEFLY revisit the concept of voice—both within and beyond Carol Gilligan's engagement with that word. In her 1993 "Letter to Readers," cited earlier, Gilligan reflects on how her understanding of voice was expanded and refined through the work of women in theater. She notes that they "have an understanding of voice which is physiological and cultural as well as deeply psychological." More specifically, she cites Kristin Linklater's helping her to differentiate between "a voice that is an open channel—

connected physically with breath and sound, psychologically with feelings and thoughts, and culturally with a rich resource of language—and a voice that is impeded or blocked." Additionally, she learned:

> ...from working with [Normi] Noel to pick up relational resonances and follow the changes in people's voices that occur when they speak in places where their voices are resonant with or resounded by others, and when their voices fall into a space where there is no resonance, or where the reverberations are frightening, where they begin to sound dead or flat.

Gilligan summarizes her evolving reflections on voice as:

> ...something like what people mean when they speak of the core of the self. Voice is natural and also cultural. It is composed of breath and sound, words, rhythm and language. And voice is a powerful psychological instrument and channel, connecting inner and outer worlds.[50]

In his posthumously published, *The Art of Voice,* poet Tony Hoagland, writing in the context of poetic principles and practice, reflects variously on voice. He calls it "the distinctive linguistic presentation of an individual speaker," and "the mysterious atmosphere that makes [the poem] memorable, that holds it together and aloft like the womb around an embryo." He describes voice as being "more primary than any story or idea the poem contains," as something through which "we may learn how someone else does it—that is, how they live, breathe, think, feel and talk," and as that which embodies "a convincingly complex version of the world and of human nature."[51]

So voice both includes and transcends the physical sounds we make when we speak, or the gestures and countenance we employ when, absent speech, we sign, or the marks on the page or screen we make when we write. It presents us and represents who we are beyond the explicit or implicit meanings of the words we express—the stories we tell and how we tell them. In this chapter we concern ourselves with the collective voice of girls and women and with the individual voice of each girl and each woman—especially amid generations of dominance by men's voices. In the larger context of this book, we are called to remember Rabbi Gellman's focus on one human being at a time, in both life and death, and to turn that focus toward each unique human voice in the Americas, Vietnam, Afghanistan, Iraq, and the rest of the world.

WE'LL BRING THIS CHAPTER TO a close by journeying back across the Atlantic, whence we began, and considering two stories that never happened. Five years after publishing *A Vindication of the Rights of Women*, Mary Wollstonecraft died due to complications of childbirth eleven days after giving birth to a daughter, who, later known as Mary Shelley, would go on to write *Frankenstein, or the Modern Prometheus*. So, a woman writes a treatise against the limiting educational expectations forced upon, and the expansive opportunities withheld from, girls and women. She gives birth to a daughter who will never know her, and who will go on to make up a story[52] about a man who, using body parts from diverse origins, creates "life" in the form of an oversized male creature with unusual strength and who is seen as ugly, terrifying and "other"—a fiend, a monster, a wretch, by his creator and those who come upon him. Nonetheless he learns language, reason, and emotion by observing and listening to those he encounters and by reading Goethe's *Sorrows of Werter*, Plutarch's *Lives,* and Milton's *Paradise Lost*. Still, his creator denies him a companion, a complement, a partner.

Victor Frankenstein's "fiend," in his recognition of and request for companionship and relationship, demonstrates the presence of and desire for the healthy feminine. Denied it, he falls back on the unhealthy masculine and sets out to destroy his creator—a move that can be seen as a desire for justice devolving into vengeance. He also begins to abhor and exile himself, which is a more complex move that blends his sense of independence, his vanquished desire for companionship, which has been replaced by a desire for isolation from humans, and, perhaps, a desire to do no further harm to them as well. This final desire arises from an explicit promise the "creature" made to his creator, if only he would give him a complement, a connection, a partner: someone like himself.

So goes, at least in part, the trajectory of the history of our collective American Shadow. We still have much work to do toward developing our desire for equal and authentic human relationships amid our diverse origins, appearances, and habitual designations of "other," and our alleged desire, as yet unrealized, to do no further harm. As with Frankenstein's creation, men yearn, some consciously, some unconsciously, for a complement—for the connection of the healthy feminine to balance the separateness of our embodied unhealthy masculine. We often confuse this yearning with weakness, which we project onto women, whom we then subjugate and oppress externally as "other." And all the while we subjugate and repress the healthy feminine within ourselves—the very thing we need in order to be "more complete," to move toward a more integrated human and a more perfect union, in every meaning of those words. Frankenstein created an exceptional creature without a companion, without another like himself. *He*, literally, had no complement—he was "the other" to all who came upon him and feared him. Though he longed for and sought connection, companionship, and relationship, he was refused and cast out because of how others saw him, not because of how he saw or actually was. It didn't end well for him or his creator. It tends not to end well any time we create *others* in the unhealthy masculine sense.

But let's not end on a bummer. Between the publications of Miller's *Toward a New Psychology of Women* in 1976 and Gilligan's *In a Different Voice* in 1982, Rosemary Sutcliff gave us her retelling of "Gawain and the Loathely Lady"[53] amid other tales from the legend of King Arthur. Here's a synopsis, which is a far cry from Sutcliff's vivid and joyful storytelling (with my occasional comments in parentheses, and permanent apologies to the late Ms. Sutcliff).

On Christmas night King Arthur agrees to help a damsel, who, engaged to a knight, saw him taken by "a creature... twice the size of a mortal man..." The creature also called Arthur a coward and told the damsel he'd brawl with the king anytime at Tarn (Lake) Wathelan. Arthur's knights, including Lancelot and Gawain, volunteer to fight their king's battle, but he honors his word to the damsel and sets out with her, and without backup, cell phone, or tracking device, to rescue her fiancé.

When he finds the creature (the Knight of Tarn Wathelan—as large as the damsel had claimed), his horse skids to a halt, and, struck by a sense of "Devil's work," Arthur is unable even to raise his sword. Knowing he's in trouble, he asks the Knight what he wants. Noting that he could easily kill or imprison the king, the Knight offers to free him if he returns on New Year's Day with the correct answer to *What is it that all women most desire?* Humiliated and enraged, Arthur agrees and spends the next week asking every "girl," ale-wife," "great lady," and "aged nun" the question. Each gives him a different answer (uh oh).

Toward the end of his fruitless week, a soft voice calls out to him, and his eyes fall upon "the most hideous creature that he had ever seen," with "a nightmare face," "only one eye," and a "shapeless gash" for a mouth (a.k.a. the Loathely Lady). She says she knows what's going on with the Knight of Tarn Wathelan, and that she can help Arthur with the question. He offers advance gratitude—promising her anything, if she actually helps him. She cautions the desperate king to hear her terms before agreeing, so he listens and then swears his oath to her. She whispers the answer to the question, he laughs because it is so obvious once known, and then he asks her what she wants in return (I would have wanted this information before swearing the oath, but I'm no Arthur).

The Loathely Lady tells him to go settle things with his tormentor and then to return to her to complete their deal. Arthur agrees, first teases his opponent with some wrong answers and then provides the right one, which enrages the Knight, who realizes that his "hideous and misshapen" sister, Ragnell, the only other who knew the answer, has helped the king. Nonetheless, the Knight keeps his word and releases Arthur, who returns to Ragnell. When she tells the king she wants to marry a knight from his court, his immediate response is that it's impossible. She questions his honor. Arthur, being Arthur, vows to keep his word.

He returns to the castle and admits to the queen and his knights that he got in way over his head and made a promise that he cannot fulfill himself. He tells them of the help he received from Ragnell (not mentioning her appearance) and of her desire to marry a knight. The knights, being men, think it's no big deal and ask only, "Is she bonnie?" to which the king responds that she's "the most hideous and misshapen woman that I ever saw." Silence envelops the room. Then some of the knights, remembering themselves, step up. Gawain is the most zealous, but Arthur insists that he see her first before committing to wed her.

They journey to Tarn Wathelan the next day and collectively gasp when they see Ragnell. Gawain keeps his word, and they all ride back to the castle for the wedding, which unfolds more like Gawain's funeral, reluctantly attended.

At night's end, the newlyweds retire to their chamber, spend time freshening up separately, and Ragnell finally approaches Gawain from behind and beckons his gaze. He turns and sees "the most beautiful maiden that he had ever seen," still sporting the Loathely Lady's gown and jewelry. Bewildered, Gawain asks her where his wife is (smooth, G).

Ragnell explains that she had been under a spell, and that his marrying her half freed her, so now she would be fair for half the day and foul for half. She also tells him that he gets to choose whether she's fair or foul by day or night. Gawain notes how hard the choice is, and first utters that she should be fair at night for him alone. She notes that by day she would then be exposed to the pity and ridicule of the fair ladies of the queen's court. Gawain admits his selfishness, reverses his choice, and Ragnell acknowledges that his reversal is truly a lover's answer, *and* that *she* would prefer being fair for him alone since he means more to her than the court ladies do (phew!). Finally, Gawain (head spinning but hanging on) tells her that her suffering is beyond his, that she is wiser than he, and that ultimately the choice is hers to make and he will be content with whatever she chooses.

She embraces him and they laugh and cry together. By allowing her to choose her own way (what all women most desire—the answer to the %*#?! question), Gawain has broken the other half of the spell (way to go, G!), and Ragnell will be her fair self 24/7. She explains the spell's fine print to him, and the next day the bewildered but happy castle inhabitants continue the wedding celebration sans concerns about Gawain's demise.

They live for seven happy years together, during which Gawain becomes gentler, kinder and more steadfast. After seven years, Ragnell leaves, or dies—it's not clear—and Gawain went "hollow of heart for her sake" until his own death.

AMID AND DESPITE IGNORANCE, ARROGANCE, fear and the consequent subjugation that have prevented and still prevent women from getting to choose their own way, the healthy feminine navigates and transcends the finite power of the unhealthy masculine. Beneath the metaphorical and sometimes literal burden of men's feet upon women's necks, the healthy feminine integrates the healthy masculine and manifests an increasingly resilient strength that is fundamental to continuing the infinite game of Life—and to welcoming all who want to play. But only if we invite, allow, advocate, engage, and embrace such a trajectory.

Trails of Tears & Broken Treaties, the Third Colorado Regiment, & the Only Good Indians[1]

*What is the sound of the end of play, and what
feelings does that sound bring up in you?*[2]

This chapter does not mention the vast majority of both extant and extinct Native American nations, and only fragments of the histories of those that are mentioned are explored. Rarely does it reveal the everyday moments of any individual's life. Beginning to understand the scope and scale of these histories is important, and it feels feeble and obvious, yet essential to write that. You can begin to take a macro view of 500-plus years of the interactions between Native Peoples, Europeans, and Americans through the following resources. All links were accurate as we went to press.

- Dr. Claudio Saunt's Digital Projects are available at: http://www.claudiosaunt.com/#projects. The projects include "The Invasion of America," which provides an interactive visual guide to the expansion of the United States across North America: https://usg.maps.arcgis.com/apps/webappviewer/index.html?id=eb6ca76e008543a89349ff2517db47e6.
- A 90-second video of the U. S. expansion from 1776 through 2010, which is linked to the interactive guide, is directly available here: https://www.youtube.com/watch?v=pJxrTzfG2bo
- The History of Land Cessions in the United States may be available here (it disappeared and reappeared as I wrote): https://archive.org/tream/annualreportofbu218smit#page/696/mode/2up

- An interactive Timeline of Native History via the National Institutes for Health's National Library of Medicine provides an overview that goes beyond healing traditions: https://www.nlm.nih.gov/nativevoices/timeline/index.html

Also, the complex history of the Bureau of Indian Affairs, as well as its current manifestation, is for the most part missing from these pages. An exploration of these two sites and one book (among many more) will provide some insight into the bureau.

- https://www.bia.gov/
- https://www.archives.gov/research/native-americans/bia
- *Custer Died for Your Sins: An Indian Manifesto* by Vine Deloria, Jr. (1988/1969).

SOME FIVE-HUNDRED-PLUS YEARS AGO, European explorers and colonizers began bumping into the land masses that are now known as South, Central, and North America and the various islands of the Caribbean—including, but not limited to what are now known as Cuba, the Dominican Republic, Haiti, Jamaica, Puerto Rico, the Bahamas and the Virgin Islands. The indigenous peoples who inhabited these areas include the Taíno, Aztec, Lakota, Yucatán, Iroquois, Inca, Nez Perce, Huron, Apache, Cherokee, Navajo, Olmec, Inuit, Toba, Quechua and Chibcha, among many, many, many more. Many more.

While our focus is on the section of North America that became known first as the United Colonies, and then as the United States of America circa 1776, it is important to remember that the indigenous peoples had been on these lands for some 10,000 to 20,000 years when the English, Spanish, Portuguese, and French met, interacted with, and eventually colonized them.[3] Slaughter, rape, removal, and betrayal often characterized the colonization process, which in contemporary parlance is a literal cancelation process, as the invaders interpreted different languages, technologies, and cultural beliefs and rituals as "lesser" (or, as some of us might say today, not "woke") and the practitioners sometimes as "innocents" and sometimes as "savages" (much as some science fiction imagines more advanced beings arriving on earth and being taken aback by twentieth- and twenty-first-century human ignorance, savagery, violence, and war).

With the above as a brief historical overview, and to the point of this writing, the federal government of the United States entered into hundreds of treaties with diverse American Indian tribes between 1778 and 1871 and, for all practical purposes, has broken part or all of every treaty, even to the point of the Supreme Court's 1903 decision in *Lone Wolf v. Hitchcock,* which held that Congress has the power to modify or terminate Native American treaties without the Native Americans' consent.

We'll zero in on several examples here, from among thousands, which is another way of saying that most of the details of the interactions between the United States, some of the individual states, and the diverse American Indian nations that were gradually removed and betrayed will not appear on these pages. Also not included are the histories of the North American indigenous peoples from before the Europeans arrived or their histories during the early fighting between the English, Dutch, French, and others for control of the "New World." Much more occurred before, during, and between the episodes summarized below. Among the examples cited, the specific, lived experience of each oppressed individual and each oppressor can only be imagined by those of us who are upset today by a slow internet connection, a flight delay, poor cell reception, wearing a mask for the common good, or spilt milk in any iteration.[4]

AFTER THE ARRIVAL OF THE EUROPEANS AND the establishment and settling of New Netherlands, New France, and New England—in what are now parts of the northeastern U. S. and southeastern Canada, and before there was a United States—the Iroquois Confederacy, also known as the People of the Longhouse and composed at first of the Seneca, Cayuga, Onondaga, Mohawk, and Oneida, and later the Tuscarora, navigated various agreements, conflicts, and commerce with both the Europeans and other indigenous nations. As the Europeans competed with each other through both violence and negotiation for the land on which the Iroquois and other nations lived, the indigenous peoples found themselves in positions of defending the land that sustained them or choosing one European country over another. In what is known as both the French and Indian War and the Seven Years War, the Iroquois sided with the British. During the American Revolution, they attempted to stay neutral, but eventually the Oneida and Tuscarora sided with the colonists and the other four nations sided with Britain. At the war's end, the Iroquois Confederacy was devastated, and they ceded lands to the United States through the Treaty of Fort Stanwix in 1784 and the Treaty of Canandaigua in 1794.

This pattern of arrival and intrusion, violence and commerce, acquisition of land through treaty, and acquisition of more land through violence, treaty, and treaty betrayal as more Europeans arrived or as something of value was discovered in the land did not begin or end with the Iroquois experience. And, in much more subtle iterations at various scales, it continues today.

IN 1813 AND 1814, TENNESSEE LANDOWNER, slaveholder, and militia general Andrew Jackson "marched through the Creek Nation, torching villages and killing residents." Between 1,200 and 1,300 men, women, and children were killed in the battles at Tallushatchee, Talladega, and Horseshoe Bend.[5] Called "Sharp Knife by the Indians," he and his troops "had slain thousands of Cherokees, Chickasaws, Choctaws, Creeks and

Seminoles"[6] —so it was no surprise that when he became president in 1829 he initiated and encouraged a decade of legislation, court decisions, military actions, treaties, and treaty betrayals designed to remove Native Americans from land east of the Mississippi River. The 1830 "Act to provide for an exchange of lands with the Indians residing in any of the states or territories, and for their removal west of the river Mississippi" is an example of euphemism at its best (or worst).

The House vote on the Act was expected to be close, so undecided members were reminded that the bill was important to Jackson, that those who opposed it would be considered "traitors and recreants," and that the president would work to unseat them in the next election—a tactic that is alive and well in the current century. The Act passed in the Senate 28-19, and in the House 102-97, with sixteen of the 102 *yes* votes attributable to the "three-fifths compromise." The slave states garnered sixteen votes because they could include "three fifths of all other Persons," (in this case, slaves), for tax and representation purposes. Said differently, in the absence of the votes these states received for owning slaves, the Act would have lost in the House by a vote of 86-93 (four of the "compromise" votes voted "no" and one abstained).[7] Eventually the "exchange of lands" would open up millions of acres of former Cherokee, Chickasaw, Choctaw, Creek and Seminole lands to southern planters and their slaves in Florida, Georgia, Alabama, Mississippi, Tennessee, and North Carolina, and thousands of native peoples would die from exposure, cholera, starvation, and exhaustion as they were forced west. Others, who resisted, would die in battle with federal troops, state militia, and armed citizens.

In his attempts to convince the peoples he wanted to remove that removal was in their best interests, Jackson gave an army major the following instructions: "Say to my red Choctaw children, and my Chickasaw children to listen.... Say to the chiefs and warriors that I am their friend...." and if they move west of the Mississippi, "There, beyond the limits of any State, in possession of land of their own, which they shall possess as long as the Grass grows or water runs. I will protect them and be their friend and father."[8] Upon passage of "the Act to provide for an exchange of lands..." Jackson remarked that he had done "my duty to my red children," and any failure of his good intentions toward them would be due to "their want of duty to themselves." He concluded that he had done everything in his power and would "now leave the poor deluded creeks & cherokees to their fate, and their annihilation."[9]

The discovery of gold in 1829 (effectively exhausted by 1835) in Alabama, Georgia, South Carolina, North Carolina, and the Cherokee nation, added prospectors to the mix of planter-politicians, the enslaved, and native peoples. As the gold-seekers intruded on their land, the Cherokees attacked them, "prompting white Georgians to retaliate."[10] In coming years, the discovery of gold in various territories west of the Mississippi, along with the first iteration of "manifest destiny" in 1845 and its subsequent embrace,[11] would bring a virtually incessant flow of trespassers onto "Indian Territory." A complementary flow of state and federal government betrayals made it clear that Native Americans should not trust the treaties, and that Andrew Jackson's words, that "an ample district west of the Mississippi" would "be guaranteed to the Indian tribes, as long as they shall occupy it" were meaningless.[12]

In other areas, other resources were confiscated. Less attractive than gold, and in most ways more practical, lead sulfide was mined and used "for religious purposes and to produce paint pigment" by native peoples long before Europeans arrived. As its usefulness for ammunition became known, mining became a for-profit endeavor, and in the late 1820s U. S. citizens were intruding on Sauk lands in what are now parts of Illinois and Wisconsin. By 1831 most of the Sauks abandoned their homes and moved west of the Mississippi, but about a thousand of them returned in 1832, leading to the U.S.-Sauk War and to President Jackson's desire to "deter others from the like unprovoked hostilities by Indians on our frontier." Jackson's deployment of federal troops began shortly after a cholera outbreak arrived along the St. Lawrence River. The outbreak would make its way south and west by steamboat and land, killing soldiers and native peoples for months as the troops confronted the Sauks. Further south, Choctaw refugees were marched between 200 and 350 miles through cold, flooded swamps and infected by the troop-transported disease along the way.[13]

"Trail of Tears," perhaps the most well-known phrase that attempts to depict the times, places, sufferings, and betrayals of Indian Removal, refers generally to the events of the 1830s and more specifically to the Cherokee nation's removal in 1838. Some 2,858 refugees were forced to travel some 1,200 miles by steamboat and some 12,496 were forced to travel by foot and wagon for 2,050 miles over three different routes. Approximately 986 of the 15,354 refugees—about 7 percent, died during the journey; another 2,500 died in holding camps and due to various causes.[14] Estimates put the total number of Indians removed during this decade at around 100,000, with 15,000 refugee deaths along the way.[15] Said differently, an infant, a child, a woman, or a man was forced to leave her or his home 100,000 times and travel hundreds of miles by foot, horse, wagon, or boat in horrible conditions. One of these individuals died 15,000 times.

The removal process was persistently characterized by diverse tactics such as "legal coercion" in which state governments like Georgia and Alabama passed laws that made the deportees' lives intolerable if they chose not to leave[16] (which was exacerbated by the native victims' not having the right to testify in court if they stayed and were arrested). Since treaties were negotiated in English and had to be translated for tribal leaders and then explained to the rest of the tribe, those being fleeced were negotiating in a foreign language. Beyond language was the larger cultural disparity—the Anglo-American legal system was based on perspectives that were foreign to the indigenous nations. The native peoples' common proclivity toward sharing and taking others at their word worked against them in dealing with the federal and state governments, the northern banker-land speculators, and the southern slaveholders—all of whom wanted their land. The condescension of the "woke" white Christians led to widely held beliefs that conversion to land ownership, farming, Christianity, and other beliefs and activities—that is, cancelation of tribal cultures—was in the best interests of the Indians and, in fact, was a sign of the intruders' benevolence and care. A century-plus later, the United States would perpetrate updated iterations of this cultural ignorance, arrogance, and violence in Vietnam, Afghanistan, and Iraq.

The willingness of the "Great Father" and his people in Washington City to break promises and treaties when it was in their best interest to do so rendered the treaty process meaningless. When precious minerals were discovered, when planter-politicians coveted more Indian land, or when more Europeans arrived at the shore, the intruding treaty makers ignored and forgot the treaties. Speculative and manipulative financial arrangements that relieved the Indians of their familiar, ancestral, prime, fertile lands included collusion among profiteering banks and "land companies" that resulted in payments of as little as $1.25 per acre to the victims, with those acres then resold to white U.S. citizens and slaveowners for $30 or $40 per acre. If all of this were not enough, the U.S. government billed those being deported for the costs of deportation. The Chickasaw, for example, paid for census costs, travel costs for military officers, government office furniture, survey costs for the lands they were being exiled to, salaries of the clerks who kept the books, and even the newspaper ads used to announce the sale of the land from which they were being removed.[17]

The Choctaw and Chickasaw nations signed their own respective treaties and suffered through their own unique circumstances of expulsion from their lands. The Creeks would fight a second war against the United States and local militia in 1836 before succumbing. While most Cherokees and Seminoles eventually were removed or killed, many stood their ground. In 1838, the resistant Cherokees were subject to a mix of "squatters, prospectors and marauders" who, with the government's tacit approval and occasional assistance, began to occupy their land, steal or destroy their sources of basic sustenance, and render their lives "wretched and intolerable."[18] Their formal expulsion, the "Trail of Tears" alluded to above, took place between May and October of 1838, with just under one thousand of the fifteen thousand refugees dying along the way. The Seminoles asserted that the 1830 "Indian Removal Act" and the controversial 1832 Treaty of Payne's Landing violated the 1823 Treaty of Moultrie Creek that granted them twenty years on some four million acres in central Florida.[19] They resisted the deportation, and, from 1835 through 1842, they engaged in a protracted conflict known as the Second U. S. Seminole War. At that war's end, with the Seminoles defeated but not vanquished, the U.S. Congress passed "An Act to provide for the armed occupation and settlement of the unsettled part of the peninsula of East Florida." This Act granted that adult male settlers who cultivated at least five acres of land in eastern Florida for five years would receive 160 acres of land and one year of rations from the federal government, and required the settlers to serve in the militia, as needed, to fight the Seminoles.[20]

The Creek, Chickasaw, Cherokee, Choctaw and Seminole tribes would eventually become known as the Five Civilized Tribes, and were dealt with as one entity by the Bureau of Indian Affairs.

By 1850, MUCH OF THE FORMER CHICKASAW, CHOCTAW, CREEK AND CHEROKEE land was inhabited by slaves and their owners in the forced labor camps in the south, and tensions continued to mount between abolitionists and slaveholders and between federal power and states' rights advocates. That some tribal people had begun to adapt to the whites' ways, attend their schools, and purchase both land and slaves exacerbated the conflict between these adapters and those who embraced their cultures of birth. By the time the Civil War began, amid the complexities of their views on slavery, what secession would mean for them, desires for tribal sovereignty, and the immediacy of caring for their families, American Indians found themselves fighting each other "in a white man's war."[21]

Further north and west, while the Union and Confederate armies devastated the land and each other, and for some years thereafter, federal troops faced off with the Cheyenne, Arapaho, Comanche, Lakota, and others. In 1864, in response to a series of skirmishes between soldiers, miners, settlers, and Indians, John Evans, governor of the Colorado Territory, issued an order to "friendly Cheyennes and Arapahos" to report to Fort Lyon for protection since the "Great Father" was angry. Black Kettle, of the Southern Cheyenne, along with other chiefs, wanted peace, and agreed to travel to Fort Lyon, but was concerned that his people would be attacked on the way there by federal troops or the Colorado militia. He sent One Eye and Eagle Head as envoys toward Fort Lyon with a letter that expressed his agreement and requested that troops come to his camp and escort his people—more than two thousand Cheyenne and Arapaho—to the fort.[22]

Having fewer than two hundred mounted troops under his command at Fort Lyon, Major Edward W. Wynkoop, known to the Cheyenne as "Tall Chief Wynkoop," did not immediately trust the request, but after conferring with his officers, decided to make the trip, holding One Eye and Eagle Head as both guides and hostages. When he made it clear he would kill them upon any hint of betrayal, One Eye responded, "The Cheyennes do not break their word. If they should do so, I would not care to live longer." Wynkoop would later say that his conversations with his two hostages shifted his view of Indians. "I felt myself in the presence of superior beings..." whom he had previously thought to be "cruel, treacherous and bloodthirsty."[23] They arrived at the Smoky Hill camp in five days, and after sitting together agreed that Wynkoop, Black Kettle and other chiefs would ride to Denver to make peace with Governor Evans and Colonel Chivington.

When they arrived Evans wanted nothing to do with the Indians and expressed to Wynkoop that they needed to be punished before peace could be attained. When Wynkoop persisted on behalf of the Indians, Evans asked, "But what shall I do with the Third Colorado Regiment if I make peace? They have been raised to kill Indians, and they must kill Indians."[24] Evans finally relented and met with the chiefs, but neither a clear agreement nor a sense of peace was reached. Wynkoop was ordered to return to Fort Lyon. The Arapaho joined him there, while the Cheyenne moved their camp from Smoky Hill to Sand Creek. For his efforts the young Major Wynkoop fell into disfavor with his superiors and was relieved of his command at Fort Lyon.

In November 1864 Colonel John M. Chivington arrived at Fort Lyon. Angered by several officers who wanted to honor Wynkoop's and Black Kettle's desires for peace, he proclaimed, "I have come to kill Indians, and believe it is right and honorable to use any means under God's heaven to kill

Indians."[25] Although Black Kettle gathered women and children beneath both an American flag and a white flag of surrender, Chivington slaughtered the Cheyenne men, women and children in their camp at Sand Creek, with atrocities corroborated by soldiers at the scene. Every dead man, woman and child was scalped, and "in many instances their bodies were mutilated in the most horrible manner—men, women and children's private parts cut out..."[26] That Black Kettle and others escaped was attributed to the drunkenness and lack of discipline among Chivington's men. The slaughter led to a Congressional hearing, and many Indians who had trusted the peace process no longer did:

> In a few hours of madness at Sand Creek, Chivington and his soldiers destroyed the lives or the power of every Cheyenne and Arapaho chief who had held out for peace with the white men. After the flight of the survivors, the Indians rejected Black Kettle...and turned to their war leaders to save them from extermination.[27]

In January 1865 a coalition of Cheyenne, Arapaho and Sioux warriors retaliated, attacking wagon trains and military outposts, scalping those they attacked, and ripping out miles of telegraph wire. When they returned to their camps, they danced in celebration of their attempts to avenge the Sand Creek Massacre, but they knew that the soldiers would return. Some three thousand Cheyenne, Arapaho, and Sioux marched north toward Powder River country to join the Teton Sioux and Northern Cheyenne. Black Kettle, along with 400 older men and women, headed south toward Oklahoma and held to his desire to make peace with the whites. The Southern Cheyenne and Arapaho peoples eventually abandoned any claim to the Colorado Territory. [28]

These patterns of intrusion, resistance, violence, negotiation, treaty, betrayal, more violence, and new intrusions continued as settlers, prospectors, and explorers intentionally or ignorantly trespassed on lands that the government had agreed was "Indian Territory." By late 1866 the Cheyenne, Arapaho, and Sioux continued what was essentially guerilla warfare against the settlers, prospectors, and soldiers who had been sent to protect them, and who continued to intrude onto Indian hunting grounds in northern Wyoming, especially along the Bozeman Road near Fort Phil Kearney. The tribal leaders claimed that the whites' use of the Bozeman Road violated the Fort Laramie Treaty of 1851, which was initially broken shortly after it was signed due to a rush for gold. On December 21, 1866, the coalition of tribes set a series of decoys near the fort and lured the soldiers, led by Captain William T. Fetterman, into an ambush. When the fighting was done, all of the soldiers, some 80 or 81, who were ambushed were dead; almost 200 Indians were killed or wounded.

Colonel Henry B. Carrington, who had been sent to the area to guard the road and establish forts along it, was stunned by what became know as the Fetterman Massacre and the "mutilations—the disembowelings, the hacked limbs" that accompanied it. He would later write an essay, pondering the "savagery" and "paganistic beliefs" that would lead the Indians to "commit the terrible deeds" they did. Dee Brown suggests that, "Had Colonel Carrington visited the scene of the Sand Creek Massacre…he would have seen the same mutilations—committed upon Indians by Colonel Chivington's soldiers. The Indians who ambushed Fetterman were only imitating their enemies…"[29]

These ongoing battles and small skirmishes along the Bozeman Road are often called Red Cloud's War, after the Oglala chief who, in June 1866, had refused to sign a treaty at Fort Laramie when Colonel Carrington arrived with several regiments and orders to build more forts along the Powder River. In the summer of 1867 new Indian Commissioner

Nathaniel Taylor attempted to restart negotiations with Red Cloud, inviting him to meet in western Nebraska with Taylor's team of commissioners and General William T. Sherman, known to the Indians as "Great Warrior Sherman." Again, Red Cloud refused to attend, but he sent several envoys. Sherman's offer of money and clothing for more access to land was not what the Indians wanted or expected to hear, but the parties agreed to meet again in November at Fort Laramie. Red Cloud made it clear on November 9 that he would only attend if the soldiers abandoned the three forts long the Powder River. The commissioners left, but sent Red Cloud a peace offering of tobacco, which he said he would smoke and enjoy, and he reiterated that he would come to Fort Laramie only after the soldiers were gone.

In the spring of 1868, the commissioners and Sherman again arrived at Fort Laramie, and Red Cloud kept them waiting until he could see that the forts were abandoned. Other tribal chiefs signed the treaty on April 29 and May 25, but it would not be until July that troops began to leave the first of the three forts, C. F. Smith, followed by Fort Phil Kearney, and lastly Fort Reno. When the last of the soldiers was gone from C. F. Smith, Red Cloud's warriors burned every building; the Cheyenne, led by Little Wolf, did the same at Phil Kearney. On November 6, 1868 Red Cloud and others signed the Fort Laramie Treaty, Article I of which begins, "From this day forward all war between the parties to this agreement shall forever cease."[30]

Among the specifics of the treaty were the geographic boundaries for the Great Sioux Reservation and also for unceded Sioux territories "north of the North Platte River and east of the summits of the Big Horn Mountains," which "no white person or persons shall be permitted to settle upon or occupy any portion of the same; or without consent of the Indians, first had and obtained, to pass through the same."[31]

Simply put, no whites could occupy, settle, or pass through these territories without permission from the Indians.

Also within the treaty were financial, service, and material considerations to be provided by the United States to the tribes, including real estate (preferably to be farmed), clothing, and English education, all of which would be administered by federal agents. Effectively, the treaty provided a) restrictions and rules by which the indigenous peoples could use the land that they had lived on for centuries, b) the opportunity to become citizens of the nation that was taking their land, and c) a written process through which they would gradually be expected to adopt the white culture while abandoning their own. Three years later the U. S. Congress would amend what is known as the Indian Appropriations Act of 1871 with a final paragraph that ended treaty-making with any Indian tribe or individual Indian. No new treaties would be entered into, and the tradition of breaking old ones would continue to flourish.[32]

Twenty-one days after the Fort Laramie Treaty was signed, Black Kettle, who had continued his quest for peace after the Sand Creek Massacre and had settled along the Washita River in what is now Oklahoma, was killed in a raid led by Lieutenant Colonel George Custer. In response to bands of young Sioux and Cheyenne warriors who continued to attack settlers and soldiers in Kansas and the Oklahoma territory, General Philip Sheridan had given Custer orders to "destroy [the hostile tribes'] villages and ponies, to kill or hang all warriors, and bring back all women and children."[33] Earlier in November Black Kettle and others had ridden some 100 miles to Fort Cobb to ask General William B. Hazen for permission to move their lodges closer to the fort for protection. Hazen denied the request and assured him they would be safe where they were. Black Kettle arrived home on November 26, 1868, the night before Custer carried out Sheridan's orders without identifying who was in the village and ignoring or not knowing that the village was on reservation land. Custer's men killed 103 Cheyenne men, 11 of whom were warriors, and captured 53 women and children.[34]

In response to the "successful" attack, Sherman encouraged Sheridan to continue to kill hostile Indians but to order those who were friendly to come to Fort Cobb to surrender. Led by Little Robe, some of the Cheyenne who survived Washita River arrived at the fort, as did some Arapaho, led by Yellow Bear. When Tosawi, chief of the Comanches, arrived, he introduced himself to Sheridan, saying, "Tosawi, good Indian." Sheridan replied, "The only good Indians I ever saw were dead." The quote would be repeated by word of mouth until it became "The only good Indian is a dead Indian."[35]

AT THE TIME OF THE FORT LARAMIE TREATY of 1868, the federal government believed the Black Hills, *Paha Sapa*—effectively the spiritual center of the world for the Sioux—to be barren, useless land. In the treaty's language, this area was north of the North Platte River and west of the Big Horn mountains, where no whites were permitted to pass through or settle without permission. Rumors of gold in the Black Hills, however, confirmed during an 1874 expedition led by now General Custer, attracted prospectors onto the sacred land. President Grant both denounced the treaty violation and sent a commission to convince the Sioux to allow the prospectors temporary access to the Black Hills. Within two years the Homestake mine was discovered and the towns of Deadwood, Lead, and Rapid City were founded by gold prospectors on Sioux land in direct violation of the treaty. In 1877, Spotted Tail, one of the signatories to the 1868 treaty, would observe that "These promises have not been kept.... All the words have proved to be false."[36]

By this time the government was using the language of "agency" or "friendly" Indians to refer to those who had agreed to live on reservations, leaving only to hunt in the unceded territories, as the treaty allowed. Those who were not living on the reservations were labeled "hostile," but when the "friendly" hunters returned to the reservation, they were angered by the increasing numbers of gold prospectors and settlers arriving on their sacred land. Red Cloud trusted the government to uphold the 1868 treaty, but many of the younger warriors did not. They left the reservation to follow Sitting Bull, Crazy Horse and others who had never lived on a reservation, and who were adamantly opposed to giving the whites access to the Black Hills and to selling the land.

On September 20, 1875, commissioners sent by President Grant set themselves up beneath a large tarpaulin. They were accompanied by 120 soldiers from nearby Fort Robinson in northwestern Nebraska, and they were met by various chiefs and several thousand Indians along the White River in the vicinity of the Red Cloud and Spotted Tail Agencies. Knowing that the Sioux would not sell the *Paha Sapa,* the visitors offered to rent the land and remove the gold for as long as there was gold to remove, after which the Indians could do what they wanted with what was left of their land. The commissioners made their case by saying it would be hard for the "government to keep the whites out of the hills."[37] They also expressed the government's interest in the unceded Powder River and Bighorn Mountain areas, which were important Indian hunting grounds. Neither of these requests was attractive to the chiefs, and both sides agreed to meet again three days later. This September 23 meeting effectively ended before it began when Crazy Horse's envoy, Little Big Man, announced his intention to kill any chief who favored selling the Black Hills. The commissioners decided to return to Fort Robinson, but met secretly with twenty chiefs several days later at the Red Cloud Agency where they made two offers—

one to buy the hills for $6,000,000 and another to lease the hills for $400,000 a year.

The chiefs rejected both offers. Even if they had agreed to one of these offers, the agreement would have no legal bearing without the consent of 75% of the adult males affected by the lease or sale: Article XII of the Fort Laramie Treaty of 1868 stipulates that:

> No treaty for the cession of any portion or part of the reservation herein described which may be held in common, shall be of any validity or force against the said Indians unless executed and signed by at least three-fourths of all the adult male Indians occupying or interested in the same...[38]

The commissioners returned to Washington, D. C., reported their failure, and recommended that Congress ignore the chiefs, designate an appropriate sum for the Black Hills, and force the Indians to sell—in essence, a final offer.[39] In the ensuing nine months, white settlers and prospectors continued to trespass through Sioux lands and into the Black Hills, and bands of Indians stood their ground and attacked them. The government realized that many of the non-agency Indians were armed and better fed than those on the agencies and issued an order that all Indians report to their agencies by January 31, 1876 or suffer military consequences. The War Department authorized General Sheridan to move against the "hostile Sioux," and on June 25, 1876 George Custer would once more engage Indians in battle with slipshod or no reconnaissance. He died, along with the soldiers of the 7th Cavalry who were under his direct command, at Greasy Grass Creek. A nation that claimed that neither its laws nor its military could prevent its citizens from trespassing and settling on Native American lands did find ways to use its military to break the laws inherent in the treaties it had made with the

Indians. In 1877 Congress passed "An act to ratify an agreement with certain bands of the Sioux Nation of Indians and also with the Northern Arapaho and Cheyenne Indians" in direct violation of Article XII of the Fort Laramie Treaty, effectively taking the Black Hills without consent of 75% of adult male Indians. Literally at the time, and metaphorically since then, if "thar's gold in them thar hills," American leadership has proven to be untrustworthy.

THIS PATTERN OF AGREEMENT, BETRAYAL, AND VIOLENCE would continue, simplified by the 1871 treaty ban that prevented new treaties from being made and broken. There were moments, nevertheless, that engendered hope. On May 12, 1879, in the U. S. District Court in Omaha, Nebraska, Judge Elmer S. Dundy ruled in favor of Ponca Chief Standing Bear in *Standing Bear v. George Crook.* Brigadier General Crook had been negotiating with and fighting Indians for over a decade, and his admiration and sympathy for their resilience and courage had gradually grown. He was also aware that his government was not keeping the promises they ordered him to make to the Indians.

After treaties in 1858 and 1865, Ponca land was erroneously ceded to the Sioux at the April 29 signing of the 1868 Fort Laramie Treaty. The Ponca were then moved under an Appropriations Bill to Indian Territory in August of 1876 and, not accustomed to the "hot country" of Indian Territory (present-day Oklahoma), decided to return to their homeland along the Niobrara River in Nebraska. In 1877 the government enforced the removal back to a new reservation in the "hot country." Standing Bear's wife, Shines White, and daughter, Prairie Flower, died on the forced 600-mile march south, and his twelve-year-old son, Bear Shield, died in 1878. Unwilling to bury his son in unfamiliar land, Standing Bear set out for

Nebraska in January 1879, leaving the reservation without permission.

General Crook caught up with them, took the small band of Poncas into custody, and began to escort them back south. Camped at Fort Omaha, Crook listened to Standing Bear's story and enlisted the help of an editor at the *Omaha Daily Herald,* who published the story, which was picked up by other newspapers. The publicity led attorneys John L. Webster and Andrew Poppleton to file a *writ of habeas corpus* under the provisions of the 14th Amendment on behalf of Standing Bear. Because the geographic boundaries of the United States were in a constant state of flux, Native Americans' status as "persons" (much less citizens) under the Constitution was ambiguous at best, and, in response to the writ, the U. S. attorney argued that Standing Bear was neither a person nor a citizen capable of filing suit.

With Standing Bear's legal personhood at stake, Judge Dundy ruled that "an Indian is a person within the meaning of the laws of the United States," that "no rightful authority exists for removing by force any of the [Indians] to the Indian Territory," and that they "must be discharged from custody." Despite his name's appearance in the case title, General Crook was among the first to congratulate the chief after the ruling. Standing Bear buried his son on their tribal lands near the Niobrara River, where he was also buried upon his death in 1908.[40]

The victory was real for Standing Bear and those Ponca who returned to the Niobrara River with him. After the court's ruling, Standing Bear's brother, Big Snake, requested permission to leave the reservation and join Standing Bear in the north, and the Ponca agency administrator, William H. Whiteman, denied his request. Big Snake tested Whiteman by traveling to the Cheyenne Reservation, which was still in Indian Territory, and Whiteman contacted the Commissioner of Indian Affairs in D.C. just nine days after Judge Dundy's decision. In short order, under orders from the Secretary of the Interior, General Sherman assured General Sheridan that the order of the U.S. District Court in Omaha "does not apply to any other than that specific case." Big Snake was arrested and accused of crimes he had not committed. Unarmed, he was beaten by four soldiers and then shot and killed. The incident was investigated and nothing was done.[41]

On September 18, 2018, a statue of Standing Bear was officially dedicated as one of Nebraska's two representative historical figures in the U. S. Capitol's Statuary Hall.[42]

AMID THE VIOLENCE, THEFT, AND BETRAYALS, CHRISTIAN MISSIONARIES of various denominations were busy trying to save the Indians' souls and competing for exclusive salvation rights on the respective reservations. Buying and selling slaves had been okay with about half of the Christian nation, and trespassing, stealing land, and killing Indians was common practice with significantly more than half. The Native Americans' reverence for the land, water, sky, and all the other-than-human beings catalogued in the first two chapters of Genesis was mysterious to the missionaries, who only seemed to remember verse 1:26, which put "man" in charge of the whole shebang. They seemed to forget, or ignore, that young Indian males quested for visions and that Elders relied on such visions, much as Jesus (and Moses, Buddha, Mohammed, and others) had. Instead, they told their prospective converts that such personally engaging and challenging rituals were unnecessary as long as they learned and abided by some specific words and regularly attended a fairly predictable ritual. In the ever-present context of violence, theft, and betrayals at the hands of the Europeans and Americans, historian and activist Vine Deloria, Jr. suggests that "[n]o missionary ever realized that it was less the reality of his religion, and more the threat of extinction that brought converts to him."[43]

In 1883 in order to further codify what Indians could and could not do, the federal government established the Court of Indian Offenses, which, among other rulings, banned a variety of traditional practices such as the Sun Dance and specific "medicine men" healing rituals and defined marriage in terms of Christian tradition. During the 1870s the government had already appointed Protestant denominations to manage more than seventy Indian agencies and the Catholics established their own Bureau of Catholic Indian Missions.[44] In 1934, under Commissioner of Indian Affairs John Collier, the Indian Reorganization Act, which took steps to return to the Indians their right to exist as a separate culture, was passed. It would not be until 1978 that the American Indian Religious Freedom Act would be passed, allowing American citizens of Native American lineage to fully exercise that part of their First Amendment right. In 1994 the Act would be amended to allow, in all states, the use of peyote for religious purposes.[45]

By 1890, the 60 million acres of the Great Sioux Reservation, as identified in the Fort Laramie Treaty of 1868, had been reduced, first to about 22 million acres in 1877 due to government's and prospectors' interest in gold and other minerals, and then further reduced to 12.7 million acres through the Dawes (General Allotment) Act of 1887. The Dawes Act ended the tribes' communal holding of land and allotted set acreage to individual Indians, who were required to farm the land for twenty-five years. Any land that was not so allotted would be sold to the public.[46] With this further encroachment on the 1868 Fort Laramie Treaty, both the missionaries and the government became concerned in October 1890 when word arrived at the Cheyenne River, Rosebud, Pine Ridge, and Standing Rock reservations—each a remnant of the former Great Sioux Reservation—that

Wovoka, who was seen as a Messiah of the Paiutes, had had a vision in which, if the Indians danced what later became known as the Ghost Dance, their ways of life would return, the dead would be brought back to life, and they would be protected from the bullets of the whites who would die in a great flood. Indians from various tribes traveled to hear Wovoka speak, learn the dance, and bring his message back to their people. At Standing Rock, when Sitting Bull heard of this vision, although he did not believe the dead could come back to life and he was not a teacher of the Ghost Dance, he did not object to his people taking part.

The government tried to stop this "pernicious system of religion" that advocated passionate dancing and singing in order to end trespass, betrayal, violence, and theft, and became increasingly frightened by what they did not understand. When the agency police, backed up by the U. S. Cavalry, arrived to arrest Sitting Bull in his cabin at Standing Rock on December 15, 1890, he did not resist, but some of his people fired on the police. Sitting Bull, unarmed, was shot and killed by two agency policemen, Bull Head and Red Tomahawk. Dee Brown makes the case that if not for the Ghost Dance and the belief in Wovoka's vision, the Sioux may have gone to war yet again with the United States following Sitting Bull's killing. They didn't. The government, through the military, continued to try to shut down the Ghost Dance and disarm the Indians.[47]

On December 28, 1890 some 120 men and 230 women and children, led by pneumonia-stricken Chief Big Foot, were on their way to seek refuge with Red Cloud at Pine Ridge after hearing of Sitting Bull's death. When they encountered U. S. troops, they surrendered to Army Major Samuel Whitside near Wounded Knee Creek. Colonel James Forsyth, in command of the 7th Cavalry, arrived shortly thereafter. The following morning, surrounded by both Whitside's and Forsyth's troops, and with four Hotchkiss guns in the distance, the Indians piled their weapons on the ground as requested. Amid the weapon surrender, one shot rang out. Then many more. Then the Hotchkiss guns opened up. Most of the Indians were unarmed; some retrieved weapons when the shooting began.

When the shooting stopped, more than 150 men, women, and children were dead. Some of the wounded crawled away and died later. Four wounded men and forty-seven wounded women and children were carted away in wagons. Twenty-five soldiers were killed and thirty-nine wounded, many by their own bullets and shrapnel.[48] The victims were not protected from the bullets of the whites by Wovoka's vision; the whites seemed equally unaffected by Jesus's ideas about loving each other, even three days after Christmas. Neither of these two messiahs' prophecies or teachings seemed to have done anyone any good.

OVER THE COURSE OF JUST FIFTY-TWO YEARS, the U. S. used its military to defeat the Confederate rebellion, massacre surrendered Indians at Wounded Knee, and fight in World War I. Some tribes supported the North in the Civil War and some supported the South. The Sioux defended themselves to no avail at Wounded Knee, and a group of Choctaw men whose parents and grandparents had been removed from their lands in the 1830s enlisted to fight in World War I and later became known as the first "Code Talkers," using their native language so enemy spies could not understand messages. Fortunately for the United States, when, as young men, some of these eventual Code Talkers attended the Bureau of Indian Affairs' boarding schools, where their native language was banned, they ignored the rule when they could and retained their language of origin. Some thirty-three tribes, most famously the Navajo, would similarly serve in World War II. Decades after they served, the Honoring the Navajo Code

Talkers Act of 2000 and the Code Talkers Recognition Act of 2008 publicly recognized their efforts.[49]

World Wars and belated recognition aside, the twentieth century brought with it the 1924 "Indian Citizen Act," which provided citizenship to all Native Americans born in the U. S. but did not provide the right to vote, which was reserved to the states until 1957.[50] The new century also brought focused efforts to terminate the scant remnants of treaties that had not yet been broken, the unique cultures of the respective extant tribes, and any legislation that had been passed for tribal benefit. The House Concurrent Resolution 108 of 1953, for instance, set in motion the termination of federal assistance to tribes and the relocation of reservation Indians to urban centers. That same year, Public Law 280 took from the tribes and gave to the states jurisdiction over any "offenses committed by or against Indians in the Indian country." Effectively, Indians would be given all the blessings and curses enjoyed by U. S. citizens if they would just, finally, give up their lands, their culture, and their tribal sovereignty and fully assimilate into the country that persistently betrayed them.[51]

While some 113 tribes were terminated through Resolution 108, opposition to the policy grew in the decades that followed. As of 2013, according to the Native American Roots online diary, "78 of the 113 terminated tribes have been recognized again by the United States government and 35 now have casinos; 24 of these tribes are considered extinct; 10 have state recognition but not federal recognition; and 31 are landless."[52]

The trespass, promises, betrayals, theft, and violence that characterize the trajectories and trails of tears and broken promises demanded that Native Americans live on increasingly smaller and useless tracts of land or leave the tribe and assimilate into the dominant culture. Reservations were and are lands in which the government, prospectors, and homesteaders saw no value, and if gold, uranium, or upgraded greed shifted the valuation, new trespass or betrayal followed.

In November 1969 Indians representing more than fifty tribes sailed to and occupied the abandoned federal prison on Alcatraz Island in San Francisco Bay. They identified themselves as "Indians of All Tribes" and offered to buy the desolate, abandoned chunk of rock for some $24.00 worth of glass beads and red cloth. Using the standards of the reservation system in the United States, they cited, among other things, Alcatraz's isolation, its history as a prison, and lack of adequate transportation, fresh water, sanitation facilities, oil or mineral rights, health care or education facilities, and farming or hunting land as evidence that it would make a perfect reservation. The occupation lasted nineteen months, with as many as 600 occupants at its peak. In June 1971 U. S. Marshals removed the final 15 protestors.[53]

In the early 1970s, "54 percent of the adult males on the Pine Ridge reservation were unemployed, one-third of the families were on welfare or pensions, alcoholism was widespread, and suicide rates were high. The life expectancy of an Oglala Sioux male was forty-six years."[54] In February 1973, several hundred Oglala Sioux, led by the American Indian Movement (AIM), occupied the town of Wounded Knee and declared it liberated from the control of what they claimed was the corrupt and often violent leadership of tribal council leader Dick Wilson and his "Guardians of the Oglala Nation" (GOONs), a private militia. The FBI, U. S. Marshals, Wilson's GOONs, and the police of the Bureau of Indian Affairs (BIA) surrounded the town. Electricity was shut off, no food or supplies were allowed in, a pilot who airdropped supplies was arrested, and shots were fired, resulting in two Indian deaths and the paralysis of a marshal. The occupiers, citing the 1890 massacre, refused to surrender their arms until the government officers did as well. A truce was called, the government agreed to revisit the Fort Laramie Treaty of 1868, 120 occupiers were arrested, two of the organizers—AIM members Dennis Banks and Russell Means—were indicted and found not guilty, and the verdict was upheld on appeal.

The government claimed that while it was valid, the 1868 treaty was superseded by "eminent domain." In the three years following the occupation, with Dick Wilson still leading the tribal council, Pine Ridge had the highest per-capita murder rate in the United States.[55]

SEVEN YEARS AFTER THE OCCUPATION of Wounded Knee, the U.S. Supreme Court ruled that in 1877 the U.S. government had in fact illegally taken the Black Hills in violation of the 1868 Fort Laramie Treaty. The 1980 ruling upheld a 1979 Court of Claims decision that called on the U. S. to pay $17.5 million plus 5% annual interest, which at the time totaled about $106 million. The Sioux refused to take the settlement, which is now worth more than $1 billion, asserting that the land was never for sale, that money was not just compensation, and that the value of the gold, timber, and other resources removed from the area is significantly greater than the money offered.[56] The issue has not been resolved as this book goes to press.

In April 2009 both houses of Congress agreed on S. J. Res. 14, a resolution "To acknowledge a long history of official depredations and ill-conceived policies by the Federal Government regarding Indian tribes and offer an apology to all Native Peoples on behalf of the United States." Just over one thousand words in length, the apology acknowledged some serious transgressions, such as the 1830 Indian Removal Act, "many" treaty violations, "unlawful acquisition of recognized tribal land," "the Sand Creek Massacre," and "the forcible removal of Native children from their families." It also embraced embarrassing euphemisms: "the arrival of Europeans in

North America *opened a new chapter* in the history of Native Peoples," (italics added). As is traditional, each statement that sets the context for the necessity of the resolution begins with "Whereas"—a form that was echoed by poet, writer, and artist, Layli Long Soldier, a citizen of the Oglala Lakota Nation and the United States, in her 2017 book of poems, *Whereas,* which became a National Book Award Finalist.[57]

By the time S. J. Res. 14 was signed on December 19, 2009 by President Obama, the House had added it to H. R. 3326, which became Public Law 111-118, more commonly known as the Department of Defense Appropriations Act, 2010. All of the context-setting "Whereas's" (the reasons for the apology) were gone, leaving a 270-word "Sec. 8113" on page 45 of the 67-page law, immediately below Sec. 8112's provision that "up to $15,000,000 shall be available for the purpose of High Priority National Guard Counterdrug Programs."[58] Neither publicity nor ceremony marked the signing of what was left of the apology, which, in light of its final disposition and location, makes an ambiguous and sad type of sense. Fortunately, Long Soldier based some thirty pages of her book on the proposed, and not the final language. With its rigidity, euphemism, and relentless "Whereas's," S. J. Res. 14 is a more honest statement than Public Law 111-118's Sec. 8113.

More recently, the Dakota Access Pipeline debate, which began in 2014, has continued through three administrations and has drawn national and international attention through protests and arrests near the Standing Rock reservation in North Dakota.[59] In better news, in a both literal and symbolic reversal (of sorts) of the smallpox, measles and cholera that Europeans and Americans shared with Native Americans, tribal leaders in Minnesota, Colorado, New Mexico, and Oklahoma began sharing COVID-19 vaccinations in March of 2021 with local people who were not tribal members.[60]

In his reflections on the respective experiences of Native Americans and African Americans in *Custer Died for Your Sins,* Vine Deloria, Jr. suggests that whites treated Native Americans like "wild animals" who had to be tamed and assimilated so their land and resources could be taken, and that they treated African Americans like "draft animals" who had to be dominated and threatened so they would do their work and know their place. Native Americans were invited in at the cost of their land and their culture—treaties were made and relentlessly broken. African Americans were kept out, even amid almost 200 years of legislation to the contrary—laws were passed and went relentlessly unenforced.[61]

Early on, native peoples who would become Americans had a 'home court' advantage, so to speak—they knew and had an intimate, generations-long relationship with the land that both attracted and overwhelmed the newcomers. The Africans who would become Americans were torn from the lands, cultures, and families they knew and dropped into slavery, becoming involuntary newcomers amid and apart from the newcomers who tore them away. Deloria concluded in 1969 that "The white man must no longer project his fears onto other groups, races and countries. Before [he] can relate to others, he must forgo the pleasure of defining them…. [and] must learn to stop viewing history as a plot against himself."[62]

If people from another country (or beings from another galaxy) with superior firepower and what they thought was an advanced culture invaded the United States and began the process of raping our daughters, spouses, and mothers and killing those we love while stealing our land and making promises they would never keep, most of us would consider such behavior wrong, evil, heinous, or, by golly, just plain unfair. Yet this is exactly what the predominantly English explorers, settlers, and colonizers, who were escaping tyrannical monarchy, did in the years before 1776. The subsequent, post-1776 United States government continued those actions on the North American continent between what are now the Mexican and Canadian borders.

In a July 1868 conference at Fort Rice (in what is now North Dakota) leading up to the signing of the Fort Laramie Treaty, Chief Gall, a Hunkpapa warrior, made this very point to the government and church negotiators:

> We were born naked and have been taught to hunt and live on the game. You tell us that we must learn to farm, live in one house and take on your ways. Suppose the people living beyond the great sea should come and tell you that you must stop farming and kill your cattle, and take your houses and lands, what would you do? Would you not fight them?"[63]

As we who choose to identify as citizens of the United States drag ourselves, kicking and screaming, deeper into the third decade of the twenty-first century, Joy Harjo is in her second term as the first Native American U. S. Poet Laureate and Deb Haaland is in her first term as U. S. Secretary of the Interior and is the first Native American to serve as any cabinet secretary. The respective journeys that each of these women travels deserves more exposition than either gets on this page. Dr. Lewis Mehl-Madrona integrates his Cherokee, Oglala Lakota and European ancestries with his Stanford University psychiatric training and brings the gift of a narrative-relational approach to healing to his clients and patients.[64] Considering these three notable examples, a question arises. How are the rest of the individual members of the Mvskoke (Creek), Pueblo of Laguna, Cherokee, Oglala Lakota, and hundreds of other tribes faring today? There is neither a single nor a simple answer.

Dr. Eduardo Duran served in the Navy in Vietnam and has worked for decades with indigenous peoples in areas of healing intergenerational trauma, substance abuse, and grief, among other challenges. He has worked with people from more than one hundred tribes, and his own ancestry includes Apache, Lakota, and Italian roots. When he is referred to as a "mixed-blood," he jokes that he is "mixed-up blood" and he sees himself as someone who is "working hard to try to be a human being with a good heart."[65]

His humor and gentle manner are evident in interviews, and it's not a stretch to suggest that Dr. Duran has been chosen or appointed by something larger than himself on a regular basis. While he chose to study psychology, the particular trajectory of his work with native peoples seems to have chosen him. Once, while he was still a doctoral student and an intern focusing on addictions, suicide, diabetes, and other problems in a native community in California, an Elder told him that those weren't problems, and that the people who visited him wanted to talk about their dreams—not these other troubles. She told him he needed to go into the mountains and listen to the spirits, which he did. There he found that "nobody [was] talking, or at least I wasn't listening." He began, however, to hear from those who shared their dreams the language of "soul wounds" and "spiritual injuries." Prepared for cognitive behavioral therapy, not dream work, he listened and began to ask the dreamers what they thought about their dreams. His deep listening and genuine questions seemed to help them.[66]

As his on-the-job training in dream work continued, a Community Health Representative (CHR) told him that another Elder, Tarrence, who was paralyzed from the neck down, wanted to see him—a second choosing. Duran resisted for a while, but the CHR persisted, showing up in her truck and demanding he get in. Tarrence lay in a bed in a room in a shack at the top of a hill, looking "totally like a skeleton" with "bags of body fluids hanging" from the bed, and Duran anxiously reviewed possible diagnoses in his mind. Tarrence smiled "a crooked smile...to one side of his face" and said,

"Don't think that way, there's other realities," which increased his visitor's anxiety. Then Tarrence laughed and asked Duran if he had "ever seen the colors." The young intern was not sure if that was a sign of "schizophrenic process or a Zen koan," and was so upset by the encounter that he "almost lost consciousness." He grew even more unsettled when this man, who would become his spiritual teacher, asked to see him again.

Eduardo Duran visited this Elder for the next three years, during which time Tarrence laughed a lot and shared things that made no "sense with a rational mind." Then, two days before his death, he explained his teachings in detail, in a "very rational, very linear" way in which "things connected to each other." Duran reflects that Tarrence had probably given him a transmission of knowledge and energy in the first minute of their initial encounter, but he had been unable at the time to receive and understand what was transmitted.[67]

As he continued to work with his clients, Duran began to get the feeling that there were "other people in the room that can't be seen," whose presence left after the session. Realizing it might not be wise to share this impression with his clinical supervisor, he shared it instead with a traditional healer named Bill who showed up unexpectedly in his office—the third choosing (in my interpretation). Rather than confirming that Duran was overworked and needed rest or sharing some traditional story that would explain his sense of the presence of others, Bill told him that "the reason you are feeling that is because they are there," and that everything we do affects the next seven generations and also the previous seven.[68] More specifically, Bill told him that between 1870 and 1900 eighty percent of the ancestors of the communities with whom he was currently working had been exterminated. Dr. Duran continues:

> And he went on to explain that when that happens…a lot of times people don't have time to really cross over and be in

harmony with the ancestors. And he says, "Because of natural law, the only place that this healing can happen is here, in the same place where the injury happened." So he said that what I was experiencing is that the ancestors and the unborn ones of the people I was working with are showing up to the therapy session, hoping that their relative here heals themselves because when they heal themselves, that heals them in the spirit world.[69]

Eduardo Duran was chosen a fourth time in 2012 when he received a call from one of the 13 Grandmothers.[70] She told him of the Grandmothers' plan to gather in Lame Deer, Montana, traveling there from Oklahoma along the same path on which native people were killed by the U. S. Army. The Grandmothers wanted him to speak to those gathered because of his work with historical trauma. He resisted, she countered, and she finally told him that he was "appointed" and really couldn't get out of it. He went, did his talk, and stayed an extra day in order to join the ceremonial feast. On the morning of the feast, a woman approached him and told him that someone who claimed to be Custer's great-niece wanted to talk to him. Thinking it was a joke, he played along, but the great-niece identified herself as Alisha Custer and said she had come to the gathering because she "wanted to offer an apology on behalf of my uncle." Duran told her it probably wasn't a good idea—with more than a thousand native people present—but she persisted. He took the request to a representative for the Grandmothers, they discussed it and decided that Custer's great-niece should apologize. They also decided that Dr. Duran should introduce her, which he did, invoking both Black Kettle and Custer in his introduction.

The apology brought tears, sacred silence, and catharsis. The feast followed, tears were shed, and much else—too much for these pages—arose. Several days later Eduardo Duran dreamed of a ceremony with General Custer in attendance. At the

General's request, Dr. Duran taught him how to make an offering of atonement.[71]

Don't think that way, there's other realities. What we and others do, and what is done to us and others lives on, especially if it's not recognized, resolved, integrated, and, when appropriate, atoned for. Tarrence's seven-word message to Eduardo Duran might be easily co-opted by those who are trying to win some finite intra- or inter-cultural game with "alternative facts," misinformation, intolerance, canceling, or outright lies. In the infinite game, which is played amid the embrace of intra-, inter- and transcultural experience—within, among, and beyond cultures—other states of consciousness and other ways of seeing and being are indeed available, and can be found at the mystical core of every religion and within other practices beyond religion.

Whereas I don't pretend to know the details of the impact of Custer's great-niece's apology at the Grandmothers' 2012 gathering in Montana, I do know the impact of apology and atonement in my own life—both offered and received. So I am willing to pretend to know that what Alisha Custer offered was more from the heart, more specific, and more meaningful than the "Apology to the Native Peoples of the United States" buried on page 45 of Public Law 111-118, Section 8113, of the Department of Defense Appropriations Act, 2010.

As Black Kettle said, "Why don't you talk, and go straight, and let all be well?"[72]

Chapter Five

Slavery, Jim Crow, Civil Rights & Everything Was Going to Change Now

Who must lose in order for you to win?[1]

WHEN WE SPEAK OR WRITE about slavery in the conventional history of the United States of America, we tend not to hear or read too much about the actual moments of invasion of the diverse African[2] communities, the violent kidnappings, the wretched conditions for those who made it onto the ships, the watery graves of those who died in transport, the *feelings* that any one of these human beings felt amid those unimaginable episodes, and the many subsequent episodes of being bought and sold and charged with forced, unpaid, backbreaking daily labor. That sentence itself does a feeble job of capturing the enormity of the horror inherent in these acts.

Here's a disturbing observation: it's a step in the right direction that a white police officer, Derrick Chauvin, was found guilty of murdering George Floyd, who was black, and that Travis McMichael, Gregory McMichael, and William Bryan, all of whom are white, were found guilty of murdering Ahmaud Arbery, a black man. Had these two murders been the first of their kind—outside of any historical context—they would, in Rabbi Gellman's words, still "be worthy of such a gathering and such a grief." That they occurred in the historical context of two-hundred-plus years of American history is the catalyst for tens of thousands of individuals gathering and grieving in public in the twenty-first century, not just in the United States, but around the world. In this chapter, we'll remember both history and context as we explore race in the contemporary United States.

Remember those first victims arriving in the colony of Virginia in 1619, and also those who arrived earlier throughout the islands of the Caribbean and in Central and South America, where collectively more than 90% of enslaved African peoples landed. Remember those who continued to arrive for the next two-hundred-plus years.

Remember that the men who conceived of, argued about, and wrote down what remains an extraordinary experiment of governance also decided that these individuals, who had been torn from their homes and their families, were deemed to be worth 60% of a full human being for tax and representation (of their owners) purposes. Without slave labor, wealthy plantation owners and politicians would not have fared as well as they did—if fare well they would have at all. While the rationale for this "three-fifths compromise" was to convince slave state planter-politicians to sign what would become the U.S. Constitution—providing them with additional seats in the House of Representatives and additional electoral votes in presidential elections based on the number of slaves they owned—the compromise's consequences effectively included the valuing of each slave as three-fifths of a human being.

Remember that the Emancipation Proclamations in 1862 and 1863 announced but could not enforce the freedom of formerly enslaved people.

Remember that the 13th Amendment to the U. S. Constitution, which made slavery unlawful in 1865, was followed almost immediately by the formation of the Ku Klux Klan in Pulaski, Tennessee, and remember that the U. S. was among the last of the slave-trading and slave-owning countries to ban both trading and owning enslaved human beings.[3]

Remember that the 14th Amendment in 1868 guaranteed citizenship to any person born or naturalized in the United States, prevented any state from depriving citizens of life, liberty, or property without due process and from denying any citizen equal protection of the laws. Notice and remember that 150-plus years later, our nation still struggles to manifest this particular destiny of equality.

Remember that the 15th Amendment in 1870, which granted formerly enslaved males the right to vote, was followed by decades of lynchings, beatings, local Jim Crow policies, and Black Code laws, especially in the South. Remember that such abominations prevented these U.S. citizens from exercising their right to vote (and other rights)—through threats and violence, through convict leasing, and through low level bureaucracy that included "testing" that no white man, including the testers themselves, had to endure or could have passed as a prerequisite to voting.[4]

Remember that *lynching,* often used to refer to *hanging,* is not limited to that particular means of terror, and also refers to torture and execution by a mob—for real or imagined and major or minor transgressions—without a trial or other access to due process. It is an act of killing and an act of terrorizing those who know it could happen to them. As referred to above, on May 25, 2020, Derek Chauvin, abetted by his three colleagues, knowing their actions were being recorded on video, slowly killed George Floyd in daylight, in front of witnesses, with the apparent authority of the city of Minneapolis and the state of Minnesota behind him (about which he was mistaken). That was a lynching. Minneapolis fired him on May 26, and Minnesota found him guilty of second- and third-degree murder and second-degree manslaughter on April 20, 2021. His firing and conviction differentiate this lynching from most that occurred in the past.

Historically, lynchings have included beatings, burnings, shootings, stabbings, hangings, and other torture, sometimes in combination, and were often announced in advance in local newspapers and on posters, and attended by hundreds and sometimes thousands of white spectators, including children.[5] The Equal Justice Initiative's research documents the number of lynchings between 1877 and 1950 in Mississippi: 654; Georgia: 589; Louisiana: 549; Arkansas: 492; Alabama: 361; Texas: 335; Florida: 311; Tennessee: 233; South Carolina: 185; Kentucky: 168; North Carolina: 123; Virginia: 84; Oklahoma: 76; Missouri: 60; Illinois: 56; West Virginia: 35; Maryland: 28; Kansas: 19; Indiana: 18; and Ohio: 15 with another 34 lynchings scattered among other states, for a total of 4,425.[6]

Earlier, the twelve-year period between 1865 and 1876, euphemistically known as *Reconstruction,* carried with it an immediate backlash against former slaves by those who had, in losing the war, also lost their primary means of economic success—slave labor. Rather than focusing their energy on reconstructing the economy through honorable means, many of these people, often in mobs, chose instead to reconstruct the manner in which they would demean those whose imprisonment and labor had served them so well. Amid ongoing investigations, the Equal Justice Initiative has documented thirty-four mass lynchings during Reconstruction and at least 2,000 total lynchings during that time. To be clear, these acts of terror are *in addition to* the 4,425 that were to follow.[7]

Calling again on Rabbi Gellman's reminder that individual lives get lost in such statistics, white mobs terrorized, tortured, and executed a black human being more than 6,425 times in less than eighty years. In most cases local and state government tolerated these crimes, and when the federal government attempted to pass anti-lynching laws, the lynching states' governments argued for states' rights, passed their own laws, and didn't enforce them.[8]

Almost exactly halfway through this 1877-1950 period, while lynching was an ever-present terrorist threat for blacks in the South, World War I "disrupted European immigration …just as the industrial North needed more workers" and the prospect of moving away from the terror and toward work and a new start in the North led to what "would become one of the largest mass relocations in American history." Over the course of almost five decades, the Great Migration would bring some six million blacks from the South to the North and West.[9]

Emphasizing how far we had not come as human beings, on May 31, 1921, some thirty months after World War I's end, what is known as both the Tulsa Race Massacre and the Tulsa Race Riot effectively destroyed the Greenwood district of Tulsa. At the time, Oklahoma was just fourteen years old as a state, and Tulsa, like virtually every city in every state throughout the country, was segregated. Greenwood was the black section, and Greenwood Avenue, especially the 100 block, was known as "Black Wall Street" because of its prosperous businesses—which included hotels, doctors, attorneys, restaurants, theaters, insurers, real estate offices, and more. Beyond its businesses, Greenwood's thirty-five blocks included schools and churches that served its some 10,000 residents. It was a thriving community of professionals, craftspeople, unskilled laborers, children, parents, and grandparents. It was also a black community in an American time of Jim Crow laws, public lynchings, and segregation.

When, on May 30, 1921, seventeen-year-old white elevator operator Sarah Page screamed, and nineteen-year-old black shoe-shiner Dick Rowland ran from the elevator in the Drexel Building in Tulsa, a white clerk in a nearby store heard the scream, saw Rowland running, and called the police. The following morning, May 31, Rowland was arrested. The *Tulsa*

Tribune ran the headline, "Nab Negro for Attacking Girl in Elevator."

Armed whites gathered outside the courthouse and demanded that the sheriff give them Rowland. He refused. Later, armed blacks arrived and offered to help protect the teenager. Again the sheriff refused. Eventually the two groups clashed and shots were fired. In less than twenty-four hours, thousands of whites devastated the Greenwood district: thirty-five blocks were burned to the ground; between 100 and 300 people, mostly black, died; another 800 were injured; some 1,200 homes were destroyed and another 200-plus were looted; some 6,000 blacks were detained, some for their own safety, for up to eight days by the National Guard. No one—not one single person—was ever prosecuted for the violence, arson, and theft.

Sarah Page expressed a desire not to prosecute the case, and charges against Rowland were dropped. The chief of detectives said on June 2 that the text that accompanied the *Tulsa Tribune* headline was misleading and went beyond what appeared in the police report. No one knows definitively what actually happened in the elevator, but it is assumed that Rowland and Page had regular encounters since the segregated restroom he was required to use was on the top floor of the building, which had just one elevator. A commonly accepted narrative is that Rowland tripped while entering the elevator and fell against Page, who screamed; he panicked and ran—an appropriate response in that situation for a young black man in the United States in 1921.[10]

Relevant both then and now, the racial context of any moment exacerbates what might otherwise, and perhaps someday will, be an unremarkable event. In addition to the ongoing lynchings and Jim Crow denial of rights in the context of the violent end of slavery's violence, the resentments of the lower rungs of the dominant caste (in this case, struggling whites) toward those in the subordinate caste who are prospering beyond what the dominant caste expects or thinks fair (prosperous blacks) played a role here. Pulitzer Prize winner, Isabel Wilkerson, in *Caste: The Origins of Our Discontents,* makes a powerful case for using the word "caste" to characterize the divisions within American society that are more often spoken about in terms of race or class—the respective impacts of which she both acknowledges and differentiates from caste:

> It is the fixed nature of *caste* that distinguishes it from *class,* .... [which] is an altogether separate measure of one's standing in a society, marked by a level of education, income and occupation.... [that] can be acquired through hard work and ingenuity or lost through poor decisions or calamity. If you can act you way out of it, then it's class, not caste.[11]

The Greenwood District's doctors, educators, attorneys, entrepreneurs and other professionals (and not *just* these professionals), through effort and ingenuity, had achieved a standing in society—a social class—that surpassed that of many of the Tulsa whites who would eventually burn down their black neighbors' businesses and homes. Operating deep below the surface of the visible, changeable class indicators, however, was (and in many cases still is) the inherited-at-birth mark of caste. Still, the less fortunate, less prosperous folks on those lower rungs of the dominant caste are conditioned to believe and expect that they are superior to everyone in the subordinate caste. When the lower-caste rises above the upper, Wilkerson tells us:

> ...the natural human response from someone weaned on their caste's inherent superiority is to perceive a threat to their existence, a heightened sense of unease, of displacement, of fear for their very survival. *"If the things that I have believed are not true, then might I not be who I thought I*

was?" The disaffection is more than economic. The malaise is spiritual, psychological, emotional. Who are you if there is no one to be better than?[12]

So when they failed to kidnap an arrested, frightened, and lower-caste Dick Rowland from the courthouse jail for a public lynching, and when other members of his subordinate caste, some of whom were World War I veterans, exhibited the audacity to try to protect him, the members of the dominant caste canceled much of the evidence of the work, prosperity, resilience, and humanity of those who were supposed to be inferior. By burning it down.

Each of us knows at least one superficial and perhaps short-lived, but no less real, example of this type of unfolding *within* our own caste, class, race, family, and circle of friends. Someone surprises us or we surprise them with an unexpected success or prosperity that exceeds what the surprised party thinks possible. Who am I or who are you, as the surprised party, now that my expectation is proven false? Some of us may experience this surprise as an uninvited, private, and uncomfortable thought that we acknowledge and dispel and then authentically celebrate the other's success (because it's about *us* or *all of us*). Some of us might experience it as an insurmountable insult or transgression that ends or permanently damages whatever relationship there was (because it's about *me*). In either case, if the reaction goes unexamined—if we don't do the work of investigating the fear and resentment that arises in us due to another's unexpected success—it will recur.

While statistics and dates can be manipulated to render lynchings as historical artifacts—events of the past— James Baldwin reminds us (below, 118) that history "is present in all that we do." Among others human beings, Ahmaud Arbery was lynched in Georgia in 2020; James Craig Anderson was lynched in Mississippi in 2011; James Byrd, Jr. was lynched in Texas in 1998; Matthew Shepard, who was white and gay, was lynched in Wyoming also in 1998; and Timothy Coggins was lynched in Georgia in 1983.[13] Byrd and Shepard have a Hate Crimes Prevention Act named after them. What differentiates these more recent lynchings from those that took place between 1865 and 1950 is that chances are better now that the murderers will be pursued, apprehended, tried, and convicted—unless they are law enforcement officers. It remains to be seen if Derek Chauvin's conviction marks a turning point or is an exception. He is appealing his conviction.

Remember the Supreme Court's 1896 *Plessy v. Ferguson* ruling that upheld the constitutionality of racial segregation, honoring the "doctrine" of "separate but equal" public facilities, which in practice were definitely separate and rarely, if ever, equal.

Remember the 1954 Supreme Court decision in *Brown v. the Board of Education of Topeka* that held that *Plessy* effectively violated the 14th Amendment's "equal protection" provision, since segregated public facilities in the South, including schools, were in fact not equal. And consider the experience of the fourteen-year-old son of Alabama sharecroppers who had taken to heart the words of the Pike County Training School's librarian, who encouraged her students, "My dear children, read. Read *everything*." He would later describe his "feeling of jubilation" when he read in every newspaper he could find on that May 1954 morning about the *Brown* decision:

> Everything was going to change now. No longer would I have to ride a broken-down bus almost forty miles each day to attend classes at a 'training' school with hand-me-down books and supplies. Come fall I'd be riding a state-of-the-art bus to a state-of-the art school, an *integrated* school.

Consider his realization as he began his sophomore year in the fall of that same year "by climbing onto the same beat-up school bus and making the same twenty-mile trip to the same segregated high school I'd attended the year before.... nothing in my life had changed."[14] John Lewis would go on to dedicate his life—literally putting it on the line—to working toward the change that would effect the manifest equality and the Beloved Community he yearned for.

Remember the Civil Rights Act of 1964 and the Voting Rights Act of 1965, and think deeply about why these two acts were even necessary in light of the hundred years of declarations, proclamations, amendments, and decisions that preceded them. And remember the 2013 Supreme Court decision in *Shelby v. Holder* that struck down part of the 1965 law, once again allowing several states and selected other voting districts to change their election laws without federal approval.[15] In the wake of fabricated stories that the 2020 presidential election had been rigged and stolen, many states with Republican governors and legislatures began various approaches to limiting voting rights. Georgia was the first to achieve this on March 25, 2021, prompting President Biden to remark, "This is Jim Crow in the twenty-first century. It must end." While the state's governor, Bryan Kemp, signed the bill into law behind the closed doors of his office, Georgia State Patrol officers arrested state legislator, Park Cannon, for knocking on the governor's door in order to speak with him.

In the wake of all of the above remembrances—most of which mark only legal, political, and historical signposts and don't touch actual moments in the lives of slaves, former slaves, their descendants, or other people of color—remember that Jim Crow laws and segregated facilities still dominated the South until midway through the twentieth century. When young men and women, mostly black and some white, marched peacefully in protest against this illegal segregation they were met with beatings and arrests ordered by governors, mayors, and other officials and carried out by state and local law enforcement officers and volunteers who seemed to believe that equal rights for blacks would somehow limit the rights of whites, that these blacks seemed not to know their place, and that violence was the way to prevent equality.

Consider reading or hearing these words from or about your government:

> "I want to tell you, ladies and gentlemen, that there's not enough troops in the army to force the Southern people to break down segregation and admit the nigra race into our theaters, into our swimming pools, into our homes, into our churches."
> - South Carolina Governor and presidential candidate, Strom Thurmond, October 7, 1948[16]

> "Nigguhs hate whites, and whites hate nigguhs. Everybody knows that deep down."
> - Alabama Governor, George C. Wallace[17]

> "This new cause—or rather the true question of the war revived—is the supremacy of the white race and along with it and strengthening it, the reassertion of our political traditions, and the protection of our ancient fabrics of government."
> - Edward A. Pollard, *The Lost Cause Regained*, c. 1868[18]

> "We are determined to take our country back. We are going to fulfill the promises of Donald Trump. That's what we believed in, that's why we voted for Donald Trump. Because he's going to take our country back. And that's what we gotta do."
> - David Duke, former Knights of the Ku Klux Klan grand wizard and Louisiana State Representative[19]

Consider that millions of U.S. citizens live this history and its consequences every moment of their lives.

> "History, as nearly no one seems to know, is not merely something to be read. And it does not refer merely, or even principally, to the past. On the contrary, the great force of history comes from the fact that we carry it within us, are unconsciously controlled by it in many ways, and history is literally present in all that we do."
> - James Baldwin[20]

It is easy to entertain a selective embrace of Baldwin's assertion that we carry history within us and that it is present in what we do. Each of us, to the extent we are willing or unwilling to examine this history within us, is in varying degrees ignorant of the history of those whose lives and ancestry are different from our own. Yes, we know some of the signposts, events, and dates that our schooling may have provided, but not what the dignities and disasters of these histories feel like within the hearts of the descendants of both the oppressed and the oppressors. Authentically exploring such feelings requires courage and support.

Bessel van der Kolk, Judith Herman, Gabor Maté, Eduardo Duran, Laura Calderón de la Barca, Peter Levine, Thomas Hübl, and Resmaa Menakem, among others, deepen our understanding of history's presence with individual, collective, intergenerational, and body-based approaches to working with trauma. They explore, amid much else, what has been passed down, generation to generation, in our bodies, including the trauma held and passed down in the bodies of both the oppressed the oppressors. They acknowledge the trauma caused by Europeans and then Americans against Africans and Native Americans, and also the trauma that generations of oppressed, lower-class Europeans brought across the Atlantic with them. In a 2020 interview, Resmaa

Menakem spoke to the relationship between unacknowledged trauma and the passage of time: "The march of time decontextualizes trauma. So trauma in a person, over time, can look like personality. Trauma in a family, over time, can look like family traits. Trauma in a people, over time, can look like culture."[21] Each of us carries the past in our bodies, and purely cognitive approaches alone do not resolve what the body holds. We will return to this work with trauma in subsequent chapters.

Some who would minimize the histories of slavery, Jim Crow, and more subtle forms of American oppression of blacks point out that no one in twenty-first-century America is a slave, that many blacks are not descendants of slaves, and that many blacks are as or more successful than many whites today. They also, in an effort to honor *their* family histories, decry the removal of the Confederate flag and monuments that glorify Confederate politicians and soldiers who fought against the United States and in favor of the slave labor camps of southern plantations.[22]

Several points warrant attention. First, a genuine desire to honor the lives and places of one's ancestors is natural, understandable, and admirable. Second, such honoring, if it is to be honorable, needs to be honest. Third, if one's ancestors kidnapped, beat, enslaved, and killed others, and fought for the right to continue committing these acts, even a modicum of empathy and compassion should lead an average human being to consider the impact these monuments might have on the descendants of the victims. The Confederate uprising against the United States, among other goals, fought to retain the slaveholding states' right to secede from the union if they were not happy with what other states or the federal government was doing. Such secession would allow the Confederacy to continue to operate an economic system that relied on the denial of rights to and forced labor by human beings whose ancestors, or who themselves, had been kidnapped from their homelands. As noted in Chapter Four, the land on which this forced labor took place had often been taken by fraud, threat, or force from Native Americans, specifically for the expansion of the for-profit, slave-labor-camp "plantations."[23] This two-pronged denial of human rights catalyzed the nation's growth.

During the 150-plus years since the United States defeated the Confederate rebellion at great cost to each side, that the leaders of and participants in the pro-slavery Confederacy have been recognized with statues and monuments, as well as with military base, street, and school names, is consistent with the conventional human habit of honoring leaders and those we've lost. Such honoring does not take place in a content- and context-free vacuum. The monuments and statues were erected, the bases, streets, and schools were named, and the Confederate flag was flown, some claim, in the name of "heritage, not hate." Such claims, even if truly not hateful, ignore what each of the names and symbols meant and means to those who were enslaved and to their generations of progeny. We don't honor individual violent criminals (of any ethnicity or skin pigmentation) with statues or memorials—even if they're "only" one-time offenders. The Confederate statues and monuments should not be destroyed—lest the history they depict be forgotten. They belong in museums, along with complete and honest accounts of the history they represent, which includes their fight to continue to enslave human beings.

In contrast, government-funded monuments and statues and base, street, and school names that honor those who did the forced physical labor that kept much of the Confederate economy going are meager.[24] On national, state, and local levels, publicly funded acknowledgments of and memorials to the 305,000-plus human beings who were kidnapped, shipped, bought, sold, and tortured and the approximately 4,000,000 total who were either kidnapped and shipped or born into slavery through 1865 are rare, as are any acknowledgments of the additional thousands who were lynched and denied their basic rights thereafter. For some reasons, honoring these lives has not been embraced in the consciousness of Americans—certainly not to the extent that we have memorialized the men who enslaved them and fought to keep them enslaved. When government-funded statues or memorials are proposed to honor former slaves, those who fought to free them, or those who continued in the twentieth century to fight for true equality, they are often locally funded, it takes years for approval, and, if they are approved and built, they are often vandalized.[25]

There are no monuments or statues of Hitler in Germany. No military bases, streets, or schools are named after him. Instead, as Isabel Wilkerson points out, there is the Memorial to the Murdered Jews of Europe in Berlin—2,711 concrete structures on 4.7 acres, with "no sign, no gate, no fence, no list of the 6 million. The stones are as regimented as the Nazis and as anonymous as the captives shorn of identity in the concentration camps."[26] There are the more than 70,000 "stumbling stones," *Stolpersteine,* not just in Germany, but in various cities across Europe. These engraved brass plates are embedded in sidewalks in front of the doors through which Holocaust victims were abducted by their persecutors. Most of the plates are personalized in the language of the victim, with an introduction, "Here lies" or "She lived here," followed by the victim's name, date of birth, and, if known, the dates of their abduction and murder, along with name of the death camp. Sometimes more than one camp is listed. Sometimes the victim was liberated from the camp, and that date is provided.

The bunker in which Hitler spent his final weeks is paved over with an ordinary parking lot near some nondescript office and apartment buildings. On the day that Wilkerson visited, "the blue Volkswagen parked next to the white minivan" marked the spot that was thirty feet above where the bunker had been.[27] Writing as a self-described "American Jew from the South who has lived in Berlin for decades," philosopher and writer Susan Neiman makes clear that "Germany has no monuments that celebrate the Nazi armed forces, however many grandfathers fought or fell for them. Instead, it has a dizzying number and variety of monuments to the victims of its murderous racism."[28]

Prior to the 2020 protests following George Floyd's murder in Minneapolis, the Equal Justice Initiative had identified at least 1,575 Confederate monuments in twelve southern states, including Virginia: 375; Texas: 137; Tennessee: 100; South Carolina: 91; North Carolina: 195; Mississippi: 175; Louisiana: 65; Kentucky: 50; Georgia: 160; Florida: 59; Arkansas: 50; Alabama: 100. *Most were erected in the twentieth century, and many after the 1960s.*[29] These are the same twelve states that led the way in lynching.

Among those who have been so memorialized, Andrew Jackson, the aforementioned Tennessee landowner, slaveholder, Indian killer and remover, militia general, and U.S. president, has been, and still is to many, an American hero. More than fifty towns, cities, counties, parks, and statues honor him. He still gazes out from our twenty-dollar bills, and though Harriet Tubman is scheduled to replace him someday, her clandestine process for conducting slaves to freedom seems to have been more efficient than our contemporary process for the redesign of paper currency. Germans and Americans have expressed significantly different collective responses to their respective atrocities. One accurate, albeit incomplete, explanation is that many Americans do not yet fully acknowledge or accept all of our nation's comparatively brief, and often savage, history and the complementary ignorance, arrogance, violence, and greed that still stand in stark contrast with our as-yet unrealized proclamations of freedom, equality, and justice for all.

Consider now our video archive, recorded in the past thirty-plus years, that documents the beating, choking, and shooting of unarmed black men by law enforcement officers. Examine this body of video evidence in the context of the above historical synopsis, and ask yourself the following questions:[30]

- What is it about some of us such that we are unable to understand, feel empathy, or express compassion for the African-American (or the American-Indian, or, as we'll see in chapters six and seven, the Vietnamese, Afghan or Iraqi) experience in the history of the United States?
- Would I or we feel different and take action if unarmed white, blonde-haired, blue-eyed young women (or, fill in another demographic here _______) were being similarly beaten, choked, or shot by police officers (whether or not these young women had been historically oppressed)?
- What is it about some of us who think we're working toward equal rights for all that we evoke our alleged "wokeness" so unskillfully that we antagonize and alienate the very people (that is, *everyone*) we need as allies?
- What is it that I and those I love have to lose if every United States citizen (or everyone on the planet) really did enjoy equal opportunity and protection of the law?
- What is it that I and those I love have to gain if every United States citizen (or everyone on the planet) really did enjoy equal opportunity and protection of the law?
- What can I do, and why don't I do what I can, to work toward the Fourteenth Amendment's equal protection of the laws for all Americans?

CONSIDER THAT FROM AT LEAST the 1950s through this book's publication (and undoubtedly and unfortunately beyond), when human beings who are discriminated against and those who support them exercise their First Amendment rights through nonviolent demonstrations or protests, those who would deny them their rights or fear their actually attaining equality and equal protection of the laws, accuse them with sweeping generalizations, labels, and insults such as *un-* or *anti-American, Marxist, communist, socialist* or *leftist.*

This concern with communist influence on and exploitation of "the militant force of the Negro civil rights movement" was evident in J. Edgar Hoover's directing the FBI to discredit Dr. Martin Luther King, Jr. and others in the movement.[31] An eloquent, more nuanced, and very clear opinion piece, published on September 14, 2020 by American Enterprise Institute Senior Fellow, Danielle Pletka, continues this tradition of sweeping generalizations. After agreeing with virtually every major criticism of the then-White House occupant—criticisms that every one of his opponents would openly embrace—Pletka wrote that "Democrats may force" her to vote for him:

> But I fear the leftward lurch of the Democratic Party even more.... I fear that former vice president Joe Biden would be a figurehead president, incapable of focus or leadership, who would run a teleprompter presidency with the words drafted by his party's hard-left ideologues.... The corrosive left-wing extremism of 2020 would be ascendant, while a smiling President Biden assures the country that everything is fine. Trump, for all his flaws, could be all that stands between our imperfect democracy and the tyranny of the woke left.[32]

Hyperbole, generalizations, and loss of personal agency aside, anything that a Democratic president does to help lower- and middle-income Americans will, as a matter of course for Pletka and others, be characterized as "corrosive left-wing extremism." Getting elected officials to spend trillions to bomb and then rebuild other nations (which is labeled *national security*) has always been a lot easier than getting them to fund programs that help American citizens (which is labeled *social-ism*). We'll say more about the "tyranny of the woke left" (and the apparently sleepy right) in Chapter Nine. For now, some historical images of the connections between civil rights and Communism speak for themselves. Simply type "race mixing is Communism" into the search bar of your browser and ask for images.

This desire to enforce the U.S. Constitution and its Amendments equally among all Americans is typically characterized as un-American, "leftist," "socialist," and "Marxist" by an outspoken faction of traditionally white, ultra-conservative elites and leaders and that subset of citizens who take them at their word. Note the specifics of "outspoken faction," which is not a blanket critique of tradition, whites, or conservatives. It is an indictment of Americans who insist on conflating social programs with socialism, Marxism, and Communism (except when the beneficiaries are the likes of Chrysler, Harley Davidson, Lockheed, Goldman Sachs, Wells Fargo, and others). We'll say more about this selective socialist bogeyman in Chapter Eight.

Our interstate highway system, our national parks, our national defense, and our local education, law enforcement, and fire departments are socialized infrastructures and organizations. Medicare and Medicaid are social programs. I have been able to find exactly no one in any (or no) political party who refuses to drive on the highways or visit the parks, or who turns away the fire department or who returns their Social Security, Medicaid, or Medicare benefits or their COVID-19 stimulus payments in protest against socialism.

THIS HISTORY AND THESE CURRENT EVENTS, as Rabbi Gellman reminded us in 2001, impacted and continue to impact one life millions of times. Jonathan Bass's *He Calls Me by Lightning* shares with us one such life. Seventeen-year-old Caliph

Washington's after-midnight drive from Birmingham through Lipscomb and toward his home in Bessemer, Alabama on July 12, 1957 would change his life forever. When Washington first saw the headlights behind him after he had dropped off three friends, they represented just another car on the late-night road, but when they got up to his bumper, he grew concerned. In the Jim Crow Alabama of 1957, the chance that members of the Ku Klux Klan or some other night riders were in the car behind him was both possible and probable—a self-preservation mindset for a black man. When two gunshots rang out, Caliph floored his father's Chevy and the chase vehicle kept pace.

Once in Bessemer, Washington made a series of turns and loops through a familiar neighborhood, honking his horn as he sped past, hoping to rouse some help. The pursuing headlights disappeared and reappeared in his mirror through the turns. When the chase car reappeared with a revolving red light on top, he pulled over, but with no idea about why he had been chased and shot at. He thought he was evading certain harm— even death. Alone in the chase car was a single driver—a thirty-seven-year-old circus performer and rookie officer, who was directly disobeying his chief when he chased and shot at what he thought was an illegal whiskey runner.

Caliph Washington complied with James "Cowboy" Clark's demands to get out of the car, raise his hands, and submit to a pat down. When asked, Washington said he had no whiskey and Clark's search found none. Still, he unholstered his weapon and raised it to strike the teenager. The two scuffled, the pistol discharged, and Clark fell to the ground. Evidence would later point to the bullet's having ricocheted off the vehicle. Caliph Washington ran and was caught two days later.

He was indicted and convicted of first-degree murder, which carried a death sentence, by an all-white jury on October 10, 1957. His execution was scheduled for December

10. After the judge pronounced the sentence, he asked the seventeen-year-old if he had anything to say regarding why he should be spared the death sentence. Caliph responded, "Because it was self-defense."

He appealed, and over the next thirteen years would be retried twice. In 1959, he was again sentenced to death, and, in 1970, he was sentenced to forty years for second-degree murder. He appealed each conviction. Between 1959 and 1964 he would receive fourteen death-row stays of execution—including five on the eve of the execution, and at least one after his head had been shaved in preparation. His 1970 conviction was overturned in 1971, after which he was released on bail and allowed to return home. That same year he met and began dating Christine Luna, an Italian-American VISTA worker from Long Island.

The Bessemer district attorney announced plans for another trial, and a grand jury again indicted him in January 1972. He pleaded not guilty, and when political disruptions in Bessemer delayed the trial's start, Caliph Washington went about his life. He and Christine Luna married and brought six beautiful children into the world. He worked with a vending company and a television station, and committed himself to helping young black men avoid the difficult path he had been given. He formed the Salvation Club basketball team and served as pastor of the St. John's Missionary Baptist Church. The Reverend Caliph Washington died on May 24, 2001 at the age of sixty-one.

Twenty-eight days later, on June 21, 2001, Circuit Court Judge Mac Parsons read through the old files of the open case that had not been acted on since the early 1970s and dismissed all charges against Caliph Washington.[33]

In a larger context, Caliph Washington's life from 1957 through 1972 was consistent with the upheaval in America during those years: the civil rights movement's sit-ins, freedom rides, marches, and protests, and the consequent beatings and arrests of those who sat, rode, marched, and protested; the assassinations of Medgar Evers, Denise McNair, Addie Mae Collins, Cynthia Wesley, Carole Robertson, John F. Kennedy, James Chaney, Michael Schwerner, Andrew Goodman, Malcolm X, Martin Luther King, Jr., and Robert Kennedy, among others; the passing of the Civil Rights and Voting Rights Acts; and the escalation of the war in Vietnam. What this larger context does not convey, and what Bass so eloquently and painstakingly provides in *He Calls Me by Lightning* are the local histories of and specific characters in Bessemer and the greater Jefferson County, Alabama area that caused, exacerbated, and occasionally somewhat mitigated Caliph Washington's imprisonment.

What none of us can comprehend, unless we've been on death row, are Caliph Washington's physical, emotional, mental, and spiritual experiences of imprisonment, more than a dozen execution dates, and more than a dozen reprieves, five of which were granted on the eves of electrocution.

JUST OVER A QUARTER CENTURY AFTER Caliph Washington was introduced to death row and eighteen years before the posthumous dismissal of the case against him, a Harvard Law student had his first encounter with a death-row inmate during an internship in Georgia with the Southern Prisoners Defense Committee (now the Southern Center for Human Rights). The experience so moved Bryan Stevenson that he continued to work with death-row inmates after his graduation, and in 1989 founded the Equal Justice Initiative (EJI) in Alabama. Since then, EJI continues to work tirelessly on issues of criminal justice reform, racial justice, and public education. Their Legacy Museum: From Enslavement to Mass Incarceration, and the National Memorial for Peace and Justice, both in Montgomery, Alabama, stand in stark contrast to the

Confederate monuments and statues throughout the south.[34] The good news is that, in this third decade of the twenty-first century, organizations like the Equal Justice Initiative, the Southern Center for Human Rights, the Southern Poverty Law Center, and others are doing the work they do. The sad news is that these organizations are necessary in a country that boasts of its freedom and justice for all.

One particularly striking irony inherent in our nation's trajectory toward a more perfect union is the willingness of black Americans to fight abroad for democratic principles that they are not fully experiencing at home. World Wars I and II were fought amid the heights of Jim Crow and the terror of lynching. The Korean War and the earliest days in Vietnam were fought before the Civil Rights and Voting Rights Acts were passed, and all four of these conflicts took place amid the Great Migration, which was in effect bounded chronologically by World War I and Vietnam.

Despite their willingness to fight for their country, blacks were segregated, even in the military, through the end of World War II, a segregation that was ended, at least formally, by President Truman's July 26, 1948 Executive Order 9981 (the formal implementation of which was completed in 1954).[35] The executive order came about when senators from the South threatened to filibuster any attempt by Congress to enact the 1947 recommendations of Truman's Commission on Civil Rights, which included anti-lynching and anti-poll tax laws.

That it was Truman who found himself historically situated to issue this order speaks to the intersection of the human capacity for growth and perspective-taking with the machinations of political expedience. When Truman was a twenty-seven-year-old corporal in the National Guard and still a captive of the white supremacist cultural givens of his

Missouri upbringing, he wrote in 1911 that "one man is just as good as another so long as he's honest and decent and not a nigger or a Chinaman."[36] The Truman who inherited the Oval Office thirty-four years later, months before the end of World War II, soon came face to face with the beatings and lynchings of black veterans upon their postwar returns to the South. Among many, Sergeant Isaac Woodward, still in uniform, was beaten and blinded by the police in South Carolina on his bus ride home to his wife in North Carolina. The trouble began when he asked the driver if he could use the men's room at a stop; the driver said no, then relented, and notified the police at the following stop. They beat him and blinded him.[37]

Truman also faced the political realities that his chances for victory in the 1948 election were in jeopardy as white southern Democrats opposed his attention to civil rights. At the same time, pressure from civil rights organizations also made it clear, as evidenced in the words of A. Philip Randolph on March 22, 1948, that "...[Negroes] will never bear arms again until all forms of bias and discrimination are abolished." Randolph later told the Senate Armed Services Committee that he "personally will advise Negroes to refuse to fight as slaves for a democracy they cannot possess and cannot enjoy."[38]

Our work continues regarding race and the U. S. military. From a leadership perspective, General Colin Powell served as the first black chairman of the Joint Chiefs of Staff from 1989 through 1993. Since then, no other person of color has served in that role. Admiral Mike Mullen, now retired, who served as chairman of the Joint Chiefs from 2007 through 2011 under both Presidents Bush and Obama, appointed General Lloyd Austin as Director of the Joint Staff in 2009 with a directive to diversify the directors and vice-directors of the Joint Staff, which he did. Nonetheless, by the time General Austin was confirmed as the first black Secretary of Defense on January

22, 2021, all of the Joint Staff directors and vice-directors were white; just one was a woman.[39]

This rise and fall of military leadership diversity takes place amid the duality of being black in the unique culture of a given service branch while living the larger experience of being a black man or woman going about his or her life in the United States. This duality took on a painfully acute and visible presence in the images of a white police officer kneeling on the neck of a handcuffed black man in Minneapolis on May 25, 2020. Among the many responses to that day, Air Force General Charles Q. Brown, Jr. delivered a message from his head, heart, and gut regarding what he was thinking about some eleven days after George Floyd's death and four days before he would be confirmed as the first black Air Force Chief of Staff. His reflections—from his school days of "trying to fit in" through the delivery of his nearly five-minute monologue—conveyed his full emotions around "the many African-Americans that have suffered the same fate as George Floyd." He recollected those times that "my comments were perceived to represent African-Americans' perspective, when it was just my perspective informed by being African-American" and "the frank and emotional conversations my wife and I have had with [our two sons] just this past week as we discussed the situations that have led to the protests around our country." His message also served as an invitation to the Air Force community to let him know what *they* were thinking about, and many of them did.[40]

On March 21, 2021, *60 Minutes* aired a segment entitled, "Race in the Ranks: Investigating Racial Bias in the U.S. Military."[41] The piece features interviews with Secretary of Defense Austin, Air Force Chief of Staff General Brown, and Admiral Mullen—already mentioned above—and includes brief clips with Air Force Chief Master Sergeant Michael Holland and Senior Master Sergeant Sapphira Morgan in conversations with Lieutenant General Brad Webb. The conversations with General Webb are part of the Air Force's "Real Talk" program, in which service members of various ranks get to talk directly with Webb on diversity issues.[42] Webb, whose service includes 3,700 flying hours and commanding the Air Force Special Operations Command, now leads the Air Education and Training Command, one part of which is researching and taking concrete action on diversity, including but not limited to race, in the Air Force. The recurring themes in the conversations include the experience of not being listened to, especially when you're the only black person in the room; assumptions by others that the white person you're with is in charge or of superior rank; a lack of trust that the chain of command will address racism and equality; a consistently higher probability of discharge due to misconduct and court martial; and a need to shift posture and voice so as not to appear intimidating.

That late Secretary of State Powell, Secretary of Defense Austin, General Brown, and others have risen to the positions they held and hold is evidence of progress—whether we measure from 1865, 1948 or 2009. That the Air Force convened its "Real Talk" program and that Chief Master Sergeant Holland and Senior Master Sergeant Morgan, among many others, still serve amid racially unlevel playing fields is evidence of work yet to do. Both are true: we have progressed, and we have more to do.

It's worth noting that the positions held by black (or white) generals and cabinet secretaries are no more indicative of the everyday experiences of black (or white) junior officers, enlisted men and women, or civilians than the top positions in other professions are representative of the experiences of those in entry-, mid-, and even many high-level jobs—whether in business, science, entertainment, academia, government, or the military. The often-vitriolic push and pull between *look at all the progress we've made as a country* (see all the non-black faces in the demonstrations following George Floyd's murder) and *look at how much remains to be done* (see the white police officer kneeling on George Floyd's neck long enough to kill him, in broad daylight, with support from fellow officers) characterizes much of Americans' usually unskillful attempts to talk about race (and other divisive issues). We'll turn our attention there now.

This chapter's preceding pages provide some context for current "conversations" on race in America. What we say and do today emerges through individual, collective, intergenerational, body-based psychology, memory and worldview—both conscious and unconscious. From concrete steps being taken by military leaders to voluminous facts, opinions, myths, and hyperbolic catastrophizing about the dangers of *antiracism* and *critical race theory* (CRT), our respective voices arise in the present through the past, informed by our cultural givens and developed (or not) through the choices we make and the company we keep.

In the opening pages of *Stamped from the Beginning,* historian Ibram X. Kendi defines a racist idea as "any concept that regards one racial group as inferior or superior to another racial group in any way."[43] In *How to Be an Antiracist,* he complements that definition with these thoughts:

> To be antiracist is to think nothing is behaviorally wrong or right—inferior or superior—with any of the racial groups. Whenever the antiracist sees individuals behaving positively or negatively, the antiracist sees exactly that: individuals behaving positively or negatively, not representatives of whole races.

He continues: "Racist ideas fooled me nearly my whole life.... I realized there is nothing wrong with any of the racial groups and everything wrong with individuals like me who think there is something wrong with any of the racial groups."[44]

Kendi is clear, first, that *to be antiracist differentiates individual behavior from race.* For instance, the respective behaviors of Donald Trump and Timothy McVeigh are not representative of all white people, just as those of Clarence Thomas and John Allen Muhammad are not representative of all blacks. Second, he owns and reflects on his own earlier racist views: "*there is... everything wrong with individuals like me who think...*" Take a moment to get clear: do you agree or disagree with his first assertion, and to what extent do you relate to the second? What does *your* honest, critical self-reflection reveal about your past or present beliefs and opinions with regard to race?

Kendi shares with us that he and his work with antiracism are works in progress. (Imagine if all of us admitted to being works in progress.) He shares insight into his own development, and, using *skillful means*, reflects on his experience of a Shadow aspect of antiracism:

> I closed myself off to new ideas that did not *feel* good. Meaning I shopped for conceptions of racism that fit my ideology and self-identity.
>
> Asking antiracists to change their perspective on racism can be as destabilizing as asking racists to change their perspective on the races. Antiracists can be as doctrinaire in their view of racism as racists can be in their view of not-racism. How can antiracists ask racists to open their minds and change when we are closedminded and unwilling to change? I ignored my own hypocrisy, as people customarily do when it means giving up what they hold dear. Giving up my conception of racism meant giving up my view of the world and myself. I would not without a fight.[45]

Juxtapose Kendi's sense of "giving up my view of the world and myself," with Wilkerson's earlier description of the lower rungs of the dominant caste (that is, struggling whites): *"If the things that I have believed are not true, then might I not be who I thought I was?"*[46] Giving up our views of the world or discovering that what we knew or believed is not true is, in many ways, a little death—the demise of earlier, less inclusive, less comprehensive worldviews. These little deaths are essential developmental moves in which we transcend limiting aspects of earlier views (those people are inferior), include healthy aspects of those earlier views (I love people who are like me), and begin the process of integrating the new, emerging view (those people are actually quite like me (gulp), so I guess I (should) love them). Development is not a smooth, linear process. It includes zigs, zags, steps forward, and steps backward. We'll develop this further in Chapter Eleven.

With an embrace of Kendi's view of antiracism, we'll turn now to critical race theory, which, prior to 2020, was a phrase most Americans had never heard. As described by Richard Delgado and Jean Stefancic:

> The critical race theory movement (CRT) is a collection of activists and scholars engaged in studying and transforming the relationship among race, racism and power…. that includes economics, history, setting, group and self-interest, and emotions and the unconscious…. [and] questions the very foundations of the liberal order, including equality theory, legal reasoning, Enlightenment rationalism, and neutral principles of constitutional law.[47]

So, critical race theory *studies, transforms,* and *questions* individual and group views, beliefs and attitudes as well as systems, infrastructure, institutions, and processes. Emerging in the 1970s, CRT was built on the insights of the "critical legal studies and radical feminism" movements (among much else) and began to address the slowing and stalled legal progress that had begun during the 1960s civil rights movement. Its current iteration, according to the authors, includes "Asian American," "LGBT," "Muslim and Arab," "American Indian," "Middle Eastern," and "South Asian" groups, all of which have their own priorities but "continue to maintain good relations under the umbrella of critical race theory."[48]

The scope and scale of CRT are extensive. Delgado and Stefancic acknowledge that not all CRT adherents would agree with everything in their text, but that "many would agree with" the propositions that "racism is ordinary, not aberrational"; that "white-over-color ascendancy" serves whites in various ways so there is little motivation to end it; that "the dominant society racializes different minority groups at different times" based on need, such as labor; that "no person has a single, easily stated, unitary identity"—we each live at the intersection of various identifying factors; and that those who have been oppressed, who have a "unique voice of color," might "be able to communicate" to whites some things they might otherwise not know.[49] Check in for a moment with your levels of (dis)comfort and (dis)agreement with the above.

Note that critical race theory is *critical* in that it analyzes, as in 'critical thinking helped me understand myself more clearly'—and is not necessarily fault-finding, as in 'he criticized the quality of my work.' It has to do with *race* and also includes gender, ethnicity, sexual orientation, and identity issues. And it is a *theory*, which is an idea or system of ideas or principles that can be investigated and tested to see if it adequately and accurately explains something. In this case, CRT investigates and tests the manner in which attitudes, beliefs, systems, and processes in the U. S. actually work for or against specific individuals or groups. Critical race theory has been around for decades in various iterations, primarily, but not only, in legal scholarship. Media mention, in all of its manifestations prior to 2019 was rare, and usually pointed to *intersectionality,* which we'll explore below, not to the larger body of critical race theory.

That began to change in the summer of 2020 when some city employees in Seattle who had to attend an anti-bias training sent documents from the training to journalist Christopher Rufo. They chose him because his reports on homelessness had "outraged Seattle's homelessness activists" to the point that someone posted his photo and home address on utility poles in his neighborhood and harassed him and his family on social media—ugly behavior that has become increasingly popular in the land of the free-ish and home of the not-so-brave. Rufo explored the Seattle anti-bias documents, invited others to send him more material from such trainings, and found within them the common threads of Robin D'Angelo's *White Fragility* and Kendi's *How to Be an Antiracist,* which he connected to critical race theory. He decided CRT was "the perfect villain" through which conservatives could battle "elites." In Rufo's words, "Its connotations are all negative to most middle-class Americans," and "Strung together, the phrase 'critical race theory' connotes hostile, academic, divisive, race-obsessed, poisonous, elitist, Anti-American," and "it's the label critical race theorists chose themselves."[50]

Rufo published his views locally and soon landed on Fox's Tucker Carlson Show in September 2020. That national exposure led to a phone call from Mark Meadows, Donald Trump's chief of staff, which led to an invitation to D. C., which led to an executive order "that limited how contractors providing federal diversity seminars could talk about race." Rufo continues to battle the "CRT Goliath" through various means, including "his must-read Twitter feed." Here's a sample from March 15, 2021, at 3:14 pm:

> We have successfully frozen their brand- 'critical race theory" – into the public conversation and are steadily

driving up negative perceptions. We will eventually turn it toxic, as we put all of the various cultural insanities under that brand category.[51]

As with other alleged or former journalists across the political spectrum, Rufo seems to have severed any ties he had with journalism. Some of what he points to when he's not hyperbolically branding carries some partial truths. *Truths,* because some folks who require or facilitate diversity/anti-bias/anti-any-ism workshops *are* unskillful at best, mean-spirited and/or ignorant at worst, and seem not to have done enough (or any) of their own work. They profess to believe in equality for all, and are out to save the world—through finger-pointing and guilt-invoking. *Partial,* because very few of the unskillful, undoubtedly well-intentioned workshop facilitators are, themselves, critical race theorists, and many other folks who facilitate such trainings are extraordinarily skillful at opening doors, hearts, and minds. Perhaps not even Christopher Rufo knows whether he would have chosen this path had the goons in Seattle not harassed him and his family because they disagreed with something he wrote. Now he harasses critical race theorists because he disagrees with some things they've written. The pot and the kettle are at it again.

Mike Gonzalez, in Acton Institute's *Religion & Liberty,* writes that "many have now heard of 'critical race theory' because...Donald Trump launched an attack against it," and characterizes CRT as "an offshoot of critical theory, as is... critical legal theory [and] other spinoffs...of all types of ethnic and gender studies. Put together, they amount to what I and many others call the 'grievance industry'." He christens critical theory as "the main philosophical school of identity politics," and "an unremitting attack on all of America's norms and traditions." His hyperbolic "unremitting" and "all" notwithstanding, Gonzalez ignores the identity politics inherent in the norms and traditions that enslaved African identities, removed Native American identities, incinerated Vietnamese, Afghan and Iraqi identities, and subjugated female identities.

This singlemindedness, which ignores larger contexts unless they serve his preconceptions, allowed him to write the following sentence in September 2020 after two police officers were shot and injured in the protests that ensued after the trial in which no officers were charged for the killing of Breonna Taylor: "When one sees hard-Left rioters in the streets shooting two police officers, attacking restaurants and stores, and in turn attracting the attention of armed right-wing militants, one shudders."[52] Indeed. This context-free rhetoric, despite an obviously different *content,* is consistent with the unskillfully designed and executed anti-bias trainings that incited Rufo. Skillful, appropriate, and effective approaches to creating awareness, shifting behaviors, and transforming systems and processes concerning race, gender, ethnicity, culture, orientation, and identity do exist. Not everyone who would like to design or facilitate them is competent to do so, as not everyone who flushes the toilet is a competent plumber and not everyone who wins an election is a competent leader.

Among CRT's tenets, *intersectionality* has arguably received the most mainstream attention, perhaps to the delight *and* chagrin of Kimberlé Crenshaw, who coined the term and who commented thus about the ruckus around it: "This is what happens when an idea travels beyond the context and the content." Journalist Joan Coaston clarifies that Crenshaw's "this" refers to three debates often conflated as one:

> one based on what academics like Crenshaw [actual critical race theorists] actually mean by the term, one based on how activists seeking to eliminate disparities between groups have interpreted the term [for example, (un)skillful workshop presenters, among others], and a third on how some

> conservatives [like Rufo, Gonzalez, et. al.] are responding to
> its use by those activists.[53]

When Crenshaw published "Demarginalizing the Intersection
of Race and Sex" in the University of Chicago Legal Forum in
1989, she focused on how black women were treated in the
courts in three cases.[54] Here's my oversimplified synopsis of
one case: black female plaintiffs lost a discrimination suit
against a company that did hire a representative number of
black men—checking the race box—and a representative
number of white women—checking the sex box. The court,
having those two boxes checked, did not have a precedent—a
race *and* sex box to check, when it came to black women,
whose identities intersected around race and sex. Thus, legally,
there was neither race nor sex discrimination, despite de facto
race-sex discrimination. The applications of intersectionality
have since expanded to include traits in addition to race and
sex. Since we all live lives at the intersections of multiple
characteristics, all of us can be served well by a skillful application of intersectionality—and disserved by an unskillful application thereof.

Some folks have charted selected traits into "privileged" and
"oppressed" categories,[55] which, skillfully wielded to create
awareness or to better understand a specific case, might be
useful. An example would be a *white, heterosexual, cisgender
male* (four privileged traits), who struggles holding a job and
getting along with people. That he was drafted, *traumatized,*
and *disabled* (two oppressed traits) in Vietnam captures him in
a more integrated, complex and fully human light. His identity
includes the intersection of these six traits, among others.

Some of these same folks unskillfully claim—in workshops,
lectures, tweets, podcasts, and interviews—that if you're living
at the intersection of all or mostly privileged traits, you're
guilty, you're a colonizer and you're an oppressor. And, if

you're living at the intersection of all or mostly oppressed traits, you're colonized, oppressed and a victim. This is a sweeping, generalizing example of unskillful means, exacerbated by a *performative contradiction*, which, in this case offers a conclusion that contradicts the original assertion: *we're working toward equality for all; you're privileged, a colonizer and an oppressor—even if you've never colonized or oppressed anyone—so, you are not equal.* Such behavior, however well-intentioned, misidentifies critical race theory, misuses intersectionality, and invites Christopher Rufo and others, funded by their own Goliath, to "turn [critical race theory] toxic" as a "brand category."[56]

In *Woke Racism,* linguist John McWhorter characterizes those I describe as unskillfully misidentifying and misusing CRT as having formed a de facto new "religion" that betrays blacks in America. He calls members of the religion, regardless of race or ethnicity, "the Elect," and points to a "Catechism of Contradictions" they follow. I agree with his general observations and most of his conclusions. I also believe he discards some babies with the bathwater, as in his selective critiques of Ibram X. Kendi and Ta-Nehisi Coates and his generally equating practicing "Elects" with critical race theorists.[57] As I've developed this point in this chapter, McWhorter's "Elects" are those who *misuse* CRT in the extreme and not the scholars who work to develop and apply it.

STANDING VERY CLOSE TO THEIR glass houses, Americans launch racial stones from both sides of various streets, facilitated by online catapults, trolls, and drones, while pointing very similar, crooked fingers at each other. Not all of us do this. And those who do seem more concerned with winning a particular, finite battle by landing a particular stone than in manifesting an authentic, infinite (or even finite) end to the conflict. Were they to put their stones down, take a breath or two, really look, and listen, they might find true peace. Rarely does anyone want to be the first to disarm and truly look and listen. Such acts require courage and trust.

Our navigation of race in twenty-first-century America travels a spectrum that includes the extremes of conservatism and liberalism and their moderate cousins. The dominant American worldview is group-centric—it's about *us.* And of the many, many fractured "usses" that are trying to win something along the spectrum, too many operate in the unhealthy realm of us *against* them, as opposed to us *with* or us *and* them. Occasionally, me-centric individuals appear, such as the forty-fifth president, and their self-interest makes matters worse. Once in a while, a few world-centric—it's about *all of us*—folks attempt to honor the partial truths and challenge the limitations—the dignities and disasters—of all the stones thrown, including their own. Heads on a swivel, they often have to duck stones from multiple directions.

This chapter depicts current American narratives about race in the context of America's racial history and juxtaposes these narratives with those in the preceding two chapters and those in the two chapters that follow as evidence of what we need to heal and what we have to unpack and own from that long, invisible Shadow bag we drag behind us.

Ample evidence exists of racial progress in America. It can be seen in our individual and collective views and behaviors, and in culture and society. Competing with this progress is the sometimes overt and sometimes covert progress of racism. As Ibram X. Kendi makes clear, both are true:

> I did not see a *singular* historical force taking steps forward and backward on race…. I saw a *dual* and *dueling* history of racial progress and the simultaneous progression of racism. I saw the antiracist force of equality and the racist force of inequality marching forward, progressing in rhetoric, in tactics, in policies.

....

And racist progress has consistently followed racial progress.[58]

Jim Crow and lynching followed the end of slavery. The "wars on crime and drugs"—declared by Richard Nixon and escalated by subsequent administrations—and the consequent mass incarceration of black men followed the civil rights progress of the 1960s. In a 1994 interview with author and journalist Dan Baum, Nixon advisor and counsel John Ehrlichman, who was convicted for his role in the Watergate scandal, admitted the following:

> The Nixon campaign in 1968, and the Nixon White House after that, had two enemies: the antiwar left and black people.... [and] by getting the public to associate the hippies with marijuana and blacks with heroin, and then criminalizing both heavily, we could disrupt those communities. We could arrest their leaders, raid their homes, break up their meetings, and vilify them night after night on the evening news. Did we know we were lying about the drugs? Of course we did.[59]

Similarly, the focused mobilization against critical race theory followed the national and international multiracial demonstrations and protests that resulted from George Floyd's murder (and those murders that preceded it).

To close, let's bring this back to each of us. Consider your honest responses, with a focus on race, to the following questions:

1. What do I truly want (and not want) for myself?
2. What do I truly want (and not want) for others?
3. What do I truly want (and not want) in my relationships with others?

4. How would I behave if I truly embodied these responses?[60]

Finally, practice both deep honesty and self-compassion as you reflect on this last question. How, and to what extent, are you exacerbating or alleviating racial tensions in your relationships with yourself and with others?

Chapter Six

Dominoes, Defoliation, Death, & Democracy

How might war be engaged without killing?[1]

THE MASS GRAVES AT HUÈ
by Doug Anderson[2]

After the siege of Huè and the enemy withdrawal,
it was impossible to tell which dead were ARVN,
NVA, or civilian, blackened as they were.
And so those who buried them, kind in their exhaustion,
wearing cloth masks against the stench and
pushed beyond all thought into the realm of ghosts,
dragged the bodies into mass graves and covered them,
without regard to who they were and where they stood
in this long and mindless war, and so as the land
became fertile there, the vines and flowers thrived.
Would that our dead have been buried
with them and our brotherhood be known.

DECADES BEFORE THE U. S. INVASION of Iraq in 2003, the United States invaded Vietnam—initially with "advisors" and eventually with bombs, troops, and bullets. After its defeat in World War II, Japan was forced to leave the former French colony,

Indochina—as Vietnam, Laos, and Cambodia were then known—which it had occupied during the war. After Japan's departure, France's attempt to reassert control of the area was thwarted by the popular support of the Viet Minh—who wanted Vietnamese independence and opposed the French colonizers, the Japanese occupiers, and eventually, the American invaders—for Ho Chi Minh. Under his leadership, on September 2, 1945, the "Proclamation of Independence of the Democratic Republic of Vietnam" emerged. It borrowed language and concepts from both the American and French revolutions, and it listed grievances against the French colonizers in 1945, much as the British colonists, who would eventually identify as Americans, had done against their British governors in 1776. The Vietnamese proclamation begins:

> "We hold truths that all men are created equal, that they are endowed by their Creator with certain unalienable Rights, among these are Life, Liberty and the pursuit of Happiness." This immortal statement is extracted from the Declaration of Independence of the United States of America in 1776. Understood in the broader sense, this means: "All peoples on the earth are born equal; every person has the right to live to be happy and free."[3]

In 1945 the leadership of Vietnam saw fit to clarify and revise the American declaration, replacing "all men" (the second time it appeared) with "all peoples" and making explicit their belief that equality and "the right to live to be happy and free" applied to everyone "on the earth." Absent were the American exclusions-by-language of women, indigenous peoples, and enslaved peoples.

In 1945 and 1946 Ho Chi Minh wrote repeatedly to President Truman and other world leaders, and at least once to the United Nations, asking for humanitarian aid from the "great world powers" and relief organizations because some two million Vietnamese had died of starvation in the final years of World War II. Neither the U. S. president nor the other leaders nor the United Nations responded. Ho concluded that "We apparently stand quite alone; we shall have to depend on ourselves." In the United States, Ho's letters were classified Top Secret and would not become known until the Pentagon Papers were published in 1971. At least two explanations for Truman's lack of response have been offered: 1) the CIA never let the president see the letters; and 2) he saw them and chose not to respond. Neither explanation bodes well in light of the next forty years. When the French began their eight-year war against Ho Chi Minh's government and its followers in 1946, the U. S., first under Truman and then under Eisenhower, helped arm the French and financed most of the French effort.[4]

With the 1949 Communist victory in China, and the faith that the Viet Minh had in Ho Chi Minh, the U. S. articulated and began to act on the "domino" theory—that if one Southeast Asian country were to succumb to Communism, the rest would follow suit, and that if free elections were allowed, Vietnam, Laos, and Cambodia would be controlled by Communists. Said differently, the U. S. wanted to stop the possible spread of Communism in the region by preventing free democratic elections. By 1954, the French military effort had failed. In July of that year, the international agreements in Geneva provided that:

> A provisional military demarcation line shall be fixed, on either side of which the forces of the two parties shall be regrouped after their withdrawal, the forces of the People's Army of VietNam to the north of the line and the forces of the French Union to the south.
>
> The provisional military demarcation line is fixed as shown on the map attached [at the 17th parallel].

> It is also agreed that a demilitarized zone shall be established on either side of the demarcation line, to a width of not more than 5 Kms. from it, to act as a buffer zone and avoid any incidents which might result in the resumption of hostilities.

The agreements further stipulated that:

> ...no military base under the control of a foreign State may be established in the regrouping zones of the two parties, the latter having the obligation to see that the zones allotted to them shall not constitute part of any military alliance and shall not be utilized for the resumption of hostilities or in the service of an aggressive policy.[5]

National elections for a unified Vietnam were scheduled for July 1956 under the supervision of the Member States of the International Supervisory Commission. The signatories to the agreements were the Democratic Republic of Vietnam (later known as North Vietnam), France, China, the Soviet Union, and the United Kingdom—all, with the exception of the first, were interested outsiders. The State of Vietnam (later known as South Vietnam) and the United States, which acknowledged the agreements, did not sign.

In April 1953, just over a year *before* the agreements were signed, President Eisenhower had delivered his "The Chance for Peace" speech to the American Society of Newspaper Editors. Widely known as the "Cross of Iron" speech, it celebrates the end of World War II, warns of the Soviet Union's post-war behaviors, and argues both against the costs of war and for hope, freedom, and democracy:

> The 8 years that have passed have seen that hope waver, grow dim, and almost die. And the shadow of fear again has darkly lengthened across the world.... In that [1945] spring of victory the soldiers of the Western Allies met the soldiers

of Russia in the center of Europe. They were triumphant comrades in arms....

This common purpose lasted an instant and perished. The nations of the world divided to follow two distinct roads. The United States and our valued friends, the other free nations, chose one road. The leaders of the Soviet Union chose another. The way chosen by the United States was plainly marked by a few clear precepts, which govern its conduct in world affairs.

First: No people on earth can be held, as a people, to be enemy, for all humanity shares the common hunger for peace and fellowship and justice.

Second: No nation's security and well-being can be lastingly achieved in isolation but only in effective cooperation with fellow-nations.

Third: Any nation's right to form of government and an economic system of its own choosing is inalienable.

Fourth: Any nation's attempt to dictate to other nations their form of government is indefensible.

And fifth: A nation's hope of lasting peace cannot be firmly based upon any race in armaments but rather upon just relations and honest understanding with all other nations.

....

In reflecting on possible consequences of the growing divide, Eisenhower declared that:

The worst is atomic war. The best would be this: a life of perpetual fear and tension; a burden of arms draining the wealth and the labor of all peoples; a wasting of strength that defies the American system or the Soviet system or any system to achieve true abundance and happiness for the peoples of this earth.

Every gun that is made, every warship launched, every rocket fired signifies, in the final sense, a theft from those who hunger and are not fed, those who are cold and are not clothed. This world in arms is not spending money alone. It is spending the sweat of its laborers, the genius of its scientists, the hopes of its children.

The cost of one modern heavy bomber is this: a modern brick school in more than 30 cities. It is two electric power plants, each serving a town of 60,000 population. It is two fine, fully equipped hospitals. It is some 50 miles of concrete highway.

We pay for a single fighter with a half million bushels of wheat. We pay for a single destroyer with new homes that could have housed more than 8,000 people. This, I repeat, is the best way of life to be found on the road the world has been taking.

This is not a way of life at all, in any true sense. Under the cloud of threatening war, it is humanity hanging from a cross of iron.[6]

Beginning almost immediately, and continuing for the next twenty-plus years in Vietnam and in various places around the globe to the present day, the United States would violate Eisenhower's first, third, fourth, and fifth precepts, and engage an ongoing national debate about the second. The Soviets and Chinese would exacerbate the situation, but they didn't claim to adhere to these same precepts.

The U.S. Congress and State Department considered Vietnam a strategic piece of property in Southeast Asia, and so they moved to prevent the national election and to set up a government in South Vietnam. Toward that end, in 1955 they funded, encouraged, promoted, and essentially inserted Ngo Dinh Diem, a Catholic who had been educated in a French school for colonial administrators and later exiled from Vietnam for four years, as the head of the new "country," South Vietnam, which was predominantly Buddhist. So, a returning exile, who was Catholic and educated by the French, would be in charge of a primarily Buddhist country that was "essentially the creation of the United States." Diem replaced provincial leaders with his own men, refused to allow the national election (with the tacit approval of the American government), imprisoned opponents and critics, favored land-lords over peasants, and consequently grew less and less popular with the peasants in the south.[7]

When Diem inaccurately castigated all Viet Minh, a name that carried patriotic meaning among the peasants, as Communists, the CIA realized that his criticism was inadver-tently helping the Communists recruit new members. The intelligence agency introduced the label *Viet Cong* as a replacement for Viet Minh in 1956, and the new name caught on in the 1960s in America, to a lesser degree in Saigon, and even less so in the rest of Vietnam. One Vietnamese reporter put it plainly: the Viet Cong "look like the Viet Minh...act like the Viet Minh, and that's what these people have always called them."[8] For a variety of cultural, historical, and political reasons, including his alienation of the peasants in the south, his often dictatorial and ruthless style of governing, and his often less-than-cooperative interactions with his American sponsors, Diem would be assassinated in a November 1963 coup led by his generals and assisted by the CIA.

Under Presidents Truman, Eisenhower, and Kennedy the U.S. first ignored and then incrementally opposed Ho Chi Minh in the north; set up, supported, and eventually disposed of Diem in the south; and increased the presence and levels of engagement of U. S. military advisors. President Johnson, with the financial blessings of Congress, then officially sent U. S. combat forces to Vietnam without declaring war. Johnson and Nixon each escalated specific aspects of the undeclared war both on the ground and in the air, persistently deaf to the echoes of President Eisenhower in 1961 and General Maxwell Taylor in 1964, each of whom marveled at the consistently high morale, resilience, and recuperative abilities of the

National Liberation Front (NLF, also known as the "Viet Cong") forces—even after they became prisoners of war.[9] The preceding paragraph paints thirty years with broad brush strokes. Selected details follow.

One man, imperfect though he was, who saw and heard clearly during his days as an American advisor to the South Vietnamese military, was Lt. Col. John Paul Vann. The battle of Ap Bac was launched on January 2, 1963 with a mission to seize a Viet Cong radio transmitter. Vann, who advised and helped plan the attack would watch it unfold from a spotter plane. At the battle's end, the Viet Cong guerillas had killed or wounded approximately four of the attackers for every one of their own; they had killed three Americans and wounded eight, and they had disabled five American helicopters. A combination of fog, incorrect intelligence, tension between Vann and some U.S. helicopter pilots, the Viet Cong's commitment to learning how to fight against the helicopters, and reluctance on the part of some ARVN officers to lead and fight in a way that might upset their superiors and their president contributed to this result. Vann, at times skillfully and at times unskillfully, would later speak and write the truth about what had happened at Ap Bac. He and other advisors who were present would see their reports ignored and generally dismissed by everyone from General Paul Harkins, who wanted Vann fired, on up through the Joint Chiefs, Defense Secretary McNamara, and the president.[10]

In his Pulitzer-Prize-winning, *A Bright Shining Lie*, journalist Neil Sheehan contrasts the perspectives of U.S. generals at the beginning of World War II with those at the beginning of the country's involvement in Vietnam:

> Eisenhower and Patton and their United States Army of 1943 [which chief of staff, General George Marshall, had referred to as a "third-rate power"] had been small men in a

world of big men. Their personal survival, the survival of their army, and the survival of their nation had been at stake. And they had been afraid that they might lose.

Many of the generals who were involved in the Vietnam conflict in the early 1960s had been junior officers in World War II. In Sheehan's view, some of them "had become so accustomed to winning from the later years of that war that they could no longer imagine they could lose…. They assumed they would prevail in Vietnam simply because of who they were."[11] When Lt. Col. John Vann wrote his report after the disputed failure at Ap Bac in January 1963 and General Paul Harkins refused to pass it along to his superiors, Harkins couldn't see—or refused to believe—that Vann's concerns were legitimate. The general would not accept that Vann, who had planned the battle and watched it unfold differently from the way he had hoped it would, had been right. Harkins was reporting to and working for men who wanted to measure success by numbers: body count, kill ratio, "number of operations reported launched…aircraft sorties flown and the tonnage of bombs dropped."[12] Vann, who had won a Bronze Star for his work in supply and logistics in the early days of the Korean War, was not oblivious to statistics. He was already an attentive and skillful strategist and tactician, and he was deeply concerned with what any numbers *meant* to those who were doing the actually fighting. He was upset by and concerned with all he had experienced at Ap Bac. With few exceptions, his concerns fell on deaf ears.

The men who would authorize the generals first to train the South Vietnamese and then to take on their fight were also subject to the limitations of their post-World War II cultural givens and worldviews. Emerging from that war as a world leader, if not the savior of the free world, the United States turned its attention to living well at home, spreading democracy abroad, and thwarting the spread of Communism.

THE AUGUST 1964 GULF OF TONKIN INCIDENT, documented in part through a series of confused and confusing reports now historically discredited and occasionally still debated, resulted in an almost unanimous vote in both houses of Congress to give President Johnson the power to fully engage the U. S. military in Southeast Asia. (Thirty-seven years later, due to the events of September 11, 2001 and despite any alleged lessons learned—or not learned—in Vietnam, Congress would give George W. Bush an updated version of that same essentially blank check to "fight terror" anywhere on the planet. We'll explore how that went in Chapter Seven). So, the Congressionally-approved *official* bombing of the north began in 1964. After the Ia Drang battle in 1965, General Westmoreland requested troops in five-figure increments, and by 1968 more than half a million American military personnel were on the ground in Vietnam.

From the mid-1960s through 1974, Buddhist monks and at least two American citizens would set themselves on fire in protest first against the Diem regime and then the war itself; letters from young U. S. combatants arrived in their parents' mailboxes depicting the horrors they were both seeing and committing; images of the carnage appeared nightly on the television news; protests erupted around the United States; young men burned their draft cards; African Americans, especially in the South, who were still denied the full freedom, equality, and suffrage of their citizenship, spoke to the hypocrisy of being asked to fight for someone else's freedom; the Ohio National Guard shot and killed four unarmed student protestors at Kent State University; the Johnson and Nixon administrations continually lied about who and what was being bombed and how much bombing was being done.

Dissent widened to include large swaths of the country—from the more public voices of Muhammed Ali, Dr. Martin Luther King, Jr., Daniel Ellsberg, the Berrigan brothers, and Ron Kovic to the unnamed individual citizens who marched and wrote and the military personnel who began to question, to defy orders, and to "frag" officers.[13] Some, upon returning home, formed the Vietnam Veterans Against the War and the Concerned Officers Movement. American and Vietnamese combatants and Vietnamese civilians continued to die.

FREE FIRE ZONE
   by Doug Anderson[14]

The eighteen-year-old who thinks
Christ is about to rain death on commies
kicks the family altar to pieces in an old mud hut.
We set the charge, roll the det cord
into the sun, chase out the old yellow dog;
but he ambles back into the dark, curls
on the cool dirt floor, tongue dripping.
We laugh and blow it anyway; the numbing flash,
dust unfurling low to the ground,
but in a moment the dog staggers
out of the rubble wagging his whole self,
sits down before us expecting to be fed.
We leave him cans to lick, then go north through red dust.
Villagers begin to rebuild their hootches
from the trash we've left, and when in two weeks
we return, the bamboo we hacked down grown back
chest high; the same dog wobbles out of the shade,
licks the shit off a bare-bottomed brat
and sits lopsided in the sun.

On the ground, rules of engagement provided that all individuals within an area that was declared a *free-fire zone* were enemy. *Search-and-destroy* missions provided that all military-age men encountered on such missions could be killed, villages could be burned, and women and children could be sent to refugee camps. On March 16, 1968, U. S. Army Warrant Officer and helicopter pilot Hugh Thompson, Jr., along with his door gunner, Specialist Larry Colburn and crew chief, Specialist Glenn Andreotta, interrupted one such search-and-destroy mission, in which Army infantry soldiers massacred some 504 non-combatant, unarmed men, women, and children.

Thompson put his helicopter down between the soldiers and the group of civilians they were preparing to kill, ordering Colburn to open fire on the soldiers if they interfered with his attempts to save the remaining Vietnamese. This was an *it's about all of us* move that continued when Thompson called in another U. S. gunship and together they evacuated the surviving civilians to a nearby base. The massacre took place in the village of Son My, with some 347 of the 504 murders taking place in the hamlet of My Lai. Glenn Andreotta would die in combat three weeks later. The three men would be called traitors and worse for thirty years. On March 6, 1998, Thompson, Colburn, and, posthumously, Andreotta, were awarded the Soldiers Medal for heroism not involving conflict with an enemy.[15] Colonel Oran Henderson, ordered to cover up the massacre, would say in 1971 that "Every unit of brigade size has its My Lai hidden someplace."[16]

In his reflections on the killings of civilians by the U.S. Army and on Lieutenant William Calley, Jr.—the one man who was held responsible—Neil Sheehan drew an at-once striking and obvious conclusion regarding what had happened at My Lai and what was happening on a daily basis in Vietnam:

> What Calley and others who participated in the massacre did that was different was to kill hundreds of unarmed Vietnamese in two hamlets in a single morning and to kill

point-blank with rifles, pistols, and machine guns. Had they killed just as many over a larger area in a longer period of time and killed impersonally with bombs, shells, rockets, white phosphorous, and napalm, they would have been following the normal pattern of American military conduct. The soldier and the junior officer observed the lack of regard his superiors had for the Vietnamese. The value of Vietnamese life was systematically cheapened in his mind.... The military leaders of the United States, and the civilian leaders who permitted the generals to wage war as they did, had made the massacre inevitable.[17]

Sheehan indicts the worst of unhealthy masculine leadership. Be it military or civilian, local, state, or national, such leadership renders inevitable, or at least highly likely, horrors such as My Lai in 1968; the mutilation and slaughter of Cheyenne men, women, and children at Sand Creek in 1864; the massacre of Lakota men, women, and children at Wounded Knee in 1890; the more than 6,000 lynchings of blacks between 1865 and 1950; and the incineration of Tulsa, Oklahoma's Greenwood district in 1921, among other examples.

In the summer of 1967, months before the massacre, Jonathan Schell, a twenty-four-year-old reporter for the *New Yorker,* met with Robert McNamara and told him what he had observed over several weeks from the back seat of a spotter plane. Seventy percent of the 450 hamlets in Quang Ngai province had been destroyed by a combination of air and ground attacks. A British doctor estimated an annual rate of 50,000 dead and wounded civilians in Quang Ngai; a U. S. Systems Analysis formula put the number at about 33,000.

When asked if he had any of this written down, Schell gave McNamara a copy of what would become an article for the *New Yorker,* and later a book. McNamara shared Schell's writing with Ellsworth Bunker, the U. S. Ambassador to

Vietnam, who shared it with Westmoreland, who authorized an investigation that concluded "… Mr. Schell's estimates are substantially correct." Earlier, by the fall of 1966, McNamara had begun to have doubts about the war. The doubts arose from his own observations and from memos provided to him by Daniel Ellsberg—especially, but not only about the dysfunction in the Saigon government. Further fueling his doubts were a statistical analysis that demonstrated that Westmoreland's war of attrition which constantly demanded more troops "was an absurdity," and an interview with Army Lieutenant Colonel Hal Moore, who conveyed his belief, based on the battles of Ia Drang and Bong Son, that the Vietnamese were learning how to fight the Americans, and actually already had the U. S. fighting *their* way. The meeting with Schell deepened the defense secretary's misgivings.[18]

ON JUNE 13, 1971, THE *NEW YORK TIMES* published the first in a series of articles based on leaked documents from the classified top secret "Report of the Office of the Secretary of Defense Vietnam Task Force," commissioned by Secretary of Defense Robert McNamara in 1967. The Justice Department obtained a restraining order against the *Times,* which along with the *Washington Post* contested the order in court. On June 30, 1971, the Supreme Court ruled 6-3 that the newspapers could continue to publish what would become known as the Pentagon Papers. In 2011 the government declassified the complete report, about 34% of which was available to the public for the first time.[19]

The report, completed before the beginning of the Nixon presidency, provides glimpses of each administration's views on and actions in "French Indochina" from Roosevelt in 1940 through Johnson in 1968. The many lessons learned, or available for learning, provide insight into the interplay of ignorance, fear, arrogance, betrayal, violence, and uncertainty at the highest levels of the government and the military. Underlying these characteristics were the worldviews and cultural givens that led to the choices these leaders made. In reflecting on the Papers in the days after the last of the series was published in 1971, journalist Max Frankel wrote:

> The American Presidents, caught between the fear of a major war involving the Soviet Union or China and the fear of defeat and humiliation at the hands of a small band of insurgents, were hesitant about every major increase in military force. But they were unrestrained in both their public and private rhetorical commitments to "pay the price," to "stay the course" and to "do whatever is necessary." .... As the Pentagon papers show, every President from Truman to Johnson passed down the problem of Vietnam in worse shape than he had received it.[20]

An often-cited sliver from the Papers quotes a March 10, 1965 memorandum from Assistant Secretary of Defense, John McNaughton, who quantified the justification for the U. S. aims for "Action for South Vietnam" as follows:

- 70%—To avoid a humiliating US defeat (to our reputation as a guarantor).
- 20%—To keep SVN (and then adjacent) territory from Chinese hands.
- 10%—To permit the people of SVN to enjoy a better, freer way of life.
- Also—To emerge from crisis without unacceptable taint from methods used.
- Not—To "help a friend," although it would be hard to stay if asked out.[21]

With regard to the quantified bullets: we did not avoid a humiliating defeat; China did not invade and take over

Vietnam, but U. S. military action did not effect this result—Vietnam did, after the U. S. military was withdrawn; the people of Vietnam do enjoy a better, freer way of life, but not the particular version the United States tried to impose.

Concerns with individual legacies and national images amid twenty years of escalating U. S. carnage in Vietnam are highlighted by the shenanigans leading up to and during the 1968 peace talks in Paris. To be clear, the gamesmanship was not exclusive to the Americans: the leaders of South Vietnam, North Vietnam, the Viet Cong, and the Soviet Union all played. President Johnson had made it known that he was not running for reelection; Hubert Humphrey and Richard Nixon were the respective Democratic and Republican candidates. Johnson cut back on the bombing of the North and was trying to get the talks going for his own legacy and to help Humphrey. Nixon—or at least his campaign managers—worried that progress with the peace talks would help Humphrey, tried to sabotage the U. S. efforts by encouraging the South Vietnamese to delay the talks until after the U. S. election. At the time, Nixon was a private citizen, and Johnson privately accused him of treason. The Soviets preferred Humphrey to Nixon and encouraged the North to attend the talks.[22] While the older boys were posturing and passing their secret notes, the younger Vietnamese and American boys and girls were still killing each other. More Americans—one death 16,000-plus times—would die in Vietnam in 1968 than in any other year.

Nixon eventually defeated Humphrey by a margin of 0.7% of the popular vote, 43.4% to 42.7%—a difference of approximately 512,000 popular votes. (In contrast, 52 years later, Donald Trump would attempt to avoid embarrassment by authoring the fictional theft of the 2020 election, in which his losing margin was 4.5%: 51.3% for the winner, Biden, and 46.8% for the loser, Trump. This was a 7,000,000+ popular vote defeat for the incumbent. The eventual loser began incessantly to repeat the story of the fictional theft months *before* the election. We'll return to this in Chapter Ten).

This fear of humiliation has impacted and continues to impact presidents, administrations, members of Congress, military officers, and the teenagers and young adults they sent and send to fight. The need to save face, to avoid shame or embarrassment, to deny the truth—whether that truth is genuine uncertainty or the certainty that what you're doing is wrong—did not start with Vietnam. Sheehan noted in *A Bright Shining Lie* that as 1942 drew to a close, college-age men "felt that the country was in danger and they could not delay. Most young men who had turned the draft age of eighteen…and were not in uniform began to feel ashamed."[23] And in the writing that emerged through his own experience and the experiences of the men with whom he served in Vietnam, National Book Award winner Tim O'Brien wrote:

> They carried the soldier's greatest fear, which was the fear of blushing. Men killed and died because they were embarrassed not to…. They died so as not to die of embarrassment…. "I couldn't make myself be brave…. I would go to the war—I would kill and maybe die—because I was embarrassed not to."[24]

Juxtaposing these personal concerns with shame, blushing, and embarrassment with John McNaughton's calibration that 70% of the justification for escalating the U. S. military involvement in Vietnam was to avoid national humiliation again raises a clear, culturally given, unhealthy masculine flag, which was raised and waved, perhaps unknowingly, by the war's architects, and which we will continue to acknowledge, clarify, explore, and attempt to lower in the chapters ahead.

Contrasted with most of the architects, many veterans, some who volunteered and some who were drafted, have returned to Vietnam and met with their former foes, recognizing that they are in many ways more alike than different. In his memoir, *Keep Your Head Down,* Doug Anderson writes:

> Among the vets, there are as many different opinions about the war as there are vets, but a significant number of them have been drawn back to Vietnam.... There is one thing any Vietnam vet, regardless of his political views, is sure of: The custodians of the official versions lie. Governments lie. Histories lie, and few people care that soldiers and others die for the lies.[25]

For differing opinions among veterans, on the public stage we need look no further than George W. Bush's 2004 reelection campaign, which enlisted Vietnam veterans (and others) to betray Bush's opponent, Senator John Kerry. Kerry was a recipient of a Silver Medal, a Bronze Medal and three Purple Hearts for his service in Vietnam, and he spoke out against the war upon his return home. Known as the "Swiftboat" campaign, this Bush strategy, now discredited by many of the veterans who helped perpetrate it, was effective. Bush, who did not serve in Vietnam and on whose watch the 9/11 attacks occurred, was seen as a more patriotic leader than Kerry, who had fought, been wounded, been decorated, and had committed himself to a life of public service.

BY THE WAR'S END, MORE than seven million tons—fourteen billion pounds—of bombs had been dropped on Vietnam. Forty-plus years after the United States withdrew the last of its troops, former Defense Secretary Robert McNamara stands out as the strongest voice, among the architects of the war, to publicly recognize the missteps in that campaign—a campaign intended to stop the "evil out there."

In Errol Morris's documentary, *The Fog of War,* McNamara spoke of eleven lessons learned—different lessons than those he provided in his book, *In Retrospect,* both of which we'll return to in Chapter Seven. In the film, McNamara's lesson one is the need to "empathize with your enemy." He believed, in hindsight, that the U. S. was better able to empathize with the Soviets during the Cuban Missile Crisis than it was with the Vietnamese. Along with this need to empathize, the seventh lesson, "Belief and seeing are both often wrong,"[26] became real for him in his 1995 return to Vietnam.

There, former deputy foreign minister, Tran Quang Co, told McNamara in one conversation that he was "totally wrong," that he didn't know history, that the Vietnamese people had been fighting for their independence for centuries—from China, from Japan, from the French, and from the Americans, that no amount of loss would stop them, and that "We never had two Vietnams. We had only one Vietnam. But the U. S. assessed it as two Vietnams." Co went on to assert that Vietnam's biggest mistake after World War II was to consider "the U. S. a leading democratic country, which was opposed to colonialism.... We thought the U. S. would support our desire for independence. But we were wrong."[27] The strategic political and military views that U. S. leadership held about Vietnam after World War II nurtured beliefs that effectively eradicated any chance of empathy for the Vietnamese people.

Perhaps more telling in the context of this book is the culturally given, unhealthy masculine disconnect between the intellects and emotions of U. S. political and military leaders. This disconnect of head from heart accompanied McNamara on his return to Vietnam: "I may not tell you how I'm feeling. I try to separate human emotions from the larger issues of human welfare. Human welfare requires that we avoid conflict. I try not to let my human emotions interfere with efforts to resolve conflict."[28] These words capture well what was expected of smart men in positions of leadership in McNamara's generation (and still in many men today). The teachings and language of emotional intelligence, competence, and regulation—popular now—were just beginning to emerge when McNamara returned in 1995.

In his article in *The Nation* on July 7, 2009, the day after Robert McNamara died, Jonathan Schell reflected on the man, on their 1967 meeting, and on what he had told the secretary he had seen from the spotter plane. Schell recalled McNamara's request for something in writing and the fate of the document he gave him. He wrote of McNamara's gradual disillusionment with the war he had helped orchestrate, of the end of his time as Secretary of Defense, and of his eventual emotional and public repudiation of the war. Schell didn't let McNamara off the hook, but asked how many public figures of national stature have ever acknowledged their mistakes or admitted they were wrong, as McNamara did, and concluded that "If a statue is ever made to him, as probably there will not be, let it show him weeping. It was the best of him."[29]

A dissonant echo to Robert McNamara's 1995 interaction with Tran Quang Co, Doug Anderson's poem, "Letting Go," depicts a conversation between two men who were on the ground amid the fighting:

LETTING GO
> *For Bào Ninh*
> by Doug Anderson[30]

I asked him how he could not hate us.
We killed his children and left his country
a sump of chemicals and upturned graves.
Ten years in the jungle, hammered by
two-thousand-pound bombs. His job,
to gather his comrades' body parts
into something like a whole, to bury them.

He said, *We had the Chinese*
for a thousand years, and then the French,
the Japanese. You are merely the most recent.
He lit a cigarette and looked out into the smoky bar.
Finally, and I believed him, he said,
We have nothing left to hate you with.

America's willingness to incessantly bomb Vietnam—employing conventional explosives to kill humans and destroy infrastructure and using chemical-based weapons in attempts to defoliate forests and destroy trails so the enemy could not hide or travel in his own country—*was* seen as "evil" by many people on the planet *and* in the United States while it was happening. This perception deepened a divide that manifested in returning veterans being treated like criminals by antiwar activists while both Republican and Democratic administrations and Congresses perpetuated the undeclared war that claimed a U. S. military life 58,318 times, and, depending on how the counting is done, a Vietnamese military and civilian life between 1.4 and 3.5 million times on both sides.[31^]

American families who lost loved ones in Vietnam know what that loss feels like. Lt. General Harold Moore, commander of the 1st Battalion of the 7th Cavalry, and later the co-author with Joseph Galloway of *We Were Soldiers Once...and Young,* recalled that early on, in the last two months of 1965, after the battle of Ia Drang:

> The war was so new and the casualties to date so few that the Army had not even considered establishing the casualty-notification teams that later in the war would personally deliver the bad news and stay to comfort a young widow or elderly parents.... Western Union simply handed the telegrams over to Yellow Cab drivers to deliver.[32]

Moore recounts that in Columbus, Georgia his wife Julie took it upon herself to follow the cabs and support the family as the cab driver delivered the telegram. She described "those days as a time of fear; a time when the mere sight of a Yellow Cab cruising through a neighborhood struck panic in the hearts of the wives and children of soldiers serving in Vietnam."[33] The surviving veterans, along with surviving family members of that one U. S. military life that was lost 58,318 times, have had to face and navigate the facts, and their various interpretations, of the conflict as the details were gradually acknowledged by the war's composers and conductors. And Vietnamese families, whether living in small villages and the countryside or in larger cities, faced and navigated that one life lost, whether military or civilian, some 3,000,000 times during the French occupation and the subsequent invasion, bombings, and ground war that was directed from more than eight thousand miles away by the United States for over a decade.

MINE
   by Doug Anderson[34]

We make the paddy crossing fine,
but fifty meters into the trees,
the man two up in front of me steps on a mine,
loses both legs at the hip, and that's not all.
He's stunned, doesn't know how bad it is.
Can't give him morphine in that much shock.
He'll die if he's lucky.
I have less work than I thought:
the blast's heat has cauterized his wounds.
Quickly I fill out the casualty tag.
I'm bleeding too, a rivulet
of my blood blends with one of his.
When he's gone, I wash my wound.
It's not shrapnel. A shard of his
shattered bone is sticking in my arm.

The culturally given intentions and subsequently rationalized decisions of these distant architects were informed by *ignorance*, as minister Co made clear in 1995 to secretary McNamara, who gradually and publicly owned it; by *fear*, of the unknown "other" and of the humiliation that defeat might bring; by *bigotry*, grounded in both ignorance and fear, that ridicules and attacks others' views; by *violence*, the primary means of expression in war, in this case taken to *excess*; by *greed*, manifested in the dismissal of Eisenhower's warning about the military-industrial complex and the profit motive inherent therein; and by *untrustworthiness*, including why we were there, what was actually happening on the ground and in the air, and what was shared with or hidden from the American public.

We, as leaders and followers in every generation's public and private sectors, necessarily carry a level of ignorance within our cultural givens. Inevitably, we also carry the consequent fear, bigotry, violence, greed, and untrustworthiness that our ignorance nurtures. In each generation there are those who recognize and authentically strive to inform and transcend the ignorance they inherit—and there are those who choose to embrace and maintain it. This dichotomy has characterized and continues to characterize every desire and every attempt to avoid the perpetuation of the same mistakes—to embrace the movement toward true progress. It is the foundational split that informs Kendi's *"dual* and *dueling* history of racial progress and the simultaneous progression of racism."[35] It is not the only characteristic present, but it is always present.

Among the more than 2.5 million military personnel who did return home after serving in Vietnam, we now know that hundreds of thousands carried with them the effects of having been exposed to Agent Orange, the defoliant used to destroy the forests that provided cover for the enemy. Exact official numbers are difficult to come by, and the number of diseases tied to that exposure has grown over the years. Many veterans became sick and died before the connection between the chemical and their illness was made, and once it was made, help from the Veterans Administration (VA) was slow to come and frustrating to obtain. Ultimately, the impact of the herbicide has impacted and continues to impact millions of lives—in Vietnam and in the United States—including American veterans and their families as well as Vietnamese veterans, civilians, and their families.[36]

Many returning veterans also carried with them the psychological impacts of combat. In his early conversations with Vietnam veterans at the Veterans Administration in the 1970s, Dr. Bessel van der Kolk worked with a group of Marines who initially engaged with such statements as "I do not want to talk about the war." And they didn't—until one of them did. Others followed, and learning they could trust the doctor, they continued to show up, formed a new sense of comradeship, gave him a uniform, and included him as one of them. He began to see that:

> You were either in or out—you either belonged to the unit or you were nobody. After trauma the world becomes sharply divided between those who know and those who don't. People who have not shared the traumatic experience cannot be trusted, because they can't understand it. Sadly, this often includes spouses, children and co-workers.

Such "in-group bias," which we'll return to in chapters nine and eleven, can be both a blessing and a curse. At its best it is at the heart of much love, loyalty, friendship, and camaraderie; at its worst it brings much suffering, fear, bullying, and violence. Van der Kolk also began to see that "the very event that had caused them so much pain had also become their sole source of meaning. They felt fully alive only when they were revisiting their traumatic past."[37]

In the late 1970s a group of Vietnam veterans, with the help of psychoanalysts Chaim Shatan and Robert J. Lifton, lobbied the American Psychiatric Association (APA) to create a new diagnosis based on this phenomenon. Posttraumatic stress disorder first appeared in the 1980 Third Edition of the APA's *Diagnostic and Statistical Manual.* Research and treatment followed, and Dr. van der Kolk proposed a study on "the biology of traumatic memories" to the VA. Their initial rejection began with the words "It has never been shown that PTSD is relevant to the mission of the Veterans Administration." Eventually, however, "the mission of the VA has become organized around the diagnosis of PTSD and brain injury."[38] Among others who are deepening this work, Dr. Eduardo Duran, whom we met in Chapter Four, continues to expand the scope of therapy, integrating awareness of and ways to address soul wounds and intergenerational trauma.[39]

Attention to the trauma of combat predates modern science and psychiatry. "Shell shock," "soldier's heart," and "war neurosis" are among the earlier descriptors used to describe it. As Dr. Marc-Antoine Crocq and Dr. Louis Crocq noted, an awareness of the trauma of war goes back as far as the Bible's book of Deuteronomy and the writings of Herodotus, Hippocrates and Lucretius.[40] The return of hundreds of thousands of traumatized Vietnam veterans catalyzed the development of the PTSD diagnosis, which today acknowledges and serves survivors of combat, sexual assault, domestic violence, mass shootings, accidents and other catastrophic events.[41] And yet, Congress, the VA, the Pentagon, and the White House have been slower to spend money and to coordinate care for veterans than they have been to spend money on waging war itself. We'll return to this disparity in our exploration of the wars in Afghanistan and Iraq in the next chapter.

THE OPENING PAGES OF NEIL SHEEHAN'S *A Bright Shining Lie* depict the June 16, 1972 funeral of Retired Lieutenant Colonel John Paul Vann at Arlington National Cemetery. In the presence of Vann's recently divorced wife, Mary Jane, and his sons, Peter, John Allen, and Jesse, the military band began playing Pete Seeger's and Joe Hickerson's "Where Have All the Flowers Gone?" as Vann's coffin was lifted off the caisson near the grave. In attendance was a unique assembly of powerful proponents and opponents of the war. Daniel Ellsberg, General William Westmoreland, General Bruce Palmer, Jr., Lieutenant General Richard Stilwell, William Colby and Richard Komer of the CIA, Senator Ted Kennedy, Lieutenant General William Dupuy, Joseph Alsop, Lieutenant Colonel Lucien Conein, and Major General Edward Lansdale were among them. Mary Jane Vann had requested the antiwar song, which had become an anthem against this particular war, but she had not expected that her request would be honored.[42]

As Vann was laid to rest in 1972, Vietnamese Buddhist monk Thich Nhat Hahn was in in his sixth year of exile from his country. Born in 1926, he had entered the Tu Hieu Temple in Huè when he was sixteen. In the face of the war, he transcended the monastic's choice of either staying in the monastery and meditating or going out to alleviate peoples' suffering. By doing both, he effectively founded what is now known as Engaged Buddhism. A visiting scholar at both Princeton and Columbia Universities in the early 1960s, he traveled to Europe and back to the U. S. in 1966 and spoke to try to end the hostilities. While in the U. S. he met and began correspondence with both Thomas Merton and Martin Luther King, Jr., each of whom opposed the war and would die within two years—Merton, in an accident, and King by assassination. These three men, each in his own way, serve as exemplars for challenging the cultural givens of their times.

Because of his 1966 peace mission, in which he eloquently opposed the violence perpetrated by all sides in the conflict, the leaders in both Hanoi and Saigon banned this peaceful man from returning to his home. He remained in exile for thirty-nine years, teaching, writing, and opening monasteries around the world. His mindfulness retreats and his public talks welcomed everyone, from families with young children to veterans of Vietnam and other wars. Among his thirty-plus book titles, *Being Peace, Peace is Every Step, The Miracle of Mindfulness* and *Being at Home in the World* provide a sense of his mission.[43]

Amid personal turmoil, John Paul Vann pursued his relentless desire to win the war early on in a way that challenged the military and political leadership of his time. He would die when his helicopter went down in Vietnam in 1972. Thich Nhat Hahn embodied an equally relentless desire to end the war and to live and promote mindful peace—an embodiment that continued in the decades after the war ended. He died peacefully, surrounded by caregivers and disciples on January 22, 2022, in the same temple in Huè that he had entered as a sixteen-year-old. He was mourned by hundreds of thousands of human beings worldwide. Neither John Paul Vann nor Thich Nhat Hanh saw his desire fulfilled as and when he would have liked.

We'll invite the voices of some of the men who fought and wrote about this war to bring this chapter to a close.

From Tim O'Brien, in *The Things They Carried:*

> …the American war in Vietnam seemed to me wrong. Certain blood was being shed for uncertain reasons. I saw no unity of purpose, no consensus on matters of philosophy or history or law…. The only certainty that summer [1968] was

moral confusion. It was my view then, and still is, that you don't make war without knowing why.[44]

From U. S. Army Lt. General Harold G. Moore and Joseph L. Galloway, in *We Were Soldiers Once…and Young:*

> Finally—even though it took ten years, cost the lives of 58,000 young Americans and inflicted humiliating defeat on a nation that had never before lost a war—some of us learned that Clausewitz had it right 150 years earlier when he wrote these words:
>
> 'No one starts a war—or rather, no one in his senses ought to do so—without first being clear in his mind what he intends to achieve by that war and how he intends to conduct it'.[45]

From U. S. Marine Corporal John Musgrave, in *The Vietnam War: A Film by Ken Burns and Lynn Novick:*

> I only killed one human being in Vietnam, and that was the first man that I ever killed. I was sick with guilt about killing that guy and thinking I'm gonna have to do this for the next thirteen months, and I'm gonna go crazy. And I saw a Marine step on a Bouncing Betty mine, and that's when I made my deal with the devil and that I said I will never kill another human being as long as I'm in Vietnam. However, I will waste as many gooks as I can find; I'll wax as many dinks as I can find; I'll smoke as many zips as I can find. But I ain't gonna' kill anybody, y'know? Turn a subject into an object: Racism 101—it turns out to be a very necessary tool when you have children fighting your wars, for them to stay sane doing their work.[46]

Finally, we'll end as we began, with Doug Anderson, from *Horse Medicine:*

SAME OLD

by Doug Anderson[47]

On radio watch I'd see tracers floating
above the horizon, arc light
in the mountains and then seconds later,
the rumble. All far away.
I'd be grateful to not be way over there,
mosquitoes my near and only enemy.
But next noon when we were in it
and there was no night for cover,
facedown in a dry paddy with mortars
walking in and a crossfire of two snipers
pinning us flat in the heat, our artillery
taking its time, and somebody
shouting CORPSMAN UP, me getting up
to run and maybe die: there's no poetry
in that, only the immediate choking fear.
Came home to a country that watched
the war on TV at dinner. No one put down
their forks: it was all in a box,
an electronic terrarium for detached
observation. These same folks
(or their children) just keep on voting in
the clowns who'd happily make us die
over and over again, the teenage fools
who buy the snake oil one more time.
I could get a resentment over this
but no one would listen, leastwise
the ones fattening on the war.
Always a war somewhere and underneath
the crack of rifles, the sound of money
sliding down the chute, and a
whimpering of mothers over here, over there.

CHAPTER SEVEN

Lessons Not Learned:
Afghanistan, Iraq, &…

*Why do those who start wars not put
themselves at physical risk in war?*[1]

WHAT TRIES TO ESCAPE[2]

Twelve-year-old bandaged
head rests on the garish
green, red and beige pillow.
Eyes full and focused,
lips pressed together
suppress what tries to
escape. Except for
the triangle of neck,
right shoulder, and breast,
his scorched torso hides
beneath white ointment.
Three or four inches of
gauze caress the
stumps that remain
where he once
had arms.

IN SEPTEMBER 2003, SOME THIRTY-SIX years after he shared with
Robert McNamara the details of the destruction of the Quang

Ngai hamlets in Vietnam and six months after the U. S. began bombing Iraq again, Jonathan Schell wrote a long, crystal-clear sentence pointing out what "the basic mistake" of the Bush policy in Iraq *was not*. Employing some 250 words and quite a few semicolons, Schell identified eleven "grievous" but "secondary" mistakes that included sending too few troops to "run the place," recruiting from among Saddam's most brutal agencies for a new police force, privatizing parts of the Iraqi economy with no input from the Iraqi people, killing civilians, and driving away traditional allies. Schell then wrote a fourteen-word sentence, in italics and with no semicolons: *"The main mistake of American policy in Iraq was waging war at all."*[3]

WHILE THIS CHAPTER PRIMARILY CONCERNS itself with the 2003 invasion of Iraq and America's two decades of fighting and occupation in Afghanistan, it does so against the backdrop of decades of direct and indirect U. S. military and intelligence engagement in those two countries and elsewhere. Historian and U. S. Army veteran Andrew J. Bacevich characterizes these two decades of engagement, and the two decades that preceded them, as *America's War for the Greater Middle East*—the title of his 2016 book. The original, official reasons for sending our military into each country differed. In Afghanistan, the U. S. was pursuing the architects of the 9/11 attacks; in Iraq, the U. S. offered a series of sequentially discredited reasons we'll explore below. As we explore the worldviews, choices, and strategies that informed the Bush administration's deployment of U. S. troops in these two countries, we'll keep in mind President Eisenhower's post-World War II and Cold War precepts, cited in Chapter Six, and we'll take a closer look at Secretary of Defense McNamara's post-Vietnam lessons learned. We'll also consider the strategies of the three administrations that followed, culminating in the Trump administration's 2019 treaty with the Taliban, and the Biden administration's 2021 withdrawal of U. S. troops, according to the terms of that treaty.

DESPITE THE REPORTS FROM TWO separate teams of U. N. weapons inspectors—the first led by a U. S. Marine veteran, Scott Ritter,[4] whose team reported that no such weapons of mass destruction existed, and the second, led by David Kay,[5] whose report corroborated Ritter's—the U. S. began bombing Iraq on March 19, 2003. On May 1 of that year, President Bush, costumed in pilot's garb, stood on the deck of an aircraft carrier below a banner that read "Mission Accomplished," and told the world that "Major combat operations in Iraq have ended. In the battle of Iraq, the United States and our allies have prevailed."[6]

The exact number of Iraqi civilians who were killed in those six weeks in 2003, and who died subsequently in ongoing violence and as a result of the destruction of large chunks of the country's infrastructure, remains a debatable issue, ranging from a low of around 186,000 to just over a million,[7^] depending upon what is counted, how it's counted, and who is counting. Beyond Iraqi civilian deaths, by the end of 2004 "attacks on American forces averaged 87 per day, and the American death toll had passed 1000."[8^] As of December 30, 2020, more than 4,500—4,586, to be exact—American men and women in uniform had died in Iraq since the invasion. Of that number, 4,100 occurred after January 2004[9^]—eight months *after* George W. Bush proclaimed that "the United States and [its] allies [had] prevailed." We'll say more about the numerous proposed, believed, simple, and complex reasons that led Mr. Bush to order the attack on Iraq below. But first, some context.

Minutes after UA 175 flew into 2 World Trade Center on September 11, 2001, Richard Clarke, National Coordinator for

Security and Counterterrorism for both Bill Clinton and George W. Bush, arrived in the Vice President's office and conferred with Dick Cheney and National Security Advisor Condoleezza Rice. According to Clarke's account of the meeting, as reported in his book, *Against All Enemies,* when Cheney asked him what he thought, Clarke responded, "'It's an al Qaeda attack. And they like simultaneous attacks. This may not be over.'" Rice responded, "'You're the crisis manager, what do you recommend?'" Clarke had previously provided her with a preemptive checklist for post-attack protocols, and he now called for a secure teleconference to manage the crisis with "'the highest-ranking official from each department'" involved.[10] The Vice President agreed. For the next twenty-four-plus hours, Clarke would coordinate the crisis response.

At 1 AM on September 12, he went home for a shower and change of clothes. When he returned to the White House several hours later, he was expecting discussions to address preparations for any subsequent attacks, plans that might mitigate any currently known U. S. weaknesses, and updated intelligence on what had happened. As he recounts, his expectations were not met:

> Instead, I walked into a series of discussions about Iraq. At first I was incredulous…. Then I realized with almost a sharp physical pain that Rumsfeld and Wolfowitz were going to try to take advantage of this national tragedy to promote their agenda about Iraq. Since the beginning of the administration, indeed well before, they had been pressing for a war with Iraq.[11]

Later that day, according to Clarke, Rumsfeld "complained that there were no decent targets for bombing in Afghanistan, and that we should consider bombing Iraq, which, he said, had better targets."[12] Later that evening, President Bush asked

Clarke and several other advisors to see if Saddam Hussein was involved in any way. When Clarke reminded him that al Qaeda was responsible, the president acknowledged that and pressed his desire to involve Hussein: "'Look into Iraq, Saddam.'" When the president walked away, Lisa Gordon-Hagerty, Director of Combating Terrorism, shook her head and said, "'Wolfowitz got to him.'"[13]

Clarke's and Gordon-Hagerty's concerns were grounded in the reality of recent publicly known events. On the record, Rumsfeld, Wolfowitz, and sixteen others, under the banner of the Project for the New American Century (PNAC) had written to President Clinton on January 26, 1998, asking him to "enunciate a new strategy" that "should aim, above all, at the removal of Saddam Hussein's regime from power," and that required "a willingness to undertake military action[,] as diplomacy is clearly failing." The letter's authors were clear that "removing Saddam Hussein's regime from power.... needs to become the aim of American foreign policy."[14]

Subsequently, in September 2000, the PNAC issued a ninety-page report, *Rebuilding America's Defenses: Strategy, Forces and Resources For a New Century*. Part V of the report, "Creating Tomorrow's Dominant Force," which stressed the importance of seeking "to exploit the emerging revolution in military affairs"—also known as RMA—included this sentence: "Further, the process of transformation, even if it brings revolutionary change, is likely to be a long one, absent some catastrophic event – like a new Pearl Harbor."[15] The September 11, 2001 attacks provided the catastrophic event. Rather than remaining focused on the attackers, George W. Bush, under the influence of the 1998 Clinton letter signatories Rumsfeld and Wolfowitz, eventually turned his administration's attention to finding a way to invade Iraq. It would not be until May 2, 2011 under President Obama, that Osama bin

Laden, the architect of the September 11 attacks, would be found and killed.

WHEN THE BUSH ADMINISTRATION TOOK office in January 2001, Clarke found that terrorism, which had not been a hot topic of discussion during the presidential campaigns and debates, was still not a priority now that the new president was in the White House. Clarke's attempts to convey the urgency of the al Qaeda threat to National Security Advisor Rice, Vice President Cheney, Secretary of State Powell, and others was met with various levels of interest and essentially no action. As we'll see below, despite Clarke's January 25, 2001 request for a Principals Committee meeting on the threat, and despite some lower-level meetings that went nowhere, the Principals meeting did not take place until September 4, a week before the attack. In Clarke's words, the meeting "was largely a nonevent."[16]

Despite the intelligence leading up to, on, and continuing after the day of the attacks, all of which pointed to al Qaeda and none of which hinted at Hussein, the campaign to oust the Iraqi dictator was rejuvenated by the events of that day. In *America's War for the Greater Middle East*, Andrew Bacevich points out that as early as November 27, 2001, not quite two months into Operation Enduring Freedom in Afghanistan, Secretary of Defense Donald Rumsfeld told CENTCOM commander General Tommy Franks to start "gearing up" to invade Iraq.[17] Bacevich argues that when the Bush administration's mission to find and dispose of Saddam's WMD became unnecessary (because there weren't any) and the mission of liberating oppressed Iraqis became too difficult to achieve for a variety of reasons (beyond the scope of this book), opponents of the war conjured other explanations for the preemptive strike. These explanations included getting access to Iraqi oil, further protecting Israel, and allowing George W. Bush to complete his father's work by getting rid of the Iraqi dictator. Bacevich notes that none of these alternatives "were self-evidently false" and that each "likely contained at least a morsel of truth." He also notes that they all missed "the magnitude of the administration's actual ambitions," which were threefold: "establishing the efficacy of preventive war," asserting "the prerogative...of removing regimes that Washington deemed odious," and "seeking to reverse the practice of exempting the Islamic world from neoliberal standards."[18]

To summarize: the United States, and only the United States, could 1) start wars in order to prevent wars; 2) remove foreign sovereign governments through various means; and 3) impose Western values on Islamic countries and peoples that were not keeping up with U. S. standards. Or at least we could try—Eisenhower's precepts be damned. Native Americans and the Vietnamese recognize the first two of these ambitions.

The aforementioned "actual ambitions" of the Bush administration are specific manifestations of what Bacevich identifies as *Washington Rules,* in his book by that name. The rules' foundational "credo" maintains that the United States is responsible for enforcing "norms according to which the international order ought to work," and "summons the United States—and the United States alone—to lead, save, liberate, and ultimately transform the world." As such the credo "obliges the United States to maintain military capabilities staggeringly in excess of those required for self-defense."

According to Bacevich, in order to act on and not just proclaim such an expansive, self-imposed purpose—so deeply ingrained as to be invisible to its supporters and actors—"the United States has adhered since the end of World War II" to a "package of presumptions, habits and precepts." He continues:

> Call them the sacred trinity: an abiding conviction that the minimum essentials of international peace and order require

the United States to maintain a *global military presence,* to configure its forces for *global power projection,* and to counter existing or anticipated threats by relying on a policy of *global interventionism.*[19]

More generally, the United States, for more than seven decades now, has obligated itself to lead the world and has determined that it can behave in ways that it would not tolerate if any other nation so behaved—a global rendition of *do as I say, not as I do.* Trillions of dollars and millions of lives later, it's past time for revision—and time for an entirely new narrative.

Informing his assertions and conclusions, and beyond his eloquence and wit, Bacevich's *process* stands out. In both his 2005 *The New American Militarism* and the 2010 *Washington Rules,* he quite publicly embodies personal traits and practices that would serve the country and its political and military leadership (and the rest of us) well—self-reflection, critical thought, and a willingness to challenge previously accepted conventional wisdom and to change his mind even amid discomfort and disappointment. By any other name, Bacevich practices intentional, ongoing development, which at its most integrated, inevitably includes some level of Shadow work.

A West Point graduate, Vietnam veteran, retired career Army Officer, Princeton Ph. D., Professor Emeritus at Boston University, and Gold Star Father, he writes in the opening sentence of *Washington Rules* that "Worldly ambition inhibits true learning. Ask me. I know…. My own education did not commence until I reached middle age."[20] Bacevich shares with us his choice to subject "conventional wisdom…to sustained and searching scrutiny," to shed "habits of conformity acquired over decades," to recognize his earlier self as "a company man" and to own "the extent to which I had been socialized to accept certain things as unimpeachable."[21]

Beyond his scholarship and insight, Andrew Bacevich models for his readers his own process—what I would call intentional, ongoing adult development and narrative healing.

Max Fisher, writing in *Vox,* generally agrees with Bacevich, and zeroes in on the neoconservative ideology that underlay the PNAC, the January 1998 letter to Clinton, the September 2000 *Rebuilding America's Defenses* report, and the decision, promoted in the Bush White House by Paul Wolfowitz and Donald Rumsfeld, to attack Iraq in 2003:

> This ideology stated that authoritarian states were inherently destabilizing and dangerous; that it was both a moral good and a strategic necessity for America to replace those dictatorships with democracy—and to dominate the world as the unquestioned moral and military leader.

Fisher writes that the neoconservatives became obsessed with removing Saddam Hussein from power for a variety of reasons, and that "Their case was always grandly ideological, rooted in highly abstract and untested theories about the nature of the world and America's rightful place in it." The September 11 attacks confirmed their biases, at least to them, and presented an opportunity to "bring democracy to Iraq." He argues that "It was this ideological conviction, more than any piece of intelligence or lie told about it, that primarily led America into Iraq." Fisher concludes that:

> The lesson, which extends to both parties, is that a potential president's ideological views are just as important to examine and vet as are his or her policy proposals; that the line between obscure policy journals and American military action can be much shorter than we'd like to think.[22]

Beyond the particular ideological lesson that Fisher presents, and amid many well-meaning and occasionally partially accurate claims about having learned the political and military lessons of Vietnam—which we'll explore below—it is still possible and seems probable that small groups of American men and a growing but still small number of women, many with degrees from elite institutions, regardless of their political affiliations and worldviews, and whether they are elected or appointed, will commit American lives, resources, money, time, and energy to endeavors that they believe in and that end badly, or go on as if never to end. The lives, resources, and money are rarely their own. In America's invasions of Vietnam, Afghanistan, Iraq and elsewhere, ignorance of others' histories, cultures, and desires is ubiquitous, as are arrogance and hubris about America's role in the world and its capacity to fulfill it, and its predisposition to employ violence toward such fulfillment. Such traits are also at the heart of the Project for the New American Century's *Rebuilding America's Defenses.* It rarely ends well when apparently intelligent people attempt to force what they believe in on others at gunpoint, in the name of democracy, human rights, and free markets.[23]

Once again in the history of the United States, an arrogance informed by the ignorance of other cultures manifested in violence toward those cultures (and our own) in the name of helping them progress. As Doug Anderson reminded us, mothers whimper for their sons over there and over here.

NOVEMBER IN FALLUJAH[24]

She sits with
a soldier she doesn't
know, C-17 en route
to Germany. Her
son,
twenty
brain-injured
head locked in place,

lies before her.
She scratches her
eyebrow with the
ring finger on
her left hand.

CONSIDER THE RELATIONSHIPS AMONG PRESIDENT Bush's May 1, 2003, announcement that we had prevailed in Iraq, President Biden's July 26, 2021 conversation with Iraqi Prime Minister, Mustafa al-Kadhimi, about plans to conclude the U. S. combat mission by the end of the year, and the various troop withdrawals and deployments under four presidents during the eighteen years between these two dates.[25] If we begin with Truman's (and/or the CIA's) post-World War II decisions regarding Ho Chi Minh's request for help in Vietnam, the U.S. involvement spanned six presidents over thirty years. If we start with Eisenhower's supporting the French colonial conflict, it's five presidents over twenty-two years. Commence with Kennedy, and it's four presidents over fifteen years. Count as we might, neither Eisenhower's precepts nor McNamara's lessons,[26] which we'll revisit below, seem to have influenced Bush, Cheney, Rumsfeld and Wolfowitz—or the administrations that followed. Granted, these later administrations were saddled with the mess that Bush left behind, and they inherited the complexities of simultaneously conducting and trying to end the preemptive war he chose to start.

Wars don't care much about the humans who plan, fight in, or succumb to them. When we choose to create a war, as we did in Vietnam and Iraq, the death and destruction we cause often further emboldens the enemy and motivates others to get involved (Viet Cong, ISIS). Even if we have a plan in place, the plan is useless if we ignore it, and even the best plan can only anticipate, but can't predict how the war, and those who are threatened by it, will behave.

In their ongoing campaign to justify the invasion of Iraq, Rumsfeld, Wolfowitz, and others did not have an agreed-upon plan for *how* to invade, occupy, and eventually withdraw. The available (pre-9/11) plans for an Iraqi invasion called for a deployment of some half a million troops, similar in scale to that of Operation Desert Storm in 1991, which saw some 697,000 U. S. troops involved.[27] Increasingly at odds with such a large-scale operation was the aforementioned (p. 179) Revolution in Military Affairs (RMA), which foresaw a growing reliance on technology that presumably would decrease the number of ground troops needed, save American lives, minimize civilian casualties, and engage the enemy with new levels of technological speed and precision.[28] Donald Rumsfeld was a fan of the RMA; in contrast with the available plan's call for 500,000 troops, he wanted just 125,000. U. S. CENTCOM commander General Tommy Franks wanted 385,000 troops, which he then lowered to 300,000, and then to 275,000. They finally settled on 170,000.[29] To further complicate the matter, when General Erik Shinseki, the Army chief of staff, estimated several weeks before the attack that several hundred thousand troops would be required in postwar Iraq, Paul Wolfowitz called the estimate "wildly off the mark," and was backed up by Rumsfeld's assessment that Shinseki's estimate was "far off the mark."[30]

The people of Iraq are no longer dictated to by Saddam Hussein. They also suffered horribly as a result of America's 2003 attack.[31] The reasons for the U. S. invasion were false, and the final decisions concerning how many troops were needed and how much it would cost were wrong. Bush, Rumsfeld, Wolfowitz, Cheney, and their advisors and allies were wrong.

WITHIN AND BEYOND THE IGNORANCE, arrogance, and violence lurk cost, waste, and excess. As of February 2020, according to the *Military Times,* the war in Iraq had cost U. S. taxpayers some one trillion, nine hundred and twenty-two billion dollars, a number that looks like this: $1,922,000,000,000.00. That amount was funneled from American taxpayers into Iraq from 2003 forward, and does not include the costs for Afghanistan or other shorter-term post-9/11 antiterrorist actions. It does include the costs of combat, private contractors, promotion of democracy, reconstruction, veterans' care, and interest on the debt incurred to fund the war.[32]

On the same day that Deputy Secretary Wolfowitz dismissed General Shinseki's troop estimate as "wildly off the mark," he told members of Congress that the Pentagon could not know how much the war would cost "until we get there on the ground," adding that estimates ranged from 10 to 100 billion dollars.[33] He was off by about $1.8 trillion. For some perspective on what a *trillion* means, consider that one million seconds account for 11.6 *days;* one billion seconds account for 31.7 *years;* one trillion seconds account for 31,710 *years.*

With that perspective in place, consider that from October 2001 through August 2021, the U. S. Department of Defense spent more than $14 trillion (measured in 2021 dollars) for all purposes, including the wars in Afghanistan and Iraq. One third to one half of these expenditures went to private contractors, and of those, a quarter to a third have gone to just five companies—Lockheed Martin, Boeing, General Dynamics, Raytheon and Northrup Grumman, which, together contracted for $286 billion in 2019 and 2020 alone. In October 2001, Boeing vice president Harry Stonecipher announced that "the purse is now open . . . any member of Congress who doesn't vote for the funds we need to defend this country will be looking for a new job after next November." Lockheed Martin's 2020 Pentagon contracts totaled $75 billion; the U. S. State Department's budget that year was $44 billion. "In addition, weapons makers have spent $2.5 billion on lobbying over the past two decades, employing, on average, over 700 lobbyists per year over the past five years, more than one for every member of Congress."[34] Okay, boys and girls, can you find any money to address climate change, infrastructure, education, and healthcare?

If the price tag for an unnecessary war of choice itself were not worrisome enough, the status quo of greed and excess is highlighted by no-bid and cost-plus contracts for (and significant levels of waste and inefficiency among) private contractors such as former Halliburton subsidiary Kellogg Brown & Root (KBR). In no-bid (or sole-source) contracts, often justified and allowed by exigent or emergency circumstances, there is no competition—the contract recipient is a foregone conclusion.[35] In cost-plus contracts, which are common in wartime, contractors get reimbursed for expenses claimed plus an agreed-upon percentage markup, a perfect motivation for waste and inefficiency. The more they claim, the more they make.

In 2003 and 2004, the U. S. shipped some twelve billion dollars, weighing about 360 tons, in shrink-wrapped packs of $100 bills to Iraq. Those bills were dispersed, and there's no record of how much was given to whom or when. When Paul Bremer, the U.S. leader of the Coalition Provisional Authority (CPA), was questioned about this, he responded that the packages of bills, sent from the U. S. Federal Reserve to Baghdad, belonged to the Iraqi people and that "the CPA discharged its responsibilities to manage these Iraqi funds on behalf of the Iraqi people."[36] In other words, the inability to account for $12 billion minted in the U. S. and sent from the Federal Reserve Bank in New York to Baghdad is okay because the funds were appropriated for Iraqi, not American, use. After we reduced significant chunks of Iraq's infrastructure to rubble, Bremer also advocated holding looters accountable by shooting them. In this case, he was overruled.

This lack of accountability is not exclusive to the post-9/11 war in Iraq. On September 10, 2001, the day before the attacks, Secretary of Defense Donald Rumsfeld spoke about "an adversary that poses a threat, a serious threat, to the security of the United States of America." He identified the threat as "the Pentagon bureaucracy—not the people, but the processes, not the civilians, but the systems, not the men and women in uniform, but the uniformity of thought and action that we too often impose on them." He admitted that "According to some estimates we cannot track $2.3 trillion in transactions."[37] He was not speaking about *missing* money, but about a bureaucracy that was unable to competently manage and account for its majority share of American taxpayers' money—much like those of us who earn and spend money but do not use a check register or refer to credit or debit card statements. We know we have income, we know we spend it, but we can't tell you where it went, when it went, or for what purpose it was spent. In our case, it's *ours* to mismanage. In the Pentagon's case, it's *ours* that *they're* mismanaging.

In Iraq, accusers and deniers have faced off for years about the particulars of U. S. government expenditures on luxury vehicles and accommodations for contractor executives, construction workers and security and combat personnel. The face offs include details of inefficient planning and supply chains in which vehicles were trashed and replaced when they needed a flat tire changed or an oil filter replaced. Speaking out against such incidents of excess, fraud, corruption, waste, or inefficiency can be dangerous.

In 1997 Bunnatine "Bunny" Greenhouse went to work for the U.S. Army Corps of Engineers and eventually became the highest ranked civilian there. She was, in her own words, "the first black female to enter the ranks of the Corps' Senior Executive Service (SES)." In the weeks before the 2003 invasion of Iraq, she was present at a top-secret Pentagon meeting along with representatives of KBR, in which a no-bid, five-year, $7-billion Restore Iraqi Oil (RIO) contract was discussed. Greenhouse expressed concern about the contract's length and the absence of competitive bids. She was ignored and KBR received the contract. A subsequent audit revealed that KBR overcharged the United States government by $61 million for fuel purchases.

Greenhouse persisted in calling attention to the KBR contract and similar problems. For doing the job she was hired to do, she was demoted, physically retaliated against, and removed from SES in October 2004. She filed suit against the Army Corps of Engineers in 2005, and in 2011 the Corps settled and agreed to pay her full restitution for lost wages, compensatory damages, and attorneys' fees.

In her appearances before the Senate Democratic Policy Committee in 2007 and the House Committee on Oversight and Government Reform in 2009, Greenhouse testified that KBR's RIO contract "and other contracts related to the RIO contract represent the worst contract abuse I witnessed during the course of my 23-year professional career."[38]

The argument from Pentagon leadership is that no-bid contracts make sense in wartime since the transition from a current to a new contractor is expensive and time consuming. That makes sense. It doesn't justify incompetence, greed, excess, and theft. The issue persists. In October 2011, the bipartisan Commission on Wartime Contracting in Iraq and Afghanistan "concluded that between $31 billion and $60 billion of taxpayers' funds have been lost to contract waste and fraud in Iraq and Afghanistan."[39]

These persistent, underlying currents of greed, excess, untrustworthiness, and lack of accountability in support of unprovoked large-scale violence exacerbate the inherently problematic reality of war as a for-profit endeavor for a small assortment of companies and people—who don't share profits with those who risk their lives in combat.[40]

SO, WHAT HAVE WE LEARNED, or not learned? What do we deny and project despite relentless, concrete evidence of our denials and projections? President Eisenhower's post-World War II precepts and Secretary McNamara's post-Vietnam lessons provide useful lenses through which to observe U.S. engagement with post-9/11 Iraq and Afghanistan and any denials or projections inherent therein. While it is by no means a given that these mid-twentieth-century precepts and late-twentieth-century lessons are fully relevant to our early-twenty-first-century invasions and decades-long occupations, it is also not given that they are irrelevant and offer nothing to help us see ourselves more clearly. And save money. And lives.

Eisenhower's first precept that no collective people can be held as enemy since "all humanity shares the common hunger for peace and fellowship and justice" doesn't hold up if we include specific leaders—those with the power to choose violence or not, as part of "all humanity." Based on their choices and behaviors, neither Saddam Hussein nor George W. Bush and his advisors shared that hunger. Part of our projection of national Shadow is that Hussein's violence and aggression were dictatorial, wrong, and evil and that Bush's (and others') were democratic, right, and good—which raises the questions, *for whom, when* and *to what degree?*

The second precept that "No nation's security and well-being can be lastingly achieved in isolation but only in effective cooperation with fellow-nations" captures the tension, as old as the concept of nations, between isolation and intervention. The Bush administration received "effective cooperation with fellow-nations," in its initial post-9/11 pursuit of al Qaeda in Afghanistan, which took about two months. That coalition weakened significantly when Bush, without the cooperation of many allies, chose to isolate and pursue the PNAC's agenda against Hussein. In differentiating Germany's active and financial support for "the fight against international terrorism" and the Bush administration's determination to invade Iraq preemptively, Chancellor Gerhard Schröder made it clear that Germany was "not available for adventures." German foreign minister Joschka Fischer expressed opposition to the U. S. campaign to attack Iraq this way: "Our deep skepticism leads us to rejection."[41] Bush chose to ignore, or was ignorant of, this second precept. Senators and representatives who did not want to be seen as soft on war gave him the green light to attack—embracing his choice and/or his ignorance.

Almost exactly fifty years earlier, Eisenhower understood the power in cooperation among a community of individuals or nations who are committed to truth. In exploring what he calls "the constitution of knowledge," author Jonathan Rauch puts it this way: "…you are entitled to claim that a statement is objectively true only insofar as it is checkable and has stood up to checking," and "whatever you do to check a proposition must be something that anyone can do, at least in principle, and get the same result." Rauch refers to the former as the "fallibilist rule: no one gets the final say" (emphasis on *one* and *final),* and to the latter as the "empirical rule: no one has personal authority…who you are does not count" (emphasis on *one,* and *personal).*[42] Bush, Rumsfeld, Wolfowitz and others demonstrated no interest in any cooperation, community, or checking that might have exposed important truths within and about Iraq. They committed themselves to cycles of ignorance, arrogance, bullying, and violence despite the lessons their predecessors left for them.

Eisenhower's third precept, that "Any nation's right to form of government and an economic system of its own choosing is inalienable," had no followers among those who chose to invade and try to transform Vietnam, Afghanistan, and Iraq. The irony here is that the precept is grounded in a nation's right to self-determination, but the U. S. leadership that chose these wars, loyal to Bacevich's "credo" before he articulated it (p. 181), implicitly added the fine print, *as long as the government and economic system meet our approval.*

The fourth precept, "Any nation's attempt to dictate to other nations their form of government is indefensible," renders U.S. exploits in Vietnam, Afghanistan, and Iraq at best questionable and at worst indefensible.

The fifth precept, that "A nation's hope of lasting peace cannot be firmly based upon any race in armaments but rather upon just relations and honest understanding with all other nations," is the antithesis of America's unprecedented and unmatched military spending and its inclination, from Vietnam forward, to put that spending to work around the world. The U. S. operates between 500 and 800 military bases in over 70 countries.[43] No other country comes close. Neither the excessive spending nor the global presence guarantees success; nor has either led to any lasting peace at home or abroad. Witness the Taliban's August 2021 return to control in Afghanistan, which took about a month, after twenty years of U. S. combat, occupation, and attempts to train the military and local law enforcement. Witness the immediate refugee crisis and finger-pointing that followed. The debates themselves about how this tragedy is just like or not like Vietnam confirm the former.

McNamara's lessons, as he presented them in his 1995 *In Retrospect*, in some ways complement and expand upon Eisenhower's precepts, albeit in the specific context of his experience of the tragedy of Vietnam. See Appendix I for the two men's reflections juxtaposed with lessons learned after twenty years in Afghanistan (introduced below). The Bush administration, in its decisions to remain in Afghanistan after December 2001 and then to invade Iraq in 2003, proved to be as unfamiliar with McNamara's lessons as it was with Eisenhower's precepts. With only vague and shifting ideas about what the U. S. was doing in either country and what might happen when we left, it's not surprising that the ill-defined and endless mission of "fighting terror" was not accomplished—by Bush or by Obama or by Trump, all of whom spoke about getting out of Afghanistan, but did not. Biden got out, and in horribly tragic ways. The Afghan people continue to pay the price for both our arrival and our departure. What new lessons loom for America?

In August 2021 the office of the Special Inspector General for Afghanistan Reconstruction (SIGAR) released a 140-page report entitled *What We Need to Learn: Lessons from Twenty Years of Afghanistan Reconstruction*—the eleventh "Lessons Learned" report issued between 2016 and 2021. The previous titles warrant mention: *Corruption in Conflict; Reconstructing the Afghan National Defense and Security Forces; Private Sector Development and Economic Growth; Stabilization; Counternarcotics; Divided Responsibility; Re-Integration of Ex-Combatants; Elections; Support for Gender Equality;* and *The Risk of Doing the Wrong Thing Perfectly.*

Along with its statistics—2,443 U. S. troops, 1,144 allied troops, and at least 66,000 Afghan troops and 48,000 Afghan civilians *killed;* 20,666 U. S. troops and at least 75,000 Afghan civilians *injured;* $145 billion in reconstruction and $837 billion on fighting *spent*—the report notes that these "extraordinary costs were meant to serve a purpose—though the definition of that purpose evolved over time," and goes on to identify "seven key lessons" that "can be used in other conflict zones around the globe."[44]

Before we briefly acknowledge SIGAR's seven key lessons, here's the executive summary of number six, "Context" (each lesson gets its own chapter in the full report):

6. Context: The U. S. government did not understand the Afghan context and therefore failed to tailor its efforts accordingly.

Effectively rebuilding Afghanistan required a detailed understanding of the country's social, economic, and political dynamics. However, U.S. officials were consistently operating in the dark, often because of the difficulty of collecting the necessary information. The U. S. government also clumsily forced Western technocratic models onto Afghan economic institutions; trained security forces in advanced weapon systems they could not understand, much less maintain; imposed formal rule of law on a country that addressed 80 to 90 percent of its disputes through informal means; and often struggled to understand or mitigate the cultural and social barriers to supporting women and girls. Without this background knowledge, U. S. officials often empowered powerbrokers who preyed on the population or diverted U.S. assistance away from its intended recipients to enrich and empower themselves and their allies. Lack of knowledge at the local level meant projects intended to mitigate conflict often exacerbated it, and even inadvertently funded insurgents.[45]

Each of us, for good or ill, gets to choose how to react to the juxtaposition of this 2021 SIGAR key lesson summary with what President Eisenhower, disappointed as the Cold War emerged after World War II, and Secretary McNamara, reflecting on the tragedy of Vietnam, left for their respective successors regarding the importance of "context"—of other nations' cultures, values, beliefs, and systems of government and economics, especially, but not only, if we choose to attack, occupy, and try to convince them to be more like us.

In 2016, *Washington Post* journalist Craig Whitlock filed Freedom of Information Act requests with SIGAR in order to access the notes, transcripts, and recordings of the hundreds of interviews that informed the reports. Two federal lawsuits and three years later, SIGAR released over 2,000 pages of notes, with some 90% of the names and some classified information redacted. The *Post* began publishing what it had learned in early December 2019 and Whitlock's book, *The Afghanistan Papers,* was released in August 2021.

Both heartbreaking because people were dying and infuriating because leadership was lying, the information corruption within and coming out of Afghanistan perfectly paralleled the problems that had plagued the policies in Vietnam. From Neil Sheehan:

> The Vietnamese Communists were fighting a war of national independence and survival. They had to be able to record dark hours and to learn from them if they were to live to see sunny ones. The…American system was receptive only to the recording of sunny hours…."progress reports." [General] Harkins's weekly report to the Joint Chiefs and McNamara…was entitled "Headway Report." He had no "Lostway Report" for a contingency like [the battle at] Ap Bac.[46]

This reluctance to pass truth up the chain of command transcends American political and military history. In a March 9, 2022, interview, Andrei Kozyrez, a career diplomat and the Russian Foreign Minister from 1991 to 1996, remarked that any dictator or authoritarian leader surrounds himself with "yes men" who are afraid to report the truth. Speaking amid Russia's invasion of Ukraine and specifically about Russian President Vladimir Putin's political and military chain of command, Kozyrez said, "They fear to tell the boss the truth, but one day they may come…and escort him either to the grave or to retirement …. That's the tradition."[47] I'll leave it to the reader to ponder the extent to which this parallel is disturbing, comforting, or both. But back to the United States.

The Special Inspector General himself, John Sopko, told Congress in 2020 that "U. S. officials 'knew the data was bad' yet bragged about the numbers anyway." Colonel John Crowley shared that "Every data point was altered to present the best picture possible," that "truth was rarely welcome," and that "bad news was often stifled." Whitlock concluded, sadly reminiscent of Sheehan, that "careerism" led to both military officers' and diplomats' hesitancy "to pass negative assessments up the chain of command.... Nobody wanted the blame for problems of failings on their watch. As a result, regardless of conditions, they claimed they were making progress." Additional comments, cited by Whitlock, from generals and cabinet members whose words were not redacted include:

> "There was no campaign plan. It just wasn't there."
>> - General Dan McNeill

> "We didn't have the foggiest notion of what we were undertaking."
>> - Lt. General Douglas Lute

> "I have no visibility into who the bad guys are in Afghanistan or Iraq.... We are woefully deficient in human intelligence."
>> - Secretary of Defense, Donald Rumsfeld

> "From the ambassadors down to the low level, [they all say] we are doing a great job.... Really? So if we are doing such a great job, why does it feel like we are losing?"
>> - Lt. General Michael Flynn[48]

While Appendix I juxtaposes Eisenhower's precepts, both sets of McNamara's lessons learned, and SIGAR's key lessons from Afghanistan, we'll conclude our brief look at lessons not learned here with a comparison of SIGAR's key lessons with what Robert McNamara shared with Errol Morris in *The Fog of War*. First, SIGAR's key lessons:

1. Strategy: The U. S. government continuously struggled to develop and implement a coherent strategy for what it hoped to achieve.

2. Timelines: The U. S. government consistently underestimated the amount of time required to rebuild Afghanistan, and created unrealistic timelines and expectations that prioritized spending quickly. These choices increased corruption and reduced the effectiveness of programs.

3. Sustainability: Many of the institutions and infrastructure projects the United States built were not sustainable.

4. Personnel: Counterproductive civilian and military personnel policies and practices thwarted the effort.

5. Insecurity: Persistent insecurity severely undermined reconstruction efforts.

6. Context: The U. S. government did not understand the Afghan context and therefore failed to tailor its efforts accordingly.

7. Monitoring and Evaluation: U. S. government agencies rarely conducted sufficient monitoring and evaluation to understand the impact of their efforts.

In *The Fog of War,* McNamara named eleven higher level lessons, which, while based on his experience as defense secretary, are not limited to government, war, and international affairs. They may be applied to a variety of organizational endeavors and are quite general; each may be interpreted and applied differently in specific contexts. They may seem obvious, or not, to readers in the third decade of the twenty-first century and beyond—reminding us that much of what any generation can see, embrace, or critique is attributable to the dignities and disasters of preceding generations' cultural givens and choices. Many of the leaders in McNamara's generation were born around the time of World War I, lived through the Great Depression, and fought in World War II. Said differently, Presidents Kennedy, Johnson, and Nixon and

Secretary McNamara were all born before women could vote. Throughout their childhoods and early adulthoods, lynchings and Jim Crow were still rampant in the former slave states. The daily news was available through newspapers and radio broadcasts; commercial television sets became available around 1938, and not everyone could afford one.

For McNamara, these eleven lessons were painful, learned through public mistakes that carried horrible costs. The first three, especially in light of his individual strengths as a gifted and rational systems thinker, are significant departures from his public persona. Four, five and six are consistent with his strengths. Seven, eight, and ten complement each other and speak to the importance of self-awareness, knowing one's perspective (and that it is *just* a perspective), and identifying, understanding, and challenging one's cultural givens. Nine and eleven, in my reading, beg for context and clarification (as do all the others to some degree) regarding how McNamara would have defined *good, evil,* and *human nature* as he used them. I've provided my sense of selected corresponding lessons from the 2021 SIGAR report in brackets:

1. **Empathize with your enemy.** [# 6-Context; #2-Timelines]
2. **Rationality will not save us.** [#1-Strategy]
3. **There's something beyond oneself.** [#6-Context; #2-Timelines; #4-Personnel]
4. **Maximize efficiency.** [All of SIGNA's lessons, 1-7]
5. **Proportionality should be a guideline in war.** [#6-Context; #2-Timelines]
6. **Get the data.** [#7-Monitoring and Evaluation]
7. **Belief and seeing are both often wrong.** [#6-Context; #3-Sustainability]
8. **Be prepared to reexamine your reasoning.** [#7-Monitoring and Evaluation]
9. **In order to do good, you may have to engage in evil.** [#6-Context]

10. **Never say never.** [#6-Context]
11. **You can't change human nature.**[49] [#6-Context]

Bush, Rumsfeld, Wolfowitz, Cheney, Rice, and other key players who initiated the wars in Iraq and Afghanistan and chose to sustain them through five and seven years respectively, had access to voluminous public and private lessons on governance and war from a wide array of combat veterans (both enlisted and officers) and public servants beyond Eisenhower and McNamara. They chose to embrace instead what Max Fisher referred to as the "grandly ideological... highly abstract and untested theories about the nature of the world" (p. 183) upon which Wolfowitz, Rumsfeld, the PNAC, and others insisted. Indeed: *Belief and seeing are both often wrong. Be prepared to reexamine your reasoning. Empathize with your enemy. Any nation's attempt to dictate to other nations their form of government is indefensible.*

In 1951 General Omar Bradley spoke to Congress in his role as chairman of the joint chiefs and argued against General MacArthur's prescribed expansion of the Korean conflict to include large-scale bombing of major cities in China. Perhaps drawing from Aristotle, Bradley referred to MacArthur's proposal as "the wrong war, at the wrong place, at the wrong time, and with the wrong enemy." Congress heeded Bradley's warning and the U. S. did not attack China.[50] The closest voice to Omar Bradley's that George Bush and the 107th Congress had in 2001 was that of Representative Barbara Lee from California's 9th district. She was the only member of either house to vote *no* on S.J. Res. 23, which gave the president the following authority:

> to use all necessary and appropriate force against those nations, organizations, or persons he determines planned, authorized, committed, or aided the terrorist attacks that

> occurred on September 11, 2001, or harbored such
> organizations or persons, in order to prevent any future acts
> of international terrorism against the United States by such
> nations, organizations or persons.[51]

The House vote was 420-1; in the Senate it was 98-0. People around the country called Lee a traitor and worse. Some called for her impeachment. Californians in the 9th district continued to vote for her and she continues to represent them in 2022. Some folks who hated her in 2001 began to see her in a different light as the war dragged on. When the Taliban retook the country in August 2021, one month shy of the twentieth anniversary of her vote, Lee reflected, "I almost wish, in many ways, that I had been wrong. Because what's taking place today is terrifying."[52]

Representative Lee's final seven words, taken in the context of the 2021 American withdrawal from Afghanistan and the swift Taliban takeover, are clear. One could drop those seven words into any number of thousands of terrifying todays that include the billions spent by Presidents Truman and Eisenhower in support of France's attempt to recolonize Vietnam after World War II, the additional billions of dollars and tens of thousands of lives spent in Korea, the billions of dollars and millions of lives spent in Vietnam, the post-9/11 dollars and lives in Afghanistan and Iraq, and any number of other dollar and life expenditures, including but not limited to actions in the Dominican Republic (1965), Grenada (1983), Lybia (1986), the Persian Gulf (1987), Panama (1989), Somalia (1993) Bosnia (1995), Kosovo (1999), and Sudan (1998).[53]

Beyond whether any one or several of these actions did some good (which begs the questions *according to what standard* and *for whom*), as a nation we have an obligation to ourselves and the rest of the world to own and interrogate the habitual, explicit manifestations of ignorance, arrogance, fear, violence, excess, bullying, and greed that we consistently choose. How else might we have allocated these trillions of war dollars? What might each individual who died—often in vain—have done with his or her one precious life?

IF AND AS WE MIGHT CHOOSE to interrogate ourselves, we have an obligation to acknowledge how we imprisoned and interrogated those we thought might have acted against us. The tone was set early on by Vice President Dick Cheney:

> It would be inappropriate for me to talk about operational matters—specific options or the kinds of activities we might undertake going forward…. We also have to work though, sort of, the dark side, if you will. We're gonna spend time in the shadows, the intelligence world. A lot of what needs to be done here will have to be done quietly, without any discussion, using sources and methods that are available to our intelligence agencies if we're gonna be successful.[54]

In the context of the Bush administration's desire not to leave too big a footprint in Afghanistan by building prisons, our allies' reluctance to take in captives, and uncertainty about how American citizens would feel about alleged terrorists being held in federal penitentiaries, White House Counsel Alberto Gonzalez reflected, during his interview for *Turning Point,* on the use of Guantanamo Bay, which began in January 2002:

> We just started capturing people. We had limited options. You can't kill them. You don't want to release 'em because they're gonna come back and fight against you again. So we had to make some decisions about what are we gonna do with people that we capture…. We also had concerns about the rights that would attach to anyone we brought into the United States.[55]

Getting directly to the point that Gonzalez was trying to avoid, Michel Paradis, senior attorney for the Department of Defense, Office of the Chief Defense Counsel, who has represented detainees held at Guantanamo, notes that in the search that led to the choice of America's little sliver of Cuba, "the State Department said they were told to look for the legal equivalent of outer space, and that's what Guantanamo was meant to be—a place where no law applied."[56]

The Pentagon made it clear that the people brought to Guantanamo were to be called *detainees* in order to avoid following the Geneva Conventions' requirements regarding *prisoners*. When Gonzalez was asked why he used the word "quaint" to refer to some of the provisions in the Geneva Conventions, he replied:

> I used the word 'quaint' to reflect the fact that the Geneva Convention was drafted at a time when wars were between nations, not between non-nation-states, like terrorist groups, like al Qaeda. We made a determination…that it should not apply because al Qaeda was not a nation-state that had signed the Geneva Conventions, and that the Taliban had forfeited their rights for prisoner-of-war protection because in order to receive those protections you had to wear a uniform when fighting, you had to carry arms openly, you had to fight under a hierarchical structure, and you can't go around killing civilians indiscriminately and expect to receive the benefits of being a prisoner of war under the Geneva Conventions.

Getting closer to the truth behind the Bush administration's concern with the Geneva Conventions, Gonzalez continued:

> A decision was made by the National Security Council to look at enhanced interrogation techniques. George Tenet and the CIA were charged with, all right, what do you recommend. And so it was important to get clear guidance

about, all right, where is the box, and so the Department of Justice drafted legal opinions to give guidance to the CIA.

In a 2002 Department of Justice memo to the CIA, ten enhanced interrogation techniques were given the green light: 1) attention grasp; 2) walling; 3) facial hold; 4) facial slap (insult slap); 5) cramped confinement; 6) wall standing; 7) stress positions; 8) sleep deprivation; 9) insects placed in a confinement box; 10) the waterboard.[57] Gonzalez seemed to believe that those techniques work and that those who would implement them would strictly adhere to "very, very detailed instructions." He was wrong on both counts; his justifications included:

> I'm not…suggesting that they're not unpleasant or terrible, but like, walling. Walling was a technique where you put a hood around their neck to make sure they don't suffer any neck injuries, you hold them against a wall that's not secure…, and you push 'em against that wall. With…the facial slap, the palm had to be open. You could only hold the hand so many inches away from the face, and it could only strike the face on the cheek…. very, very detailed instructions about what could be done…. The head of the criminal division for the Department of Justice at the time wrote that torture is that activity which the very mention sends shivers up one's spine, such as needles under the fingernails, such as piercing of your eyeball, such as electric shocks through your genitals. We weren't anywhere close to that.

Former FBI Special Agent Ali Soufan served on the Joint Terrorism Task Force, interrogated suspected terrorists both pre- and post-9/11, and obtained valuable information without using the above-described "enhanced techniques." He presents his view of what transpired after 9/11:

> When we start arresting these people and talking to them,

it's not a rocket science to interrogate them.... [After 9/11] they didn't believe that these guys would talk, so they wanted to develop a program that's gonna be like a cookie-cutter approach. One, two, three, four and the guy's gonna give you everything. That's not how the world works. That's not how human nature works. The CIA inspector general in 2004 [concluded] that they cannot prove one imminent threat was disrupted because of enhanced interrogation techniques. There's no evidence, and this is the CIA them-selves saying that. Not me.... Torture will give you compli-ance. It does not give you cooperation. The difference be-tween compliance and cooperation is that with compliance the person will tell you whatever you want to hear for the torture to stop. They won't tell you the truth. In coop-eration, you get the truth.[58]

In a post-9/11 public statement about torture, Senator John McCain, himself tortured as a POW in Vietnam, expressed his deep concern "about who we are as a country and what we stand for and believe in." The senator continued:

America has always been an example and an inspiration to other countries throughout the world, and if we practice torture and do things that diminish and even harm the image of the United States, and motivate our enemies, then it could have profound consequences in the future...[59]

As of June 2022, of some 780 "worst of the worst" Guantanamo detainees, eighteen have been charged, five have been con-victed, and ten are still in pretrial proceedings.[60] The Bush Administration would ignore both Soufan, the experienced FBI interrogator, and McCain, the experienced and tortured former POW, among others, and go on to defend the torture, by any other name, of detainees both at Guantanamo and more infamously at Abu Ghraib in Iraq. While the torture at Abu Ghraib and Guantanamo, often of men who were never charged or found guilty of anything, and massacres like the horrors at My Lai are substantially different dehumanizing acts, each in its own way requires an objectification of the victim. As John Musgrave said about his Vietnam experience: "Turn a subject into an object: Racism 101—it turns out to be a very necessary tool when you have children fighting your wars, for them to stay sane doing their work." Here's a paraphrased revision and application of Neil Sheehan's My Lai reflection to post-9/11 U. S. prison crimes:

> *The guards and their supervisors observed the lack of regard their superiors had for the enemy. The value of life was systematically cheapened by the loss of their brothers and sisters to suicide bombers, IEDs and the meaningless deaths of civilians in bombings and firefights. The torture, by any other name, at Abu Ghraib and Guantanamo, was inevitable. The civilian and military leaders who authorized and waged war as they did made the torture inevitable.[61]*

Indeed. Violence begets violence.

At the same time that members of the Bush administration were exercising their euphemistic legal scholarship to end-run the Geneva Conventions, they were also punting away aspects of the Fourth Amendment in the name of national security through the "President's Surveillance Program" (PSP), also know as Stellar Wind—which authorized electronic surveillance (warrantless eavesdropping) of U. S. citizens. President Bush asked White House Counsel Alberto Gonzalez to keep the program a "close hold," meaning that the president would decide who would be "read in." When the program began in October 2001, only three Justice Department (DOJ) lawyers were aware of it—Attorney General John Ashcroft, Deputy Assistant Attorney General John Yoo, and Counsel for Intelligence Policy James Baker.

Between May 2003 and January 2004, Jack Goldsmith and Patrick Philbin, Assistant Attorneys General with the Office of Legal Counsel, were subsequently read in on the PSP. When they expressed their concerns about the legality of aspects of the program, then Deputy Attorney General James Comey agreed with their assessment and shared that view on March 4, 2004, with Attorney General John Ashcroft, who also agreed. Ashcroft would be hospitalized later that day with severe gallstone pancreatitis. His hospitalization would impact what happened next.

Over the next few days, the DOJ lawyers met with the White House staff multiple times. Goldsmith, Philbin, and Comey from the DOJ made it clear that certain aspects of the program had to cease, and Bush's men, Alberto Gonzalez, Andrew Card, David Addington, and others argued for renewing the program as it was. Bush instructed Cheney to meet with Congress's "Gang of Eight" on March 10 to tell them about the impasse with the DOJ and to get their views; no DOJ lawyers were invited to this meeting. Bush then instructed Gonzalez and Card "to go to the George Washington University Hospital to speak to Ashcroft, who was in the intensive care unit recovering from surgery," which they did, against the explicit wishes of Ashcroft's wife, who took the call when they announced their intention to visit. By the time they arrived, Comey—now the Acting Attorney General during Ashcroft's hospitalization—Goldsmith, and Philbin were already there. Ashcroft refused to sign the authorization and made clear that Comey was the Acting Attorney General. Both Comey, the acting Attorney General, and Ashcroft, the man on whose behalf he was acting, agreed that the PSP should not be reauthorized in its current form.

Bush signed the renewed authorization of the PSP on the morning of March 11 without the approval of anyone from the DOJ. His signing led senior members of the DOJ to threaten to resign. More meetings were held. Questions were raised regarding what Bush knew or understood and what Gonzalez had shared with him. On March 17 Bush chose "to modify certain PSP intelligence-gathering activities and to discontinue certain Other Intelligence Activities that DOJ believed were legally unsupported."[62] This decision to modify was not a concluding episode. Many of the nuts and bolts of the 2001 Presidential Surveillance Program remain classified. Corporate communications providers agreed to cooperate (that is, not to fight back) if the government ordered, rather than requested, their cooperation. Corporate and government surveillance of U. S. citizens and the efforts of those who want to limit or end it continue.[63]

AS AMERICA'S POST-9/11 MILITARY PRESENCE in Afghanistan approached two decades, and before President Biden announced that the last of the U. S. troops would be withdrawn by September 11, 2021, some veterans of the post-9/11 Afghanistan and Iraq invasions reflected on their experiences in those campaigns. Their views, published on Veterans Day in 2019, give voice to what political and military leadership from 2001 through 2021 did not want to admit.

Retired U.S. Marine Corps Captain, Lyle Jeremy Rubin recalls believing in "bringing something like democracy to Iraq and Afghanistan," but questions "how you can be a killer and be a nation-builder at the same time."

Retired U. S. Army Specialist Arti Walker-Peddakotla reflects that "Democracy doesn't come in a box. It's not something that fits every country." Through her eyes, "It's a war that we've spent $1 trillion on now...where thousands of people have died, where children are growing up and all they've ever grown up in is a war zone." She feels pained that leaving makes sense, but she believes that "Whatever we do is never going to ensure that the most disenfranchised people in

Afghanistan are going to be protected, that women are going to have their rights protected. That is a burden that America will have to bear on its soul."

Retired U.S. Marine Corps Staff Sergeant Donald White believes that "We're creating war zones and we're creating refugees…. if you kill the wrong person you just create more insurgents." Echoing Captain Rubin's question, he asks, "How do I win the hearts and minds of the local populace by walking around with a machine gun in their neighborhood and shooting at people?"

Retired U.S. Army Major, Danny Sjursen laments that "the fact that we've gotten to this place now, in 2019, where poll after poll has shown that nearly two-thirds of Afghan and Iraq veterans have said, quote, 'The wars were not worth fighting,' is remarkable, because that's a higher rate than the American people at large who didn't serve."

Retired U.S. Army Lieutenant Colonel Daniel L. Davis, who considers himself "a conservative, a Republican," had read in 2011 "that things were on the way to getting better." His take on America's dilemma is straightforward: "You cannot accomplish with military power a political outcome. That's the big lesson we need to learn. Diplomacy and targeted military deterrence is what will keep you safe."

Major Sjursen offered this prognosis:

> Whether we leave tomorrow…or 10 years from now, the outcome is…a brutal civil war and half the country is going to fall under Taliban rule again and women are going to live in a medieval situation until the Afghan people as a whole come up with an Afghan solution to an Afghan problem.[64]

Of course, these five veterans don't speak for all veterans, but as was true with Vietnam, we again have a collective responsibility to hold accountable those leaders who send our young men and woman off to fight and those leaders who design and orchestrate that fight. What we chose to do was to re-elect George W. Bush in 2004 despite his choosing, under the influence of Rumsfeld, Wolfowitz, Gonzalez, and others, to authorize torture, to illegally surveil U. S. citizens, and to invade Iraq in 2003—an action that diverted military and intelligence resources from the effort to bring to justice the al Qaeda architects of the 9/11 attacks and disable their network of terror. As others have written and said, attacking and occupying Iraq, an oil-rich Arab nation, undercut the multi-nation coalition that supported the U. S. after September 2001 and probably helped the recruitment efforts of those who were inclined to attack the U. S. See again Eisenhower's second and fifth precepts and McNamara's ninth lesson in *In Retrospect.*

As U. S. troops departed Afghanistan in July and August of 2021, the Taliban moved swiftly, as anticipated and predicted, into areas that the occupiers vacated. Many combatants and local authorities who had worked with and been trained by the Americans, fled, gave up, or both, while the U. S. scrambled to get Afghan interpreters out of the country. While hindsight may or may not be 20-20, it can often be illuminating, and annoying. Earlier options for an American departure had presented themselves.

As early as November 2001 Taliban leader Mullah Muhammad Omar reached out to soon-to-be-interim-Afghan-president, Hamid Karzai about a possible surrender. Omar demanded nothing other than amnesty—a deal that Karzai (who would be the Afghanistan version of Vietnam's Diem—without the assassination) was interested in making. The Taliban were defeated and had little or no leverage for negotiation. Donald Rumsfeld's response to Omar's offer was that "The United States is not inclined to negotiate surrenders." No deal was made. Nineteen years later the U. S. wanted to get out. In February 2020, Donald Trump, the man about whom *The Art of the Deal* was written, negotiated an American troop-withdrawal agreement with a much more powerful Taliban, which was now poised to control the country. Trump's successor, President Joe Biden, honored the agreement. Chaos and tragedy ensued.[65] The familiar, professional-grade blend of ignorance, arrogance, violence, untrustworthiness, and humiliation avoidance once more guided the way, buttressed with self-serving narratives and partisan bickering.

One exception to the partisanship has been the leadership of General Mark Milley, chairman of the Joint Chiefs since September 2019, who was nominated by Donald Trump. Milley would come not to trust Trump and admit in 2021 to having privately conferred with his top officers and his Chinese counterpart in order to minimize any chance that the president would start a war with China. He was more loyal to the country and its constitution than to any particular Oval Office occupant. After the August 2021 Afghanistan exit, the general testified that the war "wasn't lost in the last 20 days or even 20 months. There's a cumulative effect to a series of strategic decisions that go way back," including shifting our focus in 2003 to Iraq and never dealing with Pakistan's claiming to be an ally while harboring terrorists.[66] In contrast with Milley's loyalty to the country, Congressional Republicans, amnesiacs when it came to Bush's and Trump's twelve-year oversight of the war, grilled Milley and criticized Biden; Congressional Democrats, amnesiacs regarding Obama's eight years, honored Milley, and defended Biden.

The U. S. withdrawal from Afghanistan first and foremost impacted the Afghan people, especially those who cooperated with the U. S. It also impacted active-duty U. S. and Afghan military personnel as well as diplomats, veterans, and, of course, the Taliban. Each of these groups warrants attention, but what *about* those who threw their lot in with the Americans against the Taliban? Yes, many American-trained soldiers and police officers abandoned their posts, but their unpredictability in battle had been known for years.[67] Vietnamese veterans who were trained by and who fought alongside U. S. troops in the 1960s and 1970s experienced their own painful American withdrawal, and their pain resurfaced as they watched the Afghanistan exit.

Ly Kai Binh, a gunnery sergeant in the South Vietnamese Marine Corps, saw his own experience in what the Afghans faced as America withdrew. The U. S. approached Vietnam with abundant supplies, equipment, and air support. "'They taught us to fight like rich men, even though we were living as poor men. And after they left we had to ration bullets. We couldn't afford to fight the way they taught us to.'" After the U. S. left and the Saigon regime surrendered, Binh was imprisoned, escaped, and found his way to the U. S. Learning of the U. S. withdrawal from Afghanistan, he reflected, "'I am an American citizen now. I understand we have to protect our country's interests. We have been at war so long. But still, we need to keep our promises. That was not done in Vietnam. I don't know if it can be done now.'"

Uc Van Nguyen, a pilot and Lieutenant Colonel in the South Vietnamese Air Force, who was trained to fly helicopters in Texas, still carries bitter memories of the U. S. withdrawal from his country:

> We wanted to fight, but no supplies, no fuel, no rockets. And the Americans did not help like they said they would. I think in the end we felt betrayed. We never thought it could happen to us, never in your mind do you think you will lose your country, but then it happens and there is no way to reverse it.[68]

I think in the end we felt betrayed. In Afghanistan, the respective impacts of the U. S. arrival, its twenty-year occupation, and its departure were experienced differently in cities like Kabul and in the rural and mountainous areas where some seventy percent of Afghans live. East and slightly north of Kandahar, in the village of Sinzai, white flags "mark the precise spots where U. S. airstrikes killed Afghans." Zabiullah Haideri, whose "shop was shattered by an airstrike in 2019 that killed 12 villagers," says that "'everyone here hated the Americans.'" "'They murdered civilians and committed atrocities.'" With the end of the firefights, bombings, and drone strikes, village imam Mohammed Omar reflects that people "'can move freely now anywhere. Death has disappeared.'" With the Taliban back in power in August 2021, it remained to be seen if they could govern. International aid had paused and people were hungry.[69]

By January 2022, David Miliband, president and CEO of the International Rescue Committee, reported that Afghanistan was "nearing economic collapse and the breakdown of virtually all basic services." He added that only "2% of Afghans have enough food to eat," and that "9 million people [are] at risk of famine, including 1 million children at risk of dying from starvation." Miliband lays out a plan that includes increasing humanitarian aid but that relies on "a shift in the mindset of the West" regarding economic sanctions that are designed to hurt the Taliban, but that are killing the Afghan people.[70]

As reported by Anand Gopal, in the Sangin Valley northwest of Kandahar, women now recall the cyclical, complex conflicts among multiple factions. Village elders, Soviet Communist occupiers and the mujahideen who opposed them, brutal warlords such as Amir Dado, corrupt and violent militias like the Ninety-third Division, the Taliban, and the U.S. invaders and occupiers are all remembered by the women in the valley. One woman, Shakira, lost sixteen members of her family over time to gunfire, IEDs, and "*buzzbuzzaks*"—the word that describes U. S. drones in the countryside. She recalls when the Taliban disabled Dado and the Ninety-third Division, and she remembers her shock when, after defeating the Taliban, the Americans befriended Dado, making him an intelligence officer, and reinstated the Ninety-third Division as an ally. Unlike women in Kabul who were exposed to almost twenty years of international aid and the slow increase of their human rights, many women in the countryside village "were unwilling to judge the [Taliban] against some universal standard—only against what had come before."

Gopal, who reported on Sinzai and the Sangin Valley, observes that "the Taliban takeover has restored order to the conservative countryside while plunging the comparatively liberal streets of Kabul into fear and helplessness."[71] As for the men in the countryside, some were coerced to join the Taliban, and some, seeing their families and friends killed by the outsiders, volunteered—much as their predecessors had joined the mujahideen against the Soviets and as the South Vietnamese had joined the Viet Cong against the Americans. Lessons not learned.

While the words referred specifically to Iraq, the careful selection of "Major combat operations" at the beginning of President Bush's May 1, 2003 statement allowed it to carry at least some morsel of truth, depending upon what "major" meant to the respective speechwriters, the speech deliverer, and the speech receivers. It's clear now that we had not prevailed in Iraq in 2003. Similar denials and misleading statements about progress in Afghanistan span four administrations over twenty years.[72] The missions, however hindsight and history might define them, have not been accomplished in either country.

IN THEIR FINAL REPORT, THE 9/11 Commission, after hearing a wide range of both private and public testimony, concluded that "Perhaps the most incisive of the advisors on terrorism to the new [Bush] administration was the holdover Richard Clarke."[73]

Under oath, Clarke spoke openly about his frustration with National Security Advisor Rice's delays and lack of urgency in her response to the information he provided her as early as January 25, 2001—less than a week after Bush's inauguration. As noted above, a National Security Council Principals meeting on the al Qaeda threat that Clarke requested on that date did not take place until September 4, 2001—one week before the attack on the United States. Further evidence of his integrity and clarity emerged, when, asked by the commission, Clarke admitted that had his policy advice been acted on when he first offered it, there was no *guarantee* it would have prevented the September 11 attacks.

In some fifteen hours of closed testimony before the commission, Clarke was asked about what was known and what had been done before the attacks, what led up to them, what might have prevented them, and what could be done to prevent future attacks. In the first ninety seconds of his subsequent March 24, 2004 public testimony to the 9/11 Commission, with some family members of those who had died in the attacks present and the cameras rolling, he began with an apology and a request for forgiveness:

> I welcome these hearings because of the opportunity that they provide to the American people to better understand why the tragedy of 9/11 happened and what we must do to prevent a recurrence.
>
> I also welcome the hearings because it is finally a forum where I can apologize to the loved ones of the victims of 9/11. To them who are here in this room [he pauses, turns and acknowledges them], to those who are watching on television, your government failed you, those entrusted with protecting you failed you, and I failed you. We tried hard, but that doesn't matter because we failed.

And for that failure, I would ask—once all the facts are out—for your understanding and for your forgiveness.[74]

Just days before his March 24 testimony, Clarke's book, *Against All Enemies,* was released. Several commission members pressed him on what they read as inconsistencies between his fifteen hours of closed testimony and what he wrote in the book. Clarke responded:

> In the fifteen hours of testimony, no one asked me what I thought about the President's invasion of Iraq. And the reason I'm strident in my criticism of the President of the United States is because by invading Iraq—something I was not asked about by the commission, it's something I chose to write about a lot in the book—by invading Iraq the President of the United States has greatly undermined the war on terrorism.[75]

Intelligent, articulate, informed, opinionated, clear, direct, compassionate, and composed, Clarke embodied what public service can be. When his testimony ended, many in the room—including 9/11 victims' family members—applauded, surrounded him, shook his hand, and hugged him. Clarke's 2004 comments about Bush and Iraq and the knowledge, insight, and integrity that informed them went unheeded— just as Eisenhower's precepts and McNamara's lessons continued to be ignored.

As the third decade of the twenty-first century continues to unfold, Afghanistan is once again under Taliban control—two decades after George Bush and his senior cabinet members ignored the intelligence on al Qaeda, invaded Afghanistan and Iraq, stood under the *Mission Accomplished* banner, and told the world that we had prevailed in Iraq.[76] While many soldiers, sailors, pilots, and Marines succeeded in specific missions, it would be the height of arrogance to intimate, much less explicitly claim that any larger mission—known and clear at the time of each invasion—has been accomplished.

In the early 1990s, amid Robert McNamara's reflections on and regrets about America's post-World War II trajectory (and with additional insights from his post-Korea, post-Vietnam, post-Cold War, and post-Desert Storm observations), he offered another lesson, or perhaps a warning, for those who might be interested: "In the postwar years, the United States had the power—and to a considerable degree exercised that power—to shape the world as we chose. In the next century, that will not be possible."[77] Indeed.

WE HAVE NOT LEARNED THE lessons of Vietnam. Nor is it clear that we're ready to learn anything as a result of our not having learned from Vietnam. Our post-9/11 ignorance and arrogance, characterized by phrases such as *you're either with us or you're with the enemy; wanted, dead or alive;* and *bring 'em on* deceive us. We live amid Eisenhower's *perpetual fear and tension,* with *a burden of arms draining our wealth and labor,* and with *every gun that is made, every warship launched, every rocket fired,* we somehow refuse to believe we're *hanging from a cross of iron* as we continue to play the familiar, well-worn, monophonic groove of all the danger out there in those other countries, religions, parties, networks, neighborhoods, and people. We refuse to listen to any sustained multichannel messages that might implicate and even save us.

The *we* and the *us* in the preceding paragraph refer to many civilian and military leaders. As important, these first-person plural pronouns also tap on the shoulder of every U. S. citizen who votes or doesn't vote, who complains and refuses to act, who acts and refuses to be accountable for his, her, or their actions, or who accepts conspiracies, cultural givens, or the status quo without concern, reflection, or even rudimentary critical thought.

The number of Vietnam veterans who have been debilitated or killed by Agent Orange exceeds those who died during the war. The deaths are in the hundreds of thousands and the disabilities are estimated to be more than a million.[78] The numbers for the Vietnamese people are higher still. The "Global War on Terror" has given its veterans the respiratory and cancer-related consequences of burn pits, diesel exhaust, and other toxins beyond the immediate dangers of combat. As the Vietnam veterans and their families struggled and continue to struggle to get the Pentagon, Congress, the Veterans Administration, and the rest of us to acknowledge and address what they brought home, so now do the veterans of Afghanistan and Iraq, along with their families, struggle to get their service-related healthcare needs acknowledged as costs of war—just like the hundreds of billions of dollars paid to private contractors. In support of the 2021 bill (cosponsored by New York Senator Kristen Gillibrand and Florida Senator Marco Rubio) that would expedite services for these veterans, commentator Jon Stewart noted, "That's the total cost of war. That's the true cost of war. And you can't just have money for war and the toys of war and not for the consequences of it."[79]

In an October 2021 conversation on this topic, Army Sergeant Isiah James (Ret.), a Senior Advisor for the Black Veterans Project, provided this fully human perspective:

> I think we're looking at it the wrong way, Admiral. I truly, truly do. And I mean no disrespect. But instead of talking about the next war—as somebody who has actually taken human life…. I don't ever want to see another war. There is no such thing as a just war. There are two rules in war: young men will die, young women will die, and somebody has to walk the point. There is never a just war…. but any

time—we're talking about the cost of war in human dollars. $6 trillion is not worth one human life on either side. So let us not forget how Americans are suffering, millions of Iraqis and people in Afghanistan, and Africa, which we don't even talk about, are suffering from the same effects of the burn pits and stuff that we don't even get to.[80]

The admiral Sergeant James addressed was Admiral Mike Mullen (Ret.), who had expressed his conviction, and his agreement with the rest of the panel, that the state of veterans' healthcare treatment was inexcusable, and that the Pentagon and the Veterans Administration had to work together to address the issue. In an earlier comment about the makeup of the military that fought in Iraq and Afghanistan, Admiral Mullen referred to "the debate that has to occur before we go to war the next time." In his response, excerpted above, Sergeant James speaks through a perspective that includes *all of us.* He embraces the human beings in Afghanistan, Iraq, and parts of Africa. In caring about Americans, and not just Americans, he embodies and integrates healthy feminine traits such as mercy, care, and compassion with healthy masculine traits such as wisdom, independence, and justice. Imagine holding your hand over your heart and saying these words: "...with liberty, justice, compassion, mercy, wisdom, care, and love for all." And imagine fully embodying those final two words.

WE'LL END WITH A POEM for the children who suffer in war—regardless of their country or the nature of the war, and whether they suffer in a refugee camp, in a shelter, in a hospital, at a mall, in a theater, on a playground, in a school, or at home. And we'll dream of and for the children, who, perhaps, one day will not suffer in war and for the adults who work to re-create a world that is a gift to open eyes.

~

THIS OPEN EYE[81]

Swollen shut the right
eye seeps semi-clotted
blood that streams
and blotches a map of
hell across the three-
year-old face. Wide
open, the left eye
appears injury-free –
untouched, but
ultimately more
lethal.
Through this open
eye the child sees
the world that has
closed the other.

Chapter Eight

And That's Not All

How are you limiting yourself?[1]

BOTH BEYOND AND WITHIN THE narratives explored in chapters three through seven, other manifestations of our collective American Shadow beckon. Each, as with those we've already explored, deserves much more consideration than it gets here. As previously noted, this volume presents selected—not exhaustive—examples to make the case for our national Shadow.

It's important to remember that we're exploring denial and projection here—those tendencies to deny both historical and current uniquely American manifestations of ignorance, arrogance, fear, bigotry, violence, greed, bullying, excess, and untrustworthiness and to project them onto others. Until we recognize, own, and begin the work of integrating what we deny in ourselves and project onto others, we will continue to unconsciously embrace the underlying elements of our national Shadow and to repeat the horrors of the past, if not exactly, then in some new, more subtle manifestations.

The briefer narratives in this chapter are interdependent, in varying degrees, with each other and with the longer narratives in the previous five chapters. Among many examples, we can see this interdependence in how the historical subjugation of women impacts the foundational infrastructures and cultures of government, business, education, and other disciplines. We can see it in that the trillions of profit-producing dollars spent on making war are not available to be spent on healthcare (or anything else), even as this war-making renders quality healthcare essential in order to address the physical and psychological injuries that war produces. We can see it in how our ambivalence about and feeling separate from the planet impacts our sense of connection and how we relate to each other—across beliefs about religion, economics, gender, race, ethnicity, and sexual orientation and identity.

So here we go. Here are additional manifestations of our national Shadow.

Ambivalence About the Planet

All of the other issues explored in this book are moot if we don't address this one. We express this ambivalence through our stances on a variety of not necessarily synonymous but inevitably interrelated issues that include climate change, global warming, pollution, resource depletion, over-development, species extinction, and disease (in the broadest meaning of the word). Yes, these issues are global concerns. The U. S. contributes to them, suffers because of them, and inconsistently works to resolve them. As 'once-in-a-century' storms, fires, and floods arrive every few years if not yearly, and as glaciers melt and sea levels rise, the only ignorance we can claim is vincible and willful—and it is underwritten by greed, excess, arrogance, and untrustworthiness. Our ambivalence about the planet arises from our remarkable misperception of being apart from it rather than an intimate living part of it.

Whatever damage our pre- and early-industrial ancestors did to the planet was limited by their relatively small populations—estimated at about 770 million *globally* in 1760, and about 3.9 million in the U. S. according to the country's first census in 1790. The technology of the times also limited the variety, speed, and scale of the damage they could do.[2] At the time the industrialized polluters first raised their smokestacks and laid their waste pipes to respectively darken our skies and rivers, they didn't know what we've learned in the ensuing two-plus centuries, but they knew that they were creating waste and had to get rid of it. They also knew that population, population density, and the number of polluters were on the rise. The point here is not to let our predecessors off the hook, but to make sure we don't let ourselves off. We know more than they did, and we have more evidence of the consequences of our actions.

As we'll see in Chapter Eleven, poets Audre Lorde and Tony Hoagland each wrote about cancer as a great equalizer amid perceived differences. Our extraordinary common home is a greater equalizer still, twirling and shooting us through space with just the right conditions for life as we understand it.

Recent statistics are sobering, as have been the statistics from earlier decades. The scope and scale of evidence for planetary deterioration, global warming, climate change, and our human role in these unfoldings are vast. The specific details of the deterioration across species of flora and fauna and on our land and in our water and air are vaster still. Some of the consequences, especially of climate change, are being felt by increasingly more people in "developed" countries, but their greatest impacts are and will continue to be on people who live much closer to and connected with the natural world in our "developing" and "least developed" countries.

Selected key messages in the 2019 "Global Assessment Report on Biodiversity and Ecosystem Services," a document produced by the Intergovernmental Science-Policy Platform on Biodiversity and Ecosystem Services (IPBES), include the following. Unless otherwise indicated, each statement is a direct quote; page numbers are in parentheses:

- Nature and its vital contributions to people, which together embody biodiversity and ecosystem functions and services, are deteriorating worldwide. (10)
- Human actions threaten more species with global extinction now than ever before. (11)
- Climate change is a direct driver that is increasingly exacerbating the impact of other drivers on nature and human well-being. (13)
- Most of nature's contributions are not fully replaceable, yet some contributions of nature are irreplaceable. (22)
- Humanity is a dominant global influence on life on earth, and has caused natural terrestrial, freshwater and marine ecosystems to decline. (23)
- The global rate of species extinction is already at least tens to hundreds of times higher than the average rate over the past 10 million years and is accelerating. (24)
- Today humans extract more from the earth and produce more waste than ever before. (28)
- Land-use change is driven primarily by agriculture, forestry and urbanization, all of which are associated with air, water and soil pollution. (28)[3]

Each of these items is a header or sub-header in the report, and is followed by detailed evidence, sources, and cross-references.

Here's another view with a focus on climate change. The *Climate Change 2021: The Physical Science Basis* report from the Intergovernmental Panel on Climate Change (IPCC) includes, among much else, the following. Again, unless otherwise indicated, each item is a direct quote, with page numbers in parentheses:

- It is unequivocal that human influence has warmed the atmosphere, ocean and land. Widespread and rapid changes in the atmosphere, ocean, cryosphere and biosphere have occurred. (6)
- Each of the last four decades has been successively warmer than any decade that preceded it since 1850. (6)

- Human influence has warmed the climate at a rate that is unprecedented in at least the last 2000 years. (8)
- Observed warming is driven by emissions from human activities, with greenhouse gas warming partly masked by aerosol cooling. (9)
- The scale of recent changes across the climate system as a whole and the present state of many aspects of the climate system are unprecedented over many centuries to many thousands of years.
  - In 2019, atmospheric CO_2 concentrations were higher than at any time in at least 2 million years.
  - Global mean sea level has risen faster since 1900 than over any preceding century in at least the last 3000 years. (10)
- Many changes due to past and future greenhouse gas emissions are irreversible for centuries to millennia, especially changes in the ocean, ice sheets and global sea level.
  - Mountain and polar glaciers are committed to continue melting for decades or centuries.
  - In the longer term, sea level is committed to rise for centuries to millennia due to continuing deep ocean warming and ice sheet melt, and will remain elevated for thousands of years. (29)[4]

For at least sixty years, science, corporate profit, and economic/political power have mostly clashed and occasionally cooperated as evidence of climate change, global warming, and pollution of our land, water, and air have become increasingly harder to ignore. In his introduction to the November 1965 *Report of the Environmental Pollution Panel, President's Science Advisory Committee,* President Johnson wrote:

> ....the technology that has permitted our affluence spews out vast quantities of wastes and spent products that pollute our air, poison our waters, and even impair our ability to feed ourselves....

> Pollution now is one of the most pervasive problems of
> our society.... [T]he flow of pollutants to our air, soil and
> waters is increasing.... [O]ur present efforts in managing
> pollution are barely enough to stay even, surely not enough
> to make the improvements that are needed.[5]

In an excerpt in *The Guardian* of her 2021 book, *Our Biggest Experiment: An Epic History of the Climate Crisis,* climate campaigner Alice Bell writes that a 1974 CIA study on "climatological research as it pertains to intelligence problems," warned that "weird weather" could lead to "political unrest and mass migration." Bell chronicles the continuing emergence of this weird weather, beginning in the 1970s and still globally manifesting itself as droughts, crop failures, and floods. She posits that "debate about climate change in the last third of the 20th century would be characterised as much by delay as concern," that "fightback from the fossil fuel industries," played a role in the delay, and that fossil fuel companies do "run on science" and that "they are strategic about which bits of it they use."

Amid the scientific, corporate, and government interplay, Bell admits that:

> [O]ne of the hardest parts of writing about the history of the
> climate crisis was stumbling across warnings from the 1950s,
> 60s and 70s, musing about how things might get bad some-
> time after the year 2000 if no one did anything about fossil
> fuels. They still had hope back then. Reading that hope
> today hurts.[6]

Perhaps informing Johnson's and the CIA's concerns was the 1962 publication of Rachel Carson's *Silent Spring,* which Johnson's White House predecessor, John F. Kennedy, had acknowledged. With its specific focus on the impact of DDT and other pesticides, which Carson noted as early as 1945, *Silent Spring* "deliberately challenged the wisdom of a government that allowed toxic chemicals to be put into the environment before knowing the long-term consequences of their use." The book further asserted that "the human body was permeable and, as such, vulnerable to toxic substances in the environment.[7] The debates about human-made toxins and their impacts on land, water, air, flora, fauna, and humans continues today. Disease, death, and destruction fueled by greed.

Lack of Health and Caring

At least three distinct and related issues intersect here: the physical and mental health of each individual American; the general health of our American culture and society; and the details of if, how, and to whom healthcare is delivered in the United States. If the quote attributed to Jiddu Krishnamurti, "It is no measure of health to be well-adjusted to a profoundly sick society," is accurate, how might we assess the health of American society, how well-adjusted are we to it, and what are we to learn from and do about our assessment and adjustment?[8]

The statistics are not reassuring. The number of organizations, public and private, that address the prevalence of anxiety, depression, trauma, addiction, and suicide in the United States is itself revealing and disturbing. This was true before the emergence of COVID-19, which only exacerbated an already extensive mental health problem.[9] What might it mean to be well-adjusted in a society in which 51.5 million adults (20.6% of our adult population) suffer from "any mental illness," and 13.1 million (5.2% of adults) suffer from "serious mental illness"?[10] Or, what if "half of millennials and 75% of Gen Zers have left their job for mental health reasons"?[11] More generally, workplace stress and "burnout" are estimated to cost the U. S. economy over $500 billion annually, and it's becoming increasingly clear that changes in the workplace culture and environment, and not just helping employees practice better "self-care" are needed.[12] These statistics relate only to adults and the workplace. Anxiety, depression, and "behavior disorders" impact our children and adolescents as well.[13]

Related to anxiety, depression, and suicide is addiction to a variety of legal and illegal substances, including alcohol, nicotine, heroin, cocaine, opioids, and methamphetamine—among many others.[14] According to the Centers for Disease Control (CDC), overdose deaths were approximately 64,000 in 2016; 71,000 in 2017; 68,000 in 2018; 72,000 in 2019; and 93,000 in 2020.[15] More than 900,000 Americans died from a drug overdose between 1999 and 2019. Of those, almost 247,000 died from prescription opioids.[16] That much killing requires cooperation and/or apathy among patients/victims, pharmacies, healthcare professionals, and pharmaceutical companies.

One example: On October 21, 2020 the U. S. Department of Justice reached a federal criminal and civil settlement with Perdue Pharma and members of the Sackler family, who founded the company, for more than $8 billion, the dissolution of the company, and a repurposing of its assets for the public good. In 2007 Perdue Pharma and three of its executives had pled guilty to criminal charges for minimizing the risk of OxyContin addiction. By September 2019, the company was facing 2,900 lawsuits and filed for bankruptcy. In late summer 2021, the U.S. Bankruptcy Court completed those proceedings, dissolving the company but largely shielding the Sacklers and their remaining billions from further civil charges. None of the Sacklers will serve time. Some states appealed, and a new settlement was negotiated in March 2022. The issue, it seems, is not completely resolved.[17]

Two familiar lessons emerge from this example. First, the justice system does not provide equal protection of the laws. Those who can afford to pay attorneys for years of litigation are better protected. Second, we'll return once again to Neil Sheehan's view that the My Lai massacre was inevitable as a consequence of the political and military leadership of the time—leadership that I characterize as ignorant, arrogant, excessive and comfortable with violence. Likewise, hundreds of thousands of opioid addictions, overdoses, and deaths are, perhaps, inevitable consequences of the arrogance, greed, excess, and untrustworthiness of Perdue Pharma's founders and leaders, who were enabled by the larger for-profit-insurance-pharmaceutical-medical-government-financial-lobbying culture and infrastructure.

Here's a different view: what kind of society has 16,066 substance abuse facilities available to complete the 2020 National Survey of Substance Abuse Treatment Services?[18] And that's just the number of facilities that were both eligible and chose to participate. It provides no measure of those facilities that were ineligible or chose not to participate.

It is not a healthy society when in 2020 more than half-a-million people were homeless—including 171,000-plus individuals within families, 37,000-plus veterans, and 34,000-plus unaccompanied minors.[19] It is not a healthy society when from 2014 through 2019, an American killed someone else with a gun 40 times every day, on average; when another 63 Americans killed *themselves* with a gun every day; and another 62 Americans killed themselves by some other means. Every day. We'll say more about these numbers below. Violence in the U.S. gets its own subheading.

Despite their relevance in this conversation about health and caring, we won't list the statistics for cancer, HIV-AIDS, obesity, heart, lung, and vascular disease, aging, or other conditions through which we suffer. While these are more conventionally considered to be of the body, and not of the mind, soul, or spirit, this distinction is increasingly seen as partial at best thanks to the work of Gabor Maté, Bessel van der Kolk, Johann Hari and many others who relate the health of the body to the health of the mind, soul, and spirit.[20]

That the United States remains one of the few countries on the planet, across political and economic ideologies, that does not provide access to quality healthcare for its citizens remains a mystery to the countries that do. That alone should arouse a sense of embarrassment, or at least curiosity, for us. In the context of Assistant Secretary of Defense John McNaughton's 1965 memo that noted that 70% of our reason for being in Vietnam was to avoid a humiliating defeat, it's ironic that we don't seem humiliated by our willful denial of equal access to quality healthcare for all American citizens. That those in Congress, including the folks I vote for and sometimes agree with, provide themselves with better health insurance than the average citizen has access to is evidence enough of the disparity. It adds insult to injury.

In *Enough with the...Talking Points* I explored the problems of sweeping generalizations and characterizations—they are typically meaningless and useless. Without the excesses and lobbying that are inherent in the insurance-pharmaceutical-medical-government-financial-lobbying complex, the U. S. would be better able to provide access to affordable healthcare for all of its citizens. Without the intentional political pandering to the nonrational American fear of words like *socialism*, more Americans might notice that we already accept nationally socialized military, highways, medical subsidies for the poor (Medicaid) and the old (Medicare), and Social Security for everyone. We already rely on locally socialized law enforcement, firefighting and education. Yet, the fear of actually respecting each human being equally and the deep embrace of profits over people, among other things, seem to prevent us from providing what virtually every other country on the planet provides.

As with those who would fight for the day-to-day manifestation—as opposed to just the legislation—of equal civil rights, those who would like equal healthcare access are called socialists, and therefore demonized in America. Yet, in the healthier democracies on the planet, the people are free, it's easier to vote than in many of our United States, war is a less frequent pastime than in the United States, and their public institutions are more "socialized" than in the United States, which enables them to take care of more people than does the United States. How we suffer is an inevitable manifestation of a culture built on acquisition, accumulation, and winning all the finite games, which, you may have noticed, we don't.

While the social*ism* scare is effective, it tends to hide the underlying culprits that feed it—ignorance, arrogance, greed, and excess. The for-profit insurance-pharmaceutical-medical-government-financial-lobbying industry known as healthcare in the United States has to pay its providers fair wages and pay for the increasingly expensive infrastructure, research, and testing of modern medicine—which is true for not-for-profit healthcare systems in other countries as well. In the United States, the cost of service has to be high enough to pay excessive salaries for corporate leaders with enough left over for shareholder dividends. Premiums that for-profit insurance corporations charge must be high enough to make profits and pay dividends as well. Said differently, a relatively small number of American executives and shareholders profit from the billions of dollars of their fellow citizens' health issues.

As noted in Chapter Four, this same profit structure underlies the government's demands for and use of a variety of weapons of individual and mass destruction—from handguns, rifles, and bullets to bombs, missiles, ships, jets, and everything in-between, plus all of the infrastructure required to implement and maintain them. Private military contractor executives and shareholders reap financial rewards while U. S. military personnel, especially those who put their lives on the line, risk injury, death, and PTS, had a starting salary of

$1,833.00 per month in 2022. And many of our daughters can't afford menstrual products. Who, pray tell, *are* we?

The COVID-19 pandemic exacerbated and ultimately exposed one specific consequence of greed in the healthcare industry. A conversation with nurses, published in January 2022 by the *New York Times*, makes clear that, despite an abundance of nurses available, "America's frontline nurses are overworked, burnt out and quitting in droves.... America is facing a national nursing shortage." According to the nurses themselves, the cause of the shortage is not difficult patients, emotional overwhelm, or even COVID-19. "The biggest force that's driving nurses away: greedy hospitals. To maximize profits, American hospitals have been intentionally understaffing nurses for decades, long before the pandemic."[21] Which leads us to the relationships among money, power, things, beliefs, and people.

Prioritizing Money, Power, Things, and Beliefs Over People (and Other Living Beings)

The desire for and the importance placed on money, power, and things are connected to, if not the driving force behind, much of what manifests as American Shadow. Our theft of both land and life from Native Americans emerged from our placing a higher value on the profitable use of stolen land than we placed on people and culture. Slavery dehumanized those enslaved and provided free labor so landowners could make money without working too hard. The attacks on Vietnam, Afghanistan, and Iraq (and the occupations that followed those last two) made billions of dollars for weapons and infrastructure manufacturers and cost millions of Vietnamese, Iraqi, Afghan, and American lives. Limiting women's roles to child-rearing and housekeeping devalued their full humanity.

Beyond these specifics, this prioritizing has led to an unprecedented unequal distribution of wealth. As mentioned above and in Chapter Five, many Americans voice a non-rational fear of the words *socialist* and *socialism* whenever prospects are raised for using government funds (taxpayer dollars) to help their less fortunate fellow citizens. They don't want the government deciding who wins and who loses. They don't want those other people to get what they didn't earn because such help might make them lazy(ier). They seem less vocal when the government provides trillions to the already wealthy and fortunate in moments of difficulty. Here are a few recipients of government handouts and bailouts, often called corporate welfare: General Motors, Chrysler, Ford, Harley Davidson, Apple, Goldman Sachs, the entire airline industry, Citigroup, Bank of America, Bear Stearns, Lockheed, Wells Fargo, JPMorgan Chase, Morgan Stanley, PNC, American Express, Capital One, and many, many more needy corporations who could not make it without taxpayer assistance.[22] The argument is that some of these companies and industries are too big to fail—helping them helps the people who work for them and the national economy. That may be true(ish) and it's definitely partial. The other side of that argument seems to be that some people are too small to help. The unhealthy masculine manifestations of independence and greed trump the healthy feminine traits of compassion and care.

Others Being Othered

Ignorance, arrogance, fear, bigotry and violence inform every instance of harmful discrimination, including but not limited to that directed at Asian, Latinx, Middle Eastern, LGBTQ+, and other groups—and the many discrete communities within each of them.[23] I limited the more detailed explorations in this book to those in chapters three through seven. At the same time, I am very aware that any of the groups named (and others not named) in this paragraph can easily be focused on as examples of our "tradition" of only very slowly recognizing our common humanity across gender, culture, ethnicity, race, color, orientation, and identity differences. I chose to dedicate full chapters to the five particular narratives I did for a variety of reasons. First, the scope and scale of Native American and African American experiences are fundamental to the founding and history of the United States. Second, the Vietnam and post-9/11 wars capture our biases against Asian and Middle Eastern peoples, our repetition of both political and military mistakes, the ease and frequency with which we rely on violence, and the lessons we might learn if we genuinely explored the reasons that Native Americans, African Americans, Middle Eastern Americans, and Asian Americans are willing to serve in the U.S. military. Finally, the subjugation of women and fear of the feminine are fundamental to all of these issues—across ethnicity, race, culture, color, orientation, and identity. Within each of these narratives, women's voices were silenced while they carried and birthed and helped nurture, educate, and otherwise raise each and every one of us.

Abundant additional examples point to the tone-deaf ignorance and arrogance that often inform many powerful, often wealthy Americans' perceptions of those they perceive as different. Consider the Reagan administration's initial lack of response to the onset of the AIDS crisis, and their literally laughing about it at press conferences.[24] Consider their (and many Americans') inability to understand Ben Vereen's blackface performance honoring Bert Williams at the 1981 inauguration as the satire it was.[25] Consider their request, rejected by the songwriter, to use Bruce Springsteen's "Born in the U. S. A." during the 1985 inaugural—only to have the president still proudly refer to the song—perhaps not listening past the title or not understanding the lyrics he did hear. [26]

~

Increasing Confusion About Truth and Falsehood in the Real and Virtual Worlds

Ralph Waldo Emerson, reflecting in 1837 on a powerful technology of his time—a technology that he both contributed to and consumed—wrote:

> This is bad; this is worse than it seems. Books are the best of things, well used; abused, among the worst. What is the right use? What is the one end which all means go to effect? They are for nothing but to inspire. I had better never see a book than to be warped by its attraction clean out of my own orbit, and made a satellite instead of a system. The one thing in the world, of value, is the active soul,—the soul, free, sovereign, active."[27]

Getting a book into print in 1837 was not something you could do on your laptop, phone, or in your home office. It was a relatively rare event by twenty-first-century standards, and yet it was still possible to get into print information that was false, harmful, or both. Emerson believed that books—someone else's accumulated knowledge, imaginings or opinions—could inspire us. He also believed that they could deprive us of a direct experience of life—or even the desire for it—and render us vicarious beings, living through what others offer us, true or not. Fast-forward to instantly available streaming news, entertainment, and information—audio, visual, video and print, social media, "content creation," and deliberate mis- and disinformation. Trolling. Not becoming a satellite can be a full-time job.

Jonathan Rauch gets to the heart of the matter. Where pre-social-media-age propagandists spread false information to discredit opponents or their views, current social-media-age propagandists and trolls intentionally "flood the zone with shit" in order to "degrade the information environment *around* the reality-based community." They use a "cacophony of wild claims" in order to foster an "inability to know where to turn for truth," and they "exhaust your critical thinking," "not to persuade but to confuse: to induce uncertainty, disorientation and attendant cynicism."[28]

We saw in Chapter Three that the generation of humans who were tweens and teens in the years during which smart phones and social media began clamoring for our attention (roughly 2007-2012), were dubbed "iGen" by researcher Jean Twenge. They have grown up, phones in hand, amid this cacophony and degraded information environment that makes it hard to know where to turn for truth (and not just for them). Research suggests that we are most impressionable between the ages of 14 and 24, with a peak impressionability around age 18, and that significant events during this time deeply influence our values and sense of the world.[29] All of us face the collective dignities and disasters of our respective generations during this height of impressionability, mitigated or exacerbated by our personal experiences and circumstances.

Those of us who are committed to what Rauch refers to as the "reality-based community"—regardless of our generational identities—have an obligation, especially if we lived through the gradual degradation of the information environment, to assist those who have only known it in its current degraded condition.[30]

Our American Culture of Violence

As mentioned above, from 2014 through 2019, on average, an American killed another American with a gun 40 times every day, another 63 Americans killed *themselves* with a gun every day, and another 62 Americans killed themselves by some other means. That's 103 gunshot deaths and 125 suicide deaths, on average, per day[31]—all *before* the additional stressors of COVID-19. During the pandemic, 2020 saw the largest one-year increase on record in homicides (all causes), with

4,901 more than in 2019,[32] and the highest number of gun violence homicides, 19,436, in the last twenty years, complemented by an additional 24,156 suicides by gun.[33]

I specifically addressed our American culture of violence in 2018 with *Killing America* (Appendix II). Violence is at once a foundational element of our national Shadow and a primary manifestation of it—thus its mention here. We are immersed in it. It is and has been our status quo. Civilized nations that kill less easily and less frequently than we do look at us with sadness and incredulity. This violence is not new, and it includes, but is not limited to, our love affair with firearms. Our national denials and projections recognize violence when it is perpetrated against us, but not the violence we perpetrate against others and ourselves. Much of our post-9/11 rhetoric bears this out. This is from Representative Eric Cantor:

> I rise today in support of this resolution [to authorize the use of United States Armed Forces against those responsible for the recent attacks launched against the United States]. Civilized society has long sought to end the use of violence, but the perpetrators of terrorism and states that harbor them are the enemies of civilized society. They only understand the use of force, and the time has come to speak to them on their terms.[34]

How, then, might we reconcile this language of civilized society with our killing of civilians at Wounded Knee, in Tulsa, Dresden, Tokyo, Hiroshima, Nagasaki, Vietnam, Afghanistan, Iraq, in Littleton, Atlanta, Orlando, Charleston, Newtown, Pittsburgh, Charlotte, Red Lake, Annapolis, Las Vegas, Minneapolis, Buffalo and Uvalde—to name just a few locations? What will it take for us to acknowledge and own this part of our American nightmare? How, exactly, do we qualify as civilized amid these increasingly normalized violent acts?

While Vietnam was raging, before the onsets of mass

shootings and daily domestic gun violence, and before what Andrew Bacevich would call "America's war for the greater Middle East," Vine Deloria, Jr. reflected in 1969:

> When one examines the history of American society one notices the great weakness inherent in it. The country was founded in violence. It worships violence and it will continue to live violently. Anyone who tries to meet violence with love is crushed, but violence used to meet violence also ends abruptly with meaningless destruction.

He continues along subtle parallels with Eisenhower (whom he also criticizes) and channels McNamara and McNaughton, neither of whose writings were available to him in 1969:

> But name if you can the last peace the United States won. Victory, yes, but this country has never made a successful peace [which] requires…recognizing the fact that two distinct systems of life can exist together without conflict….
>
> The United States…. always fails to understand the nature of the world and so does not develop policies that can hold the allegiance of people…. It worries about its reputation and prestige but daily becomes more vulnerable to ideologies more realistic than its own.[35]

Dr. Martin Luther King, Jr., at New York City's Riverside Church on April 4, 1967, exactly one year before an assassin's bullet would violently end his life, reflected on his conversations with young black men, especially in the ghettos of northern cities—conversations in which he had tried to convince them that violence would not solve their problems:

> But they asked, and rightly so, 'What about Vietnam? They asked if our own nation wasn't using massive doses of violence to solve its problems, to bring about the changes it wanted. Their questions hit home, and I knew that I could

never again raise my voice against the violence of the oppressed in the ghettos without having first spoken clearly to the greatest purveyor of violence in the world today: my own government. For the sake of those boys, for the sake of this government, for the sake of the hundreds of thousands trembling under our violence, I cannot be silent.[36]

Zeroing in on one specific manifestation of American violence, Andrew Bacevich reflected on the "Bush doctrine" of preventive war after five years of it in Iraq: "Yet our actual experience with preventive war suggests that, even setting moral considerations aside, to launch a war today to eliminate a danger that *might* pose a threat at some future date is just plain stupid. It doesn't work."[37]

And again, from Doug Anderson's poem, "Same Old":

> Always a war somewhere and underneath
> the crack of rifles, the sound of money
> sliding down the chute, and a
> whimpering of mothers over here, over there.[38]

None of these insights, however, quite captures the collective and individual suffering within each manifestation of violence. Ignorance of the other breeds fear, which encourages bigotry, which makes bullying of, violence against, and betrayal of those considered to be "other" much more palatable or at least easier to justify—reinforcing the ignorant, violent cycle for each succeeding generation. Staying armed against these others feeds the greed and excess that line the pockets of a select few. We can never really have enough firepower to protect ourselves and our way of life from these frightening others and the evil they embody. And we've proven, in our ongoing embrace of violence, that it doesn't work.

In the Smithsonian Channel's documentary, *9/11: The Heartland Tapes* (to explore just one example), genuinely shocked

Americans from beyond the New York City, Washington, D.C., and Stonycreek Township, Pennsylvania areas, spoke of *lunatics* and *terrorists,* much as Representative Cantor differentiated *civilized society* and *perpetrators of terrorism,* and asked why someone would *do this*, in response to the events of that horrific September morning. Again, the persistent questions remain: Why, then, are so many of us unable to muster our shock, outrage, and empathy for the people of Vietnam, Afghanistan, and Iraq during our decades of violence there? Where is our collective grief for Africans and their descendants in America concerning our 400+ years of violence and oppression against them? Beyond Sec. 8113 of 2010's Public Law 111-118, where is our compassion for the Native Peoples of North America regarding our 500+ years of violence against and betrayal of them? What will it take to end, once and for all, the two-millennia-plus violence against and subjugation of women? Yes, some conditions have improved somewhat, sometimes, in some places, for some people, but the questions remain: who are the lunatics and terrorists and where is the civilized society in each of these scenarios? Why would anyone do these things? Good questions.

An interesting example of America's relationship with violence occurred on March 27, 2022 at the Dolby Theater in Los Angeles during the live broadcast of the Academy Awards. One talented, successful, well-known, and wealthy entertainer slapped the face of (committed battery against) another talented, successful, well-known, and wealthy entertainer who had made a joke about his wife. The slapper later apologized—more than once—and each subsequent apology seemed to carry with it increasing levels of self-awareness, regret, and remorse. The slapped stayed onstage after the slap, continued his hosting duties, and did not press charges. The slapper was not removed from the theater, detained, or arrested, and later received a Best Actor award.

Mainstream and social media coverage of the slap was immediate. It continued for days. Other celebrities (and many noncelebrities) debated who was right and who was wrong through their various *it's about us* perspectives that included supporting the slapper for defending his wife; criticizing the slapper because women can stand up for themselves; noting that protection of the laws is not equal if a celebrity can commit battery in public and not be detained or arrested; alternately criticizing or supporting the slapped because his joke was either inappropriate or well within the norms of stand-up comedy; characterizing the slapper as an example of the inherent violence of toxic masculinity; and pointing out the impact of the altercation on the artists who subsequently received awards—especially those awards that immediately followed the slap. The next night, while the slapped was performing in another city, a noncelebrity, non-slapping heckler was removed from the audience, handcuffed, and taken away by the local police—as if to punctuate the unequal protection of the laws noted above.

While the celebrities were slapping and being slapped, and while the rest of us were debating the slap, gun violence, suicide, and other violence continued in Los Angeles and across the country. We've accepted as normal and don't engage with 103 gunshot deaths a day, but we're shocked and engaged when one entertainer slaps another entertainer.[39] If that's not enough, in May 2022, correspondence in the *New England Journal of Medicine* cited CDC statistics showing gun violence surpassing motor vehicle accidents in 2020 as the number one cause of death for children and adolescents (ages 1-19).[40]

IN THE CLOSING PAGES of *The Great Gatsby,* Nick Carraway's reflections on his experiences of and with Tom and Daisy provide us with one way to look at the elements of our collective national Shadow:

I couldn't forgive him or like him but I saw that what he had done was, to him, entirely justified. It was all very careless and confused. They were careless people, Tom and Daisy—they smashed up things and creatures and then retreated back into their money or their vast carelessness or whatever it was that kept them together, and let other people clean up the mess they had made...[41]

Like Tom and Daisy, many of us are often careless and unconcerned with skillful means. We toggle between unhealthy iterations of our me- and us-centric worldviews. The developmental moves from it's all about *me,* to it's all about *us,* to it's all about *all of us,* to it's all about *all that is* perspectives take time and attention. They are real and neither automatic nor guaranteed. Most of us inhabit versions of *it's all about us*—some iteration of group-centrism—which at its healthiest can invite both intra- and inter-group cooperation. At its unhealthiest, it is the petri dish for bigotry, sexism, racism, and any other -ism we might conjure. Until enough of us grow into and embody at least a training-wheels competency with an *it's about all of us* perspective, we'll carelessly continue to embrace the boundaries of our selected -isms. We will stagger in anger and disbelief at the audacity and lunacy of horrors perpetrated against us and our selected group(s), and have no chance to grow into an even more comprehensive and inclusive *it's about all that is* perspective, which the planet is begging us to see. Obsessed with the seedlings in the eyes of others, we will continue to ignore the sequoias in our own eyes, and not be moved in the least by the audacity, lunacy, and horrors we, ourselves, perpetrate, perpetuate, tolerate, and fund.

CHAPTER NINE

Bullied, Woke, & Canceled in the Polarized State(s) of America

*What would shift if you allowed others to do as they
wish rather than force them to do as you wish?*[1]

BULLIES, AS MENTIONED BRIEFLY IN Chapter Two, often choose to bully because of their fear and/or sense of inadequacy. This is true regardless of their particular doses of ignorance, arrogance, fear, bigotry, or excess. Bullies abuse power, which may be physical, emotional, financial, political, or intellectual. Whether they are actually stronger than their victims, or only appear to be, something about the existence of their victim scares or upsets them. So, to feel better about themselves, or to feel safer, they attempt some level of physical, emotional, financial, political, or intellectual intimidation. Much has been written about, and there is some consensus on, "schoolyard" bullying and its online progeny among our children. These are important topics, and they're not our focus here.[2] Rather, we will explore broader manifestations of bullying among American adults (in the chronological sense of "adult") as these manifestations inform our Shadow exploration.

When everything or just one thing out there starts looking like a threat, it might be time to look in the mirror, seek other perspectives, and explore projections. It might be a good time to ask questions like, "What is the threat that I am or we are truly afraid of?" "How am *I*, or are *we*, a threat to others?" And "To what extent am *I* a bully here?" This doesn't mean there are not real dangers and threats out there or that if I perceive a bully, I'm probably a bully too. Again, we're looking at *disproportionate* responses to perceived threats.[3] What really is "out there" and what really is "in here"—in the workings of my own mind and of our (group's) collective unconscious?

One common arena for bullying is fundamentalism. Said differently, one manifestation of fundamentalism is bullying, which, in the broadest sense of the word tends to engage ignorance, arrogance, fear of the other, excess, bigotry, and often violence—in various forms. While many post-9/11 Americans would be quick to embrace, for example, that one source of the terrorism "out there" is fundamentalist Islam, we are slower to embrace the idea, if we are willing to embrace it at all, that white supremacy's[4] brand of terrorism, as practiced in the history of the United States, is a product of fundamentalist Christianity, among other unhealthy cultural givens. The irony here is that the genesis of Christianity was not some guy hanging out with his friends, discussing how they were somehow superior, but rather a guy who made it clear that, if nothing else, it's really important to love one another.

In each and any case, equating a religion with the violent acts of those who are nominal or even real practitioners bastardizes the religion (or at least its mystical core). But that's a discussion for another time. When we observe writing and behavior that emerged through the worldview of the cultural givens and norms of 60 CE, when, for instance, slavery in Roman, Greek and other societies was the norm, we are obligated to employ skillful means that acknowledge those cultural norms (whether or not we agree with them). Interpreting such acknowledgment as a literal endorsement or justification of slavery in the eighteenth and nineteenth centuries, or white (or any) supremacy in the twenty-first century, requires that we ignore some significant shifts in consciousness—not necessarily for everyone—that emerged in the 1,600-1,700 years between the emergence of Paul's epistles and the ratifications of the U. S. Constitution's 13th, 14th, 15th, and 19th amendments. The sentences "Slaves, obey your earthly masters with respect and fear, and with sincerity of heart…" and "Slaves, obey your earthly masters in everything; and do it not only when their eye is on you…" were written within the limitations of the cultural givens of the first century CE. By the eighteenth century CE, perceptions of slavery were shifting, and by the twenty-first century some, albeit not enough, of those shifts are manifesting in increasingly more visible ways. These same shifts in consciousness pertain to the Pauline suggestions that women "submit" to their husbands, softened perhaps, but not refuted, by the suggestion that husbands "love" their wives.[5] This suggestion that women submit to their husbands still haunts many conservative religious sects.

As the word is used here, *fundamentalist* (absolutist, bigoted, or closed), anywhere on the political spectrum and at any developmental level, refers not to the content someone holds, but to *how* he or she holds the content. *Fundamentalist* and *absolutist* are labels at times mistakenly aligned with the *content,* or the 'what' of a given belief system (for example, 'fundamentalist' Christianity or Islam is often used to refer to the literal *content* of either religion). But fundamentalism concerns itself with the *manner* in which the belief system is held—*how* one *holds* the content. Again, as *fundamentalist, bigoted,* and *absolutist* are used here, they refer to the manner in which beliefs are held. We can and do pour conservatism, liberalism, and other -isms into extreme, absolutist, and fundamentalist 'containers' or worldviews (as well as into more moderate, tolerant and authentically-open-to-dialogue containers and worldviews).[6]

When white Christian individuals, organizations, and governments enslave blacks and then free them and then grant and deny them their rights and lynch them and treat them as "less than," it is common to ascribe the label of "fundamentalist" to the perpetrators. The same is true when Muslim men hijack planes and crash them into buildings. When individuals and organizations set fire to and destroy car dealerships, especially those with large gas-guzzling vehicle inventories, in the name of saving the environment, or when individuals censor, harass, detain, and even physically attack those they feel are not "on their side" in the name of demanding respect for particular identities or groups, some folks who have no problem referring to "far-right fundamentalists," are slower, if they are able at all, to call this behavior in the name of protecting the planet or the beliefs and identities of specific groups "far-left fundamentalism." Fundamentalism, as with beauty, and perhaps most attributions, exists in the worldview of the beholder. That's not an endorsement or a minimization of fundamentalism, climate change deniers, or those who continue to sabotage efforts toward equal rights for all. It's a recognition that fundamentalism itself is content-free. Any view can be held in an extreme, narrow, absolutist manner.

Popular evocations of woke culture are also fundamentalist moves. While its approach is often, but not always, more nuanced, and based in intellectual, emotional, and social (rather than physical) confrontation, woke culture's foundational premise is that those who are woke are superior and right, and those who are not woke are inferior and wrong and don't or can't see what the woke folks can. One problem with this particular branding of others as "less than" because they are not (as) woke is that those who wield the brand never mention that there are numerous "awakenings" available to us as humans. These awakenings have been researched, identified, and studied longitudinally for decades, and any one of them can be reasonably easy to understand, but a bit tricky to recognize and embody unless you've experienced (awakened to) it.

While this book was being written, the current woke folks' particular awakening generally refers to the move from a *modern* to a *postmodern* worldview—or at least a move toward some of the perspectives that become available as this move unfolds. An example would be equal rights for all *in practice*—day in and day out, with no exceptions, which is an ongoing postmodern quest. Equal rights for all in practice would be the manifestation of the conceptual version that's written in the U. S. Constitution, its Amendments and other legislation, which together marked the beginning of a remarkable transition from a *traditional* to a *modern* worldview on the North American continent in the eighteenth century. This was a transition from monarchy to an attempt at democracy. Depending upon whose model you work with, as far as we know right now, there are anywhere from two to as many as six awakenings available *after* postmodernity, and some four or five available leading up to it.[7] In other words, those of us who wield our own wokeness today as a criticism of others are pretty much operating at a level that's in the middle of what's available, and we're not practicing skillful means. We know what we know; we're oblivious to what we don't know; and we consider those who are "other" as less than or wrong. Does this sound familiar? Again, what's important is *the manner in which the allegedly woke folks hold their beliefs or views— how they see* themselves and others, and *not* the specific content of the belief itself. If I believe in and try every day to embody and encourage true equality for all, why would I antagonize and treat as unequal those who do not yet so believe and embody?

Late Congressman John Lewis exemplified being awake and not wielding his wokeness as a weapon. After ongoing beatings at the hands of white law enforcement officers and other white boys and men and forty-plus trips to jail as a civil-rights activist (or, as he preferred, a Beloved-Community activist), he characterized his approach in Congress and in the Black Caucus as continuing "to go with my conscience, not my complexion."[8] In observing the increasing income, access, and opportunity disparities in American culture—across skin colors and ethnicities—he wrote, "We must reach out to each other *now*. We must realize that we are all in this together. Not as black or white. Not as rich or poor. Not even as Americans or 'non'-Americans. But as human beings."[9]

Late Associate Supreme Court Justice Ruth Bader Ginsberg likewise engaged equality, well, equally. Rightfully seen as a champion for women's rights among much else, she was a champion of equal protection of the laws, period. Preceding some of her more well-known litigation and her U. S. Court of Appeals and Supreme Court opinions and dissents, she prevailed, along with her husband, in the 1972 case of *Moritz v. Commissioner of Internal Revenue*, winning for Charles E. Moritz the right to claim a tax deduction as caregiver for his aged, dependent mother—a claim he was denied because he was neither a woman nor a previously married man, which the tax code at the time required.[10] Effectively, the Moritz case touched, if not turned, on the concept of *intersectionality* more than a decade before Kimberlé Crenshaw would name and advocate for it. No one called it leftist at the time.

Other woke folks predate Lewis and Ginsberg. Siddhartha Gautama famously woke around 500 BCE and, rather than weaponizing his wokeness, urged us not to take his word for anything and to wake up ourselves. The "Wide Awakes" were abolitionist supporters of Abraham Lincoln. Lead Belly reminded us of the importance of staying "woke" in order to stay alive in his commentary at the end of his "Scottsboro Boys" recording in the 1930s.

NONE OF THE ABOVE is to say that the content of belief doesn't matter. It does. But the developmental lens (one's level of wokeness or consciousness) through which we view the content impacts how we hold the content, and how we hold the content impacts what we do with and about it—our speech and our behavior. If I truly believe that my religion (or race, skin pigmentation, ethnicity, gender, orientation, identity, or political affiliation) is the one true or right one, and if I hold that belief—however provably accurate or inaccurate it might be after reflecting on and critically thinking about it—in a way that allows me to feel good about myself and others, do good in the world, and get along with those others, and if the last thing I would ever think of doing is to mock, bully, hurt or try to convert them in any way, the *content* of what I believe might be the same as the enslavers, lynchers, betrayers, abusers, censors, and bigots, but my view of and how I hold that content and those others is filtered through a more evolved, open lens. That lens allows me to see that they have a right to their beliefs as I do mine—and I understand and accept that they believe theirs is true and right. It does, however, become more difficult to hold the belief that "my _____ is the one, true, right one," as in the above example, amid the later, more inclusive, and comprehensive ways of seeing: I'm *right* and my *beliefs are true* expand into I *prefer,* or I *choose to believe,* or (gulp) I *really don't know,* when faced with as yet unproven contrary possibilities. Developmental view is a powerful component in our lives, regardless of the "content" it is viewing, and whether or not the viewer has ever heard of, believes in, or understands it. A little like gravity.

Each authentic, successive, evolving worldview is more comprehensive, inclusive, balanced, and complex than that through which it evolves. If we're willing to agree that monarchy is an earlier and less evolved system than democracy, we can see that monarchy is more partial, exclusive, imbalanced, and simple (the King or Queen decides, so do what the King or Queen says or face the consequences). Democracy is more comprehensive (it is able to hold a bigger picture beyond the royal family's perspectives and biases). It is more inclusive (it includes the voice of the people, however imperfectly). It is more balanced (as a result of the bigger picture and the people's diverse voices). And it is more complex (a bigger picture and more voices lead to more complexity). Harry and Meghan, the Duke and Duchess of Sussex, decided to step away from the British Royal Family. Their at once private and very public decision was responded to through a cacophonous mix of traditional, modern, and postmodern worldviews and opinions from around the world and resulted in both praise and bullying from many angles and many people who felt that a choice made by a married couple who love each other was somehow everybody's business.[11] Yes, that's both accurate and oversimplified. The point is that development and worldview matter and that bullying continues, albeit in different manifestations, through traditional (do what the monarchy says or else), modern (we have freedom, power, and wealth, and you don't, so know your place), and postmodern (we're more woke, so we're gonna shut you up and shut you down) perspectives. "Canceling" is the common parlance for shutting someone up or down.

At the heart of the work that each of us and all of us have to do if we truly care about each other, this country, and the world is to recognize our own biases, fears, and generalizations as we work toward a more perfect union. We have to do this regardless of who holds office in any branch and at any level of government, and how slow or fast they are at addressing what I, we, you, or they believe is important. More specifically, as we work toward true equality for all, it is essential that we do not intentionally or unintentionally exclude, demonize, or mock other groups, especially if we believe they are in some way, large or small, responsible for the lack of equality, access, and opportunity we're striving to erase. And yes, we are called to do this work even in light of perfectly legitimate and accurate questions like *Why is this so difficult? Why does it take so long? Why is this even an issue after so much suffering and bloodshed?* Et cetera.

Speak up, listen, oppose, rebut, point out the flaws in the argument or in the point of view, and engage in loud, messy debate and conversation when possible, but if you cannot or choose not to be around dissenting opinions and perspectives that you don't like, and you want them banned, then perhaps start your own totalitarian state somewhere. Speech protected by the U. S. Constitution's First Amendment matters most when we disagree. Excluding other voices or canceling people in the move toward true equality perpetuates inequality. And, yes, this is complex. Deliberately threatening, hateful speech directed at an individual or group is not protected speech. Who gets to decide what is threatening or hateful speech, how they decide, and what consequences emerge from their decisions are inherent questions within the complexity of democracy. Dictators and ruling monarchs can simplify this. All those in favor? Opposed?

Our twenty-first-century manifestation of allegedly woke folks who choose to cancel others they perceive as not being woke enough, is most commonly perpetrated by a subset of "progressives" who (believe they) are working toward equality for all. In Chapter Five we noted that John McWhorter ordained this subset as a "religion" he calls the "Elect," and that Christopher Rufo chose them to be "the perfect villain" for his critical race theory "toxic brand category." Neither members of the progressive subset nor their critics seem to show any interest in the role of development or of skillful means in their respective arguments. Both groups are silent regarding the impact of healthy and unhealthy iterations of feminine and masculine traits. They seem unaware of their own projections.

Twenty-first-century political branding aside, this work toward equality is centuries old. Wielding the language of wokeness as a weapon, canceling the voices of those perceived as not woke (enough), and then canceling the woke cancelers themselves is newer, but not new. While it was written way back in the twentieth century before the popularity of woke and cancel culture language, Nat Hentoff's book, *Free Speech for Me—but Not for Thee: How the American Left and Right Relentlessly Censor Each Other,* lives up to its title and subtitle. Here's one from among many examples:

> So a woman who considered herself a feminist but failed the pro-abortion test was banished from a place called the Yale Women's Center. As I was banished from certain centers of Jewish dialogue because I publicly criticized Israel. As Charles Mingus was told he was not black enough to play the blues. The place for free expression, as for the homeless, is in somebody else's neighborhood.[12]

The problem that some of us who claim to want equality for all have created is that, in our genuine (or alleged) *desire* for such equality, we speak and act in contradictory ways that make it clear that these so-called unwoke, sleepier-than-we-are folks are *not* equal—yet another example of employing unskillful means to attain what is, by any measure, good. Allegedly woke words and actions that claim to support a belief in and desire for equality for all, and that then implicitly or explicitly judge those perceived as not woke as unequal are contradictions. Oops.

Those who point to this behavior, mock it, and use *woke* and *cancel culture* allegations as rallying cries against what they perceive to be their progressive or liberal or leftist opponents, practice their own self-contradiction. Canceling, even before it was labeled as such, manifests in many guises and sizes in American history and current events. For instance, despite not operating in the time and place of our current, specific woke and cancel language, the white landowner-planter-politicians believed they were more woke than the black human beings they kidnapped, bought, sold, and enslaved and the native peoples they removed and/or killed. Each of these atrocities was an attempt to quite literally cancel a group perceived as being less woke. Without in any way minimizing the significant damage done to individuals and families through public shaming and canceling in the twenty-first-century, there were earlier—and by any measure more extreme—manifestations of canceling. Recall that in demanding the removal of native peoples from east of the Mississippi in the 1830s, Andrew Jackson spoke of having done "my duty to my red children," and then leaving "the poor deluded creeks & Cherokees to their fate, and their annihilation."[13] Woke indeed.

The American architects of the attacks in Vietnam, Afghanistan, and Iraq operated from the perspective of being more democratically and capitalistically woke than the leaders and people of those countries, and they were willing to cancel millions of lives to prove it. Recall that many in America tried to cancel Representative Barbara Lee after her "no" vote on September 14, 2001. Remember the 2004 Bush campaign and the Vietnam veterans who joined them to effectively Swift-boat-cancel John Kerry's military service, his Silver Star, his Bronze Star, his Purple Hearts and his presidential candidacy. The Republican party, with various degrees of effectiveness, continues to attempt to cancel its own congressional members who voted in favor of impeaching and then convicting their outgoing president due to his role in inciting the January 6 rioters' attempt to prevent the ratification of the election that denied him a second term.[14]

Allegedly woke attempts to silence, and in rare cases, to physically assault those who (the silencers think) hold sleepy views has been a disturbing extracurricular activity on many higher education campuses since 2013 or so and elsewhere for even longer. In most of the on-campus cases, students who espouse views of equality, often protest, confront, and attempt to silence and shame faculty, administrators, visitors, and other students who, they feel, have somehow slighted them or with whom they disagree.[15] They exercise their right to free speech and assembly in order to deny free speech and assembly to others, in the name of equality for all. Again. Oops. Claiming to be more woke than others and attempting to cancel them, whether explicitly or implicitly, have been and continue to be bipartisan practices throughout the partially woke and partially sleepy history of the polarized states of America.

THE CAUSES AND CONSEQUENCES OF our mutual bullying are complex and much debated. At what point does passionate disagreement become bullying behavior? Consistent with our explorations of some of the subtleties of healthy and unhealthy manifestations of developmental worldviews and feminine and masculine traits in the context of collective Shadow, we'll consider some healthy and unhealthy manifestations of disagreement.

Research (and many of our everyday experiences) points to a preference for our own group, an *in-group bias*, even among healthy individuals in healthy cultures,[16] and among many of our other-than-human mammalian pals. Research also shows that this in-group bias or preference is just that, a preference. It's not necessarily a permanent condition, and can be transcended and included (that is, we can move beyond it and still retain its benefits) such that our in-group preference can expand to include new members who used to be outsiders. This is another way to speak about the developmental moves that allow us to identify with only *me* (I'm the group), then *us* (we're the group), then *all of us* (we're all the group), then *all that is* (it's all one group).

Variations on this theme abound. One, attributed to evolutionary organizational values consultant Richard Barrett, is "There is only self-interest. What changes is the definition of the self."[17] Another is that anytime someone draws a circle to create a boundary against outsiders, simply draw a bigger circle that includes their boundary. These ideas represent the good news, so to speak. The bad news, as presented in *Survival of the Friendliest* by Brian Hare and Vanessa Woods, is that, in its unhealthy manifestations, in-group bias allows us to tolerate or participate in unfair or harmful treatment toward those we perceive to be outsiders, and in its unhealthiest manifestation, in-group bias can descend into dehumanization of others—tolerating and engaging in genocide, slavery, lynching, and other acts of extreme and ultimate cancelation.

Prospects for dehumanization increase when a group feels threatened, whether or not they actually are, and potential empathy or identity with outsiders is diminished in order to protect members of the ingroup. The outsiders, "feeling threatened in turn, dehumanize the first group, creating a feedback loop of reciprocal dehumanization,"[18] or, as Kendi puts it in a racial context, "Anti-White racist ideas are usually a reflexive reaction to White racism. Anti-White racism is indeed the hate that hate produced…"[19]

This, in turn, invites another dose of good news: *contact*—preferably close, personal, and ongoing. Hundreds of testimonials from among the thousands of people who helped Jews hide and escape during the Holocaust revealed "just one common denominator [that differentiated them from those who had not helped]: They'd all had close relationships with Jewish neighbors, friends or co-workers before the war."[20] As Hare and Woods point out:

> Contact has been demonstrated to increase tolerance toward ethnic groups such as Chinese students, black workers in South Africa, Turkish schoolchildren in Germany, and Southeast Asian immigrants in Australia…. We could not find any evidence of where contact has systematically or repeatedly failed to improve social relationships between groups.[21]

Consider this idea of contact in the context of one example of America's partisan, polarized, political bullying. (Caveat: since both sides engage, it's a unique, mutual bullying that nonetheless draws distinct in-group and out-group lines). A 2018 study demonstrated how little Republicans and Democrats knew about *the members of their own parties* and the extreme partisan views they had of each other. Several examples from the study: 2% of Republicans make more than $250k annually, but Democrats believed that 44% did. About 6% of Democrats are gay, lesbian, or bisexual, but Republicans thought it was 38%. About 20% of Republicans are seniors but Democrats thought it was just over 40%. About 24% of Democrats are black, and about 11% of Democrats belong to unions; Republicans believed those numbers were 46% and 44%.[22]

While the reasons for these disparities are too abundant to explore here, much of the motivation for our intra-American adult bullying is grounded in ignorance. Ignorance can be diminished—sometimes even eliminated—through contact, and contact, especially close, personal, ongoing contact with those with whom we disagree or who (we think) are not "like us" is exceedingly rare in our time of siloed, partisan news sources and social media algorithms that feed us what we have made clear we already believe or want. Online contact, as opposed to close, personal, ongoing contact with our perceived opponents has been shown to *increase* partisanship and deepen bias.[23] Development—which determines how we orient around *me, us, all of us,* or *all that is* perspectives needs to be, and rarely is, a part of this conversation—and it needs to be skillfully engaged.

Let's begin to bring this home with an example that is discomfiting for some of us to engage. Above we pointed to manifestations of wokeness that exclude and demonize specific elements of society—manifestations that are ironic because they're usually perpetrated by those of us who claim to embrace equal rights for *everyone.* More to the point, many lower-middle-income whites felt (and sometimes actually were) blamed, demonized, and excluded by movements toward equality for others—movements that were and are necessary, ongoing, and painstakingly slow. Using Isabel Wilkerson's language in *Caste,* these would be the folks who find themselves among the lower rungs of the dominant caste—white, but without much or any other privilege or access to power.

When the subordinate caste members' success exceeds that of the folks on lower rungs of the dominant caste—such as it did in 1921 in Tulsa's Greenwood District—the impact can be devastating. From the lower rungs of the dominant caste, the view of the subordinate caste's success often breeds a sense of resentment, unfairness, and threat, *especially,* and I would argue *only,* if that view manifests through an unhealthy *me-* or *us*-centric developmental lens. The view through an authentic, fully embodied *all of us*-centric lens celebrates others' success, and any sense of resentment, unfairness, and threat is directed at the constructs of caste (or class or race) themselves and not at someone else's success.

So those lower-rung, dominant-caste whites who were looking through a me- or us-centric lens heard themselves referred to as "privileged" while they watched their jobs disappear as the folks on the upper rungs of their own caste automated those jobs or sent them overseas, and they worried about losing their homes or not being able to afford food, medicine, or rent. They loved and worried about their kids. Did their skin pigmentation and, in many ways nominal, caste membership afford them a certain privilege that folks in America's subordinate castes did not have? Absolutely. Did anything about their actual existence feel privileged in an America marked by increasing income disparities? Absolutely not. Were some of them sabotaged, as we all are at times, by their cultural givens? Yes. But their *experience* was that they were being ignored, and often implicitly and even explicitly blamed and called racist—when what they were doing was working hard and trying to take care of their families.

In *How to Be an Antiracist,* Ibram Kendi writes that "[t]o be antiracist is never to conflate racist people with White people...." That statement, I believe, applies to the dynamic explored in the previous paragraph. Are any of the folks on the lower rungs of the dominant caste racist? Statistically speaking, undoubtedly. But it is their racism, not their lower-rung whiteness that renders them so. Kendi also writes that "Donald Trump's economic policies are geared toward enriching White male power—but at the expense of most of his White male followers, along with the rest of us."[24] Herein lies the irony of lower income whites' support for the forty-fifth president. He did nothing for them except appeal to their desire to have someone in power—preferably someone who seemed strong and was not considered a Washington insider—recognize their plight. His deception was masterful, but he was just another wealthy white guy who was looking out for himself. Indeed, very few folks on any rung in any caste were or are being served by the behaviors of Donald Trump and the party he infiltrated.[25]

Yes, feeling ignored and being blamed as a low-income, hardworking white person in twenty-first-century America is uncomfortable and unfair; feeling ignored and being blamed as a low-income black person is uncomfortable and unfair and has been going on for a long time—through a history of enslavement, lynching and Jim Crow. Some people, albeit not enough, who feel ignored and/or blamed, across race, skin pigmentation, and ethnicity, get together, honor respective histories, compare notes, work together, and understand that minimizing or mocking someone else's suffering is rarely a useful practice. It is unskillful. It does no good. The initial response to any assertion that someone else's suffering is not so bad has to be, "According to whom?"

Speaking, reading, or writing about caste, privilege, race, gender, identity—*difference*—in America understandably invites discomfort for many of us regardless of our developmental perspective. Still, our reception of and our responses to such speech and writing will be demonstrably different depending on whether we're receiving and responding from a healthy or unhealthy manifestation of a *me-, us-, all of us-,* or *all that is-centric* worldview. Development matters.

MANY OF US WHO HAVE qualified, at least chronologically, to be considered adult citizens of the United States do not behave as good or even adequate role models for our children. Our prospects for growing into wise or even moderately competent elders are bleak. This inadequacy and this bleakness are often exacerbated by cleverness, facility with language, and above average disregard for evidence-based truth, or even its close cousin, truthfulness which, as used here, refers to the authentic, informed honesty of someone who recognizes and owns past mistakes. When the alleged adults in the room, whether we're twenty-one or eighty-one, regularly resort to name-calling, distortion, sweeping generalizations, outright lies, manipulation, and various forms of bullying in order to win this or that finite game, we limit ourselves. And we limit the size of the arena for those who come after us. *Just because you're winning doesn't mean you're doing things right.*[26] That applies across and beyond the political spectrum.

In Chapter Three we noted briefly the U.S. Supreme Court's May 24, 2022 decision to overturn *Roe v. Wade* and allow state governments to regulate what women may and may not do with their bodies—essentially protecting life before birth. Hours earlier, on May 23, 2022, that same court struck down a New York State law that limited the carrying of guns outside the home, ruling that the law was too restrictive. The Court effectively took stands to protect pre-birth life and to further endanger post-birth life. In both cases, the six justices who concurred with these decisions ignored the sixty-plus percent of Americans who want to protect a woman's right to choose and who want more effective gun safety legislation.

These six justices have lifetime appointments and, chronologically, are adults. Just because they won doesn't mean they're right. The rhetoric and sloganeering on both sides of the abortion debate are not helpful. Regardless of your stance on the issue, consider and live with these questions for a while: If I believe human life begins at conception and I believe that women (and men) have the right to sovereignty over and stewardship of their own bodies, how can I best honor and hold these apparently contradictory beliefs? How might I live with the tension of this paradox and honor others who are living with it as well?

CHAPTER TEN

The Gift: One Guy's Shadow as an Unconscious Invitation to a Nation to Heal

To what extent does what you initiate oppose what others do, and to what extent does it encourage them to initiate on their own?[1]

AS MENTIONED IN THE OPENING PAGES of the Introduction, this exploration of our collective American Shadow began as a brief essay I wrote in September 2016. It made the case that the Republican candidate for the presidency, all by himself, embodied those Shadow aspects of our culture that we deny—ignorance, arrogance, fear, bigotry, violence, greed, excess, bullying, and untrustworthiness.

As this book's direction emerged and evolved thereafter, his role and his embodiment of these traits diminished in importance except for two dynamics: a gift and a threat. The gift manifests because, even when he himself doesn't actually believe what he says, he has invited, allowed, and encouraged those who share or admire the views he espouses to stand up and speak up—and they have. He has convinced millions of people, about whom he has proven he cares not a whit, to chant his name, do what he asks, and to spend money on his behalf. This is his unwitting and unconscious legacy and gift to the United States. Effectively he has said, *look at me; look at what I can get away with and look at all these people who are willing to help me get away with it while helping to pay my way.* His unintended gift is an invitation to engage in the work of healing our American narratives through an invaluable, complex, and still-unfolding process that includes owning and integrating these Shadow elements. It's up to us to unwrap this gift, continue to unfold the process, and own and integrate our projections. We'll address this unwrapping, unfolding, owning, and integrating in the next two chapters.

Intricately entwined with the gift is the threat. Almost 63 million Americans saw fit to elect him president in 2016. Below we'll sample tiny portions of the ignorance, lies, and general incompetence he demonstrated during the forty-five months he tweeted before being voted out. Yet, even in his loss to Joe Biden, more Americans—slightly more than 74 million—voted for him in 2020 than in 2016. He lost because more than 81 million Americans voted for Biden. That almost 12 million more Americans voted for him in 2020 than in 2016 is a symptom of the threat. The threat itself arises from a complex set of variables. Not everyone who voted for him did so for the same reasons.

Those of us who look beyond ourselves (and our trusted circle) for confirmation of what we read, hear, or observe need look for no further evidence of the 45th president's unfitness for the office he held. The evidence that follows is conclusive.

While both the gift and the threat may surprise many, the giver has been dropping hints for years. As Jonathan Rauch points out in *The Constitution of Knowledge,* in a 2004 NBC News interview with host Chris Matthews, the future president expressed his admiration for the Bush campaign's aforementioned and effective 'Swiftboat' attacks against decorated Vietnam veteran Senator John Kerry, calling the strategy "maybe the best spin I've ever seen," and "brilliant." When Matthews asked him what he thought about Vice President Dick Cheney's insinuation that voting for Kerry would be voting for another attack on America, the celebrity heir interviewee responded, "Well, it's a terrible statement unless he gets away with it."[2]

These two comments intimate the lessons learned from his mentor, if not Muse, Roy Cohn, the disbarred, convicted, and discredited attorney who was Senator Joseph McCarthy's chief counsel. Cohn's rules of engagement, as summarized by attorney James Zirin, a lifelong Republican, include *counterattacking and undermining your adversary if you're charged with anything; working the press; lying, and repeating the lie over and over;* and *settling the case and claiming victory.*[3] Complementing these rules is what Glenn Kessler, Salvador Rizzo, and Meg Kelly of the *Washington Post* refer to as "[a] hallmark of authoritarian regimes...to call truth into question—except as the regime defines it." They note that Russia's president Vladimir Putin's approach includes "denying obvious facts," "spouting falsehoods," and "deflecting attention with nonsensical comparisons"—tactics that Trump used and uses regularly. No wonder the American was smitten with the Russian. In July 2019, when Trump was asked for military aid by Ukrainian President Volodymyr Zelensky—whom Putin held as an enemy—Trump attempted to extort him.[4] We'll never *know* the extent to which Trump's admiration for Putin influenced his treatment of Zelensky. Nevertheless, faced with a young president who was leading his country toward the European Union and away from Putin's Russia, the American president asked for information that might discredit a political opponent in exchange for the aid requested. He tried to use the power of his office for his personal political gain.

If nothing else, the 45th president's early denial of and persistently minimal and minimizing response to the global COVID-19 pandemic, despite evidence provided by American and international scientists, and his anticipation of and response to his 2020 loss to Joe Biden are sufficient proof that, beyond their usefulness for promoting his brand, he has not cared for a moment about this country or its people—including his most ardent supporters, and including those he incited to attack the Capitol on January 6, 2021. He told them he loved them, he told them they were special, and he claimed that he and they believe in law and order, as they were vandalizing the building, threatening members of Congress, and attacking law enforcement officers. We will return to the pandemic, the election, and the attack on the Capitol below.

On July 7, 2021 this former White House occupant announced that he was suing Facebook, Twitter, and Google because he felt they had violated his First Amendment rights when they suspended his accounts. Shortly thereafter, his son appealed through their Save America PAC for donations to support the costs of the suits. Trump pays his team of attorneys to argue for his victimhood at the hands of the social media bullies, and to argue for his innocence in the death, injury, and property damage that resulted from the riot he incited.

Lawsuits are a way of life for Donald Trump—as both plaintiff and defendant. As a candidate in 2016 he had already been involved in 3,500 lawsuits—a number that has subsequently increased. His spokespeople claim that that's just business as usual for similarly sized companies, but *USA Today* reported in 2016 that contrasted with billionaires Ed DeBartolo, Donald Bren, Stephen Ross, Sam Zell, and Larry Silverstein, 45 was "involved in more legal skirmishes than all five of the others—combined."[5] He intends to retain that honor: in September 2021 the former president's lawyers filed a suit against his niece and the *New York Times* in response to the paper's 2018 report about fraud and his tax records.[6]

Or consider this: journalist Tony Schwartz ghostwrote Trump's *The Art of the Deal,* received half the $500,000 advance and half of the book's subsequent royalties.[7] Schwartz credited the book's success with allowing him to "earn more in a few weeks than I had in the whole of my working life, giving me a financial cushion that few people are ever lucky enough to enjoy." Happily married with two young children, and with the bestseller behind him, Schwartz wondered, "Why, then, wasn't I happier?"[8] To help himself answer that question, he spent five years traveling America, spending time and speaking with the likes of Ram Dass, Michael Murphy, Elmer and Alyce Green, Betty Edwards, John Sarno, Larry LeShan, Meyer Friedman, David Spiegel, Herbert Benson, Jon Kabat-Zinn, Dean Ornish, Joseph Goldstein, Jack Kornfield, Roger Walsh, Ken Wilber, Helen Palmer and Hameed Ali, among others.

So, spending the better part of two years shadowing the man who, despite losing the popular vote, would become the 45th President of the United States, and writing a book entitled *The Art of the Deal* and being paid handsomely for it convinced Tony Schwartz to spend five years interviewing a diverse array of leading researchers, scholars, teachers, writers and practitioners in science, the arts, psychology, spirituality, and consciousness itself. Based on those conversations and his own direct experience, Schwartz next wrote *What Really Matters: Searching for Wisdom in America,* which was published in 1995. A financially rewarding two years with a self-proclaimed deal artist led Tony Schwartz to search for wisdom and for what really matters in America through conversations with a wide array of leaders who were exploring the cutting edge of our human experience. Draw your own conclusions.

IN THE CONTEXT OF THE previous chapters' explorations of our collective American Shadow, we'll now explore this unintended gift that 45 offers to the United States. In his personal and public embodiment of ignorance, arrogance, fear, excess, bigotry, violence, greed, bullying, and untrustworthiness, he invites those among us who endorse these traits and those who eschew them to step up and be counted. He has made it okay to wear these traits as public badges of honor. Stated differently, through who and how he is, he has unwittingly invited to the surface the "worse angels of our nature"—the "evil out there"—that Americans do not own in themselves. The examples cited below provide a relentless, and in many ways astounding, testimony of this embodiment. Don't take my word for it. Investigate each one yourself.

Of course, that this one guy embodies the collective Shadow of the United States in no way lets the rest of us off the hook. Rather, it more firmly fastens us on the hook. His relentless sharing of these traits with us is a gift we need to unwrap together. Each of us individually and all of us collectively must find this or that shadow element within ourselves, own it, and integrate it—one discomfiting projection at a time. Whether we choose to continue to ignore our Shadow or to do the work of owning and integrating it, some suffering will be involved. The former choice continues our suffering through sustained ignorance and denial; the latter offers us the opportunity to suffer through our own growth—coming to terms with things as they are and developing toward wholeness. We'll explore these two types of suffering in Chapter Eleven.

As explored in Chapter Nine, bullies can hold a variety of views and beliefs, and they can't be trusted, except, perhaps, to continue bullying. Consciously or unconsciously, this guy is committed to the rules of Putin and Cohn. He is willing to say anything in the moment if he thinks it serves him. He is committed to repeating it over and over again, even if it's provably false. And he is ready to contradict what he has just said, or to deny having said it, or to accuse a perceived enemy of having said it.

If, as the cliché goes, everything looks like a nail when your only tool is a hammer, it can be argued that the 45th president has two hammers—a self-aggrandizing hammer and a money hammer (or perhaps just the illusion of a money hammer), so all the nails he sees are either about him, about money, or both.

While he demands loyalty from others, his own loyalty is only to himself, and betrayal of others is common currency in his means of exchange. At times, when he does find himself and one of his lies in the unavoidable crosshairs of truth, he pretends not to know anything about the lie (re-tweeting and refusing to speak against the "Q-Anon" conspiracies), or he claims he was joking (Barack Obama was the founder of ISIS). As Kessler, Rizzo, and Kelly, the fact checkers at the *Washington Post* have demonstrated, there are literally thousands of examples of these types of behavior from him—any one of which would be annoying if it came, let's say, from our ornery neighbor. When these lies or "jokes" come from the President of the United States (or any titular leader whose office carries power), our reactions may range from annoyance through incredulity, shame, and embarrassment, but the consequences may be real danger and violence. Here are a few examples to get us started, several of which we'll look at in more detail as the chapter unfolds:

- He claimed that we were going to build a wall and that Mexico would pay for it.
- He claimed that Barack Obama was the founder of ISIS and that Hillary Clinton was the co-founder. He later claimed that he was just joking. View the video to listen to and watch him. Was it a funny moment? Any evidence of a joke there?
- He claimed he was going to *repeal Obamacare in his first 100 days in office and replace it with something better, terrific and great. You'll see.* He repeated various iterations of this claim incessantly. As of Joe Biden's January 20, 2021 inauguration, Donald Trump did not get it done. He did claim to have discovered how complicated healthcare is (which we'll explore below).

- He claimed, "I've done more for black people than anyone else." He has said this in various iterations—at times limiting the claim to just presidents other than Lincoln; at other times, it seems, to anyone who has ever lived anywhere.
- He claimed, "I know more about ISIS than the generals do."
- He asserted that "[John McCain] was not a hero..."
- He effectively disappeared amid the devastating rise in COVID-19 cases and deaths in the U.S. in the weeks immediately following his loss to Joe Biden.
- He took credit for the Veterans Choice Act, which President Obama signed in 2014, by conflating it with the 2018 Mission Act, which updated the broader 2014 legislation.
- On January 6, 2021 he repeatedly incited his supporters to march to the Capitol and "stop the steal." They obeyed him, vandalized the building and the grounds, killed and injured Capitol Police and other officers, and threatened to hang and otherwise execute the vice president of the United States. He went inside, watched television, and ignored for hours his staff's pleas to tell his rioters to stop following his orders. Only when the damage was done did he tell them they were special and to go home in peace.

Compare this pattern of outright lies and intentional manipulation with the history of the United States government's breaking virtually every treaty entered into with American Indians. Compare it with the promises of equal protection of the laws for blacks (and others), which, despite the aforementioned proclamations, amendments, laws, and court decisions in 1862, 1863, 1865, 1870, 1920, 1954, 1964 and 1965, to name a few, have not been fulfilled in the day-to-day lives of many Americans. Compare Trump's falsehoods and glib utterances (if you disagree with him, you're a *loser* or you are *failing* or *fake,* which is about as substantive as he gets) to our government's attempts to hide what was really happening in Vietnam, Afghanistan, and Iraq, as we explored in earlier chapters. He embodies falsehoods and betrayals as a daily practice.

Beginning when he was the Republican candidate for president in 2016 and continuing through his loss to Joe Biden in 2020 and his ongoing refusal to accept that loss, this guy has chosen, whether consciously or not, to become a lightning rod for the fear, bullying, bigotry, misogyny, violence, intolerance, and xenophobia of the collective American Shadow.[9] He invites and allows Americans who do in fact hold racist, sexist, violent, and generally bigoted beliefs to find a champion in him—or at least in his rhetoric. He invites other Americans who do not hold such beliefs to react in horror—sometimes surprised horror, and sometimes not—at his language, his promises, and his apparent willingness to say anything—even when it is clear that he does not know what he's talking about or he *does* know and he's lying in order to manipulate voters. Or some combination of these, or something else entirely.

As the Republican candidate and president, he personified the bully that the United States or any insecure, fearful, and powerful individual or entity can be—albeit, especially in his case, often without the ability to back up his rhetoric with strong action that is grounded in authentic, inherent authority as opposed to the external, apparent, or titular authority that comes with a job or title. Again, bullies tend to bully due to fear of their own inadequacy, weakness, and incompetence— their sense of not being "enough"—and they tend to whine when someone stronger, more adequate, or more competent shows up and does what has to be done to stop their bullying. He bullied during his party's primary debates; during the 2016 presidential campaign; as the president of the United States; in his attempt to win a second term; and in his lies after he lost. He initiates daily insults directed toward his opponents, critics, and anyone with whom he disagrees, including the free press. He then claims he is being treated unfairly when someone criticizes him or simply points out what he's doing. He claims the role of victim amid his rambling, often inarticulate, fragmented, bullying insults and assaults.

As president, within one ten-day period, he publicly ridiculed and taunted[10] a woman who had accused a Supreme Court nominee of sexual assault. He proclaimed at the United Nations General Assembly that "In less than two years, my administration has accomplished more than almost any administration in the history of our country" (and was laughed at by world leaders).[11] And his claims of being a self-made billionaire were refuted by ongoing investigations that reveal he has received the equivalent of 413 million dollars from his father's real estate empire, that he has about that same amount of debt coming due, that he paid no income taxes in ten of the previous fifteen years, and that he paid just $750.00 in federal income tax in 2019. These investigations were motivated at least in part by his choosing to be the first presidential nominee and U. S. President to refuse to reveal his income tax reports.[12]

IN THE MONTHS DURING WHICH he began his run to become the Republican candidate, in the months during which he was the Republican nominee, in his four years in the White House, and in the months following his loss to Joe Biden, the already divided and dysfunctional U. S. Congress became increasingly divided and uncivil. The tenor of public discourse—within the government, in the media, and among private citizens—became increasingly insulting, intolerant, aggressive, and territorial, and was encouraged by a president who used Twitter daily to attack people—until he was banned for making ongoing, demonstrably false statements.[13] He executed his role in such a way that some members of his White House staff literally removed documents from his desk so he would not be able to sign them—an act seen by some as ethically heroic and by others as a betrayal. He discredited and withdrew from the Paris Agreement despite consensus among scientists and leaders from around the world that climate change and humanity's role in it are real and require increasingly more immediate action.[14] Perhaps the greatest evidence of his ignorance, his self-serving manipulation, and his lack of qualification as a leader can be found in the Republican party itself—in the roster of people who have left his administration,[15] and in the words and actions of past leaders in the party, many of whom organized against Trump, for Biden, or both.[16]

One of 45's most revealing public statements addressed his understanding of healthcare and healthcare reform. After relentlessly attacking the 2010 Patient Protection and Affordable Care Act (ACA) and promising to dismantle it if he became president, he pronounced, on February 27, 2017, "Now, I have to tell you, it's an unbelievably complex subject. Nobody knew healthcare could be so complicated."[17] He said this out loud in 2017 as the President of the United States. He may actually have been the only individual who did not know healthcare is a complicated issue—a remarkable ignorance in light of his relentless attacks on the ACA, which helped provide access to affordable healthcare for some 20 million of the 45- to 50-million Americans who did not previously have such access.

In light of this small sampling of specifics, perhaps his most chilling success is his ability to make statements on the record, then accuse his opponents of saying what he is saying or has just said, and *then* convince his supporters that his accusations are accurate. This is the very essence of the "projection" aspect of Shadow.[18] Of course and again, having followers who are willing to be complicit in perpetuating the projection is necessary, and the United States has no shortage of adults who, while following the leader—and not just this particular leader—are happy to take him at his word and ignore any evidence that suggests that truth, like healthcare, might be complicated—even downright complex. It *is* possible and necessary to support Black Lives Matter *and* also support law enforcement—and evidence suggests that most Americans do. It *is* possible to embrace the sanctity of *all* life and *also* to embrace every woman's right to choose what she does with her own body. The ability to hold paradox, as mentioned earlier, is an essential skill for twenty-first-century adults.

IN LATE OCTOBER 2018 ONE of the president's avowed supporters, Cesar Sayoc, Jr., was arrested and charged with sending pipe bombs, none of which detonated, to at least twelve prominent Democrats whom Trump had insulted and/or lied about during the previous decade. The bomber's intended targets included former President Obama and former Vice President Biden.[19] The 45th president was unable or unwilling to recognize and own that any of his rhetoric might encourage his more extreme, less stable followers to act on his words—a festering shortcoming that would lead to the January 6, 2021 attack on the Capitol. That most Republican members of the Senate and the House, as 2022 draws to a close, remain equally unwilling or unable to publicly and unequivocally disavow their former president's speech and behavior presents more disturbing evidence of their putting party before country. This bias is not limited to Republicans; both parties project that the "evil" is "out there" somewhere—and not within. In the case of Donald Trump, many Republicans in the House, Senate, and various state houses held fast to this chief executive's lies and disinformation in the weeks following his being voted out of office, as they explicitly supported or remained silent during his claims that the election was fraudulent. And all the while, the COVID-19 pandemic consistently set daily records for new cases and deaths in the U. S. in November and December 2020.

Another heartbreaking moment of 45's persistent lack of self-awareness was his response to a mass shooting on October 27, 2018, at the Tree of Life Synagogue in Pittsburgh, Pennsylvania. "It's a terrible, terrible thing," he said, "what's going on with hate in our country, frankly, and all over the world. And something has to be done."[20] And then he did nothing, just as he had done in response to each mass shooting during his presidency. Is he completely oblivious to the implicit and explicit hate that he espouses, or does he say these things knowingly in deliberate attempts to manipulate? The hatred and intolerance are somewhere *out there*, frankly, all over the world. He is just an observer and a victim. It has nothing to do with him. Projection indeed.

REMARKABLY, HE EVEN GETS AWAY with combining his lack of respect for women with his xenophobia. In a country that has seen powerful men toppled across diverse industries and ethnicities due to their ongoing sexual harassment and/or assault of women and, in some cases, of other men, Donald J. Trump, before becoming the president of the United States, is on record bragging about his history of grabbing women sexually. He attributes his ability to do this to his being a star.[21]

In response to both his candidacy and his early days in the White House, many women—mostly Democrats and some Republicans—who had not previously aspired to political office or who had not planned to run in 2018, challenged incumbents in the House of Representatives. After the largest voter turnout for a midterm election since 1914, the Democrats gained 41 seats in the House. On July 14, 2019, the sitting president of the United States said that four of these winning congresswomen—Ayanna Pressley of Massachusetts, Rashida Tlaib of Michigan, Alexandria Ocasio-Cortez of New York, and Ilhan Omar of Minnesota—should "go back and help fix the totally broken and crime infested places from which they came." As reported in the *Washington Post,* the president's several-tweet message proclaimed:

> So interesting to see 'Progressive' Democrat Congresswomen, who originally came from countries whose governments are a complete and total catastrophe, the worst, most corrupt and inept anywhere in the world (if they even have a functioning government at all), now loudly and viciously telling the people of the United States, the greatest and most powerful Nation on earth, how our government is to be run.[22]

The lies herein would be problematic coming from anyone—at the dinner table, in the local tavern, in a classroom, or in a boardroom. That the lies come from a sitting president of the United States, and that it was just another day and another tweet—that it was not surprising—should worry every decent U. S. citizen, regardless of political affiliation.

As with the previously mentioned and widely known complexity of the healthcare system, it is common, easily obtained knowledge that Pressley was born in Cincinnati, Tlaib was born in Detroit, and Ocasio-Cortez was born in New York—not far from where the guy who tweeted this nonsense was born. Omar was born in Mogadishu, Somalia; her family fled the country amid civil war when she was a child, and she became a U. S. citizen as a teenager. Did 45 know these facts and deliberately appeal to the racist, sexist, xenophobic views of some of his supporters by practicing his Roy Cohn lessons? Was he simply ignorant of the truth? Or is there another explanation? Any rationale is a cause for concern.

Beyond his disparagement of these four women, the president's language in these statements provides another unmistakable example of projection. In referring to "countries whose governments are a complete and total catastrophe, the worst, most corrupt anywhere in the world," he captured how the leaders of many countries and many American citizens refer to the U. S. government under his administration—especially, but not only, with regard to his navigation of the COVID-19 pandemic, climate change, and NATO.

Staying with the theme of projection, consider this excerpt from an August 4, 2020, interview that Trump had with Axios's Jonathan Swan, following the July 17, 2020 death of U. S. Representative John Lewis: "When asked if he found Lewis's life impressive, Trump responded, 'He didn't come to my inauguration. He didn't come to my State of the Union speeches. And that's OK. That's his right. And, again, nobody has done more for Black Americans than I have.'"[23] That last sentence, again, is one that 45 has repeated in various iterations. Sometimes he claims that *no president* has done more, and sometimes, as above, he makes a more universal claim that *no one* has done more. I'll leave it to the reader to investigate whether any U. S. president or any other human being has done more for blacks than Donald Trump has.

More to the point of Shadow and projection in this president's refusal, or inability, to honor the late Congressman are the Shadow traits that he embodies. He demonstrated ignorance (of who John Lewis was and is in American history). He displayed arrogance (just to think, much less say out loud in public, that "no one has done more..."). He manifests fear (inevitably, of his own life's inadequacy). He lives through greed and excess (as the fragile son of a millionaire, contrasted, for example, with Lewis's life of abundance and generosity as the durable son of sharecroppers). He is untrustworthy (as he persistently demonstrates a lack of interest in and/or the inability to understand the depth and nuance of any given situation beyond how it impacts him personally). Whether such Shadow embodiment emerges from an underdeveloped cognitive capacity,[24] an underdeveloped moral capacity, or both, it would be a handicap for anyone—and it is a grave, dangerous flaw for someone elected to the Oval Office.[25]

During his pursuit of the presidency, perhaps oblivious to any of this country's history, Donald Trump seemed to think it was a good idea to refer to one of the few African Americans who attended his rallies as "my African American." Who else would think, in the twenty-first-century United States, it's a good idea for a born-into-privilege (or any) white man to refer to any black man—or any other human—as "my _____?" The use of *my* father, mother, brother, sister, friend, or co-worker, intimates an authentic, reciprocal relationship. My African American (or my Italian American, my Dominican American, my Vietnamese American) intimates something else entirely in the context in which the candidate made the remark. Ignorance? Arrogance? Pick one, or both.

The individual in this case, Gregory Cheadle, at first seemed to accept the reference good naturedly, but after two years of the Trump presidency he left the Republican party and ran as an independent for Congress in 2020 in California's First Congressional District. He didn't win. A look at Mr. Cheadle's platform indicates a generally conservative view on most policy, and that he left the Republican party, as he states, because he sees it as pursuing a "pro-white" agenda.[26]

WE'LL RETURN NOW FOR A closer look at the 45th president's response to the COVID-19 pandemic, his 7-million-plus-popular-vote loss to Joe Biden in 2020, and the January 6, 2021 Capitol riot that he incited in an attempt to overturn the election. In each of these cases, his adherence to Roy Cohn's teachings would have made his dead mentor proud.

On January 22, 2017, less than 48 hours after his inauguration, Trump began to set the stage for his general dismissal of science, which, three years later, would inform his initial denial of and subsequent failed early response to the COVID-19 pandemic. On that 2017 date, he ordered the removal of the President's Council of Advisors on Science and Technology (PCAST) website, along with the links to all of its reports, from the White House website. PCAST had been founded in 1990 by George H. W. Bush and had received heightened attention during the eight years of the Obama administration. Trump then left the directorship of the Office of Science and Technology Policy (OSTP), which administered PCAST, vacant for two years and reduced its staff by two thirds. This action effectively left PCAST inoperative until November 2019, when he re-staffed it and limited its charge to advising him on how America could win in the global industrial future. While this charge did not include written reports, minutes of meetings were kept. According to Jason Karlawish, M. D., "The minutes of the [PCAST] meeting on February 3 and 4, 2020, include no discussion of the COVID-19 pandemic."[27]

Based on the Obama administration's engagement with science and their involvement with both the swine flu in 2009 and the 2014 Ebola outbreak in West Africa, President Obama appointed Ron Klain, who later became President Biden's chief of staff, as coordinator of the White House Ebola response. As a result of that experience, Klain warned in 2016 that the next president may very likely face a "catastrophe of historic proportions," and that amid risks like climate change, terrorism, and nuclear weapons, "the single *most likely* cause of such a nightmare scenario...is an oft-overlooked one: pandemic illness." Klain continued, advising that a "future epidemic could be transmitted by airborne means," "break out in a nation with a global megacity," or "in a center of commercial power that sends thousands of travelers around the world each day." He went on to recommend six measures the next president should take to continue and enhance America's readiness—well worth a ten-minute read.[28]

Consistent with the January 2017 removal of the PCAST site from the White House website, in May 2018 the administration disbanded the "pandemic response team"—part of the National Security Council's Directorate for Global Health Security and Biodefense. With the arrival of COVID-19 in 2020, partisans characterized that disbanding in predictably partisan ways.[29] As we'll demonstrate below, the 45th administration's response to the pandemic was consistently confusing, distrustful of science, slow to respond, and grounded at least in part in the president's fear that he would look bad if a lot of people got sick and his anger at the unfairness that something like this could happen during *his* presidency.

As we saw in chapters six and seven, not looking bad, not being embarrassed, and not being humiliated are strong enough motivators to encourage human beings to go to war or to prolong war even when they oppose it or know they cannot win. Despite having shared with Bob Woodward on February 7, 2020 that he knew the coronavirus was airborne and that it could be five times more lethal than the flu, Trump continued publicly to make believe it was no big deal.[30] On January 22 he had said, "We have it totally under control. It's one person coming in from China, and we have it under control. It's— going to be just fine." He added, "We do have a plan and we think it's going to be handled very well. We've already handled it very well…We're in very good shape and I think China's in very good shape also."[31] One week later, on January 30, 2020, the World Health Organization (WHO) declared a global health emergency, but the president's baseless nonsense and magic thinking continued. On February 10, he said, "A lot of people think that goes away in April with the heat."[32]

On February 25, 2020, Nancy Messonnier, the director of the CDC's National Center for Immunization and Respiratory Diseases, announced that coronavirus spread in the U. S. was inevitable and that "It's not a question of if but rather a question of when and how many people in this country will have severe illness."[33] The very next day, 45 said, "When you have 15 people and the 15 people within a couple of days is gonna be down to close to zero. That's a pretty good job we've done."[34] Two days later, at a rally in South Carolina, he accused the Democrats of "politicizing the coronavirus," insisting that they "have no clue, no clue," and that "this is their new hoax."[35]

The denials and delusional utterings continued: On March 20, 2020, when coronavirus cases nationwide were just over 40,000, and total deaths were 536, up, respectively, from 7,081 and 221 on March 13—*just one week earlier*, he floated the unproven and eventually debunked idea that hydroxychloroquine, a malaria drug, might work against the coronavirus, and when asked by NBC's Peter Alexander during an official coronavirus briefing at the White House what he would say to Americans who are scared, he responded, "I say that you're a terrible reporter. That's what I say. I think it's a very nasty question."[36] He then accused Alexander and others of sensationalizing.

As the cases and deaths in the U. S. continued to climb, he eventually admitted it was worse than the flu, even as he minimized and made statements that he could not back up. According to the CDC, one month later, on April 20, 2020 there were 799,011 reported cases in the U. S., 26,024 new cases that day alone, with a 7-day average of 27,577. There were also 44,539 total reported deaths, 2,060 new deaths that day, and a 7-day average of 2,271 deaths per day.[37]

Over the course of the 79 days between the November 3, 2020 election and Joe Biden's inauguration on January 20, 2021, inclusive, 14,926,674 new cases of coronavirus were reported in the U. S. and 185,408 Americans died. On January 6, 2021 while the president was inciting thousands of his followers to storm the Capitol—he and many of his minions maskless—259,471 new cases were reported and 3,873 Americans died. On January 20, Trump's final partial day in office 3,866 American citizens would die from COVID-19.

COVID-19 Data from the Centers for Disease Control (CDC)
The CDC adjusts data as new information is validated. Chart last updated on June 2, 2022.

	Cumulative Cases	New Cases on this date	7-day Average Daily Cases	Cumulative Deaths	New Daily Deaths	7-day Average Deaths
Apr. 20, '20	799,011	26,024	27,577	44,539	2,060	2,271
Oct. 20, '20	8,380,394	59,145	59,386	226,414	805	756
Nov. 3, '20	9,593,333	98,904	89,831	238,884	1,037	933
Jan. 6, '21	21,472,897	259,471	224,022	378,140	3,873	2,956
Jan. 20, '21	24,520,007	188,321	193,064	424,292	3,866	3,167
Nov. 3, '20-Jan. 20, '21	14,926,674	n/a	n/a	185,408	n/a	n/a

This son of a New York real estate developer is responsible neither for the global pandemic nor for the million-plus Americans who have died and the millions more whose lives have been changed by COVID-19. He is responsible for not taking the threat seriously at the outset, for misleading and lying to hundreds of millions of Americans—especially the tens of millions who took him at his nonsensical words—and for effectively disappearing as the chief executive in the two-plus months of his lame-duck period, except to complain over and over and over again that the election was stolen (another bit of nonsense that we'll get to below). With an average of more than 188,000 new cases and more than 2,300 new deaths reported each day between his election loss and his refusal to attend his successor's inauguration, he chose to be invisible as a leader and a man. Many in the Republican party continue to support him and grovel for his approval.

We'll never know how much suffering and how many deaths might have been prevented had he trusted the scientists, learned from other countries, took the threat seriously in early January or February, not publicly dismissed it as a "Democratic hoax," and modelled and endorsed wearing a mask.

Remembering Rabbi Gellman's perspective, one person died 424,292 times while Donald Trump was using the president's podium, his Twitter account, and phone to make up and share publicly a series of magical thoughts about how and when the pandemic would simply go away. Again:

> March 31, 2020: "It's going to go away hopefully at the end of the month, and if not, it hopefully will be soon after that."

> May 8, 2020: "I feel about vaccines like I feel about tests. This is gonna go away without a vaccine."

> June 15, 2020: "You know at some point this stuff goes away. And it's going away."

> July 19, 2020: "I will be right eventually. I said it's going to disappear. I'll say it again. It's going to disappear and I'll be right."[38]

He shares responsibility for any deaths that could have been prevented with strong, clear, accurate leadership. Had he prepared for the pandemic and led the country as the virus spread with the same relentless focus and conviction with which he prepared his election fraud lies before the election and hammered them home after his loss, the odds are good that fewer of the Americans who trusted him would have died. The Venn diagram of the 45th president's ignorance, arrogance, bullying, and fear and COVID-19's relentless spread depicts a deadly intersection.

THIS REPUBLICAN INCUMBENT LOST TO his Democratic challenger in the United States of America's 2020 presidential election by 7,060,347 popular and 74 electoral votes. After all the votes were counted, after two recounts in Georgia, and after no lawsuits Trump filed changed anything (some dismissed as groundless), Joe Biden is still the winner. Biden won

306 electoral votes and 81,284,666 popular votes; the loser collected 232 electoral votes and 74,224,319 popular votes—a popular vote loss of 4.5%. Despite losing the popular vote to Hillary Clinton four years earlier by 2,868,519 votes, he won the electoral vote, 306-232—exactly the same difference by which he lost to Biden. Said differently, if the Americans elected their president by popular vote, this guy would never have resided at 1600 Pennsylvania Avenue.

According to the BBC, he began his campaign of future-telling and lying about the election's outcome as early as April 14, 2020 with this presidential tweet: "GET RID OF BALLOT HARVESTING, IT IS RAMPANT WITH FRAUD. THE USA MUST HAVE VOTER I.D., THE ONLY WAY TO GET AN HONEST COUNT!" They report his mentioning rigged elections or voter fraud at least seventy more times between this tweet and the election.[39] On August 17, in Oshkosh, Wisconsin, he proclaimed the oft-repeated lie that "The only way we're going to lose this election is if the election is rigged."[40]

Lying about election winners and results that he does not like was not new for him. On November 7, 2012, he called Barack Obama's reelection "a total sham and a travesty," claiming that "the electoral college is a disaster for a democracy" and that "[w]e should march on Washington and stop this travesty." In the 2016 Iowa caucuses he claimed that Ted Cruz "stole it," and in October, a few weeks before the election that he eventually won *because of* the electoral college, he claimed first that "The election is absolutely being rigged by the dishonest and distorted media pushing Crooked Hillary - but also at many polling places - SAD," and then, even after Clinton conceded, he insisted that "In addition to winning the Electoral College in a landslide, I won the popular vote if you deduct the millions of people who voted illegally."[41] Roy Cohn would be proud—work the press, lie, and repeat, repeat, repeat the lie incessantly. The electoral college is good if he likes the result and a travesty if he doesn't. Unhealthy. Me-centric.

After his successful attempt to convince tens of millions of his supporters that the only way he could lose in 2020 was if the election were stolen, he launched an exponentially more chilling and dishonest post-election-loss campaign in the media and courts to avoid being seen as the loser he is. He lost that campaign too. In a remarkable litany of public lies, even by his standards, between November 4, 2020, and the January 6, 2021 attack on the Capitol, he methodically reiterated variations of his lie. Here's a sample: "We won the election by a lot," "[We]won every one of the states." "I got more votes than anyone in history." "[W]e will stop the steal." "[T]he Democrats cheat in elections." "[T]his election was rigged." He claimed that the election was "a total fraud," with "gigantic and one-sided vote dumps." He said, "we have a company that's very suspect. Its name is Dominion," and "these [Dominion] machines are controlling our country." "[W]e amassed overwhelming evidence about a fake election," he lied, and asserted that his supporters should "make no mistake this election was stolen from you, from me and from the country."[42]

He lost every legal suit he filed except one. On November 12, 2020, the "Joint Statement from Elections Infrastructure Government Coordinating Council & The Election Infrastructure Sector Coordinating Executive Committees" began with this sentence: "The November 3rd election was the most secure in American history." In response to the joint statement, on November 17, the 45th president fired Christopher Krebs, the director of the Cybersecurity & Infrastructure Security Agency.[43] On November 19, Trump's team was still spreading conspiracy theories about how the election had been stolen by Democrats, specifically regarding Communist money from Venezuela, Cuba, and China to help Joe Biden win. Whether his personal lawyer, Rudy Giuliani, or his campaign's attorney, Sidney Powell, actually believed what they said out loud is not clear, but there's still only a downside whether they did believe their claims or they knew they were spreading lies. When Powell's lies went too far—quite a feat within this group—45's team disowned her.[44]

Trump's longstanding facility with lies and his apparent unfamiliarity with truth, when combined with those media organizations that repeat and don't challenge the lies and those tens of millions of Americans who are willing to believe what he and the performance news commenters say, lead to a perfect storm of intentionally manipulative leaders and influencers with powerful platforms, complemented by millions of willfully blind, vincibly ignorant, or intentionally collaborative followers who embody what Justice Souter referred to in 2012 as our "pervasive civic ignorance." Said differently, guys like Trump are impotent alone and need other people to believe in and act on their lies. Unhealthy. Masculine. Me-centric. Arrogant. Untrustworthy. Individual.

ON A DAY DURING WHICH just under 260,000 new cases of COVID-19 and more than 3,800 new deaths due to the virus would be reported—a day on which the U. S. Congress traditionally formalizes the presidential election results—the outgoing president held a rally for his supporters, thousands of whom came to Washington, D. C. on this day at his beckoning. He incited them to march to the Capitol in order to "stop the steal." Many of them came in military and riot gear, armed with a variety of weapons; most of them chanted his name and variations on "stop the steal." They vandalized the building, stole furnishings, attacked the police, and threatened to harm the Speaker of the House and hang the Vice President. Trump encouraged and wanted to join these people, but the Secret Service prevented him from accompanying them. His speech ended at 1:11 pm, his followers marched to the Capitol, and he went inside the White House, ignored his staff and watched on television what he had incited.

As the attack unfolded, various advisors, members of Congress, and his daughter encouraged him to talk the rioters down. At 1:49 pm he tweeted a video of his rally as the Capitol Police requested help from the National Guard. At 2:24 pm, after rioters had begun chants to hang Mike Pence, 45 encouraged them, tweeting about Pence's lack of courage and how the election had been stolen. Additional presidential tweets followed at 2:38 and 3:13 pm, encouraging support for law enforcement and for the rioters to "remain peaceful." At 4:17 pm, he reiterated the stolen election lie and told the rioters to go home. At 6:01 he tweeted a connection between the riots and the stolen election, telling his rioters to "go home with love & in peace" and to "Remember this day forever!"[45]

As 2021 rolled into 2022 he continued to repeat the election fraud claims despite every secretary of state and election official in the nation—Republican and Democrat—certifying his loss and refuting any claims of election tampering. As 2022 rolls into 2023, many Republicans in Congress have not explicitly and publicly acknowledged Trump's 2020 election loss.

Historian Kathleen Belew notes that those who marched on and attacked the Capitol on January 6, 2021 represented a cross section of "different currents in right-wing politics" that included disgruntled supporters of the president who believed and were motivated by his lies about the stolen election and who were there to demonstrate. In addition, there were the Q-Anon conspiracy activists. There was also a complex mix of white-power groups that "brought with it generations of mobilization and strategy honing and cell-style terrorism and paramilitary camps and serious military-grade weapons and materiel," with origins in the post-Vietnam War era and tendencies toward overthrowing the federal government.[46] Much as the 45th president used the gullibility of some of his most fervent supporters, these more organized groups used him to forward their agendas—to stand up and stand by, so to speak. A deeper dive into the history of these groups is beyond the scope of this book, except to note that they did not go away when Trump lost. They remain part of the American fabric.

As 2022 fades into 2023, COVID-19 variant cases dwindle, and rise and dwindle and rise, and Americans scream at each other about science and the "tyranny" of wearing masks. Climate disasters and gun violence persist, and the U. S. government remains dysfunctional and partisan. Many Americans are increasingly angry and scared for a variety of reasons—the world we thought we knew is changing around us, and while most of us see ourselves as good people within the limitations of our respective worldviews, and are generally tolerant[47] of others who appear or believe differently, we don't recognize that our latent prejudices and cultural givens are alive and well.

Consistent with Kathleen Belew's distinctions above, some of the former president's supporters are outspoken bigots—including past leaders of the Ku Klux Klan and current leaders in a variety of hate groups who value a predominantly, if not exclusively, white, male, and "Christian"[48] world. Whether the loser of the 2020 election does, in fact, embrace white supremacy, or if he merely uses its language deliberately to pander to a segment of his supporters, is a big deal, but it is of less concern than the clear evidence that white supremacists see and hear in Donald Trump a chance to resurrect Edward Alfred Pollard's "lost cause" of the Confederacy—that white supremacy was both the underlying cause of the Civil War and the "true hope of the South"[49]

AGAIN, PEOPLE WHO KNOW US, and especially people who know us well, can see our Shadow and projections much more easily than we can. If I lie a lot, or if I lose often, and I am constantly pointing to others' lies and losses while denying my own, those who see me clearly will see the projection and perhaps attempt to bring it to my attention. If I'm not willing to do the work of recognizing, owning, and integrating my lies and losses, I'll simply continue to deny and project them. If I am willing, and I do the work, I will have a better chance of growing into an increasingly integrated or whole way of being in the world— I will become more fully human.

Donald Trump lost the U. S. 2020 presidential election, and he continues to exemplify this Shadow cycle of denial and projection. Through his unconscious example, he unwittingly invites us to examine our own individual and collective Shadows. If a nation averages 103 gunshot deaths a day, 63 of which are suicides, and has an additional 62 daily suicides by other means;[50] and if that same country is the only one ever to have used atomic weapons on another nation; and if it has its history in Vietnam, Afghanistan, and Iraq as noted earlier; and if its leaders refer to other countries as an "axis of evil" or an "evil empire," and proclaim to the world that "you're either with us or you're with the enemy,"[51] and if this nation has been referred to, by one of its assassinated heroes, as "…the greatest purveyor of violence in the world today…"[52] and elects a president whose slogans have been to "Make America Great Again" without being able to answer when it was great or for whom, and to "Keep America Great" even amid a pandemic and our daily domestic violent deaths, and yet continues to perpetrate and perpetuate the illusion that all the "evil" is "out there," it's safe to say there's some projection going on.

And, it's essential to remember, as noted at the beginning of this volume, that this same country can lay claim to an abundance of many equally important 'good' acts and traits as well —including its mobilization during two twentieth-century World Wars; including its investment of countless billions of dollars for domestic and international humanitarian aid when and where it's been needed; including the Centers for Disease Control and Prevention that was relied on domestically and internationally for its reliable leadership until 2016 when Donald Trump interfered with its operations; and including, despite all of its flaws, being a country that still attracts the foundational element of its existence—immigrants who want the opportunity to improve their lives. Remarkably, despite the selective anti-immigration rhetoric of the 45th president, citizens of other countries still want to come here—a credit, perhaps, to the goodness and possibility at the heart of our collective experiment and in the respective hearts of a significant majority of United States citizens, across political parties and perspectives. *And* our collective Shadow, the underbelly, is still there and must be recognized, owned, integrated and healed—an ongoing endeavor for every generation.

Again (and again), this chapter focuses on the opportunity to embrace Donald Trump's public life as the embodiment of our collective American Shadow. It in no way denies that there has been and still is significant "evil out there" that needs to be addressed or that, in the United States, there has been and still is significant "good in here," of which we can and should be proud. America has done and still does both great harm and great good. Both are true. The denial of either provides a limited, incomplete view that is dangerous and serves only to perpetuate partial truths toward some selective, limited agenda and end. As Aleksandr Solzhenitsyn wrote:

> If only it were all so simple! If only there were evil people somewhere insidiously committing evil deeds, and it were necessary only to separate them from the rest of us and destroy them. But the line dividing good and evil cuts through the heart of every human being. And who is willing to destroy a piece of his own heart?[53]

Each of us individually and all of us collectively must have the will and do the work that is necessary to be able to move beyond our convenient partial truths and our outright falsehoods, to seek other perspectives, and to hold the inevitable paradoxes that will surely emerge.

The 45th president's words and behaviors leading up to, during, and after his time in the White House allow us to see and reflect upon uncomfortable aspects of our national culture and to choose the direction we would like to take as Americans. The evil "in here" was here long before this celebrity real estate heir entered the White House, and it remains after his graceless departure. He did not create it; *it* made *him* possible, and he has invited the worse, perhaps worst, demons of our nature to surface for all to see, hear and feel. His varied fear-based, fear-inciting, self-serving, manipulative, and divisive messages are, in the words of psychiatrist and author, M. Scott Peck, grounded in a "militant ignorance." Peck wrote that "The briefest definition of evil I know is militant ignorance. But evil is not general ignorance; more specifically it is militant ignorance of the Shadow."[54] Options abound for us, including the oft-cited final words that Abraham Lincoln spoke in his first inaugural address, inviting us to be touched "by the better angels of our nature."[55]

WE'LL BRING THIS CHAPTER TO a close with the images of two men, each leading a march, some fifty-five years apart. On June 1, 2020 the 45th President of the United States walked from the White House to St. John's Episcopal Church with members of his family, his staff and others (the Chairman of the Joint Chiefs would later apologize for participating). Holding a Bible aloft, he posed in front of the church for the photographers who had been apprised in advance of his presidential walk. While he didn't pray, or enter the church, or mention George Floyd, who had been murdered a week earlier, Donald Trump preceded his walk by expressing his desire to shoot or crack the skulls of those Americans who were protesting Floyd's death.[56] His advisors explained that shooting demonstrators was not an option, but before the president and his entourage walked from the safety of the White House, various law enforcement agencies had received orders to rid the area of the demonstrators. With an array of batons, shields, tear gas, and rubber bullets, the officers cleared the area for the photo op.[57]

On March 7, 1965 future U. S. Congressman John Lewis, who had just turned twenty-five, was already a veteran of the many marches, demonstrations, beatings, and arrests that resulted from his commitment to equal rights. Along with his friend, Hosea Williams, Lewis led some 600 marchers, including "teenagers, teachers, undertakers, beauticians" from Brown's Chapel in Selma, Alabama toward the Edmund Pettus Bridge, with their final destination, Montgomery, some fifty-four miles away.[58] The marchers were sure they would be harassed and arrested—they did not expect to get all the way to Montgomery—and yet they marched, two abreast, in virtual silence from the chapel and over the bridge, where they were met, gassed, whipped, and beaten by the Alabama state police and their deputized "possemen," who were cheered on by the gathered spectators with "Get 'em! *Get* the niggers!"[59] Among various items in Lewis's backpack that day were two books—Thomas Merton's *The Seven Storey Mountain,* and Richard Hofstader's *The American Political Tradition,* both of which Lewis had read and neither of which he ever held over his head for a photo op.

Trump wanted to shoot and crack the skulls of those who demonstrated for equal rights; Lewis demonstrated for equal rights and had his skull cracked. Which of these men would you choose as a role model? Which of them would you want your children to aspire to be like?

PART III

PROSPECTS & POSSIBILITIES FOR HEALING

CHAPTER ELEVEN

So, Now What?

*How would it feel to play a game in which everyone is
invited and the purpose is to keep the game going?*[1]

FIRST, REMEMBER (OR NOTICE FOR the first time) that you have
a body. Notice that you are breathing, and keep your attention
there for a minute or so. Intentionally observe the inbreath
that fills your lungs, the pause, and the outbreath. Pretty cool.
You are actually *being* breathed. You don't choose or have to
control the process, although you can play with—hold, quick-
en, or slow—it. Before you have too much fun with this, also
notice your posture. Attune your attention to the alignment of
muscles, bones, joints, and connective tissue from head to toe,
including everything in between. Do this even if injury or
illness impacts how you are able to hold yourself.

Breath and posture: always with us, useful, important, and
influenceable.

THE PREVIOUS EIGHT CHAPTERS TOOK us on an illustrative journey through selected American narratives that disclose our
collective Shadow—the themes, episodes, moments, traits,
and general aspects of our stories that we don't recognize or
own and often project onto others. These are things that we
unknowingly practice and have practiced. This book's title and

subtitle invite us to engage the process of changing our practices and healing these narratives by owning and integrating our denials and projections. As used here, *healing* does not mean curing or fixing (which have their respective places), but coming to terms with things as they are, with an awareness of how they have been, in order to feel, think, speak, and behave in ways that are increasingly inclusive, integrated, and balanced. Coming to terms with things as they are means recognizing and accepting that things are as they are—acknowledging what's literally true in the moment—where acceptance does not necessarily mean agreeing with, being happy about, condoning, encouraging, or endorsing how things are.

When I found my sister, Anne Marie, some six hours after she had died alone in her home, my healing began with coming to terms with—recognizing and accepting—the truth of her death in that moment. When my friend and colleague, Jill, was diagnosed with incurable but treatable stage III multiple myeloma, she embraced the illness wholeheartedly, accepting what was true while engaging an array of treatments and befriending other "chemo-sabies" with whom she shared her strength. She died nine years after the diagnosis. She was not cured, but she lived as a poster-woman for healing.

In healing—coming to terms with—America's narratives, owning and integrating requires the intentional practice of truth, beauty, goodness, justice, mercy, wisdom, compassion, courage, discipline, humility, and love, among some more tangible strategies and tactics. Owning and integrating our traumatic or uncomfortable narratives is not intended to bring us to a place of *oh, no, we are a nation of ignorant, arrogant, fearful, bigoted, violent, greedy, excessive, untrustworthy bullies,* but rather to a still necessarily discomfiting but more skillful place of *oh, yes,* we *have* manifested, and *continue* to manifest ignorance, arrogance, fear, bigotry, violence, greed, excess, untrustworthiness, and bullying, *along with* deep knowing, humility, love, openness, peace, generosity, moderation, trust-worthiness, and courage in our behaviors toward each other and the rest of the world. It is from this place of paradox and integrity—of *both of these are true*—that we can develop and begin to embody our potential to be integrated, fully human beings, at work, at home, on the street, and in the best and the worst of times.

What follows explores specific approaches to working with Shadow and offers a variety of other perspectives and practices that are designed to deepen and broaden self- and other-awareness and further commit us to truth. Our intention is to consider, imagine, wonder, and wander toward and through ways of looking at, being and interacting with, sharing, and structuring our world that transcend and include our cultural givens and what we have thus far constructed for ourselves. Beginning with that pesky reminder about breath and posture, we'll journey together along paths that can help heal our collective narratives and the traumas that arise from and contribute to them. Skillful means, development, applying skillful means *to* development, intentional practice, and commitment to the broadest, deepest view possible will accompany us along the way.

We'll begin with four questions and two statements that encourage individual exploration and can be engaged as intentional practice. As the chapter progresses, we'll move into an exploration of our collective narratives. We'll consider a fifth question (the final bullet below) in Chapter Twelve.

- Who am I, really?
- Everything is a story.[2]
- What's my impact & what impacts me?
- What am I not seeing?
- Who are my people?
- I am going to die.

- For Chapter Twelve: How am I in relationship with each of the above questions and statements—and the rest of my life?

WHO AM I, REALLY?

If you're sure you know and are ready to dismiss the question, what follows may be a waste of your time—or exactly what you need. We humans have been exploring this question for as long as humans have been exploring. We've generally figured out how bones, muscles, various organs, tissues, and other cool items systemically cooperate in order for us to breathe, circulate, move, eat, digest, excrete, procreate, see, hear, feel, touch, and smell, among other functions. Amid the amazing progress we've made toward understanding the brain, folks who study that organ remind us that much remains unknown. The relationships among the brain, the heart, the gut, and (gulp) consciousness itself are still frontiers to be explored.

Here are five prospective responses to the question. They are not necessarily mutually exclusive. Add your own. Don't limit yourself to these:

1) I am a mystery that I explore more deeply every day.
2) I am a mix of elements that's worth four or five bucks.
3) I am the result of the exploits of God, Adam, Eve, and that horrible snake.
4) I am a ___-year-old, ____-generation ________-American ___________ [← your occupation] from _________.
5) I am a child of the stars.
6) Add your own here: ____________________________.

The identity story I choose, or that chooses me, provides a unique view of myself and the world and a wildly different sense of possibilities for my life. Each human being, named or unnamed, in every chapter of this book and in the history of humanity had a sense, clear or vague, conscious or unconscious, of who they (thought they) were.

We'll engage this question through distinct, interrelated perspectives—Body-Mind (or middleworld), Soul (or underworld), and Spirit (or upperworld)—and we'll clarify how these terms are used. The language of middleworld, underworld, and upperworld comes from ancient models of the cosmos.

Body-Mind, or middleworld, as used here, refers to the day-to-day lives most of us live. We do, think, and feel, and we recognize, to various degrees, the connections among doing, thinking, and feeling. Our thoughts and feelings impact our bodies and vice versa. The relations among diet, exercise, thinking, and feeling—from the impact of breath to the brain's neuroplasticity to the body's natural chemicals—are used in performance-related elite athletic and special forces trainings, as well as in recovery-related treatments for depression and trauma. In terms of our *who-am-I* inquiry, the Body-Mind perspective encourages us to assess our skills, strengths, likes, dislikes, and aspirations and eventually identify with a job, social role, or occupation. We are educators, doctors, plumbers, attorneys, nurses, stay-at-home-parents, executives, truck drivers, and landscapers. From a Body-Mind perspective, any one of those jobs can be a valid response to that pesky question famously asked by Mary Oliver, "…what is it that you plan to do / with your one wild and precious life?"

Turning now toward Soul, we learn from eco-depth psychologist, Bill Plotkin, that our "soulwork…does not correspond to a job title." Howard Thurman directs us to find "what makes you come alive." Frederick Buechner refers to "the place where your deep gladness and the world's deep hunger meet." Harvey Swift Deer speaks of "sacred dance," and William Blake wrote of being "organized by Divine Providence for Spiritual communion."[3]

This diverse language and these various takes on a similar theme begin to move us beyond job descriptions and earning an income (each of which has its place). Plotkin and Swift Deer differentiate soulwork or sacred dance from *survival* work or *survival* dance, neither of which is in any way deprecatory; they simply refer to "our way of supporting ourselves physically and economically.... our first task when we leave our parents' or guardians' home."[4] Aptitude and career tests and other Body-Mind assessments can be useful for matching us with survival work we enjoy (or at least don't dislike too much), and rarely, if ever, address soulwork, sacred dance, deep gladness, spiritual communion, what brings us alive, or what poet David Whyte calls the "one life / you can call your own."[5]

In his exploration of the underworld, Plotkin works with Soul as an ecological, rather than a psychological or spiritual, entity, referring to it as one's "ultimate place," or one's "unique ecological niche" ("eco-niche").[6] Discovering one's *ultimate place* or *unique ecological niche* in the world feels very different from getting a really good job with good pay and benefits. We encounter Soul—our ultimate place or echo-niche—through "symbol and metaphor, image and dream, archetype and myth," which Plotkin calls our "mythopoetic identity," which is revealed to us—we don't choose it or figure it out. Our task is to find and create delivery systems that allow us to "offer our unique gift to the world."[7] These delivery systems change as we develop and are not who we are. They may manifest as survival work, soulwork, or both.

On my own continuing journey, I confused delivery systems with mythopoetic identity for years, strategically and rationally trying to combine teacher, basketball coach, college administrator, workshop developer and facilitator, writer, poet, teaching artist, and professional coach. I tried out variations on *teacher-poet-writer-coach* (each a delivery system), until I was literally given (long story) *man who finds the path with light,* a mythopoetic identity that I didn't recognize and own for months. It elucidated a recurring childhood dream, which my Body-Mind, of course, wanted to edit. I have pretty much left it alone. Each of the delivery systems—teaching, writing, and coaching—allowed or allows me to find paths with light, so to speak (which includes navigating much darkness) for myself and others.

From a Spirit or upperworld perspective, self-inquiry has been around at least from the beginning of the Advaita Vedanta tradition as a means of exploring this question. One iteration guides us through asking and returning to the question, "Who am I?" in a way that gradually eliminates who and what I am *not.* When I notice what arises in awareness (*externals* like clouds, sore muscles, job title, and cars, and *internals* like emotions, thoughts, concepts, and beliefs), I objectify and eliminate what I am not, as in "This cloud arises in my awareness, but I am not this cloud," "This thought arises in my awareness, but I am not this thought," "This pain arises…but I am not this pain." Eventually I may get curious about "in whose awareness does all of this arise?" Who is this observer/witness? Who am I, *really?* Of course, this observer, or witness, or awareness itself is just another thought or concept until and unless I directly experience it. Then all heaven can break loose, until I get distracted again.[8]

Each of these perspectives offers something of value. The center of gravity of our democratic, capitalist, American culture privileges the Body-Mind, replaces or dilutes Spirit with conventional, middleworld religious beliefs and requirements that usually protect us from any direct experience of Spirit, and generally ignores Soul—as Plotkin has developed it—or uses it in a variety of often disparate ways. For clarity, it helps to present these as three different perspectives—and they are different in a relative sense. In an absolute sense, many would argue that the universe, including Body-Mind and Soul, manifests as and through Spirit. One whole Shebang.

Ram Dass, in his teachings on change, aging, and death, shared a metaphor for *waking up* through these *who-am-I* perspectives or states of consciousness: imagine that we each have a built-in television receiver that picks up planes of consciousness. Most of our receivers are tuned to pick up just one or two of the available channels. We don't pick up more because middleworld culture doesn't teach us (or know) how to fully tune our receivers. Channel one is the physical channel, where we see traits such as tall, short, old, young, heavy, light, black, brown, and white. Channel two is the psychosocial channel, where we tune into thoughts, moods, emotions, neuroses, and social roles and identities, such as happy, sad, angry, fearful, firefighter, physician, mother, father, politician, and carpenter. Ram Dass observed that most of us are happy with these two channels (which, together, correspond with the Body-Mind/middleworld perspective).

If we learn to tune into channel three, we encounter the astral plane—where we "see people in their mythos rather than in their personality structures," we see archetypes (corresponding with the Soul/underworld perspective) rather than social identities. The move to channel four allows us to "go behind all those individual differences, and you ... see another soul just like you," that has the physical, psychosocial and archetypal packaging, beyond which is another soul, again, just like you. When we flip to channel five, Ram Dass observes, "it's looking at itself looking at itself—there's only one of it. It's awareness aware of itself."[9] Channels four and five point to the Spirit/upperworld perspective.

It's easy to identify with *me-* and *us-centric* views on channels one and two; channel three facilitates a move into an *all-of-us* identity, and the programs on channels four and five are variations on *all that is.* Channels three, four, and five do not negate the apparently separate shapes, sizes, feelings, and roles of channels one and two but rather subordinate them to the increasing unity of what's available on channels three, four, and five. The center of gravity of our current U. S. culture and society is tuned to channels one and two. Some individuals have access to three, four or five. What are you attuned to?

Which leads us to story.

EVERYTHING IS A STORY

Note your immediate response to this premise. Is it, 'What do you mean—please explain?' Is it, 'Bull...?' Is it, 'Du-uh, tell me something I don't already know?' Is it, 'Thank you for confirming what I was beginning to see?' Is it something else entirely? Whatever it is fine—it's your story about the suggestion that everything is a story. Consider that if your response was in the general area of *Bull...*

The cultural givens handed down by our parents and earliest communities and experiences are stories. As (or if) we grow up, wake up, clean up, and show up, some stories hold up and some don't. Sometimes the givens that don't hold up were false when we received them and sometimes they were true—as far as anyone knew at the time—but the larger, always evolving community of truth learned more and disproved them when new evidence was found.[10] Doctors no longer recommend smoking cigarettes as a way to relax. Earth is no longer considered the center of the universe.

The stories we choose to believe and tell, as well as the stories that choose us, are powerful. Being in the position to choose our stories and not be chosen by them carries power. Mary Catherine Bateson encourages us to exercise this power:

> ...think about the creative responsibility involved in the fact that there are different ways to tell your stories. It's not that one is true and another is not true. It's a matter of emphasis

and context…. The choice you make affects what you can do next.[11]

So, let's be thoughtful about the stories we choose to tell about who we (think we—and *they*) are. The choices we make and the stories we tell matter.

Consider the specific stories that informed *your* cultural givens. What holds up? What's the most recent revision you've made, or that was made for you, where revision actually means *re-vision*—to *see again?* Look at the sweeping revisions, many ongoing, in chapters three through seven, and the specific, personal revisions shared therein. As cited earlier, Robert McNamara's 're-visioned' view owned the extent to which he and the other architects of the Vietnam war *misjudged, underestimated, failed,* and *did not recognize* a long list of people and ideas. Andrew Bacevich, informing his critiques of U. S. political and military policies, chose to shed "habits of conformity acquired over decades." Susan Faludi "put aside [her] prefigured map" in order to better understand women's and men's struggles. Ibram Kendi recognized that he had "closed [him]self off to new ideas that did not *feel* good," and that he needed to open himself up to a new story that required giving up some views.

Such seeing again is never easy and always valuable when it moves the seer toward a more comprehensive, inclusive view. Malcolm X's life stands as an exemplar of re-visioning. Two of his major re-visions—becoming a Muslim and joining the Nation of Islam while in prison and then leaving the Nation of Islam while remaining a Muslim after his 1964 Hajj—follow the developmental trajectory from *me* to *us* to *all of us.* In each case he changed his name and publicly recognized and owned his seeing again.[12]

BASED ON HIS RESEARCH WITH HOLOCAUST and other trauma survivors, sociologist Aaron Antonovsky coined the term and concept, *salutogenesis* (origins of health), and oriented his work around it. An alternative to pathogenesis (origins of disease), which characterized the conventional approaches to physical and mental health at the time of Antonovsky's studies, salutogenesis explores "how some people, some of the time, suffer less than others [and] move toward health." Antonovsky found that those who fared better in highly stressful situations embodied a "sense of coherence" (SOC), which was characterized by a *sense of comprehensibility* (this makes sense—I understand it), a *sense of manageability* (I have internal and external resources to deal with this), and a *sense of meaningfulness* (this is worthy of my investment and engagement—I find meaning it it).[13] A sense of coherence invites us to heal, to come to terms with things as they are—to understand, manage and find meaning—again, without necessarily liking or agreeing with how things are.

How we tell our stories is as important as which stories we tell. Focus only on what's wrong and get a pathogenic or illness narrative. Open up to a sense of coherence—understanding, managing, and finding meaning in what happened *amid the larger context of life*—and get a salutogenic or healing narrative. Adults model both of these narratives for children: if the child who falls down the stairs and breaks an arm is confronted with parental overwhelm, blame, anger, and fear, an illness narrative emerges in which stairs are dangerous and the child is careless or clumsy; if the child is met with parental support, concern, acceptance, understanding, and love, a healing narrative emerges in which accidents can happen, stairs are useful and fine and best engaged with care, and the child is curious and open to experience.

Illness narratives limit us, narrowly focus on a sense of wrongness, keep us stuck, and can reinforce trauma; healing narratives open up the context in which we understand what happened (wrongness may be relevant, but not primary), they can expand and free us, and they can contribute to trauma recovery. Because they focus on what's wrong, illness narratives are often tidy, brief, stagnant, and consistent. Because they emerge through and invite increasingly larger contexts, healing narratives are often messy, ongoing, progressive, and paradoxical. Explore your narratives. Be kind to yourself.

Stephen Levine wrote in *A Year to Live* about the shift that occurs when we move from the story of *my* suffering to the story of *the* suffering: "When it's 'the' cancer instead of 'my' cancer I can relate to others with the same difficulty." We all suffer, albeit in different ways, at different times, and at different levels of intensity. "Seeing the universality of our shared condition offers a broader path of healing on which to continue."[14] Once again, the move toward *it's about all of us* lovingly beckons for our attention.

Writing can be engaged as a powerful process[15] that helps open us up to increasingly larger contexts that allow us to see and feel as others see and feel—to go beneath all the individual differences, see another soul just like ourselves, *and at the same time deeply understand and embody those differences.* Going one step further, learning to embody and tell or write *someone else's* story, both helps us understand the other and often provides clarity into our own narrative.[16] There are many approaches to writing a healing narrative. Philip Simmons's *Learning to Fall,* Toni Bernhard's *How to Be Sick,* Doug Anderson's *Keep Your Head Down,* and my own *And Now, Still* are among them.

Finally, if I'm truly playing an infinite game, some questions may arise at the intersection of "who am I, really?" and "everything is a story": *Without the stories I hold and that hold me, who am I, and what's true in this moment?* Who am I and what does this moment offer without my story/ies? Ram Dass's channels four and five point toward a prospective answer. John Tarrant, in *Bring Me the Rhinoceros,* put it this way:

Everyone knows that some events are just bad and make you sad or angry, and some are good and make you glad. Yet what everyone knows might not be true. For example there might be a certain coercion to the attitude that weddings must be happy, funerals have to be sad. It could prevent you from meeting the moment you are in. What if events don't have to be anything other than what they are?[17]

What's My Impact & What Impacts Me?

What's my impact—what's the nature of the wake I'm leaving as I swim, paddle, sail, steam, or internally combust my way along the river or across the ocean of life? To what extent does my wake impact other vessels, to what extent am I aware of this impact, and what conditions does my wake create for these others—or for the river or ocean itself?

What impacts me—what is the nature of the impact on me of other vessels, the wakes they leave, and the river or ocean itself? Less metaphorically, what beliefs, behaviors, habits, cultures, relationships, environments, systems, and people affect me; to what extent, large or small, do they affect me; and what, if anything, am I doing or can I do about it?

When considering these two questions, it helps to explore the broadest, deepest view available of *my current* beliefs, behaviors, relationships, and environments. Shining the light of awareness *on* my current awareness—witnessing myself as I am—is a significant practice. What interiors and exteriors impact who and how I am? Whether, when, where, and how I choose to shine this light of awareness emerges from the story I hold about who I think I am, and the worldview—focused on *me, us, all of us,* or *all that is*—that holds my story.

Shifting cultures at large continue to offer additional givens throughout our lives. The concrete manifestation of these earliest and ongoing givens are the literal infrastructures and systems—the natural and human-made environments—in which we live our lives, from the book or e-reader you're holding right now, to the physical space you're in, to the electricity or to the sun itself that lights that space. Cultural givens and environments co-arise, co-relate, and impact each other and each of us. Beliefs and values lead to things and systems, which in turn revise and create beliefs and values—which in turn lead to new things and systems.

Intentional fire, writing, the wheel, horticulture, agriculture, gunpowder, the printing press, steam power, trains, electricity, internal combustion, the automobile, paved roads, airplanes, the assembly line, the radio, television, space travel, atomic power, computers, robotics, the World Wide Web, smart phones, social media and many other technologies shaped and shape our environment, and, in turn, they shape us. Neal Postman proposed six questions, asked from the perspective of a "normal" person, that are worth exploring each time a new technology is being developed or emerges:

1. What is the problem to which this technology is a solution?
2. Whose problem is it?
3. Suppose we solve the problem and solve it decisively, what new problems might be created because we solved the old problem?
4. Which people and what institutions might be most seriously harmed by a technological solution?
5. What changes in language are being enforced by new technologies and what is being gained and lost by such changes?
6. What sort of people and institutions acquire special economical and political power because of technological change?[18]

In 1998 Postman applied these questions, with his usual curiosity and wit, to a variety of established and emerging technologies such as voice-activated devices, "the information superhighway" the supersonic transport (SST), automobiles, antibiotics, television, mechanical clocks, computers in schools, email "conversations," and "political debates." If we use the SST Concorde as an example, question one's problem was how long it took to fly from places like New York to Los Angeles or London. The Concorde's supersonic speed decreased the flight times. As for question two's inquiry into whose problem this was, the answer was some movie stars, rock stars, corporate executives, and other wealthy folks who were willing to pay a significant premium for a quicker flight. Never profitable, the Concorde's last commercial flight occurred in 2003. Postman, an educator and social critic—no technophobe—died in 2003 and never got to meet Siri, Cortana, and Alexa—or the iPhone, the Galaxy, Facebook, Twitter, Instagram and Tik Tok. I imagine he would have enjoyed applying his questions to each.

The views, values, resources, and talents of a few people create technologies. We vote with our wallets to allow these technologies to change the environments in which we live and how we live. These changes impact our values, subsequent technologies emerge, and we vote again with our dollars. Some technologies change the lives of many for the better; some make billions of dollars for a few; some do both. If we bother to ask Postman's questions—or any questions we choose—we might notice that it's increasingly easy for many of us to type, swipe, tap, hold, or speak our consumer votes (unlike how it is for some of us to cast our political votes). We need to clearly attune to the prospective impact of every type of vote we cast. No one does, or can do, this for us.

The importance of these types of questions occurs at the intersections of *everything is a story, technological impact,* and *who we think we are.* Here are some variations on a theme:

1. How does who you think you are impact what stories you are telling yourself about the impact of the technologies you

choose to use or must engage with every day?

2. How do the stories you tell yourself impact who you think you are and the technologies you choose to use or must engage with every day?

3. How do the technologies you choose to use or must engage with every day impact the stories you tell yourself about who you think you are?

The above is not an attempt at cleverness. Spend some time with these questions in the context of the content of chapters three through ten. Identity, story, and impact matter.

What Am I Not Seeing?

This question introduces our exploration of Shadow and invites the inquiring mind to ask something like, "If I'm not seeing something, how would I even know, and how could I do anything about it?" Genuinely asked, questions themselves open the doors to knowing. If I'm aware that *I hold certain beliefs and values* (or they hold me), that *others* (seem to) *hold different beliefs and values* (or be held by them), and that *culture and society are sending me mixed signals,* then it's important to explore individual views and behaviors, shared (cultural) views, and environments/systems—and perhaps, to live and love the questions themselves, as Rilke suggested, during our explorations.

It may be helpful to call on those people, or that person, in your life who both accepts you as you are and challenges you—not for final answers, but for honest observations and genuine questions. These people or this person does not demand that you change in a certain way, but holds and moves a mirror such that what and how you see may look different when the mirror is held at various distances and angles. These are the friends or family who might qualify for Lincoln's "team of rivals" but not for Trump's "I alone can fix it."[19]

A GENERAL APPROACH TO WORKING with Shadow begins with curiosity and the desire to unpack both that long, invisible bag of repressions and denials and that unopened gift of yet-to-emerge qualities and traits. *Disproportionately* strong responses to people, events, issues, ideas, emotions, and dreams are often indications of the presence of Shadow. If a disproportionate response surfaces, these questions may begin to uncover what might be repressed, denied, and projected:

1. What is it about this situation, person, event, issue, idea, emotion, or dream, such that I respond as I do?
2. What is it about *me,* such that I respond to this situation, person, event, issue, idea, emotion, or dream as I do?
3. To what extent do my reactions or responses feel disproportionate?
4. What might I be projecting onto this situation, person, event, issue, idea, emotion, or dream that I need to explore in myself?

The first question engages through an external locus of control. It helps begin to identify the source of the disproportionate response by looking toward something *out there* that triggers the response. Getting clearer about what that *something* is moves us closer to identifying Shadow—what we don't yet see or know about ourselves.

The second question engages through an internal locus of control and is more challenging. It implicates us. Beyond our assessment, accurate or not, of something or someone "out there" is *our* disproportionate response. What is it about *me* such that I respond as I do? Ooh, is my discomfort with his ease in expressing anger related to my unowned, seething-below-the-surface rage? Is my deep admiration for her success in the art world the result of my own as-yet-unrealized creative potential? What is it, exactly, that brings up my disproportionate response? Now, I'm curious. Repressing and projecting parts of ourselves requires energy. Owning and integrating what we repress and project frees up our energy for other aspects of life.

The third question invites us to authentically consider the extent to which our response is disproportionate to the reality of the situation, person, or thing. Honest, challenging, trusted friends may be helpful here.

The fourth question explores the quality, emotion, trait, or characteristic that may be repressed, denied, and projected. Sometimes we recognize it immediately, and perhaps experience a mix of relief, guilt, or simply, *oh, THAT!* Sometimes it may be slower to emerge—harder to see and even harder to own and integrate. I once had an ongoing, disproportionate response to someone I found to be irresponsible. I tend to be over-prepared, reliable, and across-the-board responsible. My Shadow work turned up nothing for several weeks, until I realized, quite simply and directly, that I was not making much money working as a teaching poet. I felt financially irresponsible. Oh. That. Me, irresponsible? Nah. Financially? Um, perhaps, yes.

The next move, if you're up for it, is to change the "me," "I," and "my" to "the United States" or "my country" (if the United States is your country), and slightly tweak the questions to include a historical perspective:

1. What is or was it about this situation (person, event, issue, et cetera) that leads or led the United States to react as it does or did?

2. What is or was it about the United States such that it reacts or reacted to this situation (person, event, issue, et cetera) as it does or did?

3. To what extent are or were the United States' reactions and responses disproportionate?

4. What might the United States be projecting or have projected onto this situation, (person, event, or issue, et cetera) that it needs to explore as a nation?

Engaging this move to the collective level is more complex since national Shadow represents the collective impact of our individual Shadows. Doing so accurately requires critically and honestly exploring and acknowledging our diverse, individual cultural givens, identities, and stories, and owning them, to the extent we're aware of them. Chapter Two introduced those traits I believe the United States denies. Chapters three through ten provide evidence of those traits. What do you see that corroborates or refutes my view? What do you see that I didn't? What did I see that you hadn't?

Beyond the four questions, one other specific approach to Shadow exploration, developed by Ken Wilber and the folks at Integral Institute, engages the third-, second-, and first-person structures of language. This 3-2-1 process asks us to begin by writing *about* the person, thing, or issue in the *third person*, as a *he, she, they, him, her, them* or *it* that we see out there (Chris drives me crazy...). The second step is to speak with the person or thing in *second person,* as a *you,* creating a closer relationship (Chris, you drive me crazy...). Finally, we become Chris, or the trait he or she has if we know what it is, and speak in *first person* as Chris or the trait itself (I drive myself crazy...). Face it. Talk to it. Be it.

More specifically, write out each of these steps in detail: complain *about* Chris to your heart's discontent—get it all on the page. Talk *to* Chris, imagine how he or she would respond, and write the dialogue down. Finally, *become* Chris and own the projection.[20] This is not play-acting; if you truly don't see the projection, don't make believe that you do. Shadow work works best as a regular practice, and it may take some time to see what you project.

Various approaches to Shadow work are available.[21] Some can be engaged with competent, trusted peers (perhaps your team of rivals) and some require professional guidance. Working with collective Shadow, which we'll address below, begins with the individual curiosity and desire mentioned above.

"What are we missing?"—even softened to "what might we be missing?"—is an invaluable, reality-based, truth-seeking, humility-building practice that is not limited to Shadow work and is intimately involved with who we think we are, what stories we tell, and how we tell them.

SHADOW WORK INTERSECTS WITH ASPECTS of therapeutic approaches like Parts Work, Internal Family Systems, and Voice Dialogue, which embrace the idea that we have numerous parts, selves, subpersonalities, or voices within us. Think "One part of me feels…and another feels…" or "A voice inside my head insists that…" Each approach has its own method and language, but they tend to agree that some of the parts, voices, or selves are primary or dominant and some are disowned or exiled. These latter, disowned voices correlate with Shadow— that which is denied or repressed.

For example, Voice Dialogue refers to the voices (or selves, subpersonalities, or energy patterns) as either *primary* or *disowned.* The primary voices are those with which an individual identifies and which together are known as the *primary self system.* The disowned voices are those that have been partially or completely disowned and that energetically oppose the primary selves.[22] Common selves include the Protector, Controller, Caregiver, Vulnerable Child, Fixer, Perfectionist, and Inner Critic, among many. During a session, a Voice Dialogue facilitator introduces the concept of selves to an individual client (subject). Once the subject is aware of the tensions among the selves, and is not immediately identified with any one of them (a state known as the Aware Ego Process), he can then engage in dialogue with one of the selves—primary or disowned. As the subject becomes increasingly familiar with the selves, she expands her ability to make informed choices and to not be unconsciously influenced by a primary self's or a disowned self's attempts to get attention. That's a surface overview of a wonderfully rich and deep process.

This paragraph engages Voice Dialogue as metaphor *and does not suggest the process can be applied to a nation* (as will quickly become evident). Consider the United States to be a discrete, individual subject—which it is not, except, perhaps, conceptually, in some people's minds. It does have a primary system—which, *historically,* is dominated by mostly wealthy, mostly white, mostly heterosexual, mostly male selves, who, themselves, don't necessarily get along; it also has an abundance of disowned selves, too numerous to mention—that can be (perfunctorily and unskillfully) summarized as the *absence* of one or more of the following: wealthy, white, heterosexual, male. Because the country is not a discrete, individual subject, the identities and whims of various primary and disowned selves clamor and cry every day for recognition and to keep or gain power. An Aware Collective Process, or even a competent facilitator, is nowhere to be seen. End metaphor. Please reread the first sentence of this paragraph.

Again, we need to remove that sequoia from our own eyes before pointing to the seedlings in our neighbors' eyes. We need to recognize, own, and integrate what we've been consistently unable or unwilling to see, and then take each other by our hands and hearts and help our country do the same.

Who Are My People?

In the perfectly integrated, comprehensive, inclusive, and balanced universe in which most of us do not (think we) live, we can hear the cheerleaders' rhythmic, enthusiastic, and obvious response echoing around the arena: *EV-ree-one!*

Where most of us do think we live, it can be helpful to have a sense of who our people are—not in the unhealthy *us-against-the-others* sense that governs most finite games, but in the sense of realistically assessing how and with whom I might do the most good in the world as it is, with what I have to offer, without harming others, to the benefit of the whole shebang. Taking care of my, or our, little niche is often the best way to serve the greater good. The concept of "my people" is an iteration of the *in-group bias* we noted in Chapter Nine and to which we'll return below.

Often, the answer to this question lies not in some definitive choice we make but in our authentic attention to the intersections of who we think we are, the stories we choose, the impacts we both have and receive, and what we are able to uncover and own that we previously had not seen. While "my people" may be superficially identified, or at least narrowed down, through blood, geography, and chronology, they are inevitably found and known through experience, belief, and worldview. They include those I learn from and learn with and those who learn from me—whether the learning emerges in the classroom, on the street, at the checkout counter, in the healthcare office, at work, or at the kitchen table. Consider the words of Ta-Nehisi Coates, as his writing led him into "contact with more human beings."

> I had editors—more teachers—and these were the first white people I'd ever really known on any personal level. They defied my presumptions—they were afraid neither for me nor of me. Instead they saw in my unruly curiosity and softness something that was to be treasured and harnessed.[23]

The friends we choose and who choose us in childhood and adolescence, the groups we align with when we choose a craft, profession, or area of study (or one chooses us), and the individuals in our chosen craft, profession, or discipline towards whom we gravitate may provide insight and evidence, but don't necessarily define "our people." Many folks will come, stay for a while and go; others will come and stay. We begin to recognize some who stay, and even some who go, as our people. As tempting as it can be to claim everyone as our people, if we're operating primarily from a Body-Mind identity, it is difficult to live up to that claim. Entrepreneurs, marketers, self-branders, and anyone, really, who try to appeal to everyone or to a too-broad swath of humanity in order to make money or get attention, inevitably encounter problems. In the twenty-first-century, some *very* tech-smart people created and monetized social media for billions of humans, but they are still taking years to figure out some 101-level learnings about their creations in the context of human nature, culture, ethics, and democracy. Neal Postman's questions clamor for their attention.

Most of us don't have such large scope and scale problems. Our people tend to be those with whom we feel a palpable sense of connection, even if we can't define it exactly and whether or not we know them personally. If we do know them personally, they include those who do not leave the room—literally or metaphorically—when we are at our worst, middling, or best. We offer them the same fierce presence.

I AM GOING TO DIE

Regardless of who we think we are, what stories we choose, whom or what we impact and are impacted by, and who our people are, our deaths are, your death is, inevitable. Each of us is terminal. Given enough time, everyone dies.

The more intimate deaths I've experienced so far include being with my mom as she took her final breaths at the age of 83, being with my dad about twelve hours before and then three hours after he took his final breaths at 88, and being with my sister when I found her about six hours after she took her final breaths and her own life at 55 years of age.[24]

Each of us has our own dying and death stories. If we're *lucky* we get to bury our parents and older siblings, our grandparents, aunts and uncles, and others from the generations that precede us. Some of these deaths, while sad, are expected and feel natural; sometimes they are unexpected and feel tragic. The first death that touched me beyond my perceived story-norm of what was natural or expected was a high school classmate, Richie, who died due to mononucleosis, misdiagnosed as strep throat, during Christmas break his freshman year at Manhattan College. We engaged what we didn't know was our final conversation several weeks before he died, exiting the 1 train at 242nd Street after enjoying a night of college hoops at the Garden.

Additional unexpected deaths include Paul, a high school senior, stabbed to death in 1979 over a slice of pizza the night of his last day of class; Joey, a student-athlete from the class of 1982, shot to death in March of 1983; and the first-grade son of Joey's classmate, Mark—a child who lost his life in a school shooting in 2012. I can offer more examples, but you get the idea. You have your own unique experiences of loss and grief.[25]

Knowing I am going to die might motivate me to live into a story of *knowing this, why bother?* or a story of *knowing this, what will I do with my precious, limited time?*—to mention two among many possible story lines. *Who I think I am* will influence, if not fully determine, the general direction of the story I choose. So, let's take a deep, gentle inbreath, hold it, and let go a long, slow outbreath. Repeat as needed. Good. *Who am I? What's my story? .... What am I missing? Who are my people? I'm going to die.* How might I help myself heal? How might I help my country to heal?

One clear, direct reminder of the inevitability of death can be found in the writings of Zen priest and anthropologist Joan

Halifax, who has worked with the dying for more than fifty years. In her rendering of the nine contemplations of the "eleventh-century monk and scholar Atisha Dipankara Shrijnana," Halifax compares the contemplations to "a weather report warning us of a storm in our future," and she reminds us that while the forecast "cannot predict exactly when or how the storm will hit…[it] is inevitable and we'd best prepare for it."[26] Here's a synopsis of the contemplations, some paraphrased:

> 1) Each of us will die sooner or later—no one is exempt. 2) My life span decreases every day. Each breath brings me closer to death. 3) Death comes whether or not I am prepared. 4) My life span is not fixed. Death can come at any time. 5) Death has many causes—even habits and desires are precipitants. 6) My body is fragile and vulnerable—my life hangs by a breath. 7) Material resources will be of no use to me at the time of death. 8) Loved ones cannot save me at the time of death. 9) My own body cannot help me when death comes—it, too, will be lost at the moment of death.[27]

Most of us sort of know we're going to die, and many of us tend to lightly deny and not dwell on it. Neither denying nor dwelling serves us. At least four different polls conducted since 1990 tell us that just under 50% of American adults have a will,[28] which is one concrete manifestation of a Body-Mind-identified and things-and-money-based view of life. That's not a criticism. Whether one's money and possessions are of negligible or formidable volume, a will facilitates their disposition after death according to the deceased's desires, and that's better than letting strangers decide or leaving family and friends to duke it out, which some will anyway, even with a will (a traditional manifestation of it's all about *me*).

But the Body-Mind's understandable concern with the disposition of money and objects has nothing to do with who or what dies from a Soul or Spirit perspective. If we are only attuned to size, shape, color, behavior, thought, mind, mood, and role, that will be who we are, what we care for (or not), and what dies. Buried, burned, or composted, we're gone. Soul and Spirit, as referred to in this chapter, invite narratives about dying *and* living that transcend the limited, partially true Body-Mind storyline. In an absolute sense, birth and death are illusions; in a relative sense they are very real. How might it be to live that paradox as a single truth? This matters not a whit, and it is all that matters.

If each of us is simply an assembly of flesh, bone, instinct, thought, and mood—nothing but separate animated objects with a few shared traits and some noticeable differences—then *leaving the deluded Creeks and Cherokees to their fate and annihilation, decades of lynchings,* and *wasting gooks and waxing dinks* are easier to perpetrate and excuse, while no less horrific and wrong. If, however, we share an origin, a common ancestry—whether through a religious or a scientific story—and if we each have a *unique ecological niche*—our ultimate place in the world, our Soul, expressed through *mythopoetic identity* as a one-time-only manifestation of Spirit, All That Is, God, Source, Ground of Being—then it becomes a tad more difficult—it makes no sense at all—to proclaim the *supremacy of the white race,* to declare *you're either with us or you're with the enemy,* or to write, *think about it, Dr. Jill and forthwith drop the doc.* The stories we choose about who we are, really, make a difference.

Whether or not and through whatever lens we acknowledge the inevitability of death, life gives us ongoing little "practice deaths" that encourage, ask, or force us to let something go and move on in a different way. Cultural givens offer abundant little deaths as we awaken to and let go of various myths and partial truths. The friends we lose over time and distance; the dreams and goals we don't realize; the no longer needed energy, effort, and striving when we finally succeed;

the traits, beliefs, and views we leave behind if and when we move through childhood, adolescence, young adulthood, and adulthood—all of these and more can be ceremonially honored and grieved for the losses they are and as practice for the end of life.

If little practice deaths don't seem substantial enough, spend a year as if it were your last. Live as though you had just one year, or some other time frame, to live (itself, presumptuous—see Atisha's fourth contemplation above). Stephen Levine's *A Year to Live* will walk you through the process. It requires some discipline, courage, and self-compassion, and can build some habits and views that will serve you for the next fifty-two weeks, fifty-two years, or even fifty-two hours.

Across disciplines, ancient and contemporary writers offer us dignified and terrifying views of dying, and many (most? all?) of us, if we do contemplate death, would prefer to die with dignity. At the intersection of life, dignity, and death, surgeon and author Sherwin Nuland reflects on his experience that death results "all too frequently [from] a series of destructive events that involve…the disintegration of the dying person's humanity," and on his not having "seen much dignity in the process by which we die." Nuland, however, complements his surgeon's intimacy with the sterility, knowledge, precision, life, and death of the operating room with his philosopher's view and his poet's heart. "The greatest dignity to be found in death is the dignity of the life that preceded it," he tells us. If you want a dignified death, your best bet is to live a dignified life (Atisha, #5). Recalling Rilke's petition, "Oh Lord, give each of us his own death," and inviting Rabbi Gellman's *small searing death of one person,* Nuland offers his prayer that "insofar as circumstances allow, choices may be made that will give each of us his or her own death."[29]

If living a dignified life and preparing for inevitable death seem like worthwhile pursuits, these resources, among many others, may be helpful. In addition to the works noted in this chapter—Stephen Levine's *A Year to Live;* Ram Dass's *Conscious Aging;* Wayne Muller's *How, Then, Shall We Live* (below); Joan Halifax's *Being with Dying; and* Sherwin Nuland's *How We Die*—additional titles include Nuland's *How We Live* (originally, *The Wisdom of the Body);* Atul Gawande's *Being Mortal;* Sogyal Rinpoche's *The Tibetan Book of Living and Dying;* editor Sushila Blackman's *Graceful Exits;* and editor Yoel Hoffman's *Japanese Death Poems.*[30]

~

KNOWING WE ARE GOING TO die, how, then, shall we live?[31] The livings, indignities, and dyings depicted in chapters three through ten offer examples of how not to live. As an antidote, the opening pages of this chapter offer the potential benefits of paying attention to who we think we are, the stories we choose to tell and how we choose to tell them, the impact we have and how we are impacted, what we might not see—including, but not limited to, Shadow—who our people are, and the inevitability of our death. The remainder of this chapter drops down into more specific frameworks, approaches, tools, and practices that can nurture healing individually, and within families, communities, cultures, and nations.

Healthy self-discipline is required—not the discipline of the angry parent wielding a belt. In *The Road Less Traveled,* M. Scott Peck defined discipline as "the basic set of tools we require to solve life's problems," and he characterized "these tools [as] techniques of suffering, means by which we experience the pain of problems in such a way as to work through them...learning and growing in the process."[32] This toolbox contains four essential tools: delaying gratification, acceptance of responsibility, dedication to truth/reality, and balancing (learning to discipline discipline).[33] These tools may seem obvious conceptually, but they are not widely observed by many, particularly in the third decade of twenty-first-century America.

Briefly, delaying gratification requires that we engage what is painful before we, and often in order to, experience what's pleasurable. Do the hard thing first; get it out of the way. In *My Grandmother's Hands,* Resmaa Menakam describes two types of pain. *Clean pain* "mends and can build your capacity for growth" when you don't want to do or say what you know you should, and you do or say it anyway, or when you don't know what to do or say, you're worried about consequences, "and you step forward into the unknown anyway, with honesty and vulnerability." *Dirty pain* "is the pain of avoidance, blame, and denial" that arises when we respond from our "most wounded parts" or we "physically or emotionally run away."[34] Delaying gratification generally correlates with clean pain and most often encourages a salutogenic, healing narrative. Relentlessly seeking immediate gratification generally correlates with dirty pain and most often encourages a pathogenic, illness narrative.

Accepting responsibility requires that we honestly own what's ours—that we accept and engage those problems that are ours to solve. It is at the heart of healing our narratives and owning and integrating Shadow. It requires that we do the difficult work of wisely and compassionately discerning what belongs to us and what belongs to others. It challenges us to be present to and move beyond the harmful belief that either everything, or nothing, is our fault.

Individual dedication to truth or reality (used synonymously here) requires that we know what we mean by these words; collective dedication requires that we agree on these meanings or at least honor each other's meanings. As noted in Chapter One, our working definition of truth is Parker Palmer's view that "truth is an eternal conversation about things that matter, conducted with passion and discipline."[35] Truth is an unfolding part of the infinite game; it is a conversation—not the domain of one individual or group. It is important, and it welcomes and requires both deep feeling and healthy rigor.

Finally, balancing invites the disciplining of discipline and avoids obsession, rigidity, and inflexibility. It allows us to take a day off, to rest and recover, to eat the icing (or even dessert) first, to recognize that sometimes *good enough*—even if that phrase gets caught in the throat or knots the stomach—is more appropriate than best, great, or good.

Love is also required. In fact, in the absence of love, there's a good chance discipline will either be ignored or manifested in unhealthy, punitive, subjugating ways—whether self- or other-directed. As noted in Chapter One, in this volume, love refers to "the joyful acceptance of belonging," "the will to extend one's self for the purpose of nurturing one's own or another's spiritual growth," and the absence of fear.[36]

To joyfully accept belonging is a way of being that applies to all types and levels of love—love of life, self, other, family, community, thing, place, nation, planet, universe—whether sacred or superficial. We joyfully accept belonging with whom and what we love. We may do this unconsciously—it's just how we feel—or we may consciously attune to joy, acceptance, and belonging. The will to extend ourselves on behalf of our own or another's spiritual growth identifies a purpose or determination within love, and names a conscious, chosen course of action, dedicated to an increasingly more inclusive, comprehensive sense of self and other—the growth through me, us, all of us, and all that is. Finally, the absence of fear more accurately refers to *choosing to act as if fear is absent.*

We all experience fear—sometimes resulting from real, imminent danger and sometimes arising from conditioned habits of mind (which feel no less real). Fear arises for different reasons and with different levels of frequency, duration, and intensity, and it needs to be heeded amid immediate physical threat. The palpable, real, immediate fear I felt decades ago when Sparky, the green-eyed German Shepherd, clamped down his teeth on my left wrist is different from the conditioned fear of possibly embarrassing myself by putting a book out in the world. So, try this: in a way that you know you'll survive, and engaging both mind and body, bring a habitual, recurring fear to the surface; notice that in this moment you're actually safe; now let the fear go, and then feel what sensations or emotions remain in the absence of fear. Our work amid conditioned, recurrent fear (when there is no actual, imminent danger) is to recognize and process it, and to move through it as best we can.[37] The absence of habitual fear energy unshackles the energies of joyful belonging and extending ourselves in order to nurture growth.

The historical and current threads within the five narratives explored in chapters three through seven and the additional narrative threads summarized in Chapter Eight depict a nation's behaving through numerous *unhealthy,* and primarily masculine manifestations of *it's about us* that are devoid of discipline and love. Yes, there have been and are episodes of discipline and love, and there have been and are disciplined, loving groups and individuals who serve and help others. Our focus remains on what we deny and disown—the relentless ignorance, arrogance, fear, bigotry, violence, bullying, greed, excess, and untrustworthiness that pervade our histories and current events. We are a nation so impacted by, and so in denial of, our varied individual, collective, and intergenerational traumas, that we claw toward and cling to fantasies and clichés of how we think things were, or are supposed be, while we blame each other for how things are.[38]

THUS FAR THIS CHAPTER HAS focused primarily on individual work. We'll gradually shift focus now to include the collective. Forty-plus years after his early work with Vietnam vets, Dr.

Bessel van der Kolk remains a leading researcher and practitioner with trauma recovery. In *The Body Keeps the Score,* he reminds us that trauma is not limited to combat veterans, refugees, or violent crime victims. "Trauma happens to us, our friends, our families, and our neighbors." It "affects not only those who are directly exposed to it, but also those around them," and it "is unbearable and intolerable."[39] If we are to be disciplined and loving, trauma work is required in our attempts to learn who we are, to compose, revise, and heal our narratives, and to integrate Shadow. Dr. van der Kolk directly addresses our American experience with trauma:

> You have to go inside and be still by yourself. Our culture is constantly forcing people to be distracted by stuff in order for them not to feel themselves.
>
> But the only way you can be yourself is to know yourself. When you're traumatized, it becomes even more difficult to know yourself because trauma is actually NOT the story of what happened a long time ago; trauma is residue that's living inside of you now… in horrible sensations, panic reactions, uptightness, explosions, and impulses. Because trauma lives inside of you, getting to know yourself can be the scariest thing to do. It takes an enormous amount of courage to visit and befriend yourself and to feel what that uptightness is about. Having the courage to let yourself relax and to notice the flow of your body is central for recovery.[40]

As every one of us begins to grow into a healthy it's-about-*me* perspective in early childhood, we are identified with our mother or mother figure, still without a solid sense of *me.* Assuming for a moment that mom is healthy and loving, the move from the safety and limitations of identifying exclusively with her is not only developmentally necessary but also exhilarating and terrifying, as can be any shift from the familiar to the new. These earlier moves—from "no me yet," to *it's about me,* and from *it's about me* to *it's about us*—are foundational to healthy individual growth and socialization. If mom (or dad, uncle Bob, or neighbor Mike) *isn't* healthy, trauma experienced during childhood will adversely impact, if not arrest, further development.[41]

Trauma at any age is devasting. Childhood trauma is akin to damaging the foundation or frame in the early stages of building a house. Weakness in either threatens the integrity of what's yet to be built and the house itself. Trauma experienced by healthy adults, whose frames and foundations are otherwise intact, while still devastating, can be more skillfully navigated through the integrity of the sturdy foundations and frames that young children have not yet developed.

In witnessing the public hearings of South Africa's Truth and Reconciliation Commission in 1996, Dr. van der Kolk referred to Archbishop Desmond Tutu as a "master trauma therapist," who would interrupt when testimony became overwhelming and invite those gathered into a communal rhythm through prayer, song, and dance, which allowed "participants to pendulate in and out of reliving their horror and eventually to find words to describe what had happened to them." Van der Kolk credits Tutu, Nelson Mandela, Alex Borraine, and others with wanting "to make sure that the birth of South Africa was not a bloodbath...They learned from India that if a nation gets born out of bloodbath, it will never recover."[42]

If a nation gets born out of bloodbath, it will never recover. As a nation, America remains an experiment. We were conceived through the fertilization of ideas that gave voice to some and subjugated others. We were born through a bloodbath that pitted Brit against Brit on land stolen from indigenous peoples and developed by kidnapped Africans. We were raised on enslavement, land and property theft, massacre, betrayal, and peasant labor. We were reborn in an attempt to maintain the experiment through an anything-but-civil bloodbath with ourselves, from which we have yet to fully recover. And we were reborn yet again as a financial and military superpower as the result of a global bloodbath.

We regularly perpetrate and perpetuate violence against others while refusing to acknowledge and address in any effective way the everyday violence we commit against ourselves. Dirty pain, indeed. Not yet 250 years old, we're lost in a national adolescence, thinking we're invincible and immortal—despite clear evidence that we are neither. Not only have we not recovered from our bloodbaths of birth and rebirth in any whole, integrated sense, we continue to choose to bathe ourselves and others in blood, literally and metaphorically, because that is the normal we know. Yes, the preceding two paragraphs are both truthful and one-sided so we might be motivated to make the transition from the familiar cycles of dirty pain to the possible transformations of clean pain.

In *Healing Collective Trauma,* spiritual teacher and author Thomas Hübl reminds us that "[t]rauma breaks relation. Within a person, trauma fractures relation to the self and sabotages connection to the other. At the scale of the collective, traumatic disrelation is cultural and generational; it is a feedback loop."[43] In his more than fifty years of work with trauma and the body, psychologist and researcher Peter Levine emphasizes our "innate capacity for self-regulation," which "holds the key for our modern survival…beyond the brutal grip of anxiety, panic, night terrors, depression, physical symptoms and helplessness that are the earmarks of prolonged stress and trauma." Such self-regulation requires that we "develop the capacity to face certain uncomfortable and frightening physical sensations and feelings without becoming overwhelmed by them." These "primitive trembles, shakes and spontaneous body movements" comprise the language of the unspoken voice through which the body "shakes off" the impacts of high arousal and "grounds" us for whatever is next.[44] Levine tells us that the body's wisdom speaks through an unspoken voice in a language older and other than words. It is a language that transcends and is essential for every individual expression of voice explored in Chapter Three.

Trauma informs our national Shadow. Without honest recognition of and intentional steps toward healing the individual, collective, and intergenerational traumas of America's conception, birth, and rebirths, our efforts to re-vision our narratives and integrate our Shadow will be partial at best, and completely ineffective at worst.[45]

MANY WHO AUTHENTICALLY WORK TO change habits of ignorance, arrogance, fear, bigotry, violence, greed, excess, untrustworthiness, and bullying for the better, engage a debate, often with certainty on both sides, about whether it is more effective to attempt to change individual hearts and minds or to change systems. The systems-change advocates don't dismiss the importance of individual hearts and minds, but they focus on systemic biases in our capitalist democratic republic and assert that when systems change, individuals, along with their hearts and minds, adjust to them. The individual-hearts-and-minds-change advocates don't dismiss the importance of systemic change, but they focus on individual perspectives and behaviors and assert that systems are run by individuals and won't change a whit until enough individual hearts and minds within them change first.

It's a breath mint. It's a candy mint. Less filling. Tastes great. Beyond breath and beer, they're both right. They co-arise and interrelate. To take one example, movement toward the end or diminishment of violence progresses with every individual heart or mind that awakens to the idea that violence leads to more violence. Unless, however, we own our violent history and the cultures and systems built through it, the poverty, inequality, injustice, depression, and despair that often lead to violence will remain. Both individual and systemic changes are required. As a nation with a violent past and present, is it that we lack the individual hearts and minds and the willing government, for-profit, and nonprofit systems necessary to end violence? Or, not lacking these individual and systemic resources, is it that we, for some reason, *choose* not to end violence? Do we lack the resources, the will, or both?

Individual hearts and minds create and change cultures and systems, which change individual hearts and minds, which change cultures and systems. Individual perspectives, individual behaviors, collective perspectives, and natural and human-made systems interrelate and tetra-arise. A change in one affects the other three. Strategically leveraging or remedying one in a timely manner for the greater good makes sense. Consistently ignoring or privileging one or more invites partiality. These four qualities—interior, exterior, individual and collective—represent how humans have parsed and categorized "reality" for millennia—and can be useful. They are, however, parsing a single reality.[46]

If you're willing to engage Gandhi's call to be the change you want to see, here's a prospective path to follow (homework to do): continue or begin to explore your sense of who you really are; learn about and from your body; stay curious about your unique ecological niche; stay open to identifying your people; embrace and re-vision your stories as appropriate; commit to healthy development and skillful means; and accept (with laughter) that each new view brings new things for you to miss, so your Shadow work continues; include love and discipline on the journey (toward your inevitable death).

THREE TECHNOLOGIES, DEVELOPED RESPECTIVELY BY M. Scott Peck, Otto Scharmer, and Thomas Hübl, directly engage this interplay of individuals, groups, and systems. Significantly reduced snippets of their work are presented here—with apologies for the reductions.

In *The Different Drum: Community-Making and Peace,* M. Scott Peck observed, facilitated, and refined four stages of community-making during six years of intentional experiments: *pseudocommunity, chaos, emptiness,* and *community.* He and his colleagues founded the Foundation for Community Encouragement (FCE) in 1984 and convened weekend community-making experiences.[47]

Briefly, in *pseudocommunity,* individuals are nice, friendly, and polite—and they try to fake community. When the facade falls apart, *chaos* emerges, characterized by attempts to control and fix each other; chaos feels frustrating, exhausting, and further from community. Eventually, a facilitator suggests the possibility of *emptiness,* which Peck describes as the hardest, "most crucial stage"—"the bridge between chaos and community"—that requires participants to "empty themselves of barriers to communication," many of which they have just experienced in chaos. The barriers include expectations, preconceptions, ideology, and attempts to fix, solve, or control.[48] Often, many individuals ignore the initial invitation to emptiness, unwilling to let go of what they know and to surrender to the process.

Emptiness requires both the "little deaths" and rebirths of the individuals present and the larger death of the initial group. "When its death has been completed, open and empty, the group enters community. In this final stage a soft quietness descends. It is a kind of peace. The room is bathed in peace."[49] True community is not magically permanent; it must be maintained.

In *Theory U,* MIT professor and founder of the Presencing Institute, Otto Scharmer, invites leaders (all of us at some level) to explore their "blind spot"—the "inner place" and "quality of intention and attention" from which they operate. Scharmer engages a developmental approach that navigates individual, group, institutional, and global dynamics and structures, with a focus on the collective. "Presencing, the blending of *sensing* and *presence,* means to connect with the Source of the highest future possibility and to bring it into the now."[50] The process invites leaders to connect "to the deepest source, from which the field of the future begins to arise—viewing from source," by first recognizing habits and patterns (compare with Peck's pseudocommunity and chaos) and then seeing with fresh eyes, letting go of preconceptions, connecting with the stillness of source, and "letting come" what is yet to emerge (compare with Peck's emptiness).[51] Theory U engages open minds, hearts, and wills, deeply explores self and work (beyond job description and resumé, both similar to and different from Plotkin's *eco-niche*), and embraces the collective energies of co-initiating, co-sensing, co-presencing, co-creating, and co-evolving. Scharmer is playing the infinite game at organizational, institutional, and global levels:

> The real battle in the world today is…among the different evolutionary futures that are possible for us…right now. What is at stake is…the choice of who we are, who we want to be, and where we want to take the world… The real question, then, is "What are we here for?"[52]

In *Healing Collective Trauma: A Process for Integrating Our Intergenerational and Cultural Wounds,* Thomas Hübl, after several decades of engaging large groups in collective trauma integration and healing, works through what is now known as the Collective Trauma Integration Process (CTIP). The process includes three stages: *Cohering the Group, Inducing the Collective Wave,* and *Meta-Reflection.* The second stage unfolds through four *waves: processing group denial, group eruption, discerning the collective voice,* and *group clearing and integration.*[53] Hübl's work also includes Trauma Integration Processes for individual trauma (ITIP) and Ancestral/intergenerational trauma (ATIP).

These three synopses just scratch the surface of Peck's, Scharmer's, and Hübl's respective offerings, which differ in content, context, scope, scale, and intent. Amid these differences, however, they share a trajectory that moves generally from *old or current ways of being, making believe, and denial*, through *chaos, resistance, and disruption*, then through *emptiness, presence, stillness, and openness*, and into *true community, co-evolution, integration, and healing*—these last four being ongoing processes, not static end points. Peck, Scharmer, and Hübl all emphasize the importance of the collective; the need for each member therein to do individual work as well; and the need for those who lead or facilitate community, presencing, or healing to embody the energetic, spiritual, psychological, and mental competence and clarity to guide others.

Our American polarizations have us stuck in denial, disruption, chaos, and resistance to growth. Until enough of us engage the will and the available means to move collectively into emptiness, stillness, and deep listening, we'll neither own and integrate our national Shadow nor heal our individual, ancestral, and collective traumas. Such owning, integrating, and healing won't be legislated, trickled down, or magically cast upon us. Peck, Scharmer, and Hübl present opportunities for intentional engagement, practice, love, and discipline.[54]

CONTINUING OUR CONCERN WITH THE COLLECTIVE, let's return to the concept of in-group bias, which was introduced in Chapter Nine. In *Blueprint: The Evolutionary Origins of a Good Society,* Nicholas Christakis argues that "the social suite" is at the core of all societies, that we have evolved as social creatures, and that "the human ability to construct societies has become an instinct. It is not just something we *can* do—it is something we *must* do." With evidence from "unintentional communities" such as shipwrecks and other stranded groups, "intentional communities" such as Brook Farm, the Shakers, Kibbutzim, Twin Oaks, and those who "winter-over" in darkness at Antarctic research stations, and "artificial communities" such as Amazon Mechanical Turk and other crowdsourcing technologies, Christakis points to the presence of the social suite in communities that last and to the breakdown or absence of some social suite features in those that do not. These features make up the social suite:

1. The capacity to have and recognize individual identity
2. Love for partners and offspring
3. Friendship
4. Social networks [predating and including those online]
5. Cooperation
6. Preference for one's own group ("in-group bias")
7. Mild hierarchy ("relative egalitarianism," in which "we afford more prestige to some group members—typically those who can teach us things or have many connections—than to others").
8. Social learning and teaching (we're not on our own; we rely on others to teach us).[55]

In *Survival of the Friendliest: Understanding Our Origins and Rediscovering Our Common Humanity,* Brian Hare and Vanessa Woods corroborate the spirit, if not the form, of Christakis's social suite. The authors argue that our species has survived and thrived across diverse cultures and societies because of our ability to communicate cooperatively, which is essential for each feature of the social suite. Through evolutionary, anthropological, psychological, and biological lenses, they explore how in-group bias manifests in love for family and friends as well as how it manifests in the extreme, insular horrors of dehumanization, aggression, violence, and polarization, and the roles that oxytocin and serotonin play when things are good—and when things go wrong.

Hare and Woods ground their work in two foundational elements—*theory of mind* and *self-domestication.* Theory of mind refers to our ability to attribute thoughts, beliefs, values, and intentions to ourselves and others. It's how we (try to) interpret a facial expression, an ambiguous comment, or an aberrant behavior—by assessing whether it was generally rude, the result of a bad day, or a microaggression. Said differently, it's how we are able to cooperate with and trust others with or without explicit statements. Self-domestication, as the authors use it, "is…the result of natural selection," where the selection pressure is "on friendliness—either toward a different species or toward your own."[56]

The authors remind us that Charles Darwin himself wrote that "Survival of the fittest" emerged "as a proxy for the term 'natural selection,'" and that both terms refer to what is optimum for bringing viable offspring into the world. Hare and Woods cite Darwin's observation that, "those communities, which included the greatest numbers of the most sympathetic members, would flourish best and rear the greatest number of offspring." The word *fittest,* when interpreted as strongest, dominant, or most aggressive, "can make for a terrible survival strategy," "can set you up for a lifetime of stress," and make life "'nasty, brutish and short.'"[57] Consistent with Hare and Woods's favoring friendliness over physical dominance, Ken Wilber notes that in *The Descent of Man,* Darwin mentions "survival of the fittest" twice, "love" ninety-five times, and "moral sensitivity" ninety-two times.[58] The collective, popular reduction of Darwin's message is, perhaps, another manifestation of the unhealthy masculine.

Setting aside what Darwin may have meant, we do get to choose between salutogenic, friendly narratives and pathogenic, dominating narratives as strategies for our individual and collective survival. If we choose friendliness as a foundational strategy, moments will still arise in which dominance is an immediately useful tactic—such as when we are called to protect ourselves and loved ones. If our chosen foundation is dominance, opportunities for true friendliness—not to be confused with acquiescence or subservience—will be rare. Choosing and *initiating* friendliness, before knowing how others will respond, can be risky while playing a finite game. Amid the infinite game, it is not a risk at all. It is how the game is played.

All of this can be unsettling, even scary, as change inevitably is, whether it's exterior change imposed by events such as war or pandemic, or prospective interior change beckoning for our attention. As we bring this chapter to a close, we'll briefly consider a model of how and why we resist change, a lesson from a man who faced a tsunami of change, and a strategy for getting started.

For more than two decades, Robert Kegan and Lisa Laskow Lahey have researched, developed, and implemented their "immunity to change" approach to understanding and overcoming individual and organizational resistance to change. In workshops and in their 2009 book, *Immunity to Change,* they present a nuanced[59] four-column process that asks practitioners to identify *in column one,* their goals—what they are committed to changing; *in column two,* the behaviors they either engage or don't engage that obstruct the path to these goals; *in column three,* first, what they're afraid might happen if they stop or actually engage the column two behaviors, and then the competing commitments that these fears reveal; and *in column four,* the big assumptions that underlie the competing commitments.

With these steps laid out across four columns, an "immunity to change map" depicts an immune system that is designed to keep us safe:

> ...the set of big assumptions collectively makes the third-column commitments inevitable...it is clear how they

sustain the immune system: The third-column commitments clearly follow from the big assumptions and generate the behaviors in column 2; these behaviors clearly undermine the goal in column 1.[60]

As with re-visioning narratives, learning the body's unspoken voice, and owning and integrating Shadow, Kegan and Lahey's immunity to change process helps us uncover what is hidden—competing commitments and big assumptions—so we might move forward in a more integrated way.

In her culture-bearing (and, perhaps, culture-baring) book, *Radical Joy for Hard Times: Finding Meaning and Making Beauty in Earth's Broken Places,* Trebbe Johnson shares Susumu Sugawara's experience off the coast of Japan's Oshima Island as an example of, and a prospective path towards, manifesting her title. On March 11, 2011, when Sugawara saw an approaching tsunami from his boat, *Sunflower,* which he held as his friend of forty-two years, he silently bid farewell to his fellow fisherman, turned directly into the oncoming wave, and accelerated. Miraculously, he survived the primary and largest wave and the smaller waves that followed, then he gathered himself for some hours, contemplating survival and the devastation he was sure had occurred. After dark, he began the delicate voyage toward shore amid wrecked houses, boats, and other flotsam. He spent the following weeks ferrying people and supplies—for free if they could not pay and for a nominal fee if they could.

Based on Sugawara's choices, Johnson offers this template for riding "into the wave in hard times":

- You don't try to flee it; you head right into the thick of it.
- As soon as it rushes over you, you ride it. You know it's in charge, but you neither fight it nor capitulate to it. You move with it in the way you calculate is likeliest to insure your survival.

- After the onslaught of the crisis is over, you take as much time as you need to get your bearings.
- Making your way back to the familiar shore, you reach out to help others.[61]

Each step might carry different meaning for different people at different times in different circumstances. Amid these differences, again and always, is an invitation to recognize and avoid denial, accept what is, move through chaos and disruption, open to and allow emptiness, and participate in collective healing through skillful means.

Given the relentless enormities of the waves we face and what we carry individually, collectively, currently, and historically as Americans—especially amid the abundant, often discordant opinions about what needs to be done, when, and by whom—where and how does each of us, do all of us, start?

Pema Chödrön, in her appropriately titled book, *Start Where You Are: A Guide to Compassionate Living,* reminds us that any good thing we do for ourselves affects how we experience both *our* world and *the* world. She writes: "What you do for yourself, you're doing for others, and what you do for others, you're doing for yourself."[62] With that in mind, she suggests the following:

> Start where you are…. You may be the most violent person in the world – that's a fine place to start…. juicy, smelly. You might be the most depressed person in the world, the most addicted person in the world…. You might think there are no others on the planet who hate themselves as much as you do. All of that is a good place to start. Just where you are – that's the place to start.[63]

Amen. The conditions will never be exactly right. Begin. Come back to your breath and posture. No matter what you are facing or doing, invite a sense of ease. Befriend whatever arises. Surrender to Mystery.

Whether you choose to explore who you really are, to re-vision the stories you hold (or that hold you), to clarify your impact and what impacts you, to own and integrate what's currently hidden, to identify your people, to acknowledge your inevitable death—or to engage all of these or some other practice beyond the offers in this book—just begin.

You are not alone. And we're counting on you.

CHAPTER TWELVE

Expanding & Integrating the View from Here

*What boundaries limit your vision and
how might you open or remove them?*[1]

DURING MY SINGLE-DIGIT YEARS, while I still saw the world
through my cultural givens, two experiences nudged those
givens (and me) in ways that I immediately noticed, soon forgot, and fortunately recalled years later.

During one of the Marra, Eufemia, Luna, and Dalconzo
family gatherings, this time at the Luna household on Long
Island, our parents bravely packed us into various vehicles for
some excursion. I found myself in the second or third seat of
Uncle Al and Aunt Ann Luna's 1953 Chevy station wagon
with the faux wood siding.[2] At one point, amid what today
would be an unwise if not illegal number of children in a
motor vehicle, as we nudged and teased each other in the tight
space, my mother's younger sister, Ann, turned around in the
shotgun seat and directed us to *knock it off* through the familiar, formidable energy shared by the former-Eufemia sisters.
We obeyed immediately. And momentarily. When we resumed
our shenanigans, Uncle Al, without taking his eyes off the road,
suggested, "Everybody love everybody," in a voice much calm-
er than I was accustomed to hearing when being told to settle
down by an adult. I'm pretty sure my Luna cousins had heard

it before, but it was new for me. No accusation of misbehaving, no threat of punishment, no yelling—just a gentle imperative to love each other. *Hmmm.*

Three or four years later, around 1966, I found myself on another (less crowded) excursion in the backseat of the Tepikian Rambler with my best friend, Paul, and his younger brother, Bruce, who was seated between us.[3] As we drove past St. Anthony's church, I made the required, culturally given sign of the cross, and Bruce asked, "Why does Reggie do that thing with his hands when he goes past his church?" Their dad, Troy, responded, "We're Presbyterian and Reggie's Catholic. We believe the same things, but we believe some of them in different ways. One of the ways Reggie shows his belief is doing that with his hands—the sign of the cross—when he passes in front of a Catholic church." *Hmmm. We believe the same things? What about* the One True Catholic Church?

Each of these moments, along with many that preceded and many that have succeeded them, provided a gentle hammer tap on a sharp chisel that chipped away at the vulnerable surfaces of my cultural givens. This chipping away gradually exposed a fuller, freer, more whole, and integrated version of me and the world—and allowed my unique ecological niche, perhaps, expressed through my mythopoetic identity, to begin to emerge. It's a long-term project. You have your own version of this emergence, as does every named and unnamed being referred to and cited in these pages. Ask yourself: What are you holding onto? What's holding onto you? What do you need, and have the will, to let go—in order to nurture your own and others' ongoing emergence?

This final chapter juxtaposes our American narratives and collective Shadow with snippets of my own expanding views over time. As with the cultural givens in Chapter One, I share my experience neither as a prescription for others, nor as what is right, wrong, good, or bad, but simply as an invitation to you, as you peruse these pages, to explore the trajectory of your own views over the course of your life. Our national narratives and collective Shadow emerge through millions of individual views, stories, denials, and projections. My brief sharing here provides one way, among many, to explore.

THE BELIEFS AND EXPERIENCES, GROUNDED in Catholic and Italian-American dogma, that informed what my parents began to give me in 1954 stand in stark contrast with what Ta-Nehisi Coates received from his parents beginning in 1975. His parents' rejection of "all dogmas" and their pushing him "away from secondhand answers—even the answers they themselves believed"[4] were 180 degrees away from my parents' tacit but powerful belief in the United States and the Catholic Church as guides for their first-generation Italian-American experience. Further, the years between our 1954 and 1975 births included the Vietnam War, the Civil Rights Movement, multiple assassinations, a moon landing, and a president's resignation—among other nationally impactful events.

It makes perfect sense that this generational difference would account for significantly diverse worldviews, especially early on in a finite game. Consider the differences between a second-generation Italian-American kid taught to defer to dogma in 1960s Yonkers and an at-least seventh-generation[5] African-American kid taught to reject dogma (itself a kind of dogma) in 1980s Baltimore, and between the respective experiences of their fathers, an Italian-American plumber and World War II veteran and an African-American Vietnam veteran who became a member of the Black Panthers and then a university librarian. But when Coates writes to his fifteen-year-old son, "I don't know that I have ever found any satisfactory answers of my own. But every time I ask it, the question is refined," his message is essentially the same as what I share with my own son.[6] We want our kids to know that *truth is an eternal conversation about things that matter,* and that each increasingly comprehensive, inclusive, balanced, and complex perspective brings with it opportunities for more refined questions and increasingly accurate and adequate answers—whether they begin with or without dogma, in Yonkers, Baltimore, or Everytown, U. S. A.[7]

I gradually shed my unquestioning deference to authority and dogma—usually in safe, discomfiting, and occasionally humorous ways—one unfair, unsatisfactory, or confusing experience or observation of injustice at a time. Here's a simple, goofy example: I disliked the taste and texture of liver, I loved chicken, and I knew the difference. My mom once insisted that our liver dinner was chicken (no, she didn't say it was *chicken* liver). Should a seven-year-old trust his mother or his taste buds? Another example: I was fourteen when a stranger called and told my mom that he'd caught me and other kids killing wildlife along the Saw Mill River—something I hadn't done. She believed the stranger for several days (as I questioned my memory and sanity) until I proved that I had been with *her* when the incident allegedly occurred. We visited the accuser's house, he admitted he had never seen me before, and he described the kid who had used my name. I began to learn that deference to authority helped my mom navigate a deep fear of being seen as wrong, or worse, that her kids might do something wrong—especially in public. I began to see her as an increasingly fully human, imperfect, and loving being—albeit without that thought process or language at the time.

During my third year in high school, four men assisted the process of chipping away at the surface of my culturally given worldview. An assistant principal I did not know accosted me on my way to class, asked for my student ID and threatened to expel me if I didn't get my hair cut by the following Monday. This was 1970 and high schools were losing, or had already lost, their attempts to regulate the lengths of boys' hair and girls' skirts. My parents did not have a (major) problem with my hair length, but agreed it would be best to get it cut, which I did. For the first time in my life, I engaged writing—a rudimentary "healing narrative"—to work through feelings of anger and injustice. I was a naïve "good kid" who did what he was told, and I was a bit slower than many of my peers at embodying the invincibility, immortality, and rebellion of adolescence. I was blessed that the lesson came through a forced haircut and not the barrel of a gun, but, essentially, I had yet to learn to stand up for myself.

That same year, our principal, Br. Jerome Stevens, taught my English class once a week. Shattering any stereotypes of Catholic schools, he used the then new *National Lampoon* to teach parody and satire and invited us to craft poems by finding similarities in two apparently different things. For some reason I compared Christmas and death. He wrote, "Excellent! This has an extraordinary quality that not half a dozen of your class achieved. Your language is simple, but your sentence & idea structure is quite complex."[8] Catholic education was indeed universal in Brother Jerome's classroom.

The third encounter, also during my junior year, came through my radio, tuned to WNEW-FM in New York. One Sunday morning, an unfamiliar voice sang, "I have seen the mornin' burnin' golden on a mountain in the skies / achin' with the feelin' of the freedom of an eagle when she flies...."[9] As noted in Chapter One, the expectations, risks, and revelations in Kris Kristofferson's first thirty-plus years presented my sixteen-year-old mind with a capital-P sense of *Possibility* that my cultural givens did not—perhaps could not—consider.

Finally, Jerry Houston, a close friend to this day, cut me from the basketball team my senior year and offered me my first coaching job four years later.[10] During tryouts that year, I was defending a player who changed direction and sealed me off for an easy layup on a baseline inbound play under his basket. Coach Houston yelled, "Hey Reggie, are you gonna let a guy do that to you?" He seemed unconcerned that my opponent was about seven inches and forty pounds larger than I was (at 5'6" and 125 pounds). Immediately embarrassed and motivated, I heard his question as a powerful statement that height, weight, or any other perceived disadvantage neither relieved me of responsibility nor guaranteed any particular outcome—on or off the court.

With these four encounters under my belt, my still strong but disintegrating deference to authority and my dedication to basketball led me to get cut twice more—at St. John's University in New York. Even there, however, called toward an English major and hearing that a business degree would better land me a job, I deferred and majored in marketing. When Professor Robert Cascio joyfully danced a roomful of mostly disinterested business students through a nineteenth-century American literature class as if he had been a personal friend of Emerson, Thoreau, Melville, Hawthorne, Douglass, Dickinson, Whitman, and others, I realized my mistake. Some twelve years later, I would enroll in a graduate literature program.

When Coach Houston offered, I accepted the freshman basketball coaching position at my high school alma mater during my senior year at St. John's. This led, the following year, to an invitation to teach, which led to my staying for thirteen years. The lessons I learned in those years continued the broadening, deepening, and re-visioning of my worldview. I learned in the faculty room from the veteran teachers who "took me under the wing," so to speak; I learned in the classroom from the students' diverse cultural givens and levels of motivation to learn; and I learned on the court from the student-athletes who gave their all and especially from those who did not.

In 1980-1981, during a messy contract negotiation between teachers and the New York Archdiocese in which teachers' salaries were in the public eye, a student asked me, in class, why I stayed when I could make more money in a public school or in another profession. My twenty-six-year-old worldview responded that "Money has never been my primary motivation for doing anything"—a response that confused some students, reassured or inspired others, and was completely true at the time. It would take years for me to more fully understand the mixed blessing of that genuinely held perspective.

I left the high school after thirteen years and spent the next seven as an administrator at Iona College, where I earned a master's degree in English, learned more steps in Professor Cascio's literary dance across genres and eras, and then set out on my own, with no understanding of what it took to be an entrepreneur, or even to be entrepreneurial.

Beyond classroom assignments, my reading included Robert Pirsig's *Zen and the Art of Motorcycle Maintenance*, Richard Bach's *Illusions*, and Scott Peck's *The Road Less Traveled*, among many others in the late seventies and early eighties. I found Thich Nhat Hanh's *The Miracle of Mindfulness* and Jon Kabat-Zinn's *Full Catastrophe Living* in 1993—which led to a regular meditation practice—and I began reading Ken Wilber in 1996—the year in which my dad died. That same year, I met the woman I would marry and I attended a weeklong program called "Poetry and the Political Imagination." For the next decade-plus I made my living as a teaching poet.[11] My close friends joked that I had found one of the few paths that paid less than teaching in a Catholic school—and that provided no healthcare or pension benefits. I laughed and noticed that whether I was working with third-graders, senior citizens, or anyone in between, while we crafted our poems, everyone was learning about themselves—and everyone liked that.

Between 1998 and 2003 I engaged in a vision fast and other nature-based soulwork with Bill Plotkin, a year-to-live practice based on Stephen Levine's work, a mindfulness retreat with Thich Nhat Hanh, and a week of holotropic breathwork and meditation with Stan Grof and Jack Kornfield. Between 2004 and 2007, smitten by Wilber's work, I attended various integral seminars and gatherings in Colorado and Spiral Dynamics trainings in Washington, D.C. and Texas. From 2009 through 2011 I completed coach training with Integral Coaching Canada.

All of this to say that I spent most of my forties and fifties seeking broader and deeper perspectives and earning enough to live as a teaching poet, writer, and occasional workshop facilitator. While many people close to me were building significant nest eggs, my 1981 response to the high school student still impacted my view—making money was not my primary motivator. Living into my authentic place in the world was. I learned that looking in the mirror was easier for me when I struggled financially while engaging work that felt authentic than it would be if I struggled with authenticity while doing work that paid me lots of money. I'm neither bragging nor complaining here—just owning my choice. I didn't have a plan, but I was on a trajectory.

Study, training, and money aside, the years from 1993 through 2009 invited me more deeply into "life as practice." My dad lost his left leg below the knee to gangrene in 1994, spent his final two years wheelchair-bound in a nursing home, and died on Valentine's Day in 1996. After his death, I moved back to my childhood home and cared for my mom until she died in 1999. In 2003 I had both my hips replaced and also began to help my sister through bipolar disorder and depresssion—until St. Patrick's Day, 2009, when I found her dead in her home with more than three times the lethal dose of Cardizem in her system.[12] *If we're* lucky *we get to bury our parents and older siblings...*,[13] indeed. Experiencing and embodying such luck is more complex than understanding and agreeing with it conceptually. You know this. How are you holding or anticipating the "lucky" and "unlucky" deaths amid those you consider your people?

ALL OF US HAVE OUR own conscious or unconscious approaches to finding our ways, our voices, and ourselves in the world. Again, I share snippets of mine here so you might be moved to explore and honor your own. We enter the world, suddenly separate from our mothers, helpless, and dependent on the love and support of others. Despite the species-sameness we're born with—notably marked by the navel's scar of lost physical connection—most of us learn early on to notice, and often fear (or at least roll our eyes at) the dizzying differences amid our cultures, appearances, personalities, interests, aspirations, talents, and ways of being in the world. If we're observant, fortunate, or wise, we learn to recognize and embrace the paradox of our utter sameness and dazzling diversity.

Poets Audre Lorde and Tony Hoagland, decades and life experiences apart, both died of cancer. Lorde, also a powerful activist, reflects on her initial encounter with breast cancer:

> The women who sustained me through that period were Black and white, old and young, lesbian, bisexual, and heterosexual, and we all shared a war against the tyrannies of silence. They all gave me a strength and concern without which I could not have survived intact.[14]

Hoagland shares with us his experience in the cancer ward:

> ...it seems the whole world has cancer. With relief and dismay you'll realize, *I'm not special. Everybody here has cancer....* no citizens are protected by property, job description, prestige and pretensions.... You are all simply cancer citizens bargaining for more life."[15]

Lorde and Hoagland offer us preemptive gifts through their suffering. We don't *have to* wait for personal experiences of loss, disease, mass shooting, war, flood, fire, or storm to teach us that we're in this together. We can act as if we know that everyone suffers. We can extend outward our in-group bias, our joyful acceptance of belonging, and our sense of who our people are. We can act as if we know that everyone wants to experience joy, happiness, and love as well.

WHERE ALL OF THIS LEADS me, and has led, leads, and will lead others, is toward love. Throughout this book we've pointed to an *it's-all-about-me* orientation as the earliest and least inclusive view available to us. But without a healthy iteration of this view, which allows each of us to love our self and makes it possible to look in the mirror and authentically say, "I love you," to the essence of our reflection, self-love remains repressed as part of our Shadow—and this repression inevitably limits the fullness of our love for any other(s). Thich Nhat Hanh made it clear that, "Until we are able to love and take care of ourselves, we cannot be of much help to others."[16] My choosing to extend myself in order to joyfully accept belonging as, to, and with the perfectly beautiful, blemished being *I am* strengthens my will to extend myself on behalf of the perfectly beautiful, blemished beings *you, they, all of us*, and *all that is* are. Both the foundation of healthy self-love and the expansion beyond it are essential.

In her book, *Outlaw Culture,* bell hooks expressed being puzzled by folks who authentically confront one "domination" while often passively supporting or ignoring another. She pointed specifically to black men who fought against racial discrimination but ignored the plight of women, and to white women who were on the front lines of gender discrimination but ignored the racial discrimination against their black sisters. She observed that many activists act on behalf of self-interest, attempting to end "what we feel is hurting us," rather than on behalf of "a collective transformation of society, an end to politics of dominations." She concludes:

> This is why we desperately need an ethic of love to intervene in our self-centered longing for change. Fundamentally, if we are only committed to an improvement in that politic of domination that we feel leads directly to our individual exploitation or oppression, we not only remain attached to the status quo but act in complicity with it, nurturing and maintaining those very systems of domination.[17]

She clearly states the necessity for a love that moves from embracing what concerns *me* or my particular *us* to the wider embrace of *all of us* and *all that is.* Sound familiar?

Consider the words of Siddhartha Gautama, passed down by many, including Gandhi and King: "For hatred can never put an end to hatred; love alone can. This is an unalterable law."[18] Remember the words attributed to Jesus Christ: "Love one another. As I have loved you, so you must love one another."[19]

In *Across That Bridge,* John Lewis acknowledged the roles of faith, patience, study, truth, action, peace, and reconciliation in his vision for change in the United States. He also made it clear that for those who studied, trained in, and practiced nonviolence, "not simply as a tactic, but as a way of authentically living our lives—our sole purpose was, in fact, love."[20]

In response to a question from Krista Tippett in 2020, author Jason Reynolds defined antiracism in this way:

> …[it's] simply the muscle that says that humans are human. That's it. It's the one that says, "I love you because you are you." Period. That's all…. That element of "I love you because you are you" should be the most human thing we know. It should be a natural thing to say, "Look, I love you, because you remind me more of myself than not."[21]

While simple on the surface, those last eight words are subtly sophisticated and quite challenging when engaged beyond the conceptual—in the everyday world with other human beings. The prospect that *you remind me more of myself than not* recalls Aleksandr Solzhenitsyn's recognition that each human heart—each of us—carries the potential for good and evil.[22]

Those eight words also beckon Thich Nhat Hanh's remarkable poem, "Please Call Me by My True Names," which invites us to experience our "interbeing" with all things by owning and embracing the apparent opposites within us: departure and arrival; birth and death; predator and prey; joy and pain. Grounding these conceptual polarities, the poem's images deepen the invitation and further challenge us. Can we relate to the frog *and* the snake that eats it; to the starving child *and* the arms merchant; and to the twelve-year-old refugee *and* the pirate who rapes her—so we might further open the door of compassion.[23] Notice what comes up for you in response to these three paired images. To what extent does each request open or close your heart—with whom or what can you identify, or not?

In the final chapter of *Caste,* Isabel Wilkerson shares her December 2016 encounter with a plumber. She had lost her mother and her husband during an eighteen-month period, and she found herself in her flooded basement engaging unfamiliar terrain that her late husband would have handled. Wilkerson recalls that the plumber "smelled of beer and tobacco," needed a shave, had a pot belly, wore a baseball cap that she connected with Trump supporters, and didn't offer to help as she moved boxes and swept water. He seemed disinterested when she told him of her two recent losses, and he had not found the source of the leak even as he prepared to leave.

Amid her grief and her growing anger with and assumptions about him, Wilkerson "threw a Hail Mary at his humanity" and asked him about his own mother. He shared that she had died a quarter-century earlier at the age of fifty-two, and as he and Wilkerson deepened their conversation about family, longevity, and connection, he reengaged his search for the leak and eventually found corrosion atop the water heater. The chapter is titled "The Heart Is the Last Frontier."[24]

Generalized, this encounter occurs between a grieving, accomplished, professional black woman and an apparently disengaged blue-collar white man. More specifically, it is between two particular human beings, Isabel Wilkerson and an unnamed plumber, each of whom brought unique worldviews, personalities, skill sets, and experiences to their brief time together.

Had my father responded to Isabel Wilkerson's call, he would not have worn a hat, his belly would not have protruded over his belt, he would have been clean-shaven, and he may have carried a tobacco scent, but not beer. He would have asked her for the broom and swept the water himself (or given the broom to me if I had been with him). When she shared her recent losses, he would have stopped what he was doing, expressed his condolences, and asked unintrusive, genuine questions about her mom, her husband, and how she was doing. Her world as a black female journalist and author would have been beyond his experience; his world as a loving husband and father would have connected quickly with her grief as a wife and daughter. Also, I'm pretty sure the water heater would have been one of the first things he checked.

Wilkerson was able to see and engage through a more comprehensive and inclusive worldview than was the plumber—an observation intended neither to praise her nor criticize him, but simply to note what was. Aware of her grief, growing frustration, and anger, she accepted and bowed to what was within and before her and invited him into a larger, shared perspective. She appealed to his humanity through her own. *Go behind all those individual differences, and you…see another soul just like you. You remind me more of myself than not.*[25]

In the opening pages of *After the Ecstasy, the Laundry*, Jack Kornfield reflects on his relationship with the practice of bowing in mindful reverence during his time in the Buddhist forest monastery in Thailand. The expectation that he bow upon entering the meditation hall or when taking his seat for training was fine, but a later instruction to bow to anyone who had been a monk longer than he had, even if only a week longer, was more challenging. Conflicted but committed, he "began to look for some worthy aspect of each person I bowed to" and he learned to enjoy it. Eventually, "bowing became my way—it was just what I did. If it moved, I bowed to it."[26]

Healing our American narratives and integrating our individual and collective Shadows invites us to bow to ourselves, each other, and what is—not necessarily as an endorsement, but as an acknowledgment. Whether we bow literally or metaphorically, such intentional honoring of what we share and have shared—in full awareness of what we don't share and haven't shared—reminds us of an open invitation to and our ongoing conversation about things that matter. We are invited to joyfully accept our roles in and to extend ourselves in service of the infinite game that continues whether or not we choose to play, and regardless of the extent to which we understand the rules that keep the game going.

As I bring this to a close, I'm aware of the thousand or so books that line the walls of the room in which I write. Some small remnants of the cultural givens that demanded I defer to authority and know my place in relationship to that authority attempt to interrogate and warn me. *What good is another book, among so many? Who do you think you are? Look at the works you've cited, and the many more in the world you haven't even read. Look at what you chose to leave out! The country is still falling apart, as is the world, amid all of these words from all of these wise and compassionate voices.* I notice the questions and observations for what they are (and were)—and I let them go. I realize that while I *am* a tourist amid some of the specific, finite landscapes, storyscapes, and soulscapes this book turns its attention to, I am also an observant, intimate, native participant—as is each of us—in the larger, perfect infinite-scape that holds, and is, it all. What I choose to write, or not, matters not a whit, and it is the only thing that matters.

LET'S RETURN NOW TO THE final question that appears in Chapter Eleven on page 296. I've revised it so it speaks directly to you: How are you in relationship with the questions and statements that were explored on pages 295-320, and how are you in relationship with the rest of your life? Here are the other questions and statements again:

- Who am I, really?
- Everything is a story.
- What's my impact & what impacts me?
- What am I not seeing?
- Who are my people?
- I am going to die.

Asked differently, in the context of your relationships with each of these questions and statements, what is the nature of your relationships with the many narratives and the collective Shadow of the United States of America?

One striking example of how the *nature* of our relationship with anything or anyone inevitably impacts the relationship itself comes from Dr. Eduardo Duran's soul-healing work with Native Americans. He relates his experience that moving, for instance, from the Western therapeutic language of, *I am depressed* or *I have a depressive disorder* to the language of *the spirit of sadness is visiting me* has a profound effect on his patients. The move from *I am* this (identity) or I *have* this (possession) to *being visited by the spirit of* this (relationship) opens the door to conversation with the visitor, which can open the door to transforming the relationship—whether with sadness, alcohol, posttraumatic stress, or some other visitor.[27] Shifting the relationship in this way does not necessarily change or end how any particular conventional therapeutic approach is engaged—although it may. Shifting the nature of the relationship simply opens up possibilities that were not available or seen before the shift took place.

How you relate to—the nature of your relationship with—anything and anyone is at least as important as the thing or the person with whom you relate. That's true for how you relate to the narratives explored in this book and for how you relate to how I chose to explore them. It's true for how you relate to every family member, friend, co-worker, and stranger with whom you interact. It's true for every belief, value, preference, or judgment that you hold—or that holds you. It's true for the nature of your relationship with the sun, the moon, the rain, the wind, and the snow. How you choose to be in relationship with all that is is entirely up to you.

Thanks for joining me on this journey—and for reading this far.

ACKNOWLEDGMENTS

AS FAR AS I CAN TELL, beyond life and health, my primary blessing is friendship. Perhaps, more specifically, it is an abundance of close friends. My loosely held definition of a close friend is someone who has seen me at my best and my worst, who is honest with me about what they see, who isn't leaving the room when I need their presence, and who feels pretty much the same about me. Not everyone whom I acknowledge here is a close friend, but each name on these three pages belongs to someone who is generous, caring, committed, and good at what he or she does. So, thanks to you all (and especially to those folks I've omitted).

Thanks to Lois MacNaughton, who suggested that I not rush the early days of this project in order to release it as an e-book before the 2020 election. A deep bow of gratitude goes out to Doe Boyle, whose skill and care as an editor rendered this book eminently more readable, and whose enthusiasm as a reader encouraged me (and made me laugh). Any extant (too-)long, complex sentences are my choices, not her omissions. Thanks to Leslie Williams for her insights into what an early version of Chapter Three both did and didn't accomplish regarding the fear of the feminine and the subjugation of women.

I am grateful to Doug Anderson for his ongoing generosity and clarity, and the insights he shared when we met some twenty-six years ago. Thank you to Andrew Hoffer who, more than thirty years ago, taught me how to create a book and bring it into the world once the writing and editing were done. Deep bows of gratitude go out to Eduardo Duran, Maureen Walker, Trebbe Johnson, Janet E. Aalfs, Bill Plotkin, Bridgit Dengel Gaspard, and Marianela Medrano for their courage in associating their names (and reputations) with this project, and especially to Maureen, for the Foreword.

Much love to Kent Frazier, who relentlessly encourages me, and with whom I continue to co-create the Fully Human at Work project. Thanks to Joel Kreisberg, who invited me to co-create with him at just the right time. Big hugs go out to folks in my various communities of practice and play: Teaching Artists and Educators in Connecticut and throughout the country; Weaving Soulful Community's vision-fast crew; Integral Coaching Canada's practitioners around the world; departed and still present members of the Coaching and Healing group; and the magical members of the monthly meeting of men—John Cusano, Brechin Morgan, Larry Pisani, Kim Salander, and Robert Campbell—who still get along after what feels like centuries at times.

The following folks have supported me in various ways with writing projects and/or life in general: Jay Stearns, Ray DiCapua, Eileen Dulen-Jennings, Bob Killackey, Chris Rogers, Ed Nall, Marianela Medrano, Naomi Shihab Nye, Marie Pace, Kevin Snorf, Joan Hurley, Fred Krawchuk, Bruce Tepikian, Alice Stephens, Michael Sallustio, Steve Benson, Morley Wilkinson, Shari Specland, Waverly Nall, Noé Jimenez, Tami Weiss, Mike McGrath, George Sheehan, Richard Lapchick, Kevin Scanlon, Kieran Stack, Tom Rogers, Lou Duesing, Ian Percy, Ryan Leech, Cherie Beck, Robert Gambardella, Steve Georgian, Tony Manzolillo, Sherry Reiter, Morgan Smith, Rob Francess, Brian Stack, and Tom Rubens.

The aforementioned Paul Tepikian and I grew up three houses away from each other and have been friends for (gulp) sixty-two years (or so). The years and miles continue to deepen the friendship. Thank you, Paul.

I would like to acknowledge all of the scholars, journalists, historians and writers whose works I consulted during this project. For further reading, I recommend all the books in the bibliography, and many more that don't appear there. That's not helpful, I know, but it's true.

Right now, if I could only have one book to read, it would be John Tarrant's *Bring Me the Rhinoceros,* because it reminds me how my mind works—whether I'm navigating gender, identity, ethnicity, race, violence or any other issue, concept, or trait. If I could have two or three books, I would add Ken Wilber's *The Religion of Tomorrow* because of its scope and scale, and Bill Plotkin's *Nature and the Human Soul* because his soul-centric model of development reminds me of what's possible. I would add Trebbe Johnson's *Radical Joy for Hard Times,* Terry Patten's *A New Republic of the Heart,* and Jamie Wheal's *Recapture the Rapture*—each in its own way speaks to where we are in this third decade of the twenty-first century. Resmaa Menakem's *My Grandmother's Hands* does a remarkable job navigating the intersections among history, race, violence, police, trauma, and body-based practice. Ask me again in a year and the titles may differ.

For folks not familiar with poetry, *Risking Everything,* edited by Roger Housden, is a wonderful introduction to the works of various poets—both living and dead. *Against Forgetting,* edited by Carolyn Forché, and *Poetry of Witness,* edited by Forché and Duncan Wu, provide necessary and discomfiting histories of human suffering. *Unsettling America,* edited by Maria Mazziotti Gillan and Jennifer Gillan, is a late-twentieth-century anthology of multicultural poems. There are, of course, many more poets and volumes to explore.

Finally, and again, thank *you* for reading this book.

Precepts Ignored & Lessons Not Learned: Eisenhower, McNamara, and the Special Inspector General for Afghanistan Reconstruction

President Eisenhower's Precepts, 1946

1. No people on earth can be held, as a people, to be enemy, for all humanity shares the common hunger for peace and fellowship and justice.
2. No nation's security and well-being can be lastingly achieved in isolation but only in effective cooperation with fellow-nations. [Compare with McNamara, *In Retrospect,* #9]
3. Any nation's right to form of government and an economic system of its own choosing is inalienable.
4. Any nation's attempt to dictate to other nations their form of government is indefensible.
5. A nation's hope of lasting peace cannot be firmly based upon any race in armaments but rather upon just relations and honest understanding with all other nations.[1]

[Note the underlying themes of not understanding others' values, beliefs, cultures, histories, etc., of respecting differences, and of a people's right to self-determination that connect Eisenhower's #3 & #4 with McNamara's #3-5 and #8 from *In Retrospect*].

Robert McNamara's Lessons from *In Retrospect,* 1995

1. We misjudged then—as we have since—the geopolitical intentions of our adversaries...and we exaggerated the dangers to the United States of their actions.

2. We viewed the people and leaders of South Vietnam in terms of our own experience. We saw in them a thirst for—and a determination to fight for—freedom and democracy. We totally misjudged the political forces within the country.

3. We underestimated the power of nationalism to motivate a people (the North Vietnamese and Vietcong) to fight and die for their beliefs and values—and we continue to do so today in many parts of the world.

4. Our misjudgments of friend and foe alike reflected our profound ignorance of the history, culture, and politics of the people in the area, and the personalities of their leaders....

5. We failed then—as we have since—to recognize the limitations of modern, high-technology military equipment, forces, and doctrine in confronting unconventional, highly motivated people's movements. We failed as well to adapt our military tactics to the task of winning the hearts and minds of people from a totally different culture.

6. We failed to draw Congress and the American people into a full and frank discussion and debate of the pros and cons of a large-scale U.S. military involvement in Southeast Asia before we initiated the action.

7. After the action got under way and unanticipated events forced us off our planned course, we failed to retain popular support in part because we did not explain fully what was happening and why we were doing what we did. We had not prepared the public to understand...and how to react constructively to the need for changes in course.... A nation's deepest strength lies not in its military prowess but, rather, in the unity of its people. We failed to maintain it.

8.   We did not recognize that neither our people nor our leaders are omniscient.... We do not have the God-given right to shape every nation in our own image or as we choose.

9.   We did not hold to the principle that U.S. military action—other than in response to direct threats to our own security—should be carried out only in conjunction with multinational forces fully (and not merely cosmetically) by the international community.

10.   We failed to recognize that in international affairs, as in other aspects of life, there may be problems for which there are no immediate solutions.... [which] is particularly hard to admit. But, at times, we may have to live with an imperfect, untidy world.

11.   Underlying many of these errors lay our failure to organize the top echelons of the executive branch to deal effectively with the extraordinarily complex range of political and military issues, involving the great risks and costs—including, above all else, loss of life—associated with the application of military force under substantial constraints over a long period of time.... We thus failed to analyze and debate our actions in Southeast Asia...and the necessity of changing course when failure was clear...[2]

McNamara's Lessons from *The Fog of War:*

1.   Empathize with your enemy.
2.   Rationality will not save us.
3.   There's something beyond oneself.
4.   Maximize efficiency.
5.   Proportionality should be a guideline in war.
6.   Get the data.
7.   Belief and seeing are both often wrong.
8.   Be prepared to reexamine your reasoning.
9.   In order to do good, you may have to engage in evil.
10. Never say never.
11. You can't change human nature.[3]

Special Inspector General for Afghanistan Reconstruction (SIGAR), 2021

What We Need to Learn: Lessons from Twenty Years of Afghanistan Reconstruction, August 2021

1. Strategy: The U.S. government continuously struggled to develop and implement a coherent strategy for what it hoped to achieve.

2. Timelines: The U.S. government consistently underestimated the amount of time required to rebuild Afghanistan, and created unrealistic timelines and expectations that prioritized spending quickly. These choices increased corruption and reduced the effectiveness of programs.

3. Sustainability: Many of the institutions and infrastructure projects the United States built were not sustainable.

4. Personnel: Counterproductive civilian and military personnel policies and practices thwarted the effort.

5. Insecurity: Persistent insecurity severely undermined reconstruction efforts.

6. Context: The U.S. government did not understand the Afghan context and therefore failed to tailor its efforts accordingly.

7. Monitoring and Evaluation: U.S. government agencies rarely conducted sufficient monitoring and evaluation to understand the impact of their efforts.[4]

Excerpts from *Killing America*

IN SEPTEMBER 2018, DONATIONS from a group of poets, law enforcement officers, educators, attorneys, retired military officers, nurses, social workers, accountants, artists, psychologists, entrepreneurs, coaches, artists, and business executives made it possible to send a copy of *Killing America*, a book of poems, to the president, the vice president, every member of Congress and each justice in the Supreme Court. Three of the 546 recipients sent thank-you notes. One of them, Representative Rosa DeLauro, from Connecticut's Third Congressional District, addressed the book's content in her note: "As Members of Congress, one of our most sacred duties is to protect the American people. On that measure, we have failed—and doing nothing to change the current dynamic is both cowardly and shameful."

With several exceptions, the poems focused on American violence between 1993 and 2018, and included violence perpetrated by and against civilians, law enforcement officers, and members of the military. The cover letter that accompanied each book noted that violence is a trait of America's collective Shadow. The letter that accompanied the president's book appears on the last page of this Appendix.

Killing America was followed by *Enough with the...Talking Points* (Appendix III), which explores the disintegration of public and private discourse in America. *Healing America's Narratives* takes an expansive view of some of what underlies America's propensities toward violence and away from healthy discourse. The poems[1] below, along with the three poems in Chapter Seven, are from *Killing America*.

FOUND POEM: MARCH 16, 2018

The number of children killed by gunfire
in the U.S. since the 2012 mass shooting
at Sandy Hook Elementary School
in Newtown, Connecticut,
surpasses the total of American soldiers killed
in overseas combat since 9/11,
according to a Department of Defense report.

————

Ryan Sit, "More Children Have Been Killed by Guns Since Sandy Hook Than U. S. Soldiers in Combat Since 9/11," *Newsweek*, March 16, 2018, http://www.newsweek.com/gun-violence-children-killed-sandy-hook-military-soldiers-war-terror-911-848602 Accessed March 22, 2018.

A "found" poem is a selection of writing that was not written as a poem, but was "found" and rendered as a poem. The original writing might be anything—a headline, a caption, a shopping list, a to-do list, an excerpt from a letter, a judicial opinion, a home inspection report, and so on.

GOING HOME

Near Kirkuk
five soldiers watch
or work
while two wheel
the blood-soaked
gurney from the
inflated O.R. The
sergeant's leg
amputated
and discarded, time
will tell if
he
will
be
as well.

———

Johnny Dwyer, "The Wounded," *New York Times Magazine,*
March 27, 2005, pp. 24+. Photographs by Lynsey Addario/
Corbis. The poem emerged directly from the photograph.

SUPPOSED TO BE SAFE

18-year-old Terrell Bosley, a freshman at
Olive Harvey College, who plays the bass

in several church bands, is helping a friend
unload drums from his car when shots ring

out outside the Lights of Zion Missionary Bible
Church near 116th and Halstead on Chicago's South

Side. His mother, Pam Bosley, is preparing dinner
while his father, Tom, is helping their two other

sons with their homework when she gets the call
that Terrell has been shot. *We ran to the church,*

she says. Later that night, Terrell dies at the hospital.
He didn't do anything wrong. He was in college and

working a job, doing so much, doing all the right things,
she says. *And at church, a place that's supposed to be safe.*

Sarah Hoye, "Surviving 'Chi-raq': How communities take a stand against
violence," *Aljazeera America,* November 3, 2015,
http://america.aljazeera.com/watch/shows/america-
tonight/articles/2015/11/3/surviving-chiraq-chicago-communities-stand-
against-violence.html Accessed December 7, 2017; and ABC7, "Family
of teen murdered in 2006 offers $5K reward," *ABC7 Chicago,* April 4,
2012, http://abc7chicago.com/archive/8608710/ Accessed December 27,
2017.

SUNNY DECEMBER NEW ENGLAND MORNING

The children walk across the sunlit parking lot,
long, late autumn shadows falling to their left,
most, as rehearsed, hold their hands on the
shoulders of the child in front of them, some
cry, some look confused, some have their
heads down as two uniformed officers and
two plain-clothed women guide them away
from the building. The adults don't yet know
the enormity of the day and while the children
know less, some are young enough to feel the
grownups' discomfort amid the chaos of sirens,
lights, shouting and guns. Time will pass and a
Florida woman who believes the parking lot
scene and all the events of this day are a hoax
will be charged with making death threats
against a parent of one of the twenty first-
graders killed. Other survivors will be harassed
by Americans who argue the event was staged
to erode support for the 2nd Amendment, and a
Connecticut man will be charged for allegedly
phoning in a threat to the new Sandy Hook
Elementary School which replaced the school
that was demolished after the massacre.

––––––––––

The source for the opening image in this poem is a photograph by Shannon Hicks
at the *Newtown Bee*. https://api.time.com/wp-content/uploads/2018/02/shannon-
hicks-newtown-bee-sandy-hook.jpg. The photo appeared throughout the media,
including the front page of major newspapers. The subsequent details in the poem
emerged from diverse news reports in the months and years following the shooting.
Lawsuits arising from the shooting continue to be litigated.

AMBUSH

Two police officers sitting in their patrol car
in Brooklyn are shot point-blank and killed
by a man who travels from Baltimore vowing
to kill police, and who later commits suicide
with the same gun. Officers Wenjian Liu and
Rafael Ramos are in the car near Myrtle and
Tompkins Avenues in Bedford-Stuyvesant in
the shadow of a housing project when Ismaaiyl
Brinsley walks up to the passenger-side window,
assumes a firing stance and shoots several rounds
into the heads and upper bodies of the officers
who never draw their weapons. He then flees
down the street and onto a subway platform
where he kills himself as the police close in. They
recover a silver semi-automatic handgun. Brinsley
has a rap sheet that includes robbery and carrying
a concealed gun, and is believed to have shot his
former girlfriend near Baltimore before traveling
to Brooklyn. His statements on social media
suggest that he is angered about the Eric Garner
and Michael Brown cases and that he plans to kill
police officers. Authorities in Baltimore send a
warning about these threats, but it is received
too late. The shootings, the chase, the suicide
and the failed bid to save the lives of the officers
turn a busy commercial intersection on the
Saturday before Christmas into a scene of
pandemonium. The city's some 300 killings
so far this year, is a number so low as to
be unheard-of two decades ago.

Benjamin Mueller and Al Baker, "2 N.Y.P.D. Officers Killed in Brooklyn
Ambush; Suspect Commits Suicide," *New York Times,* December 20,
2014, https://www.nytimes.com/2014/12/21/nyregion/two-police-
officers-shot-in-their-patrol-car-in-brooklyn.html Accessed November
30, 2017.

1941

An unarmed West African immigrant with no criminal record
is killed by four New York City police officers who fire 41 shots
at him, hitting him 19 times, in the doorway of his Bronx
apartment building. Amadou Diallo, 22, who comes to America

from Guinea and works as a street peddler in Manhattan, dies at
the scene. Relatives and neighbors describe him as a shy, hardworking man with a ready smile, a devout Muslim who does
not smoke or drink. *He is a skinny guy. Why would the police*

shoot somebody of that nature 30 or 40 times? We see the police
and we give them all the respect we have, says his uncle, Mamadou
Diallo. The officers involved in the shooting are assigned to the
Street Crimes Unit, which focuses largely on taking illegal guns off

the street. All four, in plainclothes, use their 9-millimeter semi-
automatic service pistols, which hold 16 bullets and can discharge
all of them in seconds. Two officers, age 35 and 26, empty their
weapons, firing 16 shots each. Another, age 27, fires five times

and the fourth, age 26, four times. It is not known why the officers
begin firing. A police official, on the condition of anonymity, says
We don't know what happened, because we haven't spoken to
them, but it looks like one guy may have panicked and the rest

followed suit. An investigation begins, and no weapon is found on
Mr. Diallo. A pager and a wallet are found lying next to the body.
I think there is no reason to shoot someone more than 30
times, says Mamadou Diallo.

Michael Cooper, "Officers in Bronx Fire 41 Shots, And an Unarmed Man Is
Killed," *New York Times,* February 5, 1999,
http://www.nytimes.com/1999/02/05/nyregion/officers-in-bronx-fire-41-shots-
and-an-unarmed-man-is-killed.html Accessed December 12, 2017.

EARLY AUTUMN SOUTHWEST EVENING

The music stops.
The young women holding hands,
their tank tops, shorts, boots, long
flowing brown hair, and the young
man in a black tee, blue jeans and
boots to their right, capture a neon-
backlit American summer evening.
They run, semi-crouched, amid
food and beverage containers
strewn across the open space while
those behind them kneel, crawl,
crouch and cower along the fence,
unsure where the shooter is and
when the shooting will stop.
If ever.

––––––––––

This poem emerged from a photograph taken by David
Becker/Getty Images. The photograph appeared here, among
other places: https://www.nytimes.com/2017/10/02/us/las-
vegas-shooting-live-updates.html?_r=0 Accessed October 2,
2017.

THIS DAY OUR DAILY DEAD
- after Naomi Shihab Nye

We wonder and worry what it will take for
our country women and men to feel again

this tender gravity, this pull of and toward
kindness, the way we did when we were

very young children. We do not need our
passports, we need not travel beyond our

borders, giving ourselves this day our daily
dead as we do, rarely really seeing them

though, protected as we agree to be from the
truth of what we do and who we are. Twenty

first-graders are not enough, yet another
unarmed black man or ambushed cop is not

enough, concert and movie goers and dancers
are not enough, a shopper, bus driver and

landscaper, still not enough, high school
students, not enough. We don't know if it will

ever be time to look at the images no one wants
to see because they're too disturbing, unless

they're broken-or-burned-beyond-recognition
un-American bodies, but our relentless refusal

to look deeply at what's disturbing is itself
disturbing. Our terrified turning away from

what is traps us ever more tightly in it, as if
that ever-growing malignancy will on its own

dissipate and disappear if we make believe it's
not there, even though we feel its pressure

within our hearts every moment. *Peek-a-boo*, it
says. *How much more of me do you need? How*

much bigger do I need to be before you admit
I'm part of you, and you have the will to do

what has to be done to remove me, before the
lost voice of that vulnerable child within you

is truly able to remember and say, all gone?
How much more? Will you ever be enough?

———

After Naomi Shihab Nye's poem "Kindness"—especially the lines, "Before
you learn the tender gravity of kindness / you must travel where the
Indian in a white poncho / lies dead by the side of the road. / You must
see how this could be you, /..." The poem is embraced and recited in
schools around the world. You can read it here:
https://poets.org/poem/kindness

September 2018

The White House
Office of the President
1600 Pennsylvania Avenue, N.W.
Washington, DC 20500

Dear Donald Trump:

The enclosed book of poems, *Killing America: Our United States of Ignorance, Fear, Bigotry, Violence and Greed,* captures and comments on a series of images from late 20th- and early 21st-century America. Our unprecedented and increasingly normalized national addiction to gun violence catalyzed this project, but what began, and continues, to emerge as the project unfolds is the underlying culture of ignorance, fear, bigotry, violence and greed – at home and abroad, that both feeds and is fed by this uniquely American embrace of violence. You personally embody and help perpetuate this culture.

I, and the folks who helped make this mailing possible have no illusions about your reading this book, being moved by it, or taking any meaningful action because of it. History will look back on many current occupants of all three branches of the United States federal government – and especially on you, as many American and world citizens and leaders already do, with disbelief and disdain. Your language, general civic ignorance and spoiled-rich-white-kid arrogance evince a striking, powerful habit of self-delusion.

One of the most challenging aspects of creating this short book, beyond writing and sequencing the individual poems, was choosing which images to include, which to leave out, and how far back into the 20th century to look. Put differently, which dead school children, concert, club, church and movie goers, unarmed black men, ambushed cops, military personnel, Iraqi and Afghan civilians, other ordinary people going about their lives and anyone I may, in fact, have omitted, deserves to be excluded? How would you choose? Oh, yes. More guns – easy to say for someone who's lived a protected, privileged life as you have. You are in over your head. Please stop embarrassing those of us who understand the complexity of what we face. You, obviously, don't.

As we approached our post-Sandy-Hook-and-Columbine and pre-Orlando-and-Las Vegas 2016 elections, I wrote "Donald Trump, Collective American Shadow and 'The Better Angels of Our Nature'" in response to the ignorance, nonsense and insults coming from your mouth and phone as a candidate. You can access that here: https://reggiemarra.com/2016/09/14/donald-trump-collective-american-shadow-and-the-better-angels-of-our-nature/.

My request is that you take some time to deeply and regularly reflect on the extent to which *your* intentions and behaviors are grounded in the ignorance, fear, bigotry, violence and greed of our collective shadow – of which you embody a great deal. If you think such reflection doesn't apply to you, you are deeply and sadly mistaken. It applies to all of us. Grow up. Own your part. I'm owning mine.

With love,

Reggie Marra

Enough with the Talking Points:
Doing More Good than Harm in Conversation[1]

WHAT FOLLOWS IS AN EXCERPT FROM one example of the type of conversational exchange that led me, some six years ago, to begin a process of teasing apart those strategies, tactics, and behaviors that lead to healthy or unhealthy conversations. The process led to the publication of *Enough with the…Talking Points: Doing More Good than Harm in Conversation* in June 2020. The particular exchange excerpted below took place on social media. You can read the entire conversation, along with my review of it, online at:
https://reggiemarra.com/2020/09/12/an-example-of-a-conversation-that-does-more-harm-than-good/

The review resulted from reading the conversation through a variety of lenses that include and are not limited to the following:

- recognizing the impacts of cultural givens, personal experience, preconceptions, judgments, assumptions, labels, insults, and sweeping generalizations

- differentiating facts and opinions

- staying curious along and committed to the path of learning

- knowing your intention in conversation

- seeking and recognizing similarities as well as differences

- staying focused on the topic of the conversation

- understanding your own and others' emotions

- embodying another's story

- exploring the impact of getting or not getting your way—that is, how it feels to "win" and lose"

- understanding the difference between truthfulness and truth and committing to both.

There are more, but these will suffice. Not all of these lenses are explored in the example; they are all explored in the book.

The intention of this conversational review is to point out the types of thinking, reacting, and writing or speaking that don't do any good and that usually do harm and make things worse. My intention in the review was not to take one or another side in the *content* of the exchanges. If I missed the mark toward that end, I welcomed clear, substantive feedback that pointed to it. I obviously have views on Donald Trump and John Lewis and made a conscious effort to keep them out of my assessment of the comments.

The *primary* exchange is between 'commenters' Rick, Gus and Gary, with occasional other commenters contributing as well. The names of the commenters are pseudonyms (except mine). The first comment each commenter made is **bolded.** My review of each comment, using some of the lenses listed above, is in a smaller font, *italicized* and bulleted. My *italicized comments* refer to the statement immediately above them. I used a bulleted form to provide more white space and make the piece easier to read. (The full online version employs colored fonts toward that end). Not every comment in the thread is reproduced here; a few other folks chimed in, but did not stay in the thread; each comment that appears is reproduced unedited—including punctuation and spacing.

As you read through this, note which comments, including my italics, bring up an emotional charge for you. Get curious as to why. Explore a bit. Reflect. Think and feel critically. Commit to the truth. Note also that because of the format of social media exchanges, unless the commenter directly addresses the person he or she is responding to, it is not always clear to whom each subsequent comment is directed. This thread is a clear example of why social media generally are not effective for any kind of authentic, rational exchange of ideas or opinions. But you knew that. Here's the excerpt:

(Original Post) Reggie: "When asked if he found (John) Lewis's life impressive, Trump responded, 'He didn't come to my inauguration. He didn't come to my State of the Union speeches. And that's OK. That's his right. And, again, nobody has done more for Black Americans than I have.'"

Atta boy, Don, way to stay with the question, hold that big picture, and conclude with a whopper with a straight face.

- *Donald Trump deflected the question about John Lewis's life and spoke about Lewis's decision not to attend specific events that were important to him (Trump)—this is an example of not focusing on the topic being discussed/question asked.*

- *Trump has a history of reflecting events and questions back to himself.*

- *The final sentence in the quote is provably untrue (whether we call it a lie, hyperbole or ignorance) and is consistent with Trump's language patterns regarding himself and his plans as the best, greatest, and more than anyone else. The list of names of people living and dead, who have done more for Black Americans than Donald Trump (and most of us of any skin pigmentation) is exhaustive.*

- *"Atta boy," which is my commentary, is mildly sarcastic. A more direct approach would be something like "The President's response dodges the question asked, makes it about himself rather than the deceased, and concludes with an outright lie."*

Gus: At this point, is anyone surprised by this?
- *A straightforward comment, in the form of a rhetorical question, that indicates the writer expects this type of response from Donald Trump, and assumes that most people would agree (is anyone surprised?).*

Al: Disgusting. Exactly what a racist would say.
- *"Disgusting" is a label/characterization, which could be clarified with something like "I find the president's comment disgusting." "Exactly what a racist would say," is inflammatory and indirectly*

calls the president a racist. Something like "I find that last sentence to be racist" would comment on the sentence and not the person.

Rick: Lewis was racist and only looked out for blacks. Trump is right
- *The initial sentence here is provably untrue, insulting, and a sweeping generalization of the life of a man who has been honored for more than fifty years by whites, blacks, liberals, conservatives, and others for his courage, humility, and service.*
- *The final three words, stated as a fact, which it is not, could be clarified with "I believe Trump is right."*

Reggie: Good book. Worth reading.
https://www.amazon.com/Enough-Talking-Points-Doing-Conversation/dp/0962782890/
- *My response to Rick here is based on, first, my completely subjective but informed belief about the value of the book, and second, on my awareness that using false statements, insults, and generalizations are specific behaviors that the book explores.*
- *My response also intentionally avoids getting involved in attempts to refute or debate anything or anyone in the thread.*

[A brief exchange between Gus and a new person, Gerry, occurs here. Again, the full conversation is available at:
https://reggiemarra.com/2020/09/12/an-example-of-a-conversation-that-does-more-harm-than-good/]

Gus [to Rick]: What is your major malfunction that you write something as heinous as that?
- *This is insulting, assumptive (that someone has a major malfunction if they disagree with Gus) and inflammatory. "Heinous" is a characterization/judgment that does not consider that the other (Rick) has a worldview that differs. The whole sentence invites what follows.*

Rick [to Gus]: what's your problem with what I said . Do you have a problem with what I feel and experienced.
- *This response is measured, and asks Gus a question that is somewhat deceptive. The question asks if Gus has a problem with what Rick has felt and experienced. Gus's remark was about what*

> *Rick* wrote, *not about his feelings or experiences. This is nuanced and clarifying it is necessary.*

Gary [to Rick]: It seems your life experiences having led you to this post ignoring all of the struggles of Mr. Lewis. Putting his life on the line for people. Which is something trump does for no one. All of this convinces me that you and your life are first hand experts at what racism is.

- *Gary begins with a measured view (It seems…) and brings John Lewis's life and work back into the exchange.*
- *The second sentence, in light of putting one's life on the line, supports the first and is factual.*
- *The final sentence indirectly calls Rick a racist (expert at what racism is). This is insulting, inflammatory, a judgment, and a label.*

Rick: typical liberal answer , when someone disagrees it is automatically considered racist.
Wrong way to define racism.
That's the real issue.
Just for being a member of the black caucus makes him a racist

- *The first line includes a sweeping generalization (typical liberal answer) and an assumption (when someone disagrees it is automatically…).*
- *The second line is meaningless as written—it implies that Rick knows the wrong and right ways to define racism, but he doesn't offer either, so the five words accomplish nothing.*
- *The third line asserts that defining racism the right way is the "real issue" but again, offers no definition—adding nothing substantive to the thread. It is also asserted as a fact ("I believe" or "I think" would be less declarative), and there's no evidence that it is factual.*
- *The final line is a provably untrue generalization and seems to be based on unstated assumptions and/or preconceptions.*

Gary: Not typical. You can cast me as an easy strawman but most critical thinkers will look at your post and see the bigotry. But go ahead and cast me as "typical" while you cast yourself as an independent thinker. Because obviously you cannot hold the concept that us liberal progressives might have come to our conclusions based on our life experiences, specifically our dealings with bigots.

- *Gary's response stays with the content of what it responds to—Rick's immediately preceding comment.*

- *First, it refutes the accusation that his own previous comment is "typical," and then,* without labeling or insulting Rick, *notes the "strawman" move that Rick has made (i.e. moving the conversation from a discussion of Lewis and Trump to an attack on "typical liberal answer[s]."*

- *Gary's assertion that "most critical thinkers...bigotry" is an assumption for which he provides no evidence, and it is based on a generalization (most critical thinkers).*

- *In the next two sentences, Gary challenges Rick's claiming to be an independent thinker while characterizing Gary's response as a "typically liberal response"—a challenge that holds up rationally.*

- *The final sentence holds up as well, and might be more effective if begun with "It seems that you cannot..." rather than "Because you obviously cannot..." This revision identifies the statement as the writer's view as opposed to an obvious given (which would not be obvious or given to someone who agrees ideologically with Rick).*

- *Finally, "...specifically our dealings with bigots" is an implicit attack on/insult to Rick, which simply does no good.*

Rick: You are the bigot and an anti-American socialist who has decided that our capitalist system is flawed.
I believe in God , family and country .
Marra can give you a pretty good background on who I am.
You don't know me and call me a bigot , that's ignorance at its best.
But expected from someone like you.

- *The first sentence is an assumption, a sweeping generalization, an insult and a label that accuses Gary of something of which there is no evidence in the exchange (i.e. "who has decided that our capitalist system is flawed").*

- *The second sentence is fine, as a stand-alone. Rick is stating his beliefs. In the context of the sentence it follows, however, it seems to imply that Gary does not believe in these same things (admittedly, I'm inferring that, and, I believe, reasonably so in the context of the thread. I would defer to Rick if he offered another reason for stating his beliefs in this comment).*

- *The third sentence directly involves me (Marra), is an assumption, and is not true. I knew Rick as a high school student in the late 1970s and early 1980s.*
  - *My memory is that he was a good kid, but I have not had direct, in-person contact with him for some forty years. In terms of who he is now, my only sense of him comes through what he has written in the thread—which indicates how he views certain things, if not who he is.*
  - *Therefore, I am not qualified to give anyone "a pretty good background on who [Rick is]." I disagree with and can easily refute his calling John Lewis a racist, and I don't endorse his, or anyone else's, labels, insults, and generalizations in the thread.*
- *The fourth sentence responds to Gary's previous comment, "...specifically our dealings with bigots." Gary never calls Rick or anyone else a bigot. In context, Rick may very easily have interpreted it as though he had been called a bigot.*
- *The final sentence labels and insults Gary as ignorant. The final words ("But expected from someone like you") constitute a sweeping generalization that has no meaning other than to insult Gary.*

The thread continues through another thirteen comments (which, again, you can read online: https://reggiemarra.com/2020/09/12/an-example-of-a-conversation-that-does-more-harm-than-good/.

Gus reappears and calls Rick a "foul racist" and calls him "the reason we need Black Lives Matter." Rick calls Gus (or Gary—it's not clear) a "liberal socialist antiAmerican pig," who "should be re-educated to become normal again." Gary reminds Rick that the founders of the United States were liberals, and Rick guarantees that they were not. Gary begins to step back and comment about what he sees happening in the thread. Frank (a new participant) supports Rick's arguments and writes that people who believe as Gary does are "a cancer on our republic." Gary continues to engage, but in an ongoing attempt to point out what he sees happening. Rick softens in his response to Gary, but continues to insult Gus, who returns in kind.

- *Most of the comments in this thread do not address the content of the initial post (regarding Donald Trump's comments about John Lewis). The thread deteriorated into name-calling, insults, labels, generalizations, and in most cases, little or no evidence of self-reflection or self-awareness on the part of the participants* in the context of the thread *(i.e. every one of the participants might or might not be self-reflective or self-aware with their kids, spouse, profession or throughout his or her life; except for two brief moments, this reflection/awareness was not evident in this exchange.*
- *Social media are not designed for thoughtful, robust, informed, rational, etc. disagreement or agreement. While they are not the only place in which attempts to communicate regularly deteriorate, they tend to foster such deterioration.*
- *Of the primary participants, Gus, Rick, and Gary, and the latecomer, Frank, only Gary participated in a way that did, or attempted to do, more good than harm in the context of the exchange, according to the lenses for conversation that can be found in* Enough with the…Talking Points. *We have a lot of work to do as a species.*

In addition to the insults, generalizations, and assumptions that characterize this exchange, there is also a perspective that has become increasingly popular in the United States (some would argue especially since the 1980s): *If you disagree with* me, *you are un-American.* Underlying that perspective is some version of *I know what it means to be an American, and you don't,* or *I'm an American and you're not.* Beneath both of these is a closed mind that has forgotten, or, perhaps, never learned the volume and depth of disagreements that led to the ratification and subsequent amending of the U. S. Constitution.

Here, again, is the link to the full conversation, with commentary: https://reggiemarra.com/2020/09/12/an-example-of-a-conversation-that-does-more-harm-than-good/

NOTES

1. David Souter, Retired U. S. Supreme Court Justice, from an interview at the University of New Hampshire Law School, September 14, 2012, excerpt: https://www.youtube.com/watch?v=rWcVtWennr0; full interview: https://www.youtube.com/watch?v=yVJhXQB1TAk

INTRODUCTION

1. Inspired by James P. Carse, *Finite and Infinite Games: A Vision of Life as Play and Possibility* (Free Press-MacMillan, 1986), 3.
2. https://reggiemarra.com/2016/09/14/donald-trump-collective-american-shadow-and-the-better-angels-of-our-nature/
3. https://reggiemarra.com/2018/10/28/revisiting-donald-trump-collective-american-shadow-and-the-better-angels-of-our-nature/
4. Throughout this volume "Shadow" refers to this denial and projection of what is disowned, and "shadow" refers to other meanings of the word. The difference is explicitly stated in Chapter 2.

CHAPTER ONE – Cultural Givens & the View from Here

1. Inspired by Carse, *Finite and Infinite Games,* 62.
2. See this chapter (8-13) for a summary of my own cultural givens; and see *Enough with the…Talking Points,* (5-8+) for more on the role of cultural givens in our struggles to engage in conversations that do more good than harm.
3. Originally from "A New President,"

https://reggiemarra.com/2016/09/11/a-new-president/,
this poem has been revised to include all three branches of the
federal government. Now titled "Broken Branches" it appears in
*Killing America: Our United States of Ignorance, Fear, Bigotry,
Violence and Greed* (2018), 55-58; you can find an earlier version
of the revised poem online at:
https://reggiemarra.com/2017/10/03/1599/.

4. John Robert Lewis, (February 21, 1940-July 17, 2020) served in the
    United States House of Representatives for Georgia's 5th con-
    gressional district from 1987-2020. He became interested in the
    racial equality and justice in his teens and was a central figure in
    the Civil Rights Movement of the 1960s. He often said that his
    work included civil rights, but was really about building a Beloved
    Community that included all human beings.
    https://en.wikipedia.org/wiki/John_Lewis. American philosopher
    Josiah Royce is credited with being the originator of the phrase,
    "Beloved Community." See Jon Meacham's *His Truth Is Marching
    On: John Lewis and the Power of Hope*, (2020), 63.

5. The carefully curated and litigated story of Trump's successful
    image and finances continues to unfold. Here's one place to begin:
    Russ Buettner, Susanne Craig, and Mike McIntire, "Long-
    Concealed Records Show Trump's Chronic Losses and Years of
    Tax Avoidance," *New York Times,* September 27, 2020,
    https://www.nytimes.com/interactive/2020/09/27/us/donald-
    trump-taxes.html Accessed September 27, 2020.

6. General McChrystal's full comment is available here:
    https://www.youtube.com/watch?v=k-
    HYFziXNlY&fbclid=IwAR2Yft9Lx8Q6Ax5BD0gPYkYl_Zwonly
    RXaib-BeHmIaDHjKQ0ZJMdT28e2I.

7. This language is from Ken Wilber, *The Religion of Tomorrow,*
    (Shambhala, 2017). What follows is my application: *waking* up
    refers to engaging available *states* of consciousness such as waking,
    dreaming, and deep dreamless sleep (and is not the intended
    meaning of "woke" in popular parlance); *growing* up (closer to
    what the popular use of the word "woke" approximates) refers to
    developing through *stages* of consciousness that can be simplified
    as it's about *me,* it's about *us,* it's about *all of us,* and it's about *all
    that is; cleaning* up refers to uncovering what's repressed—such as
    Shadow; *showing* up refers to being in the world in a way that
    embodies the fullness and freedom of waking, growing, and

cleaning up with attention to the individual, collective, interior, and exterior aspects of existence. See note 11 below.

8. If we are fortunate to develop in more or less healthy ways, we begin to question what has been and is given and see how it holds up when compared and contrasted with our own direct experience of the world and the givens and direct experiences of others—part of the process of waking, growing, cleaning and showing up.

9. Thomas Merton, "The Inner Experience," *Thomas Merton: Spiritual Master.* Ed. Lawrence S. Cunningham, (Paulist, 1992), 295.

10. Ken Wilber, *Integral Spirituality: A Startling New Role for Religion in the Modern and Postmodern World,* (Integral-Shambhala, 2006), 277. "Multiplistic level" and "orange altitude" refer to the developmental level, also known as *modern* and *rational* that gave us modern science, the U.S. Constitution, and evidence-based, strategic approaches that undergird many institutions and corporations.

11. This four-part "check-in" is based on Ken Wilber's quadrants. Here's a nine-minute intro: https://integrallife.com/four-quadrants/. Various books and online resources provide a deeper dive; Wilber, Patten, Leonard & Morelli's *Integral Life Practice* (2008) present the quadrants in the larger context of integral (AQAL) theory (quadrants, levels and lines of development, gender and personality types, and states of consciousness). Terry Patten's *A New Republic of the Heart* (2018) provides a thorough, concise, practical overview of AQAL in the context of what we might do together to save ourselves and the planet. For the brave and curious deep-divers, see also Wilber's *The Religion of Tomorrow* (2017).

12. Audre Lorde, "The Transformation of Silence into Language and Action," *Sister Outsider,* (Crossing Press, 1984), 41; and *The Cancer Journals,* (Penguin, 2020/1980), 13.

13. See Jonathan Rauch's *The Constitution of Knowledge: A Defense of Truth,* (Brookings Institute Press, 2021) for a deep dive into our contemporary struggles with knowledge and truth.

14. Parker J. Palmer, *The Courage to Teach: Exploring the Inner Landscape of a Teacher's Life,* (Jossey-Bass, 1998), 104.

15. *Love,* as used in this book, includes: "the joyful acceptance of belonging," Br. David Steindl-Rast, *Gratefulness: the Heart of Prayer,* (Paulist, 1984), 167; "the will to extend one's self for the purpose of nurturing one's own or another's spiritual growth," M.

Scott Peck, *The Road Less Traveled,* (Simon & Schuster, 1978), 81; and *the absence of fear,* based on Marianne Williamson's reflections on *A Course in Miracles,* (Foundation for Inner Peace, 1976, 1992) in *A Return to Love,* (HarperPaperbacks, 1993). We'll revisit love in chapters eleven and twelve.

CHAPTER TWO – A Brief Overview of Shadow

1. Robert Macfarlane, *Underland: A Deep Time Journey,* (Norton, 2019), 11-12.
2. Robert A. Johnson, *Owning Your Own Shadow,* 3-4.
3. Robert Bly, *A Little Book on the Human Shadow,* 17-18.
4. Ibid., 26.
5. Anger is not necessarily a "bad" thing; it is clarifying. What can go wrong is how we understand and what we do with our anger.
6. We'll explore some ways to work with Shadow in Chapter Eleven. For more on Shadow, beyond what's cited above, see Bill Plotkin's *Wild Mind: A Field Guide to the Human Psyche,* 207-34; his *Soulcraft: Crossing into the Mysteries of Nature and Psyche,* 267-80; and Connie Zweig and Jeremiah Abrams, eds. *Meeting the Shadow: The Hidden Power of the Dark Side of Human Nature.*
7. Use of the word "citizens" is noted here because "American citizens" and/or "the American people" while indicating a specific legal status, are ambiguous, if not meaningless, phrases due to the diversity of beliefs, ideologies, developmental worldviews, ethnicities, et cetera, that makes up the United States, or any nation or large group. I recognize that not every "American citizen" would agree that Donald Trump personifies the collective American Shadow or even that the country has a collective Shadow. I believe, and provide evidence here, that he does, and it does.
8. See Centers for Disease Control, specifically the daily trends setting: https://covid.cdc.gov/covid-data-tracker/#trends_dailytrendscases
9. The volume of reporting and writing that details his words and behaviors since 2016 is itself formidable. Some writers hold him as their focus; others note his relationship to larger socio-cultural concerns around truth, knowledge, partisanship, discourse and democracy. From among many: Leonnig and Rucker's *I Alone Can Fix It* and *A Very Stable Genius;* Kessler, Rizzo and Kelly's *Donald Trump and His Assault on Truth;* Kakutani's *The Death of Truth;*

Bacevich's *After the Apocalypse;* Rauch's *The Constitution of Knowledge;* Esper's *A Sacred Oath.*

10. Samuel Flagg Bemis, presidential address to the American Historical Association, December 29, 1961. https://www.historians.org/about-aha-and-membership/aha-history-and-archives/presidential-addresses/samuel-flagg-bemis. Accessed March 23, 2021. See also Gaddis Smith's "The Two Worlds of Samuel Flagg Bemis," https://academic.oup.com/dh/article/9/4/295/361855, Accessed March 23, 2021, and Howard Zinn's *Declarations of Independence,* (HarperPerennial, 1991), 60-64.

11. Retired U.S. Supreme Court Justice David Souter's interview at the University of New Hampshire's Franklin Pierce School of Law, September 14, 2012, (see contents-facing page in this volume). https://www.youtube.com/watch?v=D5aM2WnpCQ8 Accessed June 27, 2018.

12. For more on how "masculine" and "feminine" are used in this volume, see Chapter Three, 36-37 and note 3.

13. Rabbi Marc Gellman, remarks at the September 23, 2001 Prayer Service at Yankee Stadium in the Bronx, New York. This excerpt is my transcription of the video from a C-Span DVD. The video is now available for free online: https://www.c-span.org/video/?166250-1/york-city-prayer-service. Hearing these words (and others from that day) as they were spoken is more powerful than reading them. Rabbi Gellman's remarks begin at 1:14:55.

14. John Tarrant, *Bring Me the Rhinoceros: and Other Zen Koans That Will Save Your Life,* (Shambhala, 2008/2004), 76.

15. Ta-Nehisi Coates, *Between the World and Me,* (One World/ Random House, 2015), 81-82.

16. Jack Gilbert, "Highlights and Interstices," *The Great Fires: Poems 1982-1992,* (New York: Knopf, 2005/1995), 56. The poem is available online at *PBS News Hour,* November 19, 2012, https://www.pbs.org/newshour/arts/weekly-poem-highlights-and-interstices, Accessed July 30, 2021.

17. A powerful example of such "fullest understanding" is Thich Nhat Hanh's poem, "Please Call Me by My True Names," which we'll return to in Chapter Twelve. You can read it here: https://plumvillage.org/articles/please-call-me-by-my-true-names-song-poem/; also available in *Call Me by My True Names: The Collected Poems of Thich Nhat Hanh,* (Parallax, 2001).

18. Jon Meacham, *The Soul of America* (Random House, 2019) ix, 277. Meacham cites Baldwin's "The White Man's Guilt" in *Ebony,* August 1965, 47. See Chapter Five, 118 for the full quote.
19. Small scale democracies existed for a time and then collapsed in Ancient Greece and Rome. For a lively overview of the U.S. Constitution, check out Akhil Reed Amar's interview with Meghna Chakrabarti, "'The Words That Made Us': Scholar Akhil Reed Amar on How to Better Understand the Constitution," *WBUR, On Point,* May 17, 2021, https://www.wbur.org/onpoint/2021/05/17/the-words-that-made-us-how-to-better-understand-the-constitution Accessed May 17, 2021. For an equally lively and more detailed exploration, see Amar's *The Words That Made Us: America's Constitutional Conversation,* (New York: Basic, 2021).
20. As used here "culture" refers to *interiors*—shared beliefs and values; "society" refers to *exteriors*—infrastructure/environment; each emerges from and informs the other.
21. Jamie Wheal, "Until We Collapse," Anthony Chene, Producer, July 27, 2021, https://www.youtube.com/watch?v=VFkmI4PxnYA Accessed August 25, 2021. The full the 40-minute interview provides context for this passage.

CHAPTER THREE: Fear of the Feminine & the Subjugation of Women: Getting Their Feet from off of Our Necks

1. Inspired by Carse, *Finite and Infinite Games,* 30-31.
2. The interplay of biology, cultural beliefs, means of production, technology and other factors impacts the respective roles that have been expected of men and women, and, historically, "allowed" by men for women.
3. Regarding *earlier/later* levels and *healthy/unhealthy* manifestations of the feminine and masculine, early levels are often referred to as "low" since our earlier development embodies lesser or smaller capacities than later development can, and usually does (contrast a healthy toddler with a healthy adult; neither is better, worse, right, or wrong and both can be "perfect" manifestations of toddlerhood and adulthood, respectively).
   - an earlier/lower, *me-centric* orientation is a necessary aspect of development that, when healthy, allows me to function in the world as a competent, confident human being. When

unhealthy, however, it takes only the self, and no one else, into consideration—others are only useful objects to be manipulated and used for *my* purposes. I'm an insider; everyone else is an outsider.

- a later/medium, *group/us-centric* orientation allows me to identify with others (family, community, religion, team, friends, nation, etc.) without losing my self-efficacy from the earlier stage. When healthy, a group-centric orientation allows my family, my community, my team, my religion, or my country to function cooperatively among other families, communities, teams, religions, and countries. When unhealthy, this orientation often pits my group *against* other groups—other groups are wrong or bad. Manifestations of the unhealthy include bigotry, caste, xenophobia, misogyny, homophobia, racism and war—tribalism at its worst.

- a later/higher *all-of-us/human-centric* (sometimes called *world*-centric) orientation allows me to still function in various groups, but to identify primarily with other human beings, period, regardless of group or tribe. While I am aware of billions of unique human beings and the various groups we identify with, when healthy, my primary orientation acknowledges and transcends individual and group differences and embraces our common humanity. When unhealthy, I can operate in an anthropocentric manner that ignores or devalues other types of life and matter—including flora, fauna, and the planet itself.

- A still later/higher, *all-that-is-centric* orientation allows me to function in embrace of myself, my groups, all of life, matter, and the whole of interior and exterior existence. This is an orientation that embodies and acts on (as opposed to just espousing) care for the planet and beyond.

Anecdotal evidence suggests that a majority of human beings on the planet live day-to-day in group- and me-centric orientations, which, again, can be healthy or unhealthy. Many people understand and even espouse the *world-* and *all-that-is-centric* orientations, sometimes referred to as "a global perspective," but have not yet developed the consciousness that allows them to *live* at these levels: that is, they (we) don't all walk the talk.

Unhealthy manifestations of the feminine concerns with care, embrace, collaboration, mercy, and compassion very generally can include a lost or missing sense of self and self-efficacy, in which I have no intrinsic identity or value and I only matter in terms of my attention to and from others. Codependency and an inability to assert oneself or to practice self-compassion are possible manifestations in both women and men.

Unhealthy manifestations of the masculine focus on rights, independence, individualism, justice, and wisdom very generally can include a lack of awareness of and concern for other individuals or groups, which makes it easier to ignore, discriminate against, exclude, persecute, abuse and otherwise devalue these "others." Aggression, lack of awareness and/or denial of emotions, and an absence of empathy are possible manifestations—available to both men and women. This characterizes much of our collective American Shadow.

4. *Benet's Reader's Encyclopedia*, (Harper & Row, 1987), 1,073.

5. *The Oxford Companion to English Literature,* Margaret Drabble, ed. 5th edition (Oxford UP, 1985), 1,030.

6. Howard Zinn, *A People's History of the United States: 1492-Present,* (Harper Perennial, 1999/1980), 119.

7. Ibid., 121. See also the American Women's History Museum: https://www.womenshistory.org/womens-history for biographies and resources that haven't made it into most school history texts.

8. Lawrence, Hurley, "U.S. Supreme Court's Ginsburg, a Liberal Dynamo, Championed Women's Rights," *Reuters,* September 18, 2020, https://www.reuters.com/article/us-usa-court-ginsburg-obituary/u-s-supreme-courts-ginsburg-a-liberal-dynamo-championed-womens-rights-idUSKBN26A003, Accessed December 10, 2020. Ginsberg's paraphrase of Grimké appears in the documentary, *RBG:* https://www.amazon.com/RBG-Ruth-Bader-Ginsburg/dp/B07CT9Q5C6/?tag=harpersbazaar_auto-append-20&ascsubtag=[artid|10056.a.34083262[src|[ch|[lt|

9. Zinn, *A People's History of the United States: 1492-Present,* 184.

10. Debra Michals. "Sojourner Truth." National Women's History Museum. National Women's History Museum, 2015, https://www.womenshistory.org/education-resources/biographies/sojourner-truth. Accessed January 12, 2021.

11. Zinn, *A People's History of the United States: 1492-Present,* 202.

12. The quotes in this paragraph are from "The Development of Relational-Cultural Theory Beginnings: Self-in-Relation," Jean Baker Miller Training Institute,

https://www.wcwonline.org/JBMTI-Site/the-development-of-relational-cultural-theory. Accessed January 13, 2021. While that site is still accessible online, the International Center for Growth in Connection, which emerged through the JBMTI, is now the primary home for RCT scholarship and work in the world: https://growthinconnection.org/

13. Jean Baker Miller, *Toward a New Psychology of Women,* (Beacon, 1986), 76-77. Miller develops the selected points I cite here in great detail.

14. Susan Faludi, *Stiffed: The Betrayal of the American Man,* (William Morrow, 1999), 594-95. Andrew Bacevich, *Washington Rules: America's Path to Permanent War,* (Metropolitan, 2010), 11; see Chapter Seven, 182-83 and note 21.

15. Carol Gilligan, *In a Different Voice: Psychological Theory and Women's Development* (Harvard UP, 1993), 33. For an overview of Gilligan's findings and excerpts of the children's responses, see pp. 24-39. One striking example of what Gilligan points to is in the nature and the power dynamic of the research interview itself, in which the girl "is answering a different question from the one the interviewer thought had been posed," and "is considering not *whether* Heinz should act in this situation ('*should* Heinz steal the drug?') but rather *how* Heinz should act... ('should Heinz *steal* the drug?'). The interviewer is asking if it's okay to take the proposed action: steal the drug; the girl is wrestling with whether other possible actions are available besides stealing (31). A different voice indeed.

16. Ibid., Wollstonecraft and Stanton, quoted in Gilligan, 129.

17. Ibid., xiii.

18. While a detailed consideration of "The Declaration of Sentiments and Resolution" that emerged from the 1848 Seneca Falls Convention is beyond the scope and intention of this book, even a surface familiarity with its contents provides a beginning sense of what was denied women at the time. Here's one place to become familiar: https://www.womenshistory.org/resources/primary-source/declaration-sentiments-and-resolution

19. Attempts to amend Title IX, or do away with it entirely, include then Republican Texas Senator John Tower's 1974 "Tower Amendment" to protect revenue-producing sports (e.g. football) from the regulation. This and subsequent attempts to amend Title IX continued for years, and included both legislation and

litigation. A bit of editorializing: opponents of Title IX typically are men, and the arguments typically involve money (funding for sports). Had girls and women historically had equal access and equal protection, and had there been no inequality, there would be no need for Title IX, and no need to oppose it. More info here: https://www2.ed.gov/about/offices/list/ocr/docs/tix_dis.html

20. Gillian R. Brasil, "Sedona Prince Has a Message for You", *New York Times,* May 29, 2021, https://www.nytimes.com/2021/05/29/sports/ncaabasketball/sedona-prince-ncaa-basketball-video.html Accessed June 10, 2021. Based on the video, the women's "weight room" was a single rack that housed 12 dumbbells; the men's facility offered at least two-dozen weight stations and multiple dumbbells, barbells, and free-weight plates. Prince's video has had an impact. See Billy Witz, "Her Video Spurred Changes in Women's Basketball. Did They Go Far Enough?" *New York Times,* March 15, 2022, https://www.nytimes.com/2022/03/15/sports/ncaabasketball/womens-march-madness-sedona-prince.html Accessed March 16, 2022.

21. Two points here: 1) the first page of Google search results for "advertising expenditures for NCAA basketball tournament" provided results for the men's tournament only; the 6th result on the second page was the first to mention the women's tournament, and *that* was an indictment of the NCAA's management of the women's tournament, well worth the read: Sally Jenkins, "The NCAA's shell game is the real women's basketball scandal," *Washington Post,* March 25, 2021, https://www.washingtonpost.com/sports/2021/03/25/ncaa-women-basketball-tournament-revenue/ Accessed September 7, 2021. 2) The interplay of greed, untrustworthiness, ignorance and arrogance, at the very least, is present here, and both feeds and is fed by wealthy powerful men (and a few women) who run corporations and universities and who (apparently) value bottom lines over equality for women.

22. Jeannette Rankin: https://history.house.gov/People/Detail/20147#biography

23. So, yes, progress is being made, *and* in light of women making up about 51% of U.S. population, currently just 25% of Senators and 27% of Representatives are women. Senate History of women in the U.S. Congress: https://history.house.gov/Exhibitions-and-Publications/WIC/Historical-Data/Women-Representatives-and-

Senators-by-Congress/;
https://www.senate.gov/artandhistory/history/common/briefing/
women_senators.htm#:~:text=Appointed%20to%20fill%20a%20
vacancy,way%20for%20other%20women%20senators;
https://cawp.rutgers.edu/list-women-currently-serving-congress

24. Nancy Pelosi:
https://history.house.gov/People/Detail/19519#bibliography

25. U.S. Senate and House salaries:
https://pressgallery.house.gov/member-data/salaries

26. Amid the abundant and conflicting explorations, rants and
thoughtful commentaries on gender pay equity that are available,
this site presented a balanced overview with recent statistics, and
other than being in favor of gender pay equity, did not seem to
skew the stats in order to make one point or another:
https://www.payscale.com/data/gender-pay-gap.
Beyond the gender gap, pay disparity ties in with race and ethnic
gaps as well. For a look at the intersection of these disparities, as
reported by the National Partnership for Women & Families in
May 2022, see:
https://www.nationalpartnership.org/our-
work/resources/economic-justice/fair-pay/quantifying-americas-
gender-wage-gap.pdf. The essential issues that arise at the intersection of the race, caste and gender inequities inherent in the
history of the United States are foundational to "intersectionality"
as articulated by Kimberlé Crenshaw, about which and whom
we'll say more in Chapter Five:
https://www.youtube.com/watch?v=ViDtnfQ9FHc
(1:54 interview excerpt from 2018);
https://www.youtube.com/watch?v=9yKX_MH2bHs
(2:58, Omega's Women and Power Series, excerpt, 2016);
https://www.youtube.com/watch?v=akOe5-UsQ2o (18:49 TED
Talk, 2016).

27. Crotti, Robert, Kusum Kali Pal, et. al. "Global Gender Gap Report",
World Economic Forum, March 2021,
https://www.weforum.org/reports/global-gender-gap-report-
2021/ Accessed March 30, 2021. For a summary of the report, see
Ivana Saric, "U.S. women won't reach pay equity with me for at
least 60 years", *Axios,* March 30, 2021,
https://www.axios.com/wef-gender-equality-2021-e7e074e0-
baa0-4c89-935a-
1a5107b2a2c1.html?utm_source=newsletter&utm_medium=emai

l&utm_campaign=newsletter_axiosam&stream=top. One more view comes from a March 7, 2022 report from *The Economist,* which found that the United States ranks a solid twentieth globally when it comes to "the role and influence of women in the workplace." Belgium, Slovakia, Poland, Italy, and Sweden are among the nineteen nations that have a better record: https://www.economist.com/graphic-detail/glass-ceiling-index?

28. What this expectation ignores is the integration of grit and grace that many women embodied when their roles were "limited" to loving their husbands, having and raising kids, cooking, and cleaning. Husbands and fathers who choose to share these responsibilities so their wives can pursue their careers learn this integration very quickly. My primary reference regarding this brief exploration of *grit* and *grace* is the work of Leslie Williams (she's not responsible for how I'm exploring). Find out more about her work as a coach, teacher and author at https://leadershift.net/. I highly recommend spending some time with her clear writing through multiple perspectives on leadership, grit and grace at https://leadershift.net/grit-grace-blog/.

29. Melinda Wenner Moyer, "'A Poison in the System': The Epidemic of Military Sexual Assault," *New York Times Magazine,* August 3, 2021, https://www.nytimes.com/2021/08/03/magazine/military-sexual-assault.html Accessed September 12, 2021.

30. Ibid.

31. Helene Cooper, "Senate Rejects Blocking Military Commanders From Sexual Assault Cases," *New York Times,* March 6, 2014, https://www.nytimes.com/2014/03/07/us/politics/military-sexual-assault-legislation.html Accessed September 13, 2021.

32. *Annual Report on Sexual Assault:* Dave Philipps, "'This Is Unacceptable.' Military Reports a Surge of Sexual Assaults in the Ranks," *New York Times,* May 2, 2019, https://www.nytimes.com/2019/05/02/us/military-sexual-assault.html Accessed September 12, 2021. For access to the DOD's annual reports on sexual assault: https://sapr.mil/. Reports indicate that men also experience sexual assault and harassment in the military, albeit significantly less frequently than women. Regarding *Fort Hood:* Sarah Mervosh and John Ismay, "Army Finds 'Major Flaws' at Fort Hood; 14 Officials Disciplined," *New York Times,* December 8, 2020, updated April 30, 2021, https://www.nytimes.com/2020/12/08/us/fort-hood-officers-fired-vanessa-guillen.html Accessed September 12, 2021.

Regarding Senator Gillibrand's 2021 proposed legislation: Jennifer Steinhauer, "After Failures to Curb Sexual Assault, a Move Toward a Major Shift in Military Law," *New York Times,* August 3, 2021, https://www.nytimes.com/2021/04/27/us/politics/military-sexual-assault.html Accessed September 12, 2021; also, Lolita C. Baldor, "Panel: End commanders' power to block military sex cases," *Associated Press,* April 22, 2021, https://apnews.com/article/sexual-assault-lloyd-austin-government-and-politics-13077b68cbaf65e8ad862a00aa3c5552 Accessed September 13, 2021; and Karoun Demirjian, "Broad overhaul of military justice system being sidelined in favor of narrower focus on sexual assault," *Washington Post,* December 5, 2021, https://www.washingtonpost.com/national-security/military-sexual-assault-reform/2021/12/04/5946b0cc-5455-11ec-9267-17ae3bde2f26_story.html Accessed December 5, 2021.

33. This language is adapted from Brett Thomas and the Integral Leadership Collaborative (2012-2015). For a deeper dive into developmental and integral models of leadership, see Bill Joiner's and Stephen Josephs' *Leadership Agility,* Bill Torbert, et. al.'s *Action Inquiry,* and Frederic Laloux's *Reinventing Organizations,* among others.

34. Susan Faludi, *Stiffed, The Betrayal of the American Man,* 13.

35. Joseph Epstein, "Is There a Doctor in the White House? Not if You Need an M.D." *Wall Street Journal* online. December 11, 2020. Accessed December 12, 2020. https://www.wsj.com/articles/is-there-a-doctor-in-the-white-house-not-if-you-need-an-m-d-11607727380. This incident feels at once small (in light of other suffering that women experience) for the theme and scope of the chapter and book, *and* it captures well the staying power of gender bias and the unhealthy masculine that underlies it—thus the decision to include it.

36. Thomas Merton, "The Inner Experience," *Thomas Merton: Spiritual Master,* Lawrence Cunningham, ed. 295. See Chapter One, note 9.

37. Ken Wilber, *Integral Spirituality,* 277. See Chapter One, note 10.

38. Northwestern University's response to Joseph Epstein's December 11, 2020 *Wall Street Journal* opinion piece: https://news.northwestern.edu/stories/2020/12/joseph-epstein-statement/?fj=1.

39. Along with Jonathan Rauch's *The Constitution of Knowledge,* which provides a clear (and often fun) exposition and analysis of the precedents and consequences of these diverse, divisive, grave and goofy information sources, Ezra Klein's *Why We're Polarized;* Greg Lukianoff and Jonathan Haidt's *The Coddling of the American Mind;* and Haidt's *The Righteous Mind* provide insight into the current state of America's troubles with truth.

40. PRRI Staff, "Understanding QAnon's Connection to American Politics, Religion and Media Consumption," *Public Religion Research Institute,* May 27, 2021, https://www.prri.org/research/qanon-conspiracy-american-politics-report/ Accessed May 31, 2021. "acceptable, true and/or desirable" are my characterizations and not Faludi's or PRRI's.

41. "State of the Period 2021: The widespread impact of period poverty on US students," https://period.org/uploads/State-of-the-Period-2021.pdf Accessed September 10, 2021. The study, commissioned by Period and Thinx, was conducted online by SKDK in spring 2021.

42. Dr. Shelby Davis, interviewed by Robin Young, "Here & Now," *NPR,* September 7, 2021, https://www.npr.org/2021/09/07/1034914097/muslim-americans-on-growing-up-in-a-post-9-11-world-access-to-menstrual-products begin 26:46 Accessed September 9, 2021.

43. Ibid. For one (search-engine generated) example, among many, of age-appropriate, medically accurate online information, see the Nemours Children's Health site: https://kidshealth.org/en/kids/menstruation.html#catperiods Again, online access to information like this is helpful; it doesn't replace what a loving parent, or trusted doctor, nurse or teacher can provide.

44. Greg Lukianoff and Jonathan Haidt, *The Coddling of the American Mind: How Good Intentions and Bad Ideas Are Setting Up a Generation for Failure* (Penguin, 2018), 146-61. Percentages are from p. 149; quote is from p. 146. Lukianoff and Haidt draw on Jean Twenge's book, *iGen,* cited below, and its Appendix A, which is available online, and which charts decades-long longitudinal studies: http://www.jeantwenge.com/wp-content/uploads/2017/08/igen-appendix.pdf

45. Jean Twenge, *iGen* (Atria, 2017), 2-7; and Lukianoff and Haidt, 146-47.

46. Lukianoff and Haidt, 152-53, citing Twenge.

47. Ibid., 149-51, 157. Lukianoff and Haidt, citing Twenge and others, note the higher rates for girls. Their book focuses, however, on the larger picture of iGen's unhealthier traits (such as learned helplessness, external locus of control, and impaired ability to navigate the difficulties of life) and the parenting styles, educational approaches, and social factors that seem to be at play.

48. The word *know,* in this and the preceding paragraph (and the rest of the book) refers to publicly validated *knowledge*, as opposed to mere shared *information* or *content*. As Jonathan Rauch writes in *The Constitution of Knowledge*, this validation comes from a network that is "large and global and impersonal and public and critical," such as the science, education, and journalism communities at their unbiased bests (71). In *The Courage to Teach,* (1988), Parker Palmer put it this way: *"To teach is to create a space in which the community of truth is practiced"* and (as noted earlier) *"truth is an eternal conversation about things that matter, conducted with passion and discipline"* (90, 104). Italics in original. Knowledge, truth, and reality are ongoing, communal conversations.

49. Claire Cane Miller, "The World 'Has Found a Way to Do This': The U.S. Lags on Paid Leave," *New York Times,* October 25, 2021, https://www.nytimes.com/2021/10/25/upshot/paid-leave-democrats.html, Accessed October 25, 2021. Eleven states have paid leave plans in place or pending: https://www.abetterbalance.org/resources/paid-family-leave-laws-chart/, Accessed October 25, 2021/August 8, 2022.

50. Gilligan, *In a Different Voice,* xvi.

51. Tony Hoagland, *The Art of Voice,* (Norton, 2019), 3, 5.

52. Mary Shelley, *Frankenstein, Or, the Modern Prometheus,* Author's Introduction. (Signet-Penguin, 2013). Daughter of Wollstonecraft and William Godwin, married to Percy Bysshe Shelley, and neighbor to Lord Byron at the time she wrote *Frankenstein,* Mary Shelley was surrounded by writers and literature, encouraged by her husband and Byron to write, and a self-described "devout but nearly silent listener" to the two men's "many and long conversations," 5. *Frankenstein* was conceived as the author lay awake in her bed one night after Lord Byron proclaimed, "We will each write a ghost story," 3.

53. Rosemary Sutcliff, "Gawain and the Loathely Lady," *The Sword and the Circle.* (Puffin-Penguin, 1981), 224-42. I deeply enjoyed

and recommend Sutcliff's version. Her love of language and storytelling is evident. I apologize for the synopsis. The origins of the story go back at least to the Middle Ages, most notably to Chaucer's "The Wife of Bath's Tale." Sutcliffe cites "a Middle English ballad" as her primary source for this rendering.

CHAPTER FOUR – Trails of Tears & Broken Treaties, the Third Colorado Regiment, & the Only Good Indians

Abbreviations for books frequently cited in this chapter:

BMH   Dee Brown, *Bury My Heart at Wounded Knee: An Indian History of the American West,* (Owl/Holt, 1970).

UR   Claudio Saunt, *Unworthy Republic: The Dispossession of Native Americans and the Road to Indian Territory*, (W. W. Norton, 2020).

1. Some folks (many of whom are white and well-intentioned) maintain that "Native American," "Indigenous Peoples," and "First Peoples," among others, should be used instead of "American Indian." I include "American Indian" along with other titles in this volume in order to honor the American Indian Movement (AIM) and the writings of Dee Brown and Vine Deloria, Jr.
2. Inspired by Carse, *Finite and Infinite Games,* 32.
3. Adam Rutherford. "A New History of the First Peoples in the Americas." *Atlantic.* October 3, 2017, https://www.theatlantic.com/science/archive/2017/10/a-brief-history-of-everyone-who-ever-lived/537942/. Accessed March 8, 2021. The article is adapted from Rutherford's *A Brief History of Everyone Who Ever Lived: The Human Story Retold Through Our Genes.* New York: The Experiment, 2017.
4. Of course, any one of these contemporary inconveniences could, in a specific circumstance, involve a life-or-death situation. Generally, this is not the case.
5. Claudio Saunt, *UR,* 48. All subsequent references to this author are to this volume.
6. Dee Brown, *BMH,* 5. All subsequent references to this author are to this volume.
7. Saunt, *UR,* "traitors and recreants," 76; impact of the three-fifths compromise on the House vote, 78-83.

8. Howard Zinn, *A People's History of the United States,* 133-34.

9. Saunt, *UR,* 97. Saunt cites *The Papers of Andrew Jackson Digital Edition,* ed. Daniel Feller (Charlottesville: University of Virginia Press: 2015). See also Chapter Nine, note 13 in this volume.

10. Ibid., 69.

11. D.S. Heidler and J.T. Heidler, "Manifest Destiny," *Encyclopedia Britannica.* https://www.britannica.com/event/Manifest-Destiny. Accessed February 9, 2021. Attributed to John L. O'Sullivan, the initial appearance of the phrase was a complaint against France and England, who he felt were acting "for the avowed object of thwarting our policy and hampering our power, limiting our greatness and checking the fulfillment of our manifest destiny to overspread the continent allotted by Providence for the free development of our yearly multiplying millions."

12. Brown, *BMH,* 5.

13. Saunt, *UR,* "deter others…," 145; cholera outbreak, 143-55.

14. Ibid., 280.

15. Elizabeth Prine Pauls, "Trail of Tears," *Encyclopedia Britannica.* https://www.britannica.com/event/Trail-of-Tears
Accessed February 10, 2021.

16. Saunt, *UR,* 74.

17. Ibid., 200-13.

18. Ibid., 270.

19. Ibid., 236-37.

20. "An Act to provide for the armed occupation and settlement of the unsettled part of the peninsula of East Florida," aka the Armed Occupation Act of 1842. Selected resources: https://myfloridahistory.org/date-in-history/august-04-1842/armed-occupation-act#:~:text=1842%20%2D%20The%20Armed%20Occupation%20Act,rations%20from%20the%20Federal%20government; https://stars.library.ucf.edu/cgi/viewcontent.cgi?article=2786&context=fhq

21. Fighting each other "in a white man's war." My synopsis over-simplifies the deep complexities of the Civil War era for Native Americans. This source focuses on the Cherokee experience: https://www.history.com/news/civil-war-native-american-indian-territory-cherokee-home-guard Accessed March 8, 2021.

22. Brown, *BMH,* 74.

23. Ibid., 77.

24. Ibid., 79.

25. Ibid., 86-87. Brown cites U.S. Congress, 39th. 2nd session. Senate Report 156, 53, 74.

26. Ibid., 87-91.

27. Ibid., 92-94.

28. Ibid., 94-96, 102.

29. Ibid., 134-37. Quotations, 137.

30. Ibid., 141-46. Full text of the Fort Laramie Treaty of 1868 and the list of signatories is available at: https://www.archives.gov/milestone-documents/fort-laramie-treaty#transcript; For a synopsis of the Fort Laramie Treaties of 1851 and 1868 and what has transpired (through 2018), see Kimbra Cutlip, "In 1868, Two Nations Made a Treaty, the U.S. Broke It and Plains Indian Tribes are Still Seeking Justice," *Smithsonian,* November 7, 2018, https://www.smithsonianmag.com/smithsonian-institution/1868-two-nations-made-treaty-us-broke-it-and-plains-indian-tribes-are-still-seeking-justice-180970741/

31. Fort Laramie Treaty of 1868, Article XVI: https://www.archives.gov/milestone-documents/fort-laramie-treaty#transcript

32. Text of the "Indian Appropriations Act" of March 3, 1871: https://reggiemarra.files.wordpress.com/2022/05/acts-of-the-forty-first-congress-of-the-united-states.pdf, 544-71 (pages refer to the Act, not the PDF); see page 570, Sec. 3 for the paragraph that ends treaty-making. See also: https://coloradoencyclopedia.org/article/indian-appropriations-act-1871. The full title of the act is "An Act making Appropriations for the current and contingent Expenses of the Indian Department, and for fulfilling Treaty Stipulations with Various Indian Tribes, for the Year ending June thirty, eighteen hundred and seventy-two, and for other Purposes." For one historical perspective on the Act, see Mark Hirsch, "1871: The End of Indian Treaty-Making," *American Indian,* Vol. 15 No. 2 / Summer/Fall 2014. https://www.americanindianmagazine.org/story/1871-end-indian-treaty-making Accessed March 7, 2021.

33. Brown, *BMH,* 168.

34. Ibid., 167-69.

35. Ibid., 170-72.

36. Ibid., 146.

37. Ibid., 282.

38. Treaty of 1868, Article XII:

https://www.archives.gov/milestone-documents/fort-laramie-treaty#transcript

39. Brown, *BMH*, 283-84.

40. *Standing Bear v. Crook:* https://indianlaw.mt.gov/_docs/fed_state/court_decisions/us-bear/us_crook.pdf Sources for the details of Standing Bear's case include Brown, *BMH*, 355-62; Jennifer Davis, "Chief Standing Bear and His Landmark Civil Rights Case," *Library of Congress.* November 21, 2019, https://blogs.loc.gov/law/2019/11/chief-standing-bear-and-his-landmark-civil-rights-case/ Accessed April 19, 2021; Poncas' History Timeline: http://ponca.com/ponca-history Accessed April 19, 2021.

41. Brown, *BMH*, 363-66.

42. Gillian Brockwell, "The civil rights leader 'almost nobody knows about' gets a statue in the U.S. Capitol," *Washington Post,* November 20, 2019, https://www.washingtonpost.com/history/2019/09/20/civil-rights-leader-almost-nobody-knows-about-gets-statue-us-capitol/ Accessed April 19, 2021.

43. Vine Deloria, Jr., *Custer Died for Your Sins,* (U of Oklahoma P, 1969/1988), 107.

44. Dennis Zotigh, "Native Perspectives on the 40th Anniversary of the American Indian Religious Freedom Act", *Smithsonian,* November 30, 2018, https://www.smithsonianmag.com/blogs/national-museum-american-indian/2018/11/30/native-perspectives-american-indian-religious-freedom-act/ Accessed May 3, 2021. The text of the "Rules Governing the Court of Indian Offenses" is available here: http://robert-clinton.com/wp-content/uploads/2018/09/code-of-indian-offenses.pdf Accessed May 3, 2021.

45. American Indian Religious Freedom Act (1978): https://www.govinfo.gov/content/pkg/STATUTE-92/pdf/STATUTE-92-Pg469.pdf#page=1. Amendment (1994): https://www.congress.gov/103/bills/hr4230/BILLS-103hr4230enr.pdf Both accessed May 3, 2021.

46. Miles Hudson, "Wounded Knee Massacre," *Encyclopedia Britannica,* December 22, 2020, https://www.britannica.com/event/Wounded-Knee-Massacre Also: The Editors of Encyclopaedia Britannica, "Dawes General Allotment Act," *Encyclopedia Britannica,* Dec. 4, 2019,

https://www.britannica.com/topic/Dawes-General-Allotment-Act. Accessed April 23, 2021.

47. Brown, *BMH*, 431-38. Also: The Editors of the Encyclopaedia Britannica, "Wovoka: American Indian prophet," *Encyclopedia Britannica,* September 27, 2020, https://www.britannica.com/biography/Wovoka Accessed April 23, 2021.

48. Brown, *BMH,* 440-45. Also: Howard Zinn, *A People's History of the United States,* 524, and https://www.history.com/this-day-in-history/u-s-army-massacres-indians-at-wounded-knee | https://www.history.com/news/remembering-the-wounded-knee-massacre | https://www.britannica.com/event/Wounded-Knee-Massacre

49. William C. Meadows, "The Code Talkers' Legacy: Native Languages Helped Turn the Tides in Both World Wars," *Magazine of Smithsonian's National Museum of the American Indian,* Fall 2020 / Vol. 21 No.3, https://www.americanindianmagazine.org/story/code-talkers-legacy-native-languages-helped-turn-tides-both-world-wars Accessed April 29, 2021. Also: National World War II Museum: https://www.nationalww2museum.org/war/articles/american-indian-code-talkers, and U.S. Department of the Interior: https://www.doi.gov/blog/honoring-native-american-code-talkers

50. "Indian Citizenship Act" Library of Congress: https://www.loc.gov/item/today-in-history/june-02/#:~:text=Indian%20Citizenship%20Act,barred%20Native%20Americans%20from%20voting. Also: National Archives: https://www.archives.gov/historical-docs/todays-doc/?dod-date=602 Both accessed April 29, 2021.

51. Termination Policy: 1953 House Concurrent Resolution 108: https://www.govinfo.gov/content/pkg/STATUTE-67/pdf/STATUTE-67-PgB132-2.pdf
1953 Public Law 280: https://www.govinfo.gov/content/pkg/STATUTE-67/pdf/STATUTE-67-Pg588.pdf Also: https://en.wikipedia.org/wiki/Indian_termination_policy Accessed April 29, 2021.

52. http://nativeamericannetroots.net/diary/1511 Accessed April 29, 2021.

53. Howard Zinn, *A People's History of the United States,* 527-29. Also: https://www.nytimes.com/2019/11/20/us/native-american-occupation-alcatraz.html and: https://www.history.com/news/native-american-activists-occupy-alcatraz-island-45-years-ago Accessed April 30, 2021. The $24.00 offer was symbolic of the price allegedly paid by the Dutch for Manhattan Island in the 1600s.

54. Ibid., 534. The summary of the 1973 Wounded Knee occupation derives from Zinn, 534-35 along with sources cited in note 55.

55. Emily Chertoff, "Occupy Wounded Knee: A 71-Day Siege and a Forgotten Civil Rights Movement," *The Atlantic,* October 23, 2012. https://www.theatlantic.com/national/archive/2012/10/occupy-wounded-knee-a-71-day-siege-and-a-forgotten-civil-rights-movement/263998/ Accessed April 29, 2021. Additional background and perspectives: https://en.wikipedia.org/wiki/Wounded_Knee_Occupation https://www.usmarshals.gov/history/wounded-knee/index.html

56. Numerous legal, historical and journalistic sources exist for this story. See Kimbra Cutlip, "In 1868, Two Nations Made a Treaty, the U.S. Broke It and Plains Indian Tribes are Still Seeking Justice," *Smithsonian Magazine,* November 7, 2018 (see note 30 for link); and Tom LeGro, et al. "Why the Sioux Are Refusing $1.3 Billion", *PBS News Hour,* August 24, 2011, https://www.pbs.org/newshour/arts/north_america-july-dec11-blackhills_08-23 Accessed May 4, 2021.

57. For more on Layli Long Soldier and *Whereas* (Graywolf, 2017): https://www.poetryfoundation.org/poetrymagazine/poems/91697/from-whereas; https://poets.org/book/whereas; and https://www.griffinpoetryprize.com/awards-and-poets/shortlists/2018-shortlist/layli-long-soldier/ among others.

58. Texts of S.J. Res. 14 (To acknowledge a long history…): https://www.congress.gov/bill/111th-congress/senate-joint-resolution/14/text and Public Law 111-118 (Dept. of Defense Appropriation Act, 2010 / Sec. 8113, p. 45): https://www.congress.gov/111/plaws/publ118/PLAW-111publ118.pdf Both accessed May 2, 2021.

59. Dakota Access Pipeline: reported throughout the media. This site carries recent updates: https://earthjustice.org/features/faq-standing-rock-litigation?

60. Sharing Covid-19 vaccinations: https://www.mprnews.org/story/2021/02/19/collaboration-between-white-earth-nation-mahnomen-co-leads-to-high-vaccination-rate-mn and https://www.the-journal.com/articles/ute-mountain-ute-tribe-offers-free-covid-vaccinations-today/

61. Vine Deloria, Jr., *Custer Died for Your Sins,* 170-74.

62. Ibid., 174-75.

63. Brown, *BMH,* 293. Brown cites D. W. Robinson. "Editorial Notes on Historical Sketch of North and South Dakota." *South Dakota Historical Collections,* Vol. 1, 1902, 151. For an overview of Chief Gall, see Robert W. Larson, "Sioux Chief Gall," *Historynet,* https://www.historynet.com/sioux-chief-gall.htm, Accessed May 7, 2021. My focus here is on the predominantly English colonizers and the founding of the United States, and not on the French, Spanish and Portuguese colonizers of what are now called Canada, various Caribbean islands, and Central and South America. For a harrowing first-person account of the arrival of Europeans on the islands of the Caribbean and in Central and South American, see Bartolemé de las Casas, *A Short Account of the Destruction of the Indies* in the bibliography.

64. Joy Harjo, 23rd Poet Laureate of the United States: https://www.joyharjo.com/; Deb Haaland, 54th United States Secretary of the Interior: https://www.doi.gov/secretary-deb-haaland; Lewis Mehl-Madrona, M.D. Ph.D.: https://www.mehl-madrona.com/.

65. Eduardo Duran, "Transgenerational Trauma, Soul Wounding and Effects on Families and Communities: The Impact of History on Present Day Chronic Illnesses," *Advances in Indian Health Conference,* (Indian Health Service: Division of Diabetes Treatment and Prevention, 2010), 2; transcript available at: https://www.ihs.gov/sites/diabetes/themes/responsive2017/display_objects/documents/media/transcripts/Duran_transcript_508c.pdf Accessed October 26, 2021.

66. Ibid., 6-7.

67. Ibid., 8-10. The Elder's name, Tarrence, was transcribed as "Clarence" in this source. The correction is from Eduardo Duran, *Healing the Soul Wound: Trauma-Informed Counseling for Indigenous Communities,* 2nd Edition, (Teachers College Press, 2019), xiii.

68. Ibid., 11-12.

69. Eduardo Duran, in conversation with Laura Calderón de la Barca, "An Indigenous Lens on Psychotherapy as a Soul Healing," *Collective Trauma Summit 2021 / Collective Healing in Action*, (Inner Science, 2021), 3. Recording and transcript are available through summit attendance or purchase.

70. The Thirteen Indigenous Grandmothers from around the world came together for the first time in October 2004 and have gathered regularly since then as "a global alliance of prayer, education and healing" at various locations on the planet for ceremony, teachings and healing.
https://www.grandmotherswisdom.org/the-grandmothers

71. Duran, "An Indigenous Lens on Psychotherapy as a Soul Healing," (2021), 19-22. Details of the Grandmothers' Montana gathering and the apology are from these pages.

72. Brown, *BMH,* 148.

CHAPTER FIVE – Slavery, Jim Crow, Civil Rights, & Everything Was Going to Change Now

1. Inspired by Carse, *Finite and Infinite Games,* 33.

2. Peoples from Senegal, Gambia, Guinea-Bissau and Mali, and west-central Africa, including what is now Angola, Congo, the Democratic Republic of Congo and Gabon were kidnapped and forced into slavery. Also, peoples from Ghana, as well as neighboring parts of the Windward Coast, now Ivory Coast, and others the Bight of Biafra, including parts of present-day eastern Nigeria and Cameroon, were taken. More detail here: https://www.history.com/news/what-part-of-africa-did-most-slaves-come-from

3. For a list of countries and the dates they ended slave-trading and (usually subsequently) slave-owning, see:
https://www.reuters.com/article/uk-slavery/chronology-who-banned-slavery-when-idUSL1561464920070322
For an overview/timeline of slavery and civil rights in the U.S. see https://www.ushistory.org/more/timeline.htm

4. Ferris State University provides examples of literacy tests from Alabama, Louisiana and Mississippi. See if you can pass:
Alabama: https://www.ferris.edu/HTMLS/news/jimcrow/pdfs-docs/origins/al_literacy.pdf
Louisiana:
https://www.ferris.edu/HTMLS/news/jimcrow/question/2012/pdfs-docs/literacytest.pdf

Mississippi: https://www.ferris.edu/HTMLS/news/jimcrow/pdfs-docs/origins/ms-littest55.pdf

5. Images of these newspaper announcements and posters, as well as photographs of the lynchings themselves are abundant and accessible online. While 21st-century sensibilities suggest that we not exhibit images of mutilated, broken bodies of American crime victims, and while that may be a good thing—especially, but not only for the families of the victims—the sanitization of the consequences of what we do and what we tolerate allows us to remain a safe step away from what's true. That's not a good thing. The images are disturbing and horrific and we should be disturbed and horrified by what they depict.

6. Equal Justice Initiative, *Lynching in America,* 39-47. These pages provide statistics along with some narrative. The volume's 90 pages provide a searing look into its title and is also available online: https://lynchinginamerica.eji.org/report/

7. Equal Justice Initiative, *Reconstruction in America,* 6-7, 40-55. As with all of EJI's publications, these pages are representative; the volume warrants a full reading. Also online: https://eji.org/report/reconstruction-in-america/

8. Equal Justice Initiative, *Lynching in America,* 48.

9. Isabel Wilkerson, "The Great Migration," in Kendi and Blain, eds. *Four Hundred Souls,* 278-82. See Wilkerson, *The Warmth of Other Suns* for the larger story (and smaller stories) of the Great Migration.

10. This synopsis (111-12) from "Emphasizing how far…" through "…United States in 1921" is derived from the following sources:
History(dot)Editors, "Tulsa Race Massacre," *History,*
https://www.history.com/topics/roaring-twenties/tulsa-race-massacre
Accessed May 24, 2021.
Tulsa Historical Society and Museum, "1921 Tulsa Race Massacre,"
https://www.tulsahistory.org/exhibit/1921-tulsa-race-massacre/
Accessed May 24, 2021.
Daniel Victor, "At 107, 106 and 100, Remaining Tulsa Massacre Survivors Plead for Justice," *New York Times,* May 20, 2021,
https://www.nytimes.com/2021/05/20/us/tulsa-massacre-survivors.html
Accessed May 24, 2021.
Matt Craig, Alain Delaquérière, Lazaro Gamio, et. al. "What the Tulsa Massacre Destroyed," *New York Times,* May 24, 2021,
https://www.nytimes.com/interactive/2021/05/24/us/tulsa-race-massacre.html?action=click&module=Top%20Stories&pgtype=Home page Accessed May 24, 2021.

"Tulsa Race Massacre," *Wikipedia,*
https://en.wikipedia.org/wiki/Tulsa_race_massacre Accessed May 25, 2021.

"Story of Attack on Woman Denied," *Tulsa World,* June 2, 1921, https://tulsaworld.com/archive/story-of-attack-on-woman-denied/article_6a43affa-7d3a-5259-a574-18f315849dbc.html Accessed May 25, 2021.

DeNeen L. Brown, "His arrest sparked the Tulsa Race Massacre. Then Dick Rowland disappeared," *Washington Post,* May 30, 2021, https://www.washingtonpost.com/history/2021/05/30/dick-rowland-tulsa-massacre-sarah-page/ Accessed May 31, 2021.

11. Isabel Wilkerson, *Caste: The Origins of Our Discontents,* (Random House, 2020), 106. Italics in original. Whether or not the reader agrees with the concept of caste here, the disaffection that arises within an alleged superior when a perceived subordinate surpasses them is the larger point. The language of "lower rungs," "dominant caste," and "subordinate caste" is Wilkerson's.

12. Ibid., 183. Wilkerson's final question becomes decreasingly relevant at later stages of healthy development (when it's about *all of us,* we celebrate each other's successes—even amid fleeting moments of envy). Beyond the immediate scope of this chapter, yet relevant to the book, Wilkerson goes on to explore caste in a 21st-century America in which some dominant members of the dominant caste incited folks on the lower rungs of that caste who were suffering physically, emotionally and economically for a variety of reasons (as were an even higher percentage of the subordinate caste, with whom they had more in common than they ever would with those who incited them), to take the country back and make it great again (178-89).

13. Omitted from this list are those lynchings carried out by on-duty law enforcement officers since, theoretically and technically, they work for the government and are not an "outside-the-law" mob, which is one of the characteristics of lynching. That said, as we've seen in the case of George Floyd, if kneeling on the neck of a man who is on the ground in handcuffs and repeatedly saying he can't breathe, while two of your colleagues help hold him down and a third controls the onlookers who are shouting at you to stop is not *outside the* law and an example of lynching, I'm not sure what would be. See note 30.

14. John Lewis with Michael D'Orso, *Walking with the Wind: A Memoir of the Movement,* (Simon & Schuster, 1998), 43-45.

15. *Shelby v. Holder* (2013): https://www.lawyerscommittee.org/project/shelby-co-v-

holder/?gclid=Cj0KCQiAnKeCBhDPARIsAFDTLTK6fD3oDcTr5vOX
c-CD_8FgR4rMO3Or6LV6RW6u3sxpo9tollq3HLAaAm3lEALw_wcB
https://www.nytimes.com/2013/06/26/us/supreme-court-ruling.html

16. Jon Meacham, *The Soul of America* (Random House, 2019), 3-4, 277-78. Meacham cites the October 8, 1948 Charlottesville *Daily Progress.* Thurmond served for 48 years as a U.S. Senator from South Carolina. He switched from the Democratic to the Republican Party in 1964 due to his opposition to the Civil Rights Act.

17. Ibid., 212, 340. Meacham cites Marshall Frady's *Wallace* (1968), 14.

18. Edward A. Pollard, *The Lost Cause Regained,* (G.W. Carleton & Co., 1868), Kindle, (HardPress, 2017), Location 2105.

19. This particular comment by David Duke is captured on video here: https://www.youtube.com/watch?v=fULPlGwjJMA. It, along with other pledges he has made in support of Donald Trump, are available in various print and online media.

20. Meacham, *The Soul of America,* ix, 277. Meacham cites Baldwin's "The White Man's Guilt," *Ebony,* August 1965, 47.

21. Resmaa Menakem, "Resmaa Menakem discusses healing racialized trauma", *Fox 11 Los Angeles,* December 11, 2020, https://www.foxla.com/video/879820 Accessed May 27, 2021.

22. Saunt, *Unworthy Republic,* 186, 357 n. 21. Saunt cites the origin of the phrase, "slave labor camp," as Peter H. Wood, "Slave Labor Camps in Early America: Overcoming Denial and Discovering the Gulag," in *Inequality in Early America,* ed. Carla Gardina Pestana and Sharon V. Salinger (Hanover, N.H.: University Press of New England, 1999), 222-39.

23. The reasons for the U.S. Civil War continue to be debated by historians, Pollard's claims of the Lost Cause of white supremacy notwithstanding. Historians generally agree on a short list of causes, but disagree on which were primary. States' rights, including the right to secede, and the expansion vs. the abolition of slavery are two of the more prominent, and inevitably related, debates. Here's one place to explore, among many:
https://www.battlefields.org/learn/articles/reasons-secession?gclid=Cj0KCQiA7NKBBhDBARIsAHbXCB7vjGu6JSD
GJD5TsH1CYEuZYvmvbBU5xmuoqWXHTkKmwwTA1jXpmQc
aAkPoEALw_wcB

24. Petula Dvorak, "America's missing slave memorials: It's time to truly acknowledge our bloody past," Perspective, *Washington Post,* August 28, 2017,

https://www.washingtonpost.com/local/americas-missing-slave-memorials-its-time-to-truly-acknowledge-our-bloody-past/2017/08/28/9beeb6d4-8c1a-11e7-8df5-c2e5cf46c1e2_story.html. Accessed February 28, 2021. The Equal Justice Initiative, cited above and below, is one example of a private organization that has committed to funding such memorials (amid other good, essential work):
https://museumandmemorial.eji.org/

25. Ibid.
26. Wilkerson, *Caste,* 343. Wilkerson provides an eloquent and disturbing contrast of the American and German responses to their respective atrocities, 333-349. See also:
Memorial to the Murdered Jews of Europe:
https://goo.gl/maps/3mX2SCfGcpX2WTYL7
Stumbling Stones:
https://www.npr.org/2012/05/31/153943491/stumbling-upon-miniature-memorials-to-nazi-victims
https://www.washingtonpost.com/news/made-by-history/wp/2018/02/06/how-a-small-stone-could-help-america-reckon-with-its-worst-history/
27. Ibid., 345.
28. Susan Neiman, "There Are No Nostalgic Nazi Memorials," *Atlantic,* September 14, 2019.
https://www.theatlantic.com/ideas/archive/2019/09/germany-has-no-nazi-memorials/597937/. Accessed February 28, 2021.
29. Equal Justice Initiative, *Segregation in America,* 112-15.
30. This reference to videos of unarmed black men being beaten, choked or shot by law enforcement officers raises strong emotion and pushback among most, if not all, of us. That the police shoot unarmed black women and unarmed white and brown men and women as well reinforces the point that some of those we appoint to protect and serve are shooting a variety of unarmed people.

In the context of the history of the United States through slavery, Reconstruction, Jim Crow, and the incessantly necessary and ongoing legislative, executive, and judicial attempts to provide equal protection as promised in the 14th Amendment, we, as a country continue to try, but have not yet succeeded in fully embodying that all lives matter. "Black Lives Matter" carries an implicit "too" after it, and it doesn't suggest that *only* black lives matter or that other lives matter *less.* I was born a cisgender, heterosexual "white" male, and expect to die that way. "Black

Lives Matter" is not a threat to me (it feels simultaneously awkward, unnecessary and essential to write that). Rather, that it needs to be spoken or written is a source of sadness and shame. *Refuting* "Black Lives Matter" with "All Lives Matter" or "Blue Lives Matter" or "xxx Lives Matter" is like refusing to respond to a particular house on fire because "all houses matter." This example is from Maureen Walker's *When Getting Along Is Not Enough: Reconstructing Race in Our Lives and Relationships* (2020), 122.

Finally, calls to "defund" or "abolish" the police are a bad idea. Calls to retrain the police and rethink our approach to public safety and policing are essential at this point in our history. This is a topic that warrants deeper attention, is beyond the scope of this book, and begs for a more detailed, honest accounting of our nation's history.

31. Before the House Appropriations subcommittee in April 1964 Hoover testified that "The [Communist] party is continually searching for new avenues in order to expand its influence among the Negroes." "In particular, it has sought ways and means to exploit the militant force of the Negro civil rights movement," and "We do know that Communist influence does exist in the Negro movement and it is this influence which is vitally important." https://www.nytimes.com/1964/04/22/archives/hoover-says-reds-exploit-negroes-fbi-chief-asserts-party.html?searchResultPosition=1

    This is not to ignore that the FBI played a role in combatting the local violence against and oppression of blacks in the South in the 1960s—it did, and that role is often characterized, especially in those states that overtly prevented blacks from voting, as the federal government's overstepping its bounds and interfering with state and local politics. The issue was that local politics were in direct violation of the 14th, 15th and 19th Amendments.

32. Danielle Pletka. "I Can't Stand Trump but Democrats May Force Me to Vote for Him." *Washington Post.* September 14, 2020. https://www.washingtonpost.com/opinions/i-cant-stand-trump-but-democrats-may-force-me-to-vote-for-him/2020/09/14/1cf10518-f6c4-11ea-a275-1a2c2d36e1f1_story.html#comments-wrapper

33. Jonathan S. Bass, *He Calls Me by Lightening: The Life of Caliph Washington and the Forgotten Saga of Jim Crow, Southern Justice and the Death Penalty,* (Liveright/Norton, 2017), "Because it was self-defense," 101. The details in this synopsis of Caliph Washing-

ton's story on pages 125-28 are drawn from Bass's book, with the exception of "six beautiful children": Christine Luna is my cousin and that characterization is my firsthand observation.

34. Bryan Stevenson's story, and the stories of some of the incarcerated people he and EJI have helped, are depicted in his book, *Just Mercy* (2014). The Equal Justice Initiative is located at 122 Commerce Street, Montgomery, AL 36104.
https://eji.org/
https://museumandmemorial.eji.org/museum
https://museumandmemorial.eji.org/memorial

35. Executive Order 9981 ending segregation in the military: https://www.archives.gov/milestone-documents/executive-order-9981 Accessed May 23, 2022.

36. Farrell Evans, "Why Harry Truman Ended Segregation in the US Military in 1948," *History,* November 5, 2020, https://www.history.com/news/harry-truman-executive-order-9981-desegration-military-1948 Accessed March 31, 2021.

37. Wilkerson, *Caste,* 227-28; and Equal Justice Initiative, *Lynching in America: Targeting Black Veterans,* 40, https://eji.org/wp-content/uploads/2019/10/lynching-in-america-targeting-black-veterans-web.pdf Accessed April 1, 2021.

38. Farrell Evans, *History,* November 5, 2020, https://www.history.com/news/harry-truman-executive-order-9981-desegration-military-1948 Accessed March 31, 2021.

39. Helene Cooper, "'Is Austin on Your List?': Biden's Pentagon Pick Rose Despite Barriers to Diversity," *New York Times,* December 9, 2020/updated January 10, 2021, https://www.nytimes.com/2020/12/09/us/politics/biden-lloyd-austin-defense-secretary.html | Accessed April 2, 2021.

40. General Charles Q. Brown, Jr., "What I'm Thinking About," online video:
https://www.pacaf.af.mil/News/Article-Display/Article/2210485/heres-what-im-thinking-about/ includes transcript; also see:
https://www.youtube.com/watch?v=UjPco68usEo | Accessed August 8, 2022.

41. "Race in the Ranks: Investigating Racial Bias in the U.S. Military," *60 Minutes,* March 21, 2021, https://www.cbsnews.com/news/us-military-racism-60-minutes-2021-03-21/ Accessed March 29, 2021. CBS has changed access to this program to subscription-only. A clip may be available here:

https://www.youtube.com/watch?v=NRiuKPKEsdo

42. The Air Force's "Real Talk" conversations take place live on Facebook and are archived on YouTube. They are not sound bites—most are over an hour, and, as the title states, real conversations. The following link got me there; search for "AETC" real talk": https://www.youtube.com/results?search_query=aetc+real+talk Most recently accessed February 27, 2022.

43. Ibram X. Kendi, *Stamped from the Beginning: The Definitive History of Racist Ideas in America,* (Bold Type/Perseus/Hachette, 2017), 5.

44. Ibram X. Kendi, *How to Be an Antiracist,* (One World/Random House, 2019), "To be antiracist…," 105; "Racist ideas…," 227. The Trump, et. al. example that follows is mine, not Kendi's.

45. Ibid., 219.

46. Wilkerson, see pp. 113-14 in this chapter, and note 12 above.

47. Richard Delgado and Jean Stefancic, *Critical Race Theory: An Introduction,* 3rd edition, (New York UP, 2017), 3.

48. Ibid., 3-4.

49. Ibid., 8-10.

50. Benjamin Wallace-Wells, "How a Conservative Activist Invented the Conflict Over Critical Race Theory," *New Yorker,* June 18, 2021, https://www.newyorker.com/news/annals-of-inquiry/how-a-conservative-activist-invented-the-conflict-over-critical-race-theory Accessed August 18, 2021. Unless otherwise noted, further references to Christopher Rufo are from this source.

51. Rod Dreher, "Christopher Rufo Vs. the CRT Goliath," *The American Conservative,* September 9, 2020, https://www.theamericanconservative.com/dreher/christopher-rufo-vs-critical-race-theory-goliath/ Accessed November 10, 2021.

52. Mike Gonzalez, "The Constitutional Way to Defeat Cancel Culture," *Religion & Liberty,* vol. 30, no. 4, Acton Institute, October 23, 2020, https://www.acton.org/religion-liberty/volume-30-number-4/constitutional-way-defeat-cancel-culture; available as a PDF through the Heritage Foundation: https://www9.heritage.org/rs/824-MHT-304/images/CancelCultureHeritage.pdf Accessed October 26, 2021.

53. Jane Coaston, "The intersectionality wars," *Vox,* May 28, 2019,

https://www.vox.com/the-highlight/2019/5/20/18542843/intersectionality-conservatism-law-race-gender-discrimination Accessed November 10, 2021.

54. Kimberlé Crenshaw, "Demarginalizing the Intersection of Race and Sex: A Black Feminist Critique of Antidiscrimination Doctrine, Feminist Theory and Antiracist Politics," *University of Chicago Legal Forum:* Vol. 1989: Iss. 1, Article 8, http://chicagounbound.uchicago.edu/uclf/vol1989/iss1/8

55. The charts on this page provide an example: https://campusmentalhealth.ca/toolkits/equity-diversity-inclusion/appendix-a/. Others are available online. For a concise, and in my reading, evenhanded, synthesis of charts like this and how they're used and misused, see Lukianoff and Haidt, *The Coddling of the American Mind* (2019), 67-71.

56. For the Rufo quote, see note 51. From among many, examples of the "others" include: Mike Pence: "Critical race theory is racism, pure and simple, and it should be rejected by every American of every race." Ted Cruz: "Critical race theory is bigoted, it is a lie, and it is every bit as racist as the Klansmen in white sheets." Regarding "their own Goliath," funding for attacks against critical race theory comes from numerous conservative sources. Here's a sampling: https://www.cnbc.com/2021/11/10/critical-race-theory-executives-rich-gop-donors-funded-attacks-during-elections.html; https://www.thedailybeast.com/right-wing-aristocrats-fund-critical-race-theory-backlash; https://www.npr.org/2021/06/24/1009839021/uncovering-who-is-driving-the-fight-against-critical-race-theory-in-schools

57. John McWhorter, *Woke Racism: How a New Religion Has Betrayed Black America,* (Portfolio-Penguin, 2021).

58. Kendi, *Stamped from the Beginning,* x-xi.

59. Dan Baum, "Legalize It All: How to win the war on drugs," *Harper's Magazine,* April 2016, https://harpers.org/archive/2016/04/legalize-it-all/. Ehrlichman's assertion has been challenged as being an oversimplification of Nixon's motivations, an attempt by a bitter Ehrlichman to discredit Nixon after Ehrlichman's Watergate convictions, and a complete fabrication. More relevant to our purpose here, the war on crime and drugs, declared by Nixon and escalated by subse-

quent administrations, did lead to the beginning of the mass incarceration of black men in the 1980s.

60. These questions are adapted from Kerry Patterson, Joseph Grenny, et. al., *Crucial Conversations: Tools for Talking When Stakes Are High,* (McGraw-Hill, 2002), 34-35.

CHAPTER SIX – Dominoes, Defoliation, Death, & Democracy

Abbreviations for books frequently cited in this chapter:

BSL   Neil Sheehan, *A Bright Shining Lie: John Paul Vann and America in Vietnam,* (New York: Random House, 1988).

PHUS   Howard Zinn, *A People's History of the United States: 1492-Present* (New York: Harper Perennial, 1999/1980).

1. Inspired by Carse, *Finite and Infinite Games,* 61.
2. Doug Anderson, "The Mass Graves at Huè," *Horse Medicine,* (New York: Barrow Street, 2015), 7. ARVN refers to the Army of the Republic of [South] Vietnam. NVA refers to the North Vietnamese Army.
3. "Proclamation of Independence of the Democratic Republic of Vietnam" (September 2, 1945); multiple sources online; here's one: http://afe.easia.columbia.edu/ps/vietnam/independence.pdf
4. Sheehan, *BSL,* 148-53 and Zinn, *PHUS,* 469-71. Sheehan puts the number of letters and telegrams from Ho Chi Minh to Truman and his Secretary of State at eleven over an 18-month period and notes that Britain, China and the Soviet Union also ignored his requests for help at the time. China and the Soviets would later provide financial and military assistance when the U.S. began financing France's efforts. "We apparently stand quite alone; we shall have to depend on ourselves," *BSL,* 149. Zinn includes an excerpt from one of Ho's letters, *PHUS,* 470-71. The U.S. State Department classified and locked away the correspondence, which would not become public until the publication of the Pentagon Papers, *BSL,* 152-53.
5. "Geneva Agreements, July 20-21, 1954," *Demarcation line and demilitarized zone:* Chapter 1, Article 1. *No military base:* Final Declaration, paragraph 5. *National election in 1956,* Final Declaration, paragraph 7.

https://peacemaker.un.org/sites/peacemaker.un.org/files/KH-LA-VN_540720_GenevaAgreements.pdf Accessed June 5, 2021.

6. President Dwight Eisenhower, "The Chance for Peace," April 16, 1953. Audio: https://www.eisenhowerlibrary.gov/eisenhowers/speeches. Text: https://www.americanrhetoric.com/speeches/dwighteisenhowercrossofiron.htm. Accessed June 5, 2021.

7. Zinn, *PHUS,* 472-73, cites the Pentagon Papers as his source for South Vietnam's being "essentially the creation of the United States." Sheehan, *BSL* develops Diem's background, arrogance, missteps, impact and demise in detail, 175-84 and 351-71.

8. Sheehan, *BSL,* 188-89, 197.

9. Zinn, *PHUS,* 475.

10. Sheehan, *BSL,* overview of Ap Bac, 204-65; statistics, 262-63; leadership's dismissing Vann's, et. al., reports, 272+.

11. Ibid., 285-87.

12. Ibid., 287-88. Robert McNamara is kinder to Harkins than is Sheehan, writing that he did not believe that Harkins or "other officers consciously misled" him, choosing instead to lay the blame on "very inaccurate information from the South Vietnamese," (McNamara, *In Retrospect,* 47-48).

13. To "frag" refers to attempting to kill a military colleague, usually an officer or NCO, so it looks like an accident. The name comes from the common weapon of choice, which was the fragmentation grenade.

14. Doug Anderson, "Free Fire Zone," *The Moon Reflected Fire,* (Cambridge MA: Alice James, 1994),19.

15. For a concise overview of My Lai, with a first-person account from then 18-year-old door gunner, Spc 4 Larry Colburn, see *Stars and Stripes,* December 21, 2016: https://www.stripes.com/larry-colburn-the-last-hero-of-my-lai-1.445593. Accessed January 5, 2021. Additional accounts:
https://www.military.com/history/hugh-c-thompson-jr.html
https://www.nytimes.com/2006/01/07/us/hugh-thompson-62-who-saved-civilians-at-my-lai-dies.html
https://www.zinnedproject.org/news/tdih/hugh-thompson-lai-massacre/
https://www.sdvfp.org/about/who-was-hugh-thompson/.
National Book Award-winning author and Vietnam veteran, Tim O'Brien, recalls arriving in My Lai with his unit in February 1969, not knowing about the massacre and wondering "why the place

was so hostile." D.J.R. Bruckner, "A Storyteller For the War That Won't End," *New York Times*, April 3, 1990, https://www.nytimes.com/1990/04/03/books/a-storyteller-for-the-war-that-won-t-end.html?searchResultPosition=1   Accessed August 8, 2022.

16. Zinn, *PHUS*, 479.

17. Sheehan, *BSL*, 689-90.

18. Details of Jonathan Schell's meeting with Robert McNamara and McNamara's growing disillusionment about the war are drawn from Sheehan, *BSL*, 686-89, and Jonathan Schell, "Remembering Robert McNamara," *The Nation*, July 7, 2009, https://www.thenation.com/article/archive/remembering-robert-mcnamara/ Accessed July 13, 2021. Hal Moore's interview is from Sheehan, *BSL*, 683.

19. See Neil Sheehan, Hedrick Smith, et.al., *The Pentagon Papers*, (New York: Racehourse, 2017). For the complete declassified report, see: https://www.archives.gov/research/pentagon-papers.

20. Max Frankel, "The Lessons of Vietnam", *New York Times*, July 6, 1971: https://www.nytimes.com/1971/07/06/archives/the-lessons-of-vietnam-pentagons-study-uniquely-portrays-the-greek.html Accessed May 13, 2021.

21. Asst. Sec. of Defense, John McNaughton's March 10, 1965 memorandum justifying ground troops in Vietnam: https://history.state.gov/historicaldocuments/frus1964-68v02/d193 Accessed May 13, 2021. See also Sheehan, Smith, et.al., *The Pentagon Papers*, (Racehourse, 2017), 442.

22. The details of 1968's election, the peace talks and Nixon's interference therewith, ongoing war, Johnson's decision not to run and then to curtail the bombing, etc. all against the backdrop of the assassinations of Martin Luther King, Jr. and Robert Kennedy, riots throughout the United States, and the "police state" Democratic national convention in Chicago are central to and beyond the scope of this chapter. Nixon's papers continue to be released. Contextual overviews include: John A. Farrell, "When a Candidate Conspired With a Foreign Power to Win an Election", *Politico*, August 6, 2017, https://www.politico.com/magazine/story/2017/08/06/nixon-vietnam-candidate-conspired-with-foreign-power-win-election-215461 Accessed May 17, 2021; Peter Baker, "Nixon Tried to Spoil Johnson's Vietnam Peace Talks in '68, Notes Show," *New York Times*, January 2, 2017,

https://www.nytimes.com/2017/01/02/us/politics/nixon-tried-to-spoil-johnsons-vietnam-peace-talks-in-68-notes-show.html Accessed May 17, 2021; and Jason Daley, "Notes Indicate Nixon Interfered With 1968 Peace Talks", *Smithsonian,* January 2, 2017, https://www.smithsonianmag.com/smart-news/notes-indicate-nixon-interfered-1968-peace-talks-180961627/ Accessed May 17, 2021.

23. Sheehan, *BSL,* 421.

24. Tim O'Brien, *The Things They Carried,* (New York: Mariner, 2009), 20, 57.

25. Doug Anderson, *Keep Your Head Down: Vietnam, the Sixties, and a Journey of Self-Discovery,* (New York: Norton, 2009), 248-49.

26. *The Fog of War,* Errol Morris, director, (Sony, 2003). Regarding McNamara's being better able to empathize with the Soviets than with the Vietnamese, the Soviets were WW II allies and more familiar; the Vietnamese were colonized enemies of the French (our allies) and culturally less familiar to Americans.

27. David K. Shipler, "Robert McNamara and the Ghosts of Vietnam." *New York Times,* August 10, 1997, https://www.nytimes.com/1997/08/10/magazine/robert-mcnamara-and-the-ghosts-of-vietnam.html. Quotes attributed to Trang Quang Co are from this source.

28. Ibid.

29. Jonathan Schell, "Remembering Robert McNamara," *The Nation,* July 7, 2009, https://www.thenation.com/article/archive/remembering-robert-mcnamara/ Accessed July 14, 2021.

30. Anderson, "Letting Go," *Horse Medicine,* 12. Bào Ninh is a Vietnamese writer who fought in the North Vietnamese Army from 1969-1975. See also: Bao Ninh, "The First Time I Met Americans," *New York Times,* September 5, 2017, https://www.nytimes.com/2017/09/05/opinion/vietnam-war-writers.html.

31. ^As with Chapter Two, 28, note 13, and Chapter Seven, 177, notes 7, 8, & 9, I refer you to Rabbi Gellman's words on page 28 of this volume regarding what gets lost when we hear or speak about large numbers of deaths. This site provides one *starting point* for calculating deaths in Vietnam: https://en.wikipedia.org/wiki/Vietnam_War_casualties#Total_number_of_deaths

32. Harold G. Moore, and Joseph L. Galloway, *We Were Soldiers Once ...and Young,* (New York: Ballantine, 2004), 351.

33. Ibid., 352.

34. Anderson, "Mine," *The Moon Reflected Fire*, 12.

35. Kendi, *Stamped from the Beginning*, x-xi. See Chapter Five, 142-43, and note 58 in this volume.

36. An extensive, albeit dated, history of the use of herbicides like Agent Orange is the Institute of Medicine's *Veterans and Agent Orange: Health Effects of Herbicides Used in Vietnam,* (National Academies Press, 1994), https://www.ncbi.nlm.nih.gov/books/NBK236356/; more current information is available at the Veterans Adm. (VA) site: https://www.va.gov/disability/eligibility/hazardous-materials-exposure/agent-orange/; and the Vietnam Veterans Memorial Fund site: https://www.vvmf.org/topics/Agent-Orange/;

37. Bessel van der Kolk, *The Body Keeps the Score,* (Penguin, 2014), 17-18.

38. Ibid., 19.

39. Eduardo Duran, *Healing the Soul Wound: Trauma-Informed Counseling for Indigenous Communities,* (Teachers College Press, 2019), 112-47.

40. Crocq, Marc-Antoine, and Louis Crocq, "From shell shock and war neurosis to posttraumatic stress disorder: a history of psycho-traumatology," *Dialogues in Clinical Neuroscience,* "March 2000, 2(1): 47-55, https://www.ncbi.nlm.nih.gov/pmc/articles/PMC3181586/ Accessed August 3, 2021.

41. The posttraumatic stress diagnosis has employed the language of "syndrome" (PTSS), and "disorder" (PTSD), and has recently been simplified (and some would say destigmatized) by some practitioners and patients by removing the final word altogether: post-traumatic stress (PTS).

42. Sheehan, *BSL*, 23-25.

43. Thich Nhat Hahn: https://plumvillage.org/about/thich-nhat-hanh/biography/ and https://thichnhathanhfoundation.org/thich-nhat-hanh Accessed May 27, 2021. Sometimes written as Thích Nhất Hạnh, I have chosen to use the presentation of his name as it appears in his books and on the above two sites.

44. O'Brien, *The Things They Carried,* 38.

45. Moore, and Galloway, *We Were Soldiers Once ...and Young,* 373.

46. John Musgrave, "This Is What We Do (July 1967-December 1967)" *The Vietnam War: A Film by Ken Burns and Lynn Novick,* Season 1, Episode 5: 16:10-17:10. The written version is my transcription from the film. John Musgrave's memoir, *The Education of Corporal John Musgrave,* was published by Knopf in November 2021 (after this chapter was written). For more information: https://www.johnmusgraveveteran.com/
47. Anderson, "Same Old," *Horse Medicine,* 9.

CHAPTER SEVEN – Lessons Not Learned: Afghanistan, Iraq, &…

1. Inspired by Carse, *Finite and Infinite Games,* 61.
2. Reggie Marra, "What Tries to Escape," *Killing America* (From the Heart Press, 2018) 21. The image from which this poem emerged originally appeared at http://www.marchforjustice.com/4.8.php, accessed May 2003 and August 9, 2006, a site that no longer exists. I have been unable to find accurate credit for the image, other than a Reuters copyright. The child, Ali Abbas, was married in 2017 and became the father of a baby boy in 2018: http://www.dailymail.co.uk/news/article-2203977/Joy-Iraq-war-orphan-lost-arms-bombing-raid-plans-wedding-childhood-friend.html | Accessed February 21, 2018; see also: https://www.dailymail.co.uk/news/article-5453719/Iraqi-severely-injured-2003-U-S-airstrike-hails-birth-son.html Accessed December 30, 2020.
3. Jonathan Schell, "The Importance of Losing," *The Jonathan Schell Reader,* (Nation-Avalon, 2004) 343-44. Originally published in *The Nation,* September 23, 2003.
4. Scott Ritter: http://www.democracynow.org/2005/10/21/scott_ritter_on_the_untold_story
5. David Kay: http://www.npr.org/2011/05/29/136765601/david-kay-wmds-that-never-were-a-war-that-ever-was
6. The quote, and Bush's entire speech, are available from most news sources: https://georgewbush-whitehouse.archives.gov/news/releases/2003/05/20030501-15.html.
7. ^https://www.iraqbodycount.org/: According to this site, again, depending on what is counted and who's counting, there have

been between 186,354 and 209,613 documented civilian deaths due to violence in Iraq between 2003 and August 8, 2022. See note 9 for a more extensive accounting of civilian and military deaths in other post-9/11 U.S. military engagements.

^Regarding notes 7, 8 & 9, I refer you again to Rabbi Gellman's words in Chapter Two, page 28, regarding what gets lost when we hear or speak about large numbers of deaths.

8. ^Stanley McChrystal, Tantum Collins, et al. *Team of Teams: New Rules of Engagement for a Complex World.* (Portfolio-Penguin, 2015), 130.

9. ^4,586 American military deaths as of December 30, 2020 (4,100 of those from 2004-2020), again, that is *after* President Bush's announcement that we had prevailed. http://www.statista.com/statistics/263798/american-soldiers-killed-in-iraq/. Last accessed June 27, 2022. See also, Neta C. Crawford and Catherine Lutz, "Human Cost of Post 9-11 Wars Direct War Deaths in Major War Zones, Afghanistan and Pakistan (October 2001 - October 2019) Iraq (March 2003 - October 2019); Syria (September 2014 - October 2019); Yemen (October 2002 - October 2019); and Other," *20 Years of War: A Costs of War Research Series,* Watson Institute, Brown University & The Frederick S. Pardee Center, Boston University, November 13, 2019, https://watson.brown.edu/costsofwar/files/cow/imce/papers/2019/Direct%20War%20Deaths%20COW%20Estimate%20November%2013%202019%20FINAL.pdf Accessed July 4, 2021. This study "tallies direct deaths by war violence. It does not include indirect deaths, namely those caused by loss of access to food, water, and/or infrastructure, war-related disease, etc."

10. Richard A. Clarke, *Against All Enemies,* (Free Press, 2004), 2.

11. Ibid., 30.

12. Ibid., 31

13. Ibid., 32.

14. Project for the New American Century's January 26, 1998 letter to President Bill Clinton, https://zfacts.com/zfacts.com/metaPage/lib/98-Rumsfeld-Iraq.pdf Accessed June 27, 2021. The PNAC, and its website, are no longer available online under that name.

15. Thomas Donnelly, *Rebuilding America's Defenses: Strategy, Forces and Resources For a New Century*, Project for the New American Century, September 2000, pp. 50-51, https://pdf4pro.com/download/rebuilding-america-s-defenses-30f72.html, Accessed June 30, 2021.

16. Clarke, *Against All Enemies,* 231-38; "largely a nonevent," 237.

17. Andrew Bacevich, *America's War for the Greater Middle East*, (Random House, 2016), 231, citing Tommy Franks, *American Soldier* (New York, 2004), 315.

18. Ibid., 240.

19. Andrew Bacevich, *Washington Rules: America's Path to Permanent War,* (Metropolitan, 2010), 11-15. Italics in original. Note the contrast with Eisenhower's post-WW II precepts (Appendix I).

20. Ibid., 1.

21. Ibid., 11.

22. Max Fisher, "America's unlearned lesson: the forgotten truth about why we invaded Iraq," *Vox,* February 16, 2016, https://www.vox.com/2016/2/16/11022104/iraq-war-neoconservatives Accessed June 27, 2021. Fisher wrote this piece in response to the February 13, 2016 Republican presidential debate in which the candidates argued whether it was lies about WMD (Donald Trump) or faulty intelligence (most other candidates) that led to the attack on Iraq.

23. "apparently intelligent," as used here refers to the traditional verbal, logical, mathematical, and rational abilities that can be applied to studying, learning, and mastering most academic disciplines, and that remain the core of formal schooling. One can excel here and fail miserably when it comes to moral, interpersonal, intrapersonal, somatic, emotional and other human characteristics and endeavors. Said differently, the intellectual gifts that manifest above the neck are just one part of what is necessary for fully developing and integrating as a human being.

24. Marra, "November in Fallujah," *Killing America.* The image from which this poem emerged appeared in Johnny Dwyer, "The Wounded," *New York Times Magazine,* March 27, 2005, 24+. Photograph by Lynsey Addario/Corbis.

25. For several perspectives on the U. S. in Iraq from 2003 forward, see: Sarhang Hamasaeed and Garrett Nada, "Iraq Timeline: Since the 2003 War," *United States Institute of Peace,* May 29, 2020, https://www.usip.org/iraq-timeline-2003-war; BBC, "Iraq profile – timeline," *BBC News,* October 3, 2018,

https://www.bbc.com/news/world-middle-east-14546763 (this site also provides a longer view of Iraqi history); and Miriam Berger, "Invaders, allies, occupiers, guests: A brief history of U.S. military involvement in Iraq," *Washington Post,* January 11, 2020, https://www.washingtonpost.com/world/2020/01/11/invaders-allies-occupiers-guests-brief-history-us-military-involvement-iraq/ All three accessed August 7, 2021.

26. See Chapter Six, 149, for Eisenhower's precepts, and this chapter, 199-200, for McNamara's lessons from *The Fog of War.* Both are available in Appendix I.

27. Shannon Collins, "Desert Storm: A Look Back," *U.S. Department of Defense,* January 11, 2019, https://www.defense.gov/Explore/Features/story/Article/1728715/desert-storm-a-look-back/ Accessed August 6, 2021.

28. Bacevich, *America's War for the Greater Middle East,* 178-79. For one reflection on the RMA, see Michael O'Hanlon, "A Retrospective on the So-called Revolution in Military Affairs," *Brookings Institution,* September 2018, https://www.brookings.edu/research/a-retrospective-on-the-so-called-revolution-in-military-affairs-2000-2020/ Accessed August 7, 2021.

29. Ibid., 248. For these numbers, Bacevich cites Michael R. Gordon and Bernard E. Trainor, *Cobra II,* (New York, 2006) 4, 29, 31-32 and Tommy Franks, *American Soldier,* 428.

30. Eric Schmitt, "Pentagon Contradicts General on Iraq Occupation Force's Size," *New York Times,* February 28, 2003, https://www.nytimes.com/2003/02/28/us/threats-responses-military-spending-pentagon-contradicts-general-iraq-occupation.html?searchResultPosition=1 Accessed August 5, 2021.

31. Here's one example: Qassim Abdul-Zahra and Zeina Karam, "Death and suffering in Iraq a painful legacy of 9/11 attacks," *AP News,* September 12, 2021, https://apnews.com/article/afghanistan-united-states-iraq-george-w-bush-middle-east-84eaa99721b433d0db1b0c12051bb117 Accessed March 7, 2022.

32. Neta C. Crawford, "The Iraq War has cost the US nearly $2 trillion," *Military Times,* February 6, 2020, https://www.militarytimes.com/opinion/commentary/2020/02/06/the-iraq-war-has-cost-the-us-nearly-2-trillion/ Accessed July 1, 2021.

33. Schmitt, "Pentagon Contradicts General..." *New York Times,* February 28, 2003. See note 30.

34. William D. Hartung, "Profits of War: Corporate Beneficiaries of the Post-9/11 Pentagon Spending Surge," Center for International Policy & Watson Institute, International & Public Affairs at Brown University, September 13, 2021; "more than $14 trillion," 4; "one third to one half," 1; "just five companies," 4-5; "the purse is now open," 3; Lockheed Martin contract and State Department budget, 4; "$2.5 billion on lobbying," 20; https://watson.brown.edu/costsofwar/papers/2021/ProfitsOfWar Accessed September 14, 2021.

35. Sharon Weinberger, "Windfalls of War: Pentagon's No-Bid Contracts Triple in 10 Years of War", *The Center for Public Integrity,* May 19, 2014 (update of original August 29, 2011), https://publicintegrity.org/national-security/windfalls-of-war-pentagons-no-bid-contracts-triple-in-10-years-of-war/ Accessed July 2, 2021.

36. David Pallister, "How the US sent $12bn in cash to Iraq. And watched it vanish", *Guardian,* February 7, 2007, https://www.theguardian.com/world/2007/feb/08/usa.iraq1 Accessed July 1, 2021. Reported throughout the media.

37. Donald Rumsfeld, "Defense Business Practices", September 10, 2001, https://www.c-span.org/video/?165947-1/defense-business-practices Accessed July 1, 2021.

38. Bunny Greenhouse's story: https://www.whistleblowers.org/news/victory-for-bunny-greenhouse/ Accessed July 2, 2021. Note: this site provides links to the transcripts of her 2007 and 2009 testimony before the Senate and House committees. Her story was covered throughout the media.

39. *The Final Report of the Commission on Wartime Contracting in Iraq and Afghanistan,* S. Hrg. 112-298, October 19, 2011, https://www.govinfo.gov/content/pkg/CHRG-112shrg72564/pdf/CHRG-112shrg72564.pdf Accessed July 3, 2021. While our focus thus far has been on Iraq, Afghanistan is as bad or worse: Graham Lanktree, "U.S. Contractor Bought Luxury Cars, Paid Fat Salaries to Partners on Afghanistan Contract, Audit Finds", *Newsweek,* August 9, 2017, https://www.newsweek.com/us-contractor-bought-luxury-cars-paid-fat-salaries-partners-afghanistan-648834 Accessed July 3, 2021.

40. Samuel Stebbins and Evan Comen, "Military spending: 20 companies profiting the most from war", *USA Today,* February 21, 2019,
https://www.usatoday.com/story/money/2019/02/21/military-spending-defense-contractors-profiting-from-war-weapons-sales/39092315/ Accessed, July 3, 2021.

41. John Hooper, "German leader says no to Iraq war," *Guardian,* August 5, 2002,
https://www.theguardian.com/world/2002/aug/06/iraq.johnhooper Accessed August 17, 2021.

42. Jonathan Rauch, *The Constitution of Knowledge: A Defense of Truth,* (Brookings Institution Press, 2021), 88-89.

43. Depending on who's measuring and what's being measured, in light of China's ongoing growth and Russia's invasion of Ukraine, ratings of military *strength* vary. The U. S. *spends* more than any other nation. Some statistics and opinions on expenditures:
https://armedforces.eu/compare/country_USA_vs_China
https://www.military.com/daily-news/2020/02/24/5-most-powerful-armies-world.html
https://www.globalfirepower.com/country-military-strength-detail.php?country_id=united-states-of-america
https://www.statista.com/chart/20418/most-powerful-militaries/
Here are two assessments of the *number of military bases:*
https://www.overseasbases.net/uploads/5/7/1/7/57170837/fact_sheet_on_overseas_bases_2018_09_17.pdf
https://www.politico.com/magazine/story/2015/06/us-military-bases-around-the-world-119321/

44. John F. Sopko, et. al., *What We Need to Learn: Lessons from Twenty Years of Afghanistan Reconstruction,* (Special Inspector General for Afghanistan Reconstruction, August 2021) vii-xi,
https://www.sigar.mil/pdf/lessonslearned/SIGAR-21-46-LL.pdf
SIGAR's other Lessons Learned reports are available here:
https://www.sigar.mil/lessonslearned/lessonslearnedreports/index.aspx?SSR=11&SubSSR=60&WP=Lessons%20Learned%20Reports

45. Ibid., x-xi. This is the executive summary of Chapter Seven (71-81) of the report.

46. Sheehan, *A Bright Shining Lie,* 287.

47. Andrei Kozyrez, interview with Ari Melber, "Kremlin vet: They'll overthrow Putin before giving him bad news about setbacks in Ukraine," *MSNBC,* March 9, 2022, https://www.msnbc.com/the-

beat-with-ari/watch/kremlin-vet-they-ll-overthrow-putin-before-giving-him-bad-news-about-russian-setbacks-in-ukraine-134995525702 Accessed March 11, 2022.

48. Craig Whitlock, *The Afghanistan Papers: A Secret History of the War,* (Simon & Schuster, 2021), Sopko and Crowley quotes, 204; "Whitlock concluded….'making progress,'" 205; "There was no…" - General Dan McNeill, xv; "We didn't have…" - Lt. General Douglas Lute, xv; "I have no visibility…" - Secretary of Defense, Donald Rumsfeld, September 8, 2003 memo, photo insert 1, #1, facing p. 12 text; "From the ambassadors…" - Lt. General Michael Flynn, 205. See also Whitlock's December 9, 2019 *Washington Post* video:
https://www.washingtonpost.com/video/world/exclusive-a-secret-history-of-the-war-in-afghanistan-revealed/2019/12/09/dd9210b9-f583-4371-bd51-ad261626fc20_video.html

49. *The Fog of War,* Errol Morris, director, (Sony, 2003). As captured in this volume, the eleven lessons are from my notes while viewing the documentary. They appear in a variety of online sources as well.

50. Bradley's quote is from Bacevich, *After the Apocalypse,* (Metropolitan, 2021), 85. Often-quoted online and variously translated from Aristotle's *Nicomachean Ethics,* Book 2, Chapter 9: "So too anybody can get angry—that is easy—and anybody can give or spend money, but to give it to the right person, to give the right amount of it, at the right time, for the right cause and in the right way, this is not what anybody can do, nor is it easy." *Aristotle: On Man in the Universe,* Louise Ropes Loomis, ed. (Walter J. Black, 1943), 111.

51. S.J. Res. 23 is available at:
https://www.govinfo.gov/content/pkg/BILLS-107sjres23enr/pdf/BILLS-107sjres23enr.pdf Accessed August 22, 2021.

52. Roxanne Roberts, "Barbara Lee doesn't feel vindicated for voting against Afghan war: 'I almost wish … I had been wrong,'" *Washington Post,* August 18, 2021,
https://www.washingtonpost.com/lifestyle/2021/08/18/barbara-lee-vote-afghanistan-war/ Accessed August 18, 2021.

53. Bacevich, *America's War for the Greater Middle East,* (2016), xiv-xv, is the source for the Middle East campaigns listed.

54. *Turning Point: 9/11 and the War on Terror*, Netflix, Ep. 3, "The Dark Side," Brian Knappenberger, director, (Netflix, 2021). Cheney was speaking on *Meet the Press*, September 16, 2001.

55. Ibid., Alberto Gonzalez interview. Unless otherwise indicated, all subsequent quotes attributed to Alberto Gonzalez are from this source and episode.

56. Ibid., Michel Paradis interview. For both photographic and verbal updates on Guantanamo, see note 60.

57. An August 1, 2002 memo from Assistant Attorney General Jay S. Bybee to Acting General Counsel of the CIA, John Rizzo describes the "very, very detailed instructions" Gonzalez refers to and authorizes them for use on Abu Zubaydah: https://www.justice.gov/sites/default/files/olc/legacy/2010/08/05/memo-bybee2002.pdf Accessed September 21, 2021.

58. *Turning Point,* Episode 3, (Netflix, 2021), Ali Soufan interview. For more on Soufan's work: https://www.soufangroup.com/team-member/ali-soufan/

59. Ibid., John McCain's public statement.

60. Carol Rosenberg, "The Secret Pentagon Photos of the First Prisoners at Guantánamo Bay," *New York Times,* June 12, 2022, https://www.nytimes.com/interactive/2022/06/12/us/guantanamo-bay-pentagon-photos.html Accessed June 13, 2022.

61. John Musgrave, Chapter Six, 172, note 46; Neil Sheehan, Chapter Six, 156-57, note 17.

62. Details of the Presidential Surveillance Program on pages 206-08 are from "(U) Unclassified Report on the President's Surveillance Program," Offices of Inspectors General, DOD, DOJ, CIA, NSA, DNI, (Report No. 2009-0013-AS, July 10, 2009), https://irp.fas.org/eprint/psp.pdf, Accessed September 21, 2021. "close hold" and "read in," 10; "Gang of Eight," 23; "…recovering from surgery," 24; details of the meeting in Ashcroft's hospital room, 23-25; "…to modify certain PSP…," 29. See also: Carrie Johnson and Ellen Nakashima, "Report: Wiretaps risked a crisis," *Philadelphia Inquirer,* July 11, 2009, https://www.inquirer.com/philly/news/homepage/20090711_Report__Wiretaps_risked_a_crisis.html

63. Elizabeth Goitein, "Rolling Back the Post-9/11 Surveillance State," *Brennan Center for Justice,* August 25, 2021, https://www.brennancenter.org/our-work/analysis-opinion/rolling-back-post-911-surveillance-state,

Accessed September 22, 2021; and Barton Gellman, "U.S. surveillance architecture includes collection of revealing Internet, phone metadata," *Washington Post,* June 15, 2013, https://www.washingtonpost.com/investigations/us-surveillance-architecture-includes-collection-of-revealing-internet-phone-metadata/2013/06/15/e9bf004a-d511-11e2-b05f-3ea3f0e7bb5a_story.html

64. Mark Hannah, Producer, and Eric Felipe-Barkin, Director, Editor and Producer, "Why These Veterans Are Demanding an End to the War in Afghanistan," Video, *New York Times*, November 11, 2019, https://www.nytimes.com/video/opinion/100000006802073/veterans-afghanistan-war.html?searchResultPosition=1 Also at: https://www.youtube.com/watch?v=m6c6ADB6CwI Accessed July 6, 2021. The opinions of the five veterans cited are from this source.

65. Alissa J. Rubin, "Did the War in Afghanistan Have to Happen?" *New York Times,* August 23, 2021, https://www.nytimes.com/2021/08/23/world/middleeast/afghanistan-taliban-deal-united-states.html Accessed August 23, 2021. "Pentagon Briefing with Donald Rumsfeld," *Washington Post,* November 19, 2001, https://www.washingtonpost.com/wp-srv/nation/specials/attacked/transcripts/rumsfeldtext_111901.html Accessed August 23, 2021. Mujib Mashal, "Taliban and U.S. Strike Deal to Withdraw American Troops From Afghanistan," *New York Times,* February 29, 2020, updated August 23, 2021, https://www.nytimes.com/2020/02/29/world/asia/us-taliban-deal.html Accessed August 23, 2021.

66. Karoun Demirjian and Alex Horton, "U. S. lost war in Afghanistan through miscalculations spanning multiple administrations, Milley tells lawmakers," *Washington Post,* September 29, 2021, https://www.washingtonpost.com/national-security/2021/09/29/afghanistan-hearing-milley-austin-mckenzie/ Accessed September 29, 2021.

67. Whitlock, *The Afghanistan Papers,* 213-25.

68. Dave Phillips, "'In the End We Felt Betrayed': Vietnamese Veterans See Echoes in Afghanistan,'" *New York Times,* July 7, 2021, https://www.nytimes.com/2021/07/07/us/vietnam-war-veterans-us-afghanistan.html?action=click&module=Top%20Stories&pgtype=Homepage Accessed July 7, 2021.

69. Sudarsan Raghavan, "'Everyone here hated the Americans': Afghans live with the Taliban and a painful U.S. legacy," *Washington Post,* October 5, 2021,
https://www.washingtonpost.com/world/asia_pacific/afghanistan-village-us-taliban/2021/10/04/e531303c-214a-11ec-a8d9-0827a2a4b915_story.html   Accessed October 5, 2021.

70. David Miliband, "The Afghan economy is a falling house of cards. Here are 5 steps to rebuild it," *CNN* Opinion, January 20, 2022, https://www.cnn.com/2022/01/20/opinions/afghan-economy-falling-house-cards-miliband/index.html Accessed March 9, 2022.

71. Anand Gopal, "The Other Afghan Women: in the countryside, the endless killing of civilians turned women against the occupiers who claimed to be helping them," *New Yorker,* September 13, 2021, (10-14, 19, 28),
https://www.newyorker.com/magazine/2021/09/13/the-other-afghan-women Accessed September 15, 2021.

72. Whitlock, *The Afghanistan Papers;* see especially pages 91-102 and 199-211. Examples abound throughout the book.

73. National Commission on Terrorist Attacks Upon the United States, *The 9/11 Commission Report,* 2004, 11.2, 348, https://9-11commission.gov/report/ Accessed July 7, 2021.

74. Richard Clarke, "Public Testimony before the 9/11 Commission," March 24, 2004,
https://www.youtube.com/watch?v=_IJaDUzag9w Accessed July 6, 2021. Excerpts from this testimony also appear in Clarke's *Against All Enemies,* 293-97.

75. Ibid., in video testimony and in *Against All Enemies,* 296-97.

76. Miriam Berger, "Invaders, allies, occupiers, guests: A brief history of U.S. military involvement in Iraq," January 11, 2020, https://www.washingtonpost.com/world/2020/01/11/invaders-allies-occupiers-guests-brief-history-us-military-involvement-iraq/ Accessed July 11, 2021.

77. McNamara, *In Retrospect,* 324. As he used the term, "postwar" refers to WW II.

78. See Chapter Six, 167-68, and note 36 regarding Agent Orange in Vietnam.

79. Regarding burn pits:
https://burnpits360.org/;
Veterans Administration site:
https://www.publichealth.va.gov/exposures/burnpits/;

PBS News Hour, May 27, 2021 (Jon Stewart quote is from this report): https://www.youtube.com/watch?v=LBTB5br6tHY; *CBS Mornings,* August 22, 2019: https://www.youtube.com/watch?v=mOk7iAiYCOw; SIGAR reported to Congress frequently regarding burn pits; here's a second-quarter report from 2013: "Alert 13-4: Observations on Solid Waste Disposal Methods in Use at Camp Leatherneck," July 30, 2013, *SIGAR Oversight,* 25, https://www.sigar.mil/pdf/quarterlyreports/2013-07-30qr-section2.pdf More recently: Kevin Freking, "House backs bill to help veterans exposed to toxic burn pits," *APNews,* March 3, 2022, https://apnews.com/article/military-veteran-burn-pit-exposure-legislation-49a461be5d50ef146a65850a5c48d2df Accessed March 7, 2022.

80. Sergeant Isiah James, (Ret.), "The Problem with War," *The Problem with John Stewart,* October 4, 2021, *Apple TV+,* https://www.youtube.com/watch?v=MCUIFNn77PU&t=111s; see also https://www.blackveteransproject.org/team.

81. Marra, "This Open Eye," *Killing America* (2018). The image from which this poem emerged originally appeared at http://www.marchforjustice.com/3.25.php, accessed April 2003 and August 9, 2006 (this site no longer exists and it did not credit the photograph). A February 21, 2018 online search led to this: http://avax.news/sad/Iraq_Wars_10th_Anniversary.html | Photo by Damir Saglj/Reuters via *The Atlantic.* The Avax site caption puts the girl's age at 4. My guess in 2003 was 3. Most recently accessed October 13, 2021.

CHAPTER EIGHT – And That's Not All

1. Inspired by Carse, *Finite and Infinite Games,* 30.

2. Global population 1760: https://www.worldometers.info/world-population/world-population-by-year/; U. S. population 1790: https://www.census.gov/content/dam/Census/library/stories/2019/07/july-fourth-celebrating-243-years-of-independence-table-1.jpg; https://www.census.gov/history/www/through_the_decades/fast_facts/1790_fast_facts.html

3. Sandra Díaz, Josef Settele, Eduardo S. Brondízio, et. al., eds., Summary for Policymakers: *The Global Assessment Report on Bio-*

diversity and Ecosystem Services, Intergovernmental Science-Policy Platform on Biodiversity and Ecosystem Services (IPBES), 2019, https://ipbes.net/sites/default/files/2020-02/ipbes_global_assessment_report_summary_for_policymakers_en.pdf Accessed October 2, 2021. The "developed," "developing," and "least developed" language is from the report. For an overview of the report, see Brad Plumer, "Humans Are Speeding Extinction and Altering the Natural World at an 'Unprecedented' Pace," *New York Times,* May 6, 2019, https://www.nytimes.com/2019/05/06/climate/humans-are-speeding-extinction-and-altering-the-natural-world-at-an-unprecedented-pace.html.

4. Valérie Masson-Delmotte, Panmao Zhai, Anna Pirani, et. al., eds., Summary for Policymakers, *Climate Change 2021: The Physical Sciences Basis. Contribution of Working Group I to the Sixth Assessment Report of the Intergovernmental Panel on Climate Change.* https://www.ipcc.ch/report/ar6/wg1/downloads/report/IPCC_AR6_WGI_SPM.pdf Accessed October 2, 2021. For an overview of the findings see Andrew Freedman, "UN report: Effects of climate change even more severe than we thought," *Axios,* August 9, 2021, https://www.axios.com/un-climate-report-global-warming-faster-ipcc-003e9e0b-ae85-4298-ad0c-09fe163b74f4.html.

5. Lyndon Johnson, Introduction to *Restoring the Quality of Our Environment: Report of The Environmental Pollution Panel, President's Science Advisory Committee,* November 1965, https://www-legacy.dge.carnegiescience.edu/labs/caldeiralab/Caldeira%20downloads/PSAC,%201965,%20Restoring%20the%20Quality%20of%20Our%20Environment.pdf Accessed October 5, 2021.

6. Alice Bell, "Sixty years of climate change warnings: the signs that were missed (and ignored)," *Guardian,* July 5, 2021, https://www.theguardian.com/science/2021/jul/05/sixty-years-of-climate-change-warnings-the-signs-that-were-missed-and-ignored, Accessed October 5, 2021.

7. Linda Lear, Introduction to the Fortieth Anniversary Edition of Rachel Carson's *Silent Spring,* (Mariner/Houghton Mifflin, 2002, 1962), xiv-xvi.

8. Jiddu Krishnamurti, https://jkrishnamurti.org/. The quote is ubiquitous and attributed to Krishnamurti. I was unable to find any verifiable written or spoken source.

9. Here are just a few organizations concerned with mental health in the U. S. See note 16 for addiction-specific organizations. Mental Health America: https://www.mhanational.org/; American Foundation for Suicide Prevention: https://afsp.org/; Centers for Disease Control and Prevention: https://www.cdc.gov/mentalhealth/; Johns Hopkins Medicine: https://www.hopkinsmedicine.org/health/wellness-and-prevention/mental-health-disorder-statistics; National Alliance on Mental Illness: https://www.nami.org/mhstats; National Institute of Mental Health: https://www.nimh.nih.gov/health

10. Numbers are for 2019. "Any mental illness" (AMI), can vary from no, to mild, to moderate, to severe impairment. "Serious mental illness" (SMI) results in "serious functional impairment" that interferes with or limits one or more major life activities." https://www.nimh.nih.gov/health/statistics/mental-illness Accessed September 28, 2021.

11. Todd Wasserman, "Half of millennials and 75% of Gen Zers have left their job for mental health reasons," *CNBC,* October 11-15, 2019, https://www.cnbc.com/2019/10/11/mental-health-issues-cause-record-numbers-of-gen-x-z-to-leave-jobs.html Accessed September 28, 2021.

12. Jennifer Moss, "Burnout Is About Your Workplace, Not Your People," *Harvard Business Review,* December 19, 2019, https://hbr.org/2019/12/burnout-is-about-your-workplace-not-your-people Accessed December 20, 2019.

13. Centers for Disease Control and Prevention, "Statistics on Children's Mental Health," https://www.cdc.gov/childrensmentalhealth/data.html Accessed September 29, 2021.

14. National Institute on Drug Abuse: "Commonly Used Drugs": https://www.drugabuse.gov/download/2918/commonly-used-drugs-charts.pdf?v=297a7d6c889a22228d2e4ab83541d494

15. Overdose deaths - Centers for Disease Control and Prevention: https://www.cdc.gov/nchs/nvss/vsrr/drug-overdose-data.htm Accessed September 29, 2021.

16. Opioids - Centers for Disease Control and Prevention: https://www.cdc.gov/drugoverdose/deaths/index.html Accessed September 30, 2021. Additional organizations that deal with

substance abuse and addiction in the U. S. include: Partnership to End Addiction: https://drugfree.org/; Substance Abuse and Mental Health Services Administration (SAMHSA): https://www.samhsa.gov/; Addiction Center: https://www.addictioncenter.com/; American Addiction Centers: https://americanaddictioncenters.org/; Shatterproof: https://www.shatterproof.org/; National Institute on Drug Abuse: https://www.drugabuse.gov/; National Institutes of Health HEAL Initiative: https://heal.nih.gov/; 2019 World Happiness Report (excerpt on addiction): https://worldhappiness.report/ed/2019/addiction-and-unhappiness-in-america/; Surgeon General (*2016* Report): https://addiction.surgeongeneral.gov/sites/default/files/OC_SpotlightOnOpioids.pdf; Surgeon General (*2018* Report): https://addiction.surgeongeneral.gov/sites/default/files/OC_SpotlightOnOpioids.pdf; SAMSA National Survey of Substance Abuse Treatment Services (N-SSATS): 2020 - https://www.samhsa.gov/data/sites/default/files/reports/rpt35313/2020_NSSATS_FINAL.pdf Accessed September 29, 2021.

17. U.S. Department of Justice Settlement with Perdue Pharma: https://www.justice.gov/opa/pr/justice-department-announces-global-resolution-criminal-and-civil-investigations-opioid; 2007 plea, 2019 bankruptcy filing and 2021 bankruptcy ruling: Jan Hoffman, "Purdue Pharma Is Dissolved and Sacklers Pay $4.5 Billion to Settle Opioid Claims," *New York Times,* September 1, 17, 2021, https://www.nytimes.com/2021/09/01/health/purdue-sacklers-opioids-settlement.html Accessed September 30, 2021. More recently: Jan Hoffman, "Sacklers and Perdue Pharma Reach New Deal With States Over Opioids," *New York Times,* March 3, 2022, https://www.nytimes.com/2022/03/03/health/sacklers-purdue-oxycontin-settlement.html Accessed March 12, 2022.

18. SAMSA "National Survey of Substance Abuse Treatment Services (N-SSATS): 2020": https://www.samhsa.gov/data/sites/default/files/reports/rpt35313/2020_NSSATS_FINAL.pdf Accessed September 29, 2021.

19. National Alliance to End Homelessness, https://endhomelessness.org/homelessness-in-america/homelessness-statistics/state-of-homelessness-2021/ Accessed January 6, 2022.

20. See Dr. Gabor Maté, *In the Realm of the Hungry Ghosts*, and *When the Body Says No,* https://drgabormate.com/; Dr. Bessel van der Kolk, *The Body Keeps the Score,* https://www.besselvanderkolk.com/; Johann Hari, *Chasing the Scream* and *Lost Connections,* https://johannhari.com/. In Chapter Eleven, we will briefly address some of the ways that the words "soul" and "spirit" are used.

21. Lucy King and Jonah M. Kessel, "We Know the Real Cause of the Crisis in Our Hospitals. It's Greed." *New York Times,* January 19, 2022, https://www.nytimes.com/2022/01/19/opinion/covid-nurse-burnout-understaffing.html Accessed January 19, 2022.

22. "Bailout Tracker," *ProPublica,* https://projects.propublica.org/bailout/list; many corporate recipients do not repay the loans in full; for a brief, humorous synopsis of this not-really-funny issue, see Jon Stewart's October 2021 clip: https://www.youtube.com/watch?v=jXZoO-FjJyQ

23. I apply the qualifier *harmful* here because *discrimination*, as commonly used nowadays, refers to treating an individual or group unfairly based on perceived differences. At its root, to discriminate means to identify differences, to differentiate. It is important to discriminate between the poison and safe mushrooms, between the troll and the authentic narrative, between fact and opinion. Also, labels such as "Asian," "Latinx," "Middle Eastern" and "LGBTQ+" fall short of discriminating among the unique cultures and individuals they attempt to capture (as "American" itself is a woefully inadequate, but sometimes useful label). Some of these labels may already be outdated by the time this book is out of my hands, so to speak. I appreciate your generous, healthy *it's-about-all-that-is* understanding.

24. German Lopez, "The Reagan Administration's unbelievable response to the HIV/AIDS epidemic," *Vox,* December 1, 2016, https://www.vox.com/2015/12/1/9828348/ronald-reagan-hiv-aids Accessed September 30, 2021. For the definitive history, see Randy Shilts's *And the Band Played On.*

25. The second half of Ben Vereen's courageous, satirical performance was seen only by those who attended the 1981 inauguration in-person, since ABC only televised the first half, leaving most who watched on television to believe that the actor had subjugated himself to the predominantly Republican attendees. Vereen paid a price for years. Cy Musiker, "What Viewers Didn't See Changed

Everything for Ben Vereen," *KQED,* February 14, 2018, https://www.kqed.org/arts/13824539/what-viewers-didnt-see-changed-everything; Accessed May 30, 2021.

26. Marc Dolan, "How Ronald Reagan Changed Bruce Springsteen's Politics," *Politico,* June 4, 2014, https://www.politico.com/magazine/story/2014/06/bruce-springsteen-ronald-reagan-107448/ Accessed May 30, 2021.

27. Ralph Waldo Emerson, "The American Scholar," *The American Tradition in Literature,* 4th ed. (Grosset & Dunlap, 1974), 601. The comma and dash, "soul,—the soul" appear in the original.

28. Jonathan Rauch, *The Constitution of Knowledge* (2021), citing Trump strategist Steve Bannon: "flood the zone…," 163; Rauch: "degrade the information environment," 164; citing *The Economist,* April 19, 2018: "cacophony of wild claims," 165; Rauch: "an inability to know where…," 166; citing Russian dissident Gary Kasparov: "exhaust your critical thinking," 166; Rauch: "not to persuade but to confuse…," 165.

29. Amanda Cox, "How Birth Year Influences Political Views," *New York Times,* July 7, 2014, https://www.nytimes.com/interactive/2014/07/08/upshot/how-the-year-you-were-born-influences-your-politics.html?searchResultPosition=1 Accessed October 6, 2021. Cox's piece is based on Yair Ghitza and Andrew Gelman, "The Great Society, Reagan's Revolution, and Generations of Presidential Voting," Working Paper, July 7, 2014, https://static01.nyt.com/newsgraphics/2014/07/06/generations2/assets/cohort_voting_20140707.pdf Accessed October 6, 2021.

30. We're not picking on iGens here. Every generation has its respective dignities and disasters (and is better able and more willing to see its own dignity and everyone else's disasters). This chapter's closing paragraph speaks to the disaster of such unhealthy group-centrism.

31. 2014-2019: 14,515 gun deaths/year avg. (not suicide) = 40/day avg; 23,094 suicides by gun = 63/day; 37,609 total annual gun deaths = 103/day: https://www.gunviolencearchive.org/ Accessed September 28, 2021. 2014-2019: 45,835 suicides/year avg. = 126*/day: https://webappa.cdc.gov/sasweb/ncipc/leadcause.html Accessed September 28, 2021. Search criteria was: *2014-2019 / all causes, races, genders and ages.* *Due to rounding, the suicides per day on the two sites differ by 1. I used the lower, 125, in the text.

32. Neil MacFarquhar, "Murders Spiked in 2020 in Cities Across the United States," *New York Times,* September 27, 2021, https://www.nytimes.com/2021/09/27/us/fbi-murders-2020-cities.html Accessed September 27, 2021.

33. Reis Thebault and Danielle Rindler, "Shootings never stopped during the pandemic: 2020 was the deadliest gun violence year in decades," *Washington Post,* March 23, 2021, https://www.washingtonpost.com/nation/2021/03/23/2020-shootings/ Accessed September 28, 2021. Gun violence ties directly to the unhealthy masculine: Mike McIntire, Glenn Thrush and Eric Lipton, "Gun Sellers' Message to Americans: Man Up," *New York Times,* June 18, 2022, https://www.nytimes.com/2022/06/18/us/firearm-gun-sales.html Accessed June 18, 2022.

34. Representative Eric Cantor (VA-R) on September 14, 2001. From Netflix, *Turning Point: 9/11 and the War on Terror,* Episode 2, "A Place of Danger." Not to pick on Mr. Cantor—many similar statements were made by members of both parties.

35. Vine Deloria, Jr., *Custer Died for Your Sins,* (U of Oklahoma P, 1988/1969), 255-56.

36. Leading up to what's cited in the text, Dr. King said, "…as I have walked among the desperate, rejected, and angry young men, I have told them that Molotov cocktails and rifles would not solve their problems. I have tried to offer them my deepest compassion while maintaining my conviction that social change comes most meaningfully through nonviolent action. But they asked…" https://kinginstitute.stanford.edu/king-papers/documents/beyond-vietnam; recording: https://www.youtube.com/watch?v=SQr_e_P-nBA

37. Bacevich, *The Limits of Power,* 163.

38. Anderson, "Same Old," *Horse Medicine,* 9.

39. This unfortunate episode is relevant here because of the light it shines on our collective Shadow. The disconnect between the reaction to a celebrity slap (not to minimize its impact on those immediately involved) and the "normalized" everyday violence and death in America is stark. In the larger picture of American violence and Shadow, this moment and the reaction to it were at once superficial and indicative of our collective denial. I respect the work of both Chris Rock and Will Smith, each of whom I experience as exceptional at what he does. (I'm sure they'd both be relieved to know this).

40. Jason E. Goldstick, Ph.D., Rebecca M. Cunningham, M.D., and Patrick M. Carter, M.D., "Current Causes of Death in Children and Adolescents in the United States," *New England Journal of Medicine,* May 19, 2022, https://www.nejm.org/doi/full/10.1056/NEJMc2201761

41. F. Scott Fitzgerald, *The Great Gatsby,* (Scribner, 1925 / Scribner Paperback, 1995), 187-88.

CHAPTER NINE – Bullied, Woke, & Canceled in the Polarized State(s) of America

1. Inspired by Carse, *Finite and Infinite Games,* 31.

2. Regarding schoolyard and online bullying: From the U. S. federal government: https://www.stopbullying.gov/bullying/what-is-bullying; From the American Psychological Association: https://www.apa.org/topics/bullying

3. Greg Lukianoff and Jonathan Haidt, in *The Coddling of the American Mind,* provide case-study and research-based insights into perceived safety and threats, along with suggestions for how to more accurately discern threats that are really out there and threats that are creations of our minds. While they're not specifically addressing Shadow, their insights are relevant to the larger American narrative(s). Also, as noted in Chapter Two, a *disproportionate* emotional response is often an indication of the presence of Shadow.

4. As used here, "white supremacy" refers primarily to the explicit beliefs, articulated, for instance, in Edward Alfred Pollard's *The Lost Cause: A New Southern History of the War of the Confederates* (1866) and *The Lost Cause Regained* (1868), that "the supremacy of the white race" was the true cause of the war and the hope of the South*—beliefs that are currently still held and acted on by various groups throughout the United States.^ Secondarily, it refers to the implicit beliefs, explicitly manifested first in the founding of the country by white men who, in their choices and behavior indicated their belief that the English (whites) were superior to others, especially but not only, the indigenous peoples of the Americas and Africa, and later (i.e. today) in biases held by many individuals, often unconsciously, and implicitly built into many institutions. Paradoxically and fortunately, these same men also gave us documents and structures

that invite and allow us to move away from mistaken ideas of supremacy—albeit slowly and imperfectly. Explicit white supremacist beliefs remain extant and available. Several excerpts from *The Lost Cause Regained* (1868), disturbing and informative, follow. Locations cited here are from the Kindle edition. Page numbers are approximations:

From Part III "The Negro Question," 112-128: "The value of the fact of the Negro's inferiority is very great." (Location 1469); "The permanent, natural inferiority of the Negro was the true and *only* defence [sic] of Slavery." (Location 1500); "In Man we find the Negro as the base of the generic [sic] column; and ascending, in order, the different races above him—the Esquimaux, the Aboriginal American, the Malay or Oceanic, the Mongolian—we at last reach in the Caucasian or the *historic* race the perfection of the highest form of the human creation." (Location 1576).

From Part IV "The True Hope of the South," 129-184: "Slavery has improved and civilized the Negro to a certain extent, and has now left him the subject of a new experiment. We would make that experiment kindly and tenderly, although we think it vain, as we believe the Negro obtains his highest development in the convenient position, of a subordinate where he copies and imitates." (Location 1891-1900); "What is the true hope of the South?—The new cause or the 'lost cause' revived.... What is that hope to which we have referred? It is the hope of a new political conflict, in which the South will stand stronger than she ever did before.... She may have to endure much before she reaches the threshold and fruition of this new controversy; but the conclusion is sure to her. This new cause—or rather the true question of the war revived—is the supremacy of the white race and along with it and strengthening it, the reassertion of our political traditions, and the protection of our ancient fabrics of government." (Location 2098-2105).

*Meacham, *The Soul of America,* 58-59, 299.

^Southern Poverty Law Center: https://www.splcenter.org/hatemap and https://www.splcenter.org/hatewatch. Not all groups listed are white supremacist.

5. Respectively, Ephesians 6:5+ (regarding slaves and masters), 5:22+ (regarding wives and husbands); and Colossians 3:22+ (slaves and masters), 3:18+ (wives and husbands) in the *NIV Study Bible,* (Zondervan, 1973, 1995). See Chapter Five, 108-09 and note 3, for a link to the years in which the slave trade, and slavery itself were

abolished in different countries. For more on what was shifting and had shifted, consider the dignities and disasters of the Enlightenment: Several places to start:
https://en.wikipedia.org/wiki/Age_of_Enlightenment
https://www.history.com/topics/british-history/enlightenment
https://www.britannica.com/event/Enlightenment-European-history & https://plato.stanford.edu/entries/enlightenment/ With regard to the twenty-first century, especially but not only amid the reign of the 45th president, we see evidence of tens of millions of Americans who really do seem to believe in equality for all, and evidence of tens of millions who seem not to so believe—or are undecided. Note again, Ibram Kendi's dual and dueling histories of racial and racist progress, Chapter Five, 142-43.

6. For an exploration of some recent manifestations of intolerant, fundamentalist liberal words and behavior, see Lukianoff and Haidt, especially, but not only, pages 53-117. Fundamentalist conversative words and behavior are more commonly noted publicly, as with SPLC's hate map and hate watch (note 4^).

7. See Chapter One, note 7 for commentary on what the word "woke" actually connotes in the context of waking up, growing up, cleaning up, and showing up. It is possible for development from one worldview to another to take place in an unhealthy or incomplete way. Wielding the new perspective as a weapon may result. The modern-to-postmodern "woke" move mentioned in the text is just one example. For further exploration, Ken Wilber's work provides a synthesis of various researchers (among much else), including Robert Kegan, who is arguably the "founder" of adult development research. Bill Plotkin's work provides a rather extraordinary and eloquent "soulcentric" model of development. A one-page diagram of Plotkin's model is available here: https://animas.org/wp-content/uploads/Eight-Stages-diagram_3-3_hi-res.png. The first chapter of his *Nature and the Human Soul* is available here: https://animas.org/books/nature-and-the-human-soul/nature-and-the-human-soul-chapter-one/ Note that these researchers study diverse aspects of human beings but that the basic movements (from partial and simple to increasingly inclusive and complex) are consistent. Ongoing adult development is itself complex. Knowing about it does not make problems disappear, but it does help clarify patterns and differentiate perspectives. Not knowing about it doesn't mean it doesn't exist. Here's a brief sampling of some of the language, moving left

to right from earlier to later development: Archaic > Magic > Mythic > Rational > Pluralistic > Integral (Jean Gebser re worldviews); Undifferentiated > Magical > Mythic-literal > Conventional > Individuative-reflective > Conjunctive > Universalizing (James Fowler re stages of faith); Socialized Mind > Self-authoring Mind > Self-transforming Mind (Kegan re adult mental capacity); some sources for further reading: Wilber, *The Religion of Tomorrow: A Vision for the Future of the Great Traditions,* 180-250, charts 190-95, (Shambhala, 2017); Kegan, *In Over Our Heads: The Mental Demands of Modern Life,* (Harvard UP, 1994); Kegan and Lisa Laskow Lahey, *Immunity to Change How to Overcome It and Unlock the Potential in Yourself and Your Organization,* 11-30, (Harvard UP, 2009); Bill Torbert, et.al., *Action Inquiry: The Secret of Timely and Transforming Leadership,* especially 65-117, (Berrett-Koehler, 2004); Plotkin, *Nature and the Human Soul: Cultivating Wholeness and Community in a Fragmented World,* (New World Library, 2008); Fowler, *Stages of Faith: The Psychology of Human Development and the Quest for Meaning,* (HarperSanFrancisco, 1981).

8. John Lewis, *Walking with the Wind,* 496.
9. Ibid., 486.
10. *Moritz v. Commissioner of Internal Revenue* (among multiple sources):
    https://law.justia.com/cases/federal/appellate-courts/F2/469/466/79852/;
    https://scholar.google.com/scholar_case?case=11568697307639967604&q=Charles+E.+Moritz%252C+Petitioner-appellant%252C+v.+Commissioner+of+Internal+Revenue%252C+Respondent-appellee&hl=en&as_sdt=2006
11. Mark Landler, "Harry and Meghan's Hard Exit," *New York Times,* January 19, updated January 21, 2020, https://www.nytimes.com/2020/01/19/world/europe/harry-meghan-royal.html?searchResultPosition=1 Accessed September 5, 2021. Emily Yahr, "Meghan tells Oprah Winfrey she had suicidal thoughts as part of the royal family: 'I just didn't want to be alive anymore,'" *Washington Post,* March 7, 2021, https://www.washingtonpost.com/arts-entertainment/2021/03/07/meghan-harry-oprah-interview-royals/ Accessed March 7, 2021.

12. Nat Hentoff, *Free Speech for Me—but Not for Thee: How the American Left and Right Relentlessly Censor Each Other* (Harper-Collins, 1992), 141.

13. Saunt, *Unworthy Republic,* 97. Saunt cites *The Papers of Andrew Jackson Digital Edition,* ed. Daniel Feller (Charlottesville: University of Virginia Press: 2015). See also Chapter Four, note 9. This critique of Jackson is not an example of unskillful means applied by a later (mine) against an earlier (Jackson's) developmental view. By the 1830s plenty of Americans (albeit not enough in positions of power) disagreed with Jackson's and others' views and policies regarding Indian removal and slavery.

14. Ten Republican representatives who voted to impeach, 2021: https://www.npr.org/2021/01/14/956621191/these-are-the-10-republicans-who-voted-to-impeach-trump; seven Republican senators who voted to convict, 2021: https://www.npr.org/sections/trump-impeachment-trial-live-updates/2021/02/15/967878039/7-gop-senators-voted-to-convict-trump-only-1-faces-voters-next-year

15. Lukianoff and Haidt, *The Coddling of the American Mind,* 81-121; and Rauch, *The Constitution of Knowledge,* 189-231. In both volumes, case studies and explorations of causes and consequences extend beyond the pages cited. Here's one, among many examples: https://www.thefire.org/cases/protesters-at-yale-threaten-free-speech-demand-apologies-and-resignations-from-faculty-members-over-halloween-email/

16. Nicholas A. Christakis, *Blueprint: The Evolutionary Origins of a Good Society,* (Little, Brown Spark, 2019), 13-14+; and Brian Hare and Vanessa Woods, *Survival of the Friendliest,* (Random House, 2021), 110-11, 143.

17. Don Beck shared this quote in a Spiral Dynamics training in 2004. For more on Richard Barrett: https://www.barrettacademy.com/about-2020/richard-barrett

18. Hare and Woods, *Survival of the Friendliest,* 170. See 102-49 for their larger treatment of in-group bias and dehumanization. The authors cite N. Kteily, G. Hodson, E. Bruneau, "They See Us as Less Than Human: Metadehumanization Predicts Intergroup Conflict via Reciprocal Dehumanization," *Journal of Personality and Social Psychology* 110, 343 (2016).

19. Kendi, *How to Be an Antiracist,* (One World, 2019), 131.

20. Hare and Woods, *Survival of the Friendliest,* 165-66, citing P. M. Oliner, *Saving the Forsaken: Religious Culture and the Rescue of Jews in Nazi Europe* (Yale University Press, 2008).

21. Ibid., 249, note 70, citing T. F. Pettigrew, "Intergroup Contact Theory," *Annual Review of Psychology* 49, 65-85 (1998).

22. Ezra Klein, *Why We Are Polarized,* (Avid Reader-Simon & Schuster, 2020), 147-49, citing Douglas J. Ahler and Gaurav Sood, "The Parties in Our Head: Misperceptions About Party Composition and Their Consequences," *Journal of Politics* 80, no. 3 (July 2018): 964-81, doi.org/10.1086/697253.

23. Ibid., See Klein's Chapter Six, "The Media Divide Beyond Left-Right," 139-70. I specify "contact" that is "close, personal, ongoing." Some research that concludes contact not only *does not moderate* opposite-group bias, but *deepens* it, is online, social-media based, and doesn't take developmental perspective into account: in a 2017 study all 1,220 survey respondents used Twitter regularly and self-identified as either Democrat or Republican—while it's possible that folks with a *me*-centric or *all-of*-us centric perspective might indicate a *preference* for one of the parties, to *self-identify* as Democrat or Republican is more typical of an *us-centric* developmental perspective. After agreeing to be exposed to tweets from the other side, "Republicans…became substantially more conservative," and "Democrats exhibited slight increases in liberal attitudes…," 160. Developmental perspective does not answer every question; it does add an essential variable to the mix; and it's missing from most of the current conversation(s) about opposition and polarization (not just from this one). It might shed light on why Republicans deepened their conservative attitudes *substantially* and Democrats deepened their liberal attitudes *slightly.* Developmental perspectives aside, Klein's treatment of polarization is insightful and clear. The study he cites is Christopher A. Bail et al., "Exposure to Opposing Views on Social Media Can Increase Political Polarization," *PNAS,* 115, no. 37 (Sept. 2018): 9216-21, https://www.pnas.org/doi/10.1073/pnas.1804840115

24. Kendi, *How to Be an Antiracist,* (One World, 2019), 129.

25. We'll look more closely at Trump's behavior and briefly explore the varied perspectives of his supporters in the next chapter.

26. Attributed to George Sheehan, from my notes. I regularly read Dr. Sheehan's *Runner's World* column, read his *Running and Being* (1978), *Personal Best* (1989), and *George Sheehan on Running to*

Win (1992) when they were published, and finished behind him in various races despite being 36 years his junior. I have been unable to find the specific source for this quote, but it's his.

CHAPTER TEN – The Gift: One Guy's Shadow as an Unconscious Invitation to a Nation to Heal

1. Inspired by Carse, *Finite and Infinite Games*, 31.

2. Jonathan Rauch, *The Constitution of Knowledge: A Defense of Truth* (Brookings Institution, 2021), 7-8. See also "The Constitution of Knowledge," *National Affairs*, Fall 2018, https://www.nationalaffairs.com/publications/detail/the-constitution-of-knowledge Accessed November 29, 2020.

3. Robin Lindley, "Trump and his 3,500 suits: Prosecutor and author reveals in interview his portrait of 'Plaintiff in Chief,'" *ABA Journal*, April 20, 2020, https://www.abajournal.com/web/article/attorney-and-author-on-his-portrait-of-donald-trump-through-more-than-3500-lawsuits Accessed July 12, 2021. Cf. note 5.

4. Glenn Kessler, Salvador Rizzo, and Meg Kelly, *Donald Trump and His Assault on Truth: The President's Falsehoods, Misleading Claims and Flat-Out Lies,* (Scribner, 2020), 261-62. The book predates Putin's 2022 invasion of Ukraine (ongoing as I type this) by two years. For more on Trump's attempt to shake down Ukraine's President Zelensky, see pages 219-48 in Kessler, et. al. and the following: Jeremy Venook and Talia Dessel, "Trump's Extortion of Ukraine: A Complete Government Shake-down," *Center for American Progress*, October 2, 2019, https://www.americanprogress.org/article/trumps-extortion-ukraine-complete-government-shakedown/ Accessed April 3, 2022; and Amber Phillips, "Who is Alexander Vindman and why does his public testimony matter?" *Washington Post*, November 19, 2019, https://www.washingtonpost.com/politics/2019/11/18/who-is-alexander-vindman-why-does-his-public-testimony-matter/ Accessed April 3, 2022.

5. Nick Penzenstadler, and Susan Page, "Trump's 3,500 lawsuits unprecedented for a presidential nominee," *USA Today,* June 1, 2016 / updated October 23, 2017, https://www.usatoday.com/story/news/politics/elections/2016/06/01/donald-trump-lawsuits-legal-battles/84995854/ Accessed July

12, 2021. See also James Zirin's *Plaintiff in Chief: A Portrait of Donald Trump in 3,500 Lawsuits* (All Points/St. Martin's, 2019).

6. Katerina Ang, "Trump sues New York Times and niece Mary Trump over tax records story," *Washington Post,* September 22, 2021, https://www.washingtonpost.com/politics/2021/09/21/trump-taxes-mary-times-lawsuit/ Accessed September 22, 2021.

7. Jane Mayer, "Donald Trump's Ghostwriter Tells All," *New Yorker,* July 18, 2016. https://www.newyorker.com/magazine/2016/07/25/donald-trumps-ghostwriter-tells-all Accessed January 31, 2021. See also: Linda Qiu, "Is Donald Trump's 'Art of the Deal' the best-selling business book of all time?" *Politifact,* July 6, 2015, https://www.politifact.com/factchecks/2015/jul/06/donald-trump/donald-trumps-art-deal-best-selling-business-book-/ Accessed March 16, 2022.

8. Tony Schwartz, *What Really Matters: Searching for Wisdom in America* (Bantam, 1995), p. 3.

9. Examples of Trump's statements are abundant and ongoing. This report correlates his language with his early loss of support from Republican leaders during his candidacy and presidency: Karen Yourish, Larry Buchanan and Alicia Parlapiano, "More Than 160 Republican Leaders Don't Support Donald Trump. Here's When They Reached Their Breaking Point." *New York Times,* August 29, 2016, updated October 9, 2016, http://www.nytimes.com/interactive/2016/08/29/us/politics/at-least-110-republican-leaders-wont-vote-for-donald-trump-heres-when-they-reached-their-breaking-point.html Accessed August 29, 2016. A sampling of the statements follows: "They're bringing drugs. They're bringing crime. They're rapists." *- June 16, 2015, on undocumented Mexican immigrants.* "He's not a war hero. He's a war hero because he was captured. I like people that weren't captured."*- July 18, 2015, on AZ Republican Senator John McCain, former pilot and POW in Vietnam.* "I know more about ISIS than the generals do. Believe me." *- November 12, 2015.* "Donald J. Trump is calling for a total and complete shutdown of Muslims entering the United States." *- December 7, 2015.* "I don't know anything about David Duke. O.K.? I don't know anything about what you're even talking about with white supremacy or white supremacists." *- March 3, 2016 after former Ku Klux Klan leader Duke endorsed aspects of Trump's message.* "I've been

treated very unfairly by this judge. Now, this judge is of Mexican heritage. I'm building a wall, O.K.? I'm building a wall." - *June 6, 2016 on Judge Gonzalo P. Curiel, a federal judge overseeing a suit against the defunct Trump University.* "If she gets to pick her judges, nothing you can do, folks. Although the Second Amendment people — maybe there is, I don't know." - *August 9, 2016 implying a connection between the right to own guns and stopping Hillary Clinton's ability to nominate judges should she win the election.*

10. Maggie Haberman and Peter Baker, "Trump Taunts Christine Blasey Ford at Rally," *New York Times,* October 2, 2018, https://www.nytimes.com/2018/10/02/us/politics/trump-me-too.html?action=click&module=Top%20Stories&pgtype=Homepage (widely reported throughout the media). The issue, beyond whether the court nominee did what he was accused of or if his accuser was telling the truth (both of which are important), is that the president of the United States saw fit to put the weight of his office, via social media, behind one side of the testimony in a Congressional hearing.

11. David Nakamura, "'People actually laughed at a president': At U.N. speech, Trump suffers the fate he always feared," *Washington Post,* September 25, 2018, https://www.washingtonpost.com/politics/people-actually-laughed-at-a-president-at-un-speech-trump-suffers-the-fate-he-always-feared/2018/09/25/990b1d52-c0eb-11e8-90c9-23f963eea204_story.html?utm_term=.841979b322c8 Accessed September 25, 2018.

12. Russ Buettner, Susanne Craig and Mike McIntire, "Long-Concealed Records Show Trump's Chronic Losses and Years of Tax Avoidance," *New York Times,* September 27, 2020, https://www.nytimes.com/interactive/2020/09/27/us/donald-trump-taxes.html?action=click&module=Spotlight&pgtype=Homepage Accessed Sept 27, 2020. An earlier stage of the investigation was released in 2018: David Barstow, Susanne Craig and Russ Buettner, "Trump Engaged in Suspect Tax Schemes as He Reaped Riches From His Father," *New York Times,* October 2, 2018, https://www.nytimes.com/interactive/2018/10/02/us/politics/donald-trump-tax-schemes-fred-trump.html?action=click&module=Top%20Stories&pgtype=Homepage Accessed October 2, 2018.

13. See note 9 for examples of Donald Trump's persistent use of deceit. See also: Glenn Kessler, Salvador Rizzo and Meg Kelly, "President Trump Has Made 4,229 false or misleading claims in 558 days," *Washington Post,* August 1, 2018, https://www.washingtonpost.com/news/fact-checker/wp/2018/08/01/president-trump-has-made-4229-false-or-misleading-claims-in-558-days/?noredirect=on&utm_term=.31fe5c8c6061 Accessed August 1, 2018. Kessler, Rizzo and Kelly eventually published *Donald Trump and His Assault on Truth* in 2020. See also: David Leonhardt and Stuart A. Thompson, "Trump's Lies," *New York Times,* June 23, 2017, updated December 14, 2017, https://www.nytimes.com/interactive/2017/06/23/opinion/trumps-lies.html Accessed June 23, 2017; An ongoing tally of false statements, "Latest False Fact-Checks on Donald Trump," is available on *Politifact,* https://www.politifact.com/personalities/donald-trump/statements/byruling/false/ Accessed August 29, 2016; Susan B. Glasser, "It's True: Trump Is Lying More, and He's Doing It on Purpose," *New Yorker,* August 3, 2018, https://www.newyorker.com/news/letter-from-trumps-washington/trumps-escalating-war-on-the-truth-is-on-purpose Accessed August 3, 2018; James Pfiffner, "Trump's lies corrode democracy, *Brookings Institution,* April 13, 2018, https://www.brookings.edu/blog/fixgov/2018/04/13/trumps-lies-corrode-democracy/ Accessed August 3, 2018; Lauren Duca, "Donald Trump Has Been Lying to the American Public, and Journalists Need to Call Him Out," *Teen Vogue,* June 1, 2018, https://www.teenvogue.com/story/thigh-high-politics-donald-trump-lying-journalists-need-to-call-him-out Accessed August 3, 2018; Ryan Teague Beckwith, "President Trump Made 1,950 Untrue Claims in 2017. That's Making His Job Harder," *Time,* January 2, 2018, http://time.com/5084420/donald-trump-lies-claims-fact-checks/ Accessed August 3, 2018.

14. Coral Davenport, "Major Climate Report Describes a Strong Risk of Crisis as Early as 2040," *New York Times,* October 7, 2018, https://www.nytimes.com/2018/10/07/climate/ipcc-climate-report-2040.html?module=inline Accessed October 7, 2018. See also Chapter Eight in this volume.

15. Kathryn Dunn Tenpas, "Tracing turnover in the Trump administration," *Brookings Institution,* January 2021,

https://www.brookings.edu/research/tracking-turnover-in-the-trump-administration/ Accessed July 19, 2021.

16. Republican groups who organized against Trump, for Biden, or both: Lincoln Project: https://lincolnproject.us/; Republican Voters Against Trump: https://rvat.org/; 43 Alumni for Biden: https://43alumniforjoebiden.com/ (renamed "43 Alumni for America" after the 2020 election); *Not a party-affiliated group,* and in existence since 2006, VoteVets, which self-identifies as a progressive organization that supports candidates in both parties, also brought a strong anti-Trump presence to the 2020 election: https://www.votevets.org/; See also Annie Karni's "The Crowded, Competitive World of Anti-Trump G.O.P. Groups," *New York Times,* October 12, 2020, updated January 21, 2021, https://www.nytimes.com/2020/10/12/us/politics/never-trump-republicans.html?action=click&module=Top%20Stories&pgtype=Homepage Accessed October 12, 2020.

17. "…Nobody knew healthcare could be so complicated": https://www.youtube.com/watch?v=5oQLf65N-AU (reported throughout the media).

18. Peter Baker, "Trump's Contradiction: Assailing 'Left-Wing Mob' as Crowd Chants 'Lock Her Up,'" *New York Times,* October 10, 2018. This is one example among many: https://www.nytimes.com/2018/10/10/us/politics/trump-rally-opponents.html?action=click&module=In%20Other%20News&pgtype=Homepage&action=click&module=News&pgtype=Homepage Accessed October 10, 2018.

19. William K. Rashbaum, Alan Feur and Adam Goldman, "Outspoken Trump Supporter in Florida Charged in Attempted Bombing Spree," *New York Times,* October 26, 2018, https://www.nytimes.com/2018/10/26/nyregion/cnn-cory-booker-pipe-bombs-sent.html?module=inline Accessed October 26, 2018; Liz Robbins, "They Were Sent Pipe Bombs. Here's What Trump Said About Them—and What They Said About Trump," *New York Times,* October 26, 2018, https://www.nytimes.com/2018/10/26/nyregion/who-received-pipe-bombs-explosives.html?module=inline Accessed October 26, 2018; Jack Healy, Julie Turkewitz and Richard A. Oppel Jr., "Cesar Sayoc, Mail Bombings Suspect, Found an Identity in Political Rage and Resentment," *New York Times,* October 27, 2918,

https://www.nytimes.com/2018/10/27/us/cesar-altieri-sayoc-bomber.html?action=click&module=Top%20Stories&pgtype=Homepage Accessed October 27, 2018.

20. Campbell Robertson, Christopher Mele and Sabrina Tavernise, "11 Killed in Synagogue Massacre; Suspect Charged With 29 Counts," *New York Times,* October 27, 2018, https://www.nytimes.com/2018/10/27/us/active-shooter-pittsburgh-synagogue-shooting.html?action=click&module=Top%20Stories&pgtype=Homepage Accessed October 27, 2018.

21. Mark Makela, "Transcript: Donald Trump's Taped Comments About Women," *New York Times,* October 8, 2016, https://www.nytimes.com/2016/10/08/us/donald-trump-tape-transcript.html Accessed October 8, 2016.

22. Felicia Sonmez and Mike DeBonis, "Trump tells four liberal congresswomen to 'go back' to their countries, prompting Pelosi to defend them," *Washington Post,* July 14, 2019, https://www.washingtonpost.com/politics/trump-says-four-liberal-congresswomen-should-go-back-to-the-crime-infested-places-from-which-they-came/2019/07/14/b8bf140e-a638-11e9-a3a6-ab670962db05_story.html Accessed July 14, 2019.

23. David Nather, "Trump declines to praise John Lewis, citing inauguration snub," *Axios,* August 4, 2020, https://www.axios.com/trump-john-lewis-inauguration-1adc0747-51b8-4990-a7d8-29290e990dc5.html? Accessed August 4, 2020. The full interview is here: https://www.axios.com/full-axios-hbo-interview-donald-trump-cd5a67e1-6ba1-46c8-bb3d-8717ab9f3cc5.html?

24. As used here, "cognitive capacity" refers to perspective-taking, or how many perspectives one is aware of and can understand. Lower cognitive capacity might be aware only of an individual's own needs and desires (it's about me). More developed capacity is aware of others (it's about us, all of us, or all that is).

25. At the heart of much of this behavior seems to be his obsession with winning and, perhaps more importantly, a deep fear of losing, that manifests in denial—throughout his business failures and including his loss to Joe Biden in 2020. See Dan Barry, "'Loser': How a Lifelong Fear Bookended Trump's Presidency," *New York Times,* November 27, 2020, https://www.nytimes.com/2020/11/26/us/politics/trump-election-

loss.html?action=click&module=Top%20Stories&pgtype=Homep
age Accessed November 27, 2020.

26. "Trump Praises to [sic] 'My African American' Supporter,"
Associated Press, June 3, 2016.
https://www.youtube.com/watch?v=nHgb8uNIcNE
Gregory Cheadle's responses and website:
https://www.pbs.org/newshour/politics/man-trump-once-called-
my-african-american-leaves-republican-party
http://www.cheadleforcongress.com/index.html

27. Jason Karlawish, "A pandemic plan was in place. Trump
abandoned it—and science—in the face of Covid 19," *STAT,* May
17, 2020, https://www.statnews.com/2020/05/17/the-art-of-the-
pandemic-how-donald-trump-walked-the-u-s-into-the-covid-
19-era/ Accessed July 21, 2021. The details of Obama's focus on
PCAST and OSTP and his successor's ignoring them are stark. The
PCAST reports removed by Trump are available in the Obama
White House Archives: "PCAST Documents & Reports," *Obama
White House Archives,* Final entry: January 13, 2017,
https://obamawhitehouse.archives.gov/administration/eop/ostp/p
cast/docsreports Accessed July 22, 2021.

28. Ronald Klain, "Confronting the Pandemic Threat," *Democracy,*
Spring 2016, No. 40,
https://democracyjournal.org/magazine/40/confronting-the-
pandemic-threat/ Accessed July 22, 2021.

29. Deb Riechmann, "Trump disbanded NSC pandemic unit that
experts had praised," *Associated Press,* March 14, 2020,
https://apnews.com/article/donald-trump-ap-top-news-virus-
outbreak-barack-obama-public-health-
ce014d94b64e98b7203b873e56f80e9a Accessed July 22, 2021. For
the partisan bickering, see: "Partly false claim: Trump fired entire
pandemic response team in 2018," *Reuters,* March 25, 2020,
https://www.reuters.com/article/uk-factcheck-trump-fired-
pandemic-team/partly-false-claim-trump-fired-entire-pandemic-
response-team-in-2018-idUSKBN21C32M Accessed July 22, 2021.

30. Nancy Cook, Meredith McGraw and Adam Cancryn, "What did
Trump know and when did he know it? Inside his Feb. 7
admission," *Politico,* September 10, 2020,
https://www.politico.com/news/2020/09/10/trump-coronavirus-
bob-woodward-412222 Accessed July 21, 2021.

31. Cameron Peters, "A detailed timeline of all the ways Trump failed
to respond to the coronavirus," *Vox,* June 8, 2020,

https://www.vox.com/2020/6/8/21242003/trump-failed-coronavirus-response Accessed July 21, 2021.

32. J. M. Rieger, "40 Times Trump said the coronavirus would go away," *Washington Post,* November 2, 2020, https://www.washingtonpost.com/video/politics/40-times-trump-said-the-coronavirus-would-go-away/2020/04/30/d2593312-9593-4ec2-aff7-72c1438fca0e_video.html Accessed July 23, 2021. Here's a selected sampling from the video: Feb 27: "It's going to disappear. One day, it's like a miracle, it will disappear." March 12: "It's gonna go away. It will go away." Aug. 7: "It's going to disappear." Oct. 22: "It will go away, and as I say, we're rounding the turn, we're rounding the corner. It's going away." Oct 31: "It's going to go away, and we are rounding, it drives them crazy, the fake news media. It's going away." See also: Eugene Kiely, Lori Robertson, Rem Rieder and D'Angelo Gore, "Timeline of Trump's COVID-19 Comments," *FactCheck(dot)org,* October 2, 2020, https://www.factcheck.org/2020/10/timeline-of-trumps-covid-19-comments/ Accessed July 21, 2021.

33. Brianna Ehley, "U.S. coronavirus outbreak inevitable, CDC official says," *Politico,* February 25, 2020, https://www.politico.com/news/2020/02/25/us-coronavirus-outbreak-inevitable-cdc-117389 Accessed July 22, 2021.

34. Rieger, *Washington Post,* November 2, 2020 (see note 32).

35. "Trump: Coronavirus is Democrats' 'new hoax'" *Telegraph,* February 29, 2020, video [a chilling betrayal of his supporters], https://www.youtube.com/watch?v=G5TZ6fTYrsE&t=2s Accessed July 22, 2021.

36. Peters, "A detailed timeline..." *Vox,* June 8, 2020 (see note 31).

37. Statistics provided in text and chart are from the CDC, specifically from the daily trends setting: https://covid.cdc.gov/covid-data-tracker/#trends_dailytrendscases Last accessed June 2, 2022. Updated numbers may vary slightly from those cited here.

38. Rieger, *Washington Post,* November 2, 2020 (see note 32). For comprehensive reporting on Trump's final year in office, including the pandemic, the loss to Biden and the January 6 attack on the Capitol, see Carol Leonnig and Philip Rucker's *I Alone Can Fix It: Donald J. Trump's Catastrophic Final Year,* (Penguin, 2021).

39. Mariana Spring, "'Stop the steal': the deep roots of Trump's 'voter fraud' strategy," *BBC News,* November 23, 2020,

https://www.bbc.com/news/blogs-trending-55009950, Accessed July 24, 2021.

40. Morgan Chalfant, "Trump: 'The only way we're going to lose this election is if the election is rigged,'" *The Hill,* August 17, 2020, https://thehill.com/homenews/administration/512424-trump-the-only-way-we-are-going-to-lose-this-election-is-if-the Accessed July 24, 2021.

41. Adam Kelsey, "Donald Trump's 2012 Election Tweetstorm Resurfaces as Popular and Electoral Vote Appear Divided," *ABC News,* November 9, 2016, https://abcnews.go.com/Politics/donald-trumps-2012-election-tweetstorm-resurfaces-popular-electoral/story?id=43431536 Accessed July 24, 2021; and Terrance Smith, "Trump has longstanding history of calling elections 'rigged' if he doesn't like the results," *ABC News,* November 11, 2020, https://abcnews.go.com/Politics/trump-longstanding-history-calling-elections-rigged-doesnt-results/story?id=74126926 Accessed July 24, 2021.

42. Larry Buchanan, Karen Yourish, Ainara Tiefenthäler, Jon Huang and Blacki Migliozzi, "Lie After Lie: Listen to How Trump Built His Alternate Reality," *New York Times,* February 9, 2021, https://www.nytimes.com/interactive/2021/02/09/us/trump-voter-fraud-election.html?action=click&module=Spotlight&pgtype=Homepage Accessed February 11, 2021. For an overview of the contexts within which these lies were told, see also Jim Rutenberg, Jo Becker, Eric Lipton, Maggie Haberman, Jonathan Martin, Matthew Rosenberg, and Michael S. Schmidt, "77 Days: Trump's Campaign to Subvert the Election," *New York Times,* January 31, 2021, updated June 15, 2021, https://www.nytimes.com/2021/01/31/us/trump-election-lie.html?action=click&module=Spotlight&pgtype=Homepage Accessed January 31, 2021. After almost a year of investigation, the House Select Committee to Investigate the January 6 Attack on the United States Capitol began public hearings in June 2022. Evidence from testimony from former Trump White House staff and family indicates that the election-fraud campaign and the January 6 attack were more well organized than originally thought and that the president orchestrated much of it. The story continues to emerge as this book goes to print. Luke Broadwater,

"'Trump Was at the Center'" Jan. 6 Hearing Lays Out Case in Vivid Detail," *New York Times,* June 9, 2022, https://www.nytimes.com/2022/06/09/us/politics/trump-jan-6-hearings.html Accessed June 10, 2022.

43. Cybersecurity & Infrastructure Security Agency, "Joint Statement from Elections Infrastructure Government Coordinating Council & The Election Infrastructure Sector Coordinating Executive Committees," November 12, 2020, https://www.cisa.gov/news/2020/11/12/joint-statement-elections-infrastructure-government-coordinating-council-election?utm_source=newsletter&utm_medium=email&utm_campaign=newsletter_axiosam&stream=top&fbclid=IwAR2RE0N2ve Xq4aVRRGYie6gHt6TgwB0l1TmqchsrrIy4eTMwpK5jg7_6ubk Accessed November 18, 2020. Weijia Jiang, "Trump fires nation's top election security official after agency said election was securely run," *CBSN* online, November 18, 2020, https://www.youtube.com/watch?v=UxAnm9pUMM0 Accessed November 18, 2020. Christopher Krebs's November 29, 2020 interview on CBS's *60 Minutes* is available here: https://www.youtube.com/watch?v=YzBJJ1sxtEA&t=630s

44. Video of the November 19, 2020 Giuliani and Powell statements as covered by the *Washington Post, Fox News* and *Reuters: Washington Post* (excerpt): https://www.youtube.com/watch?v=zTbUQQxn0w8 *Fox News* (full press conference, no longer available, was here): https://www.youtube.com/watch?v=3r7KIDXruxw *Reuters* (Giuliani and Trump distance themselves from Powell): https://www.youtube.com/watch?v=YsW7e0zGZ-M

45. Maggie Haberman and Jonathan Martin, "After the Speech: What Trump Did as the Capitol Was Attacked, *New York Times,* February 13, 2021, https://www.nytimes.com/2021/02/13/us/politics/trump-capitol-riot.html?action=click&module=Spotlight&pgtype=Homepage Accessed February 14, 2021. As this book goes into production, the January 6 Select Committee's investigation continues. Evidence of witness tampering and that Trump knew some protesters were armed is emerging. Isaac Arnsdorf, Josh Dawsey, and Carol Leonnig, "'Take me up to the Capitol now': How close Trump came to joining the rioters," *Washington Post,* July 1, 2022, https://www.washingtonpost.com/politics/2022/07/01/trump-capitol-riot-march/ Accessed July 2, 2022.

46. Kathleen Belew, interviewed by Michel Martin, "The White Power Movement's History," *PBS / Amanpour & Company,* June 25, 2021, https://www.pbs.org/wnet/amanpour-and-company/video/the-white-power-movements-history/ Accessed July 26, 2021. See also Kathleen Belew and Bill Moyers interviewed by Hari Sreenivasan, "Is Trump Laying the Groundwork for a Coup in 2024?" *Amanpour & Company,* January 5, 2022, https://www.pbs.org/wnet/amanpour-and-company/video/is-trump-laying-the-groundwork-for-a-coup-in-2024/

47. For a clear articulation of why tolerance alone is not sufficient for the healing the country needs, see Maureen Walker's *When Getting Along Is Not Enough: Reconstructing Race in Our Lives and Relationships.* Teachers College Press, 2020.

48. See the Southern Poverty Law Center's database for more on the individuals and groups who have publicly supported Trump's messages: https://www.splcenter.org/resources?keyword=Trump. Again, the use of "Christian" to refer to these groups is misleading, as is the use of "Muslim" to refer to individuals or groups who claim to kill in the name of Islam. In both cases, Christian and Muslim, these groups bastardize the religion they reference—whether in ignorance of the religion or in an intentional attempt to legitimize their bigotry/hatred/violence.

49. Pollard, *The Lost Cause Regained,* Kindle edition (Location 2098-2105). See Chapter Nine, note 4.

50. See Chapter Eight, note 31 for gunshot/suicide sources.

51. "axis of evil" was used by President George W. Bush in his January 29, 2002 State of the Union address to refer to Iran, Iraq, and North Korea: http://georgewbush-whitehouse.archives.gov/news/releases/2002/01/print/20020129-11.html; "evil empire" was used by President Ronald Reagan to refer to the Soviet Union: http://voicesofdemocracy.umd.edu/reagan-evil-empire-speech-text/. He later recanted his use of the phrase.
President George W. Bush repeated several iterations of "you're either with us, or you're with the enemy": https://www.youtube.com/watch?v=-23kmhc3P8U The fallacy of his simplistic *either-or, us vs. them,* and *no in-between* stance played itself out in real time as many nations who "were with us" and joined the alliance to find those responsible for the September

11 attacks, were neither "with us" nor "with the enemy" when the United States chose to attack Iraq in March 2003.

52. From Dr. Martin Luther King, Jr., on April 4, 1967 at New York City's Riverside Church: This site now requires registration for access: https://kinginstitute.stanford.edu/king-papers/documents/beyond-vietnam. See Chapter Eight, 238-39, and note 36.

53. Aleksandr Solzhenitsyn. *The Gulag Archipelago.* Accessed via https://www.goodreads.com/quotes/13750-if-only-it-were-all-so-simple-if-only-there

54. M. Scott Peck, *The Road Less Traveled and Beyond: Spiritual Growth in an Age of Anxiety,* (Simon & Schuster, 1997), 74.

55. President Lincoln's final paragraph reads: "I am loath to close. We are not enemies, but friends. We must not be enemies. Though passion may have strained it must not break our bonds of affection. The mystic chords of memory, stretching from every battlefield and patriot grave to every living heart and hearthstone all over this broad land, will yet swell the chorus of the Union, when again touched, as surely they will be, by the better angels of our nature."

56. Mike Allen, "Scoop: Esper says Trump wanted to shoot protesters," *Axios AM,* May 2, 2022, https://www.axios.com/mark-esper-book-trump-protesters-24e93272-2af5-423d-be3b-164daab7b43d.html; Allen cites Mark Esper's book, *A Sacred Oath* (William Morrow, 2022); and Zachary Cohen, "Top US general rejected Trump suggestions military should 'crack skulls' during protests last year, new book claims," *CNN,* June 24, 2021, https://www.cnn.com/2021/06/24/politics/bender-book-trump-milley-protests/index.html; Cohen cites Michael Bender's book, *Frankly, We Did Win This Election* (Twelve-Grand Central, 2021). Both accessed May 2, 2022.

57. Rebecca Tan, Samantha Schmidt, Derek Hawkins, et. al., "Before Trump vows to end 'lawlessness,' federal officers confront protestors outside White House," *Washington Post,* June 2, 2020, https://www.washingtonpost.com/local/washington-dc-protest-white-house-george-floyd/2020/06/01/6b193d1c-a3c9-11ea-bb20-ebf0921f3bbd_story.html Accessed June 3, 2020.

58. John Lewis, and Michael D'Orso, *Walking with the Wind,* (Simon & Schuster, 1998), 337.

59. Ibid., 340.

CHAPTER ELEVEN – So, Now What?

1. Inspired by Carse, *Finite and Infinite Games,* 6-7.
2. To further engage (or to try to disprove) that everything is a story, see David Loy's *The World Is Made of Stories,* (Somerville, MA: Wisdom Publications, 2010).
3. Mary Oliver, "The Summer Day," *New and Selected Poems,* (Beacon, 1992), 94. Bill Plotkin, *Nature and the Human Soul: Cultivating Wholeness and Community in a Fragmented World,* (New World Library, 2008), 316. Howard Thurman attribution: https://quoteinvestigator.com/2021/07/09/come-alive/. Frederick Buechner, *Wishful Thinking: A Seeker's ABC,* (HarperOne, 1993), 118-19. Harvey Swift Deer, in Plotkin, *Nature...,* 258. William Blake, *The Complete Poetry & Prose of William Blake,* David V. Erdman, ed., (U of California P, 1981), 724.
4. Plotkin, *Nature and the Human Soul,* 258.
5. David Whyte, "All the True Vows," *The House of Belonging,* (Many Rivers, 1997), 24.
6. Plotkin, "ultimate place" in *Nature and the Human Soul,* 35-38; "unique ecological niche" in *The Journey of Soul Initiation: A Field Guide for Visionaries, Evolutionaries, and Revolutionaries,* (New World Library, 2021), 6-17. A 52-minute interview with Bill is available here (there are more available): https://www.youtube.com/watch?v=uOTaKXHMabM
7. Plotkin, *The Journey of Soul Initiation,* 18.
8. This paragraph is meant to be descriptive, not instructive. My encounter with self-inquiry began with the writings of David Frawley and Ken Wilber, which led me to Ramana Maharshi's work. Here's a link to Frawley's writing from 1998: https://www.vedanta.gr/wp-content/uploads/2012/03/Frawley_SelfInquiry_ENA5.pdf. Online references to self-inquiry are abundant and unequal. Inquirer beware.
9. Ram Dass, "The Art Form of Dying," *Conscious Aging: On the Nature of Change and Facing Death,* CD, (Sounds True, 1992), Disc 2, 2:50-6:25.
10. See Jonathan Rauch's *The Constitution of Knowledge: A Defense of Truth* (Brookings Institution, 2021) for an expansive and passionate exploration of his book's title and the "community of truth."

11. Mary Catherine Bateson, "Composing a Life," *Sacred Stories: A Celebration of the Power of Stories to Transform and Heal.* Eds. Charles & Anne Simpkinson, (HarperSanFrancisco, 1993), 42-43.

12. M.S. Handler, "Malcolm Rejects Racist Doctrine," *New York Times,* October 4, 1964, https://www.nytimes.com/1964/10/04/archives/malcolm-rejects-racist-doctrine-also-denounces-elijah-as-a.html; Alex Haley, *The Autobiography of Malcolm X: As Told to Alex Haley,* (New York: Ballantine, 1992).

13. Aaron Antonovsky, "Studying Health vs. Studying Disease," Lecture at the Congress for Clinical Psychology and Psychotherapy, (Berlin, February 19, 1990), "how some … move toward health" (4); "sense of coherence" (7-8), https://www.angelfire.com/ok/soc/aberlim.html.

14. Stephen Levine, *A Year to Live: How to Live This Year as if It Were Your Last,* (Bell Tower-Harmony, 1997), 19-20.

15. James Pennebaker has led the way in decades of research that back this up. See his *Expressive Writing: Words that Heal,* co-authored with John Evans, (2014); and *Opening Up: The Healing Power of Emotions* (1990), among others. See also John Fox's *Poetic Medicine: The Healing Art of Poem-Making,* (1997). There are many more resources available.

16. See Marra, *Enough with the Talking Points,* (2020), 79-82 for more on truly embodying another's story. For a deeper dive into telling another's story as if it were our own, see the work of *Narrative 4,* which uses "story exchange" to help young (and old) people develop empathy. (Some meeting "icebreaker" exercises skim the surface of this experience: two strangers briefly share who they are and then introduce each other to a group—speaking in first-person, as if they *are* the person they're introducing. Narrative 4 goes deeper): https://narrative4.com/.

17. John Tarrant, *Bring Me the Rhinoceros,* (Shambhala, 2008/2004), 113.

18. Neal Postman, "Staying Sane in a Technological Society: Six Questions in Search of an Answer," *Lapis,* (New York Open Center, Issue 7, 1998), 53-57. Regarding the SST example, the Concorde was a joint venture of Great Britain and France. The U.S. government ceased its funding of Boeing's SST project in 1971 after four years and a billion dollars.

19. "team of rivals" is from Doris Kearns Goodwin's 2005 book on Lincoln; "I alone can fix it" is from Trump's speech at the 2016

Republican convention (later a 2021 book by Carol Leonnig and Philip Rucker). See also the David Souter quote that precedes the table of contents in this volume.

20. For more detailed 3-2-1 Shadow instructions and examples, see Ken Wilber, Terry Patten, et. al., *Integral Life Practice,* (Integral-Shambhala, 2008), 41-66.

21. See notes 2, 3 & 6 in Chapter Two, especially Plotkin's *Wild Mind,* (2013), 207-34 and *Soulcraft,* (2003), 267-80; and Zweig and Abrams, eds. *Meeting the Shadow* (1991).

22. For a practical, fun, and concise introduction to engaging Voice Dialogue on your own, see Bridgit Dengel Gaspard's *The Final 8th,* (New World Library, 2020). https://www.bridgit-dengel-gaspard.com/. See also Voice Dialogue founders, Hal and Sidra Stone's *Embracing Ourselves: The Voice Dialogue Manual,* (Nataraj-New World Library, 1989). https://www.voicedialogueinternational.com/articles/Voice_Dialogue.pdf provides an introduction from the founders.

23. Ta-Nehisi Coates, *Between the World and Me,* (One World-Random House, 2015), 62.

24. See Marra, *And Now, Still: Grave & Goofy Poems,* (From the Heart Press, 2016) for my exploration of these three deaths, among other grave and goofy considerations.

25. See Marra, *Killing America*, (From the Heart Press, 2018) and Appendix II in this volume for my exploration of these and other violent deaths in the U. S.

26. Joan Halifax, *Being with Dying. Cultivating Compassion and Fearlessness in the Presence of Death* (Shambhala, 2008), 55.

27. Ibid., 55-60.

28. Jeffrey M. Jones, "How Many Americans Have a Will?" *Gallup,* June 23, 2021, https://news.gallup.com/poll/351500/how-many-americans-have-will.aspx Accessed December 3, 2021.

29. Sherwin B. Nuland, *How We Die,* (Knopf, 1993), "all too frequently…," xvii; "The greatest dignity…," 242; "insofar as circumstances…," xvii.

30. These titles scratch the surface of what's available and are among those that continue to serve me and to which I pay sustained attention.

31. This sentence transposes one of the questions posed in Wayne Muller's, *How, Then, Shall We Live? Four Simple Questions That Reveal the Beauty and Meaning of Our Lives,* (Bantam, 1996).

32. M. Scott Peck, *The Road Less Traveled: A New Psychology of Love, Traditional Values, and Spiritual Growth,* (Touchstone-Simon & Schuster, 1978), 17-18.

33. Ibid. Peck develops each of these in detail, 16-78.

34. Resmaa Menakem, *My Grandmother's Hands: Racialized Trauma and the Pathway to Mending Our Hearts and Bodies,* (Central Recovery Press, 2017), 19-20. Menakem credits Dr. David Schnarch and Dr. Steven Hayer with popularizing the terms, *clean pain* and *dirty pain.*

35. Palmer, *The Courage to Teach*, 104. See Chapter One, 17-18, and note 14.

36. Again, "joyful acceptance..." is from Br. David Steindl-Rast; "the will to extend..." is from M. Scott Peck; *absence of fear* is based on Marianne Williamson's *A Return to Love* and the Foundation for Inner Peace's *A Course in Miracles.* See Chapter One, 18, and note 15. We'll say more about love in Chapter Twelve.

37. Fear is an experience that protects us in many cases of actual, imminent threat. Evolution over millennia has conditioned our bodies and minds to respond to real danger (flee, fight, freeze).

38. For a brief overview of language associated with trauma, see "Behind the Term: Trauma," *SAMHSA's National Registry of Evidence-based Programs and Practices,* (2016), https://calswec.berkeley.edu/sites/default/files/4-3_behind_the_term_trauma.pdf.

39. Bessel van der Kolk, *The Body Keeps the Score,* (Penguin, 2014), 1.

40. Elissa Melaragno, "Trauma in the Body: An Interview with Dr. Bessel van der Kolk," *Anchor Magazine,* No. 4, Fall/Winter 2015, https://www.dropbox.com/s/h9m8efox1k4jcbu/Anchor_Issue%2004_Online.pdf?dl=0. Archived, and syndicated to: *Daily Good,* April 21, 2018, http://m.dailygood.org/story/1901/trauma-in-the-body-an-interview-with-dr-bessel-van-der-kolk-elissa-melaragno/ Accessed December 9, 2021.

41. For an overview of what can go wrong at different levels of development, see Ken Wilber, *The Religion of Tomorrow,* (Shambhala, 2017), 186-96, 273-351. These pages focus on eight developmental levels (which are the more detailed foundations of the *me, us, all-of-us,* and *all-that-is* shorthand used in this book).

42. "master trauma specialist," and "to make sure.... never recover" in Elissa Melaragno, "Trauma in the Body..." (2015), 68; "participants to pendulate...happened to them," in Bessel van der Kolk, *The Body Keeps the Score,* (2014), 335. (See notes 40 and 39).

43. Thomas Hübl, *Healing Collective Trauma: A Process for Integrating Our Intergenerational and Cultural Wounds,* (Sounds True, 2020), 45. https://thomashuebl.com/

44. Peter Levine, *In an Unspoken Voice: How the Body Releases Trauma and Restores Goodness,* (North Atlantic Books, 2010), 15-18.

45. Individual trauma can result from a one-time event or from exposure to repeated events (complex trauma) like ongoing childhood abuse or neglect. Collective trauma impacts groups of people (war, slavery, genocide, natural disasters, etc.). Intergenerational (aka historical or transgenerational) trauma is carried forward through generations, biologically, experientially, and psychologically. These are not mutually exclusive categories. I am indebted to the work of Bessel van der Kolk, Peter Levine, Eduardo Duran, Judith Herman, Resmaa Menakem, Gabor Maté and Thomas Hübl for this chapter's overview of trauma.

46. The concepts in this paragraph are based on Ken Wilber's quadrant model. See Chapter One, 16-17, and note 11.

47. M. Scott Peck, *The Different Drum: Community-Making and Peace,* (Touchstone-Simon & Schuster, 1987), 86-135. FCE no longer seems operational, but its site remains: https://www.fce-community.org/stages_of_cb. Dr. Peck passed in 2005.

48. Ibid., 95-98. For more on barriers to communication, see also, Marra, *Enough with the Talking Points,* (2020).

49. Ibid., 102-03.

50. Otto Scharmer, *Theory U: The Social Technology of Presencing,* (Berrett-Koehler, 2009), 163. Excerpts and an executive summary of the book is available at: https://ottoscharmer.com/publications

51. Ibid., 38-39.

52. Ibid., 20.

53. Hübl, *Healing Collective Trauma,* 119-42.

54. After his death in 2005, M. Scott Peck's work with community-making is primarily available through his book, *The Different Drum,* (1987). For information on Otto Scharmer's offerings, visit https://www.presencing.org/. For information on Thomas Hübl's offerings, visit: https://thomashuebl.com/.

55. Nicholas Christakis, *Blueprint,* 13-14. See also Chapter Nine, 254-55 and note 16.

56. Brian Hare and Vanessa Woods, *Survival of the Friendliest,* (Random House, 2021), xxv-xxvi, 109-21, 180-81.

57. Ibid., xvi-xvii: "...terrible survival strategy" is the authors' own language; "...for a lifetime of stress" is attributed to R. M. Saplosky, "The Influence of Social Hierarchy on Primate Health," *Science* 308, 648-52 (2005); "nasty, brutish and short" is from Thomas Hobbes, *Leviathon* (London: A & C Black, 2006).

58. Wilber, *The Religion of Tomorrow,* 709, note 12.

59. Robert Kegan, and Lisa Laskow Lahey, *Immunity to Change,* (Harvard Business Press, 2009). The process is "nuanced," detailed, and specific and unfolds most accurately and effectively through numerous conversations and drafts (i.e. rushing through it is not a skillful approach). Their chapter 9, "Diagnosing Your Own Immunity to Change" is available here: https://mindsatwork.com/wp-content/uploads/2015/02/Chapter9.pdf

60. Ibid., 250.

61. Trebbe Johnson, *Radical Joy for Hard Times: Finding Meaning and Making Beauty in Earth's Broken Places,* (North Atlantic, 2018), 83-85, 90. Find out more: https://radicaljoy.org/. Johnson's source for Sugawara's story is Paula Hancocks, "Defiant Japanese boat captain rode out tsunami," *CNN,* April 3, 2011, http://edition.cnn.com/2011/WORLD/asiapcf/04/03/japan.tsunami.captain/index.html

62. Pema Chödrön, *Start Where You Are: A Guide to Compassionate Living,* (Shambhala, 2001/1994), 33.

63. Ibid., 34.

CHAPTER TWELVE – Expanding & Integrating the View from Here

1. Inspired by Carse, *Finite and Infinite Games,* 62. This question plays with the question at the beginning of Chapter One.

2. Aunt Ann and Uncle Al ushered my cousins Mary Ann, Christine, Paul, Rita, and Tom into the world. Christine is the dedicatee of this book. (A deep bow to all the Lunas and Washingtons).

3. Paul, Bruce, and I remain friends to this day. For a glimpse into how their dad navigated our friendship, check out Paul's 2016 "Heat" (aka "Mr. Wizard") story at the Houston Moth StorySLAM: https://www.youtube.com/watch?v=wG5CHzqJ-xs

4. Ta-Nehisi Coates, *Between the World and Me,* (One World, 2015), 28, 34.

5. In the PBS program, *Finding Your Roots,* Season 4, episode 4, "The Vanguard" (2017), Henry Louis Gates, Jr. presented records that

trace Ta-Nehisi Coates's lineage back through a fourth great-grandparent; thus, at least seven generations.

6. Coates, *Between the World and Me*, 34. My son is a first-generation Dominican-American (*technically,* my stepson), who is now thirty-three years old.

7. I'm projecting this agreement here onto Coates, whom I've never met. I "know" him only through his writing and several recorded interviews I've encountered.

8. The poem appears, with Br. Jerome's comment intact, on the final page of *And Now, Still* (From the Heart Press, 2016). His comment invited me to believe I might be a "writer" or even a "poet." The jury is still out.

9. Kris Kristofferson, "Loving Her Was Easier (Than Anything I'll Ever Do Again)," *The Silver Tongued Devil and I,* LP, (Monument, 1971). Here's a 1972 performance:
https://www.youtube.com/watch?v=HCgnbRWVvU8

10. The details of my getting cut and becoming a coach are summarized in Chapter One of *The Quality of Effort* (From the Heart Press, 2013/1991).

11. Thanks to everyone involved with the Connecticut HOT Schools program, the national Poetry Out Loud program, the Mattatuck Museum's work with poetry in the schools, the Wednesday Night Poetry Series in Newtown, Goddard College's Transformative Language Arts Network and Power of Words Conference, the National Association for Poetry Therapy, and the many schools and districts that have welcomed me.

12. I explore these dyings and deaths in some detail in *And Now, Still: Grave & Goofy Poems,* (2016). The hip replacements were due to damage I did with weights while attempting to increase my standing vertical leap in order to dunk a basketball in high school and college (I increased it from 25" to 32"—enough to touch the rim, but not to dunk. Oops.). I miss the tops of my femurs.

13. See Chapter Eleven, 316.

14. Audre Lorde, "The Transformation of Silence into Language and Action," *The Cancer Journals,* (Penguin, 2020/1980), 13, and back cover; and *Sister Outsider,* (Crossing/Ten-Speed, 1984), 41. The essay appears in both volumes.

15. Tony Hoagland, "The Cure for Racism Is Cancer," *The Sun,* Issue 513, September 2018, 13-15. Available online:
https://www.thesunmagazine.org/issues/513/the-cure-for-racism-is-cancer

16. Thich Nhat Hanh, *Teachings on Love.* (Parallax, 1998), 21.

17. bell hooks, *Outlaw Culture: Resisting Representations,* (Routledge Classics, 2006/Routledge 1994), 243-44. In making her case for love, hooks also cites Peck's "the will to extend one's self..." view and King's "I have decided to love," 247.

18. Eknath Easwaran, trans., *The Dhammapada,* (Nilgiri Press, 1985), 78.

19. John 13:34, *NIV Study Bible,* (Zondervan, 1973, 1995).

20. John Lewis, with Brenda Jones, *Across That Bridge: A Vision for Change and the Future of America,* (Hachette, 2012), 183.

21. Jason Reynolds, "Imagination and Fortitude," *On Being with Krista Tippett,* June 25, 2020, https://onbeing.org/programs/jason-reynolds-imagination-and-fortitude/

22. Solzhenitsyn, see Chapter Ten, 288, and note 53.

23. Thich Nhat Hanh, "Please Call Me by My True Names," *Call Me by My True Names: The Collected Poems of Thich Nhat Hanh,* (Parallax, 2001); the poem is available online at: https://plumvillage.org/articles/please-call-me-by-my-true-names-song-poem/; see also Chapter Two, note 17.

24. Isabel Wilkerson, *Caste: The Origins of Our Discontents,* (Random House, 2020), 371-75.

25. *Go behind...just like you:* Ram Dass, Chapter Eleven, 300. *You remind me...than not:* Jason Reynolds, this chapter, 349-50.

26. Jack Kornfield, *After the Ecstasy, the Laundry: How the Heart Grows Wise on the Spiritual Path,* (Bantam, 2000), ix-xi.

27. Eduardo Duran, in conversation with Laura Calderón de la Barca, "An Indigenous Lens on Psychotherapy as a Soul Healing," *Collective Trauma Summit 2021 / Collective Healing in Action,* (Inner Science, 2021), 9-10. For more information and an excerpt from a case study regarding alcohol, see Eduardo Duran's *Healing the Soul Wound,* 61-79.

APPENDIX I

1. President Dwight Eisenhower, "The Chance for Peace," April 16, 1953. See also, Chapter 6, note 6. Audio: https://www.eisenhowerlibrary.gov/eisenhowers/speeches. Text: https://www.americanrhetoric.com/speeches/dwighteisenhowercrossofiron.htm. Accessed June 5, 2021.

2. Robert S. McNamara, *In Retrospect: The Tragedy and Lessons of Vietnam,* (Vintage, 1996), 321-23.

3. *The Fog of War,* Errol Morris, director, (Sony, 2003). As captured in this volume, the eleven lessons are from my notes while viewing the documentary. They appear in a variety of online sources as well.

4. John F. Sopko, et. al., *What We Need to Learn: Lessons from Twenty Years of Afghanistan Reconstruction,* (Special Inspector General for Afghanistan Reconstruction, August 2021) vii-xi, https://www.sigar.mil/pdf/lessonslearned/SIGAR-21-46-LL.pdf

APPENDIX II

1. Poems are from Reggie Marra, *Killing America: Our United States of Ignorance, Fear, Bigotry, Violence, and Greed,* (From the Heart, 2018): "Found Poem: March 16, 2018," 2; "Going Home," 23; "Supposed to Be Safe," 11; "Sunny December New England Morning," 8; "Ambush," 13; "1941," 15; "Early Autumn Southwest Evening," 19; "This Day Our Daily Dead," 102; letter to the president, (final unnumbered page in the book).

APPENDIX III

1. Reggie Marra, *Enough with the...Talking Points: Doing More Good than Harm in Conversation,* (From the Heart, 2020). The full conversation review is available online at: https://reggiemarra.com/2020/09/12/an-example-of-a-conversation-that-does-more-harm-than-good/.

BIBLIOGRAPHY

The bibliography includes several titles that are relevant to but not cited in the text.

Anderson, Doug. *Horse Medicine.* New York: Barrow Street Press, 2015.

—. *Keep Your Head Down: Vietnam, the Sixties, and a Journey of Self-Discovery.* New York: Norton, 2009.

—. *The Moon Reflected Fire.* Cambridge, MA: Alice James, 1994.

Bacevich, Andrew. *After the Apocalypse: America's Role in a World Transformed.* New York: Metropolitan/Henry Holt, 2021.

—. *America's War for the Greater Middle East: A Military History.* New York: Random House, 2017.

—. *The Limits of Power: The End of American Exceptionalism.* New York: Metropolitan/Henry Holt, 2008.

—. *Washington Rules: America's Path to Permanent War.* New York: Metropolitan/Henry Holt, 2010.

Bass, S. Jonathan. *He Calls Me by Lightning: The Life of Caliph Washington and the Forgotten Saga of Jim Crow, Southern Justice, and the Death Penalty.* New York: Liveright/Norton, 2017.

Bateson, Mary Catherine. "Composing a Life." *Sacred Stories: A Celebration of the Power of Stories to Transform and Heal.* Eds. Charles & Anne Simpkinson. San Francisco: HarperSanFrancisco, 1993. 39-52.

Benét's Reader's Encyclopedia. 3rd edition. New York: Harper & Row, 1987.

Bernhard, Toni. *How to Be Sick: A Buddhist-Inspired Guide for the Chronically Ill and Their Caregivers.* Somerville, MA: Wisdom, 2010.

Blackman, Sushila, ed. *Graceful Exits: How Great Beings Die – Death Stories of Tibetan, Hindu, & Zen Masters.* New York: Weatherhill, 1997.

Blake, William. *The Complete Poetry & Prose of William Blake.* David V. Erdman, ed. Berkeley: U of California P, 1981.

Bly, Robert. *A Little Book on the Human Shadow.* New York: Harper & Row, 1988.

Brown, Dee. *Bury My Heart at Wounded Knee: An Indian History of the American West.* New York: Owl/Holt, 1970.

Buechner, Frederick. *Wishful Thinking: A Seeker's ABC.* New York: HarperOne, 1993.

Burns, Ken, and Lynn Novick. *The Vietnam War: A Film by Ken Burns and Lynn Novick.* PBS, 2017. Episodes 1-10 accessed April-May 2021 via Amazon Prime.

Christakis, Nicholas A. *Blueprint: The Evolutionary Origins of a Good Society.* New York: Little, Brown, Spark, 2019.

Clarke, Richard A. *Against All Enemies: Inside America's War on Terror.* New York: Free Press/Simon & Schuster, 2004.

Chödrön, Pema. *The Places That Scare You: A Guide to Fearlessness in Difficult Times.* Boston: Shambhala, 2002.

—. *Start Where You Are: A Guide to Compassionate Living.* Boston: Shambhala, 2001/1994.

Coates, Ta-Nehisi. *Between the World and Me.* New York: One World-Random House, 2015.

Dass, Ram. *Conscious Aging: On the Nature of Change and Facing Death.* CD. Boulder: Sounds True, 1992.

de las Casas, Bartolemé. *A Short Account of the Destruction of the Indies.* Nigel Griffin, ed. and trans. New York: Penguin, 1992.

Deloria, Vine, Jr. *Custer Died for Your Sins.* Norman, OK: University of Oklahoma Press, 1988 / New York: Macmillan, 1969.

Duran, Eduardo. *Healing the Soul Wound: Trauma-Informed Counseling for Indigenous Communities.* 2nd Edition. New York: Teachers College Press, 2019.

—. "Transgenerational Trauma, Soul Wounding and Effects on Families and Communities: The Impact of History on Present Day Chronic Illnesses." *Advances in Indian Health Conference.* Rockville, MD: Indian Health Service: Division of Diabetes Treatment and Prevention, 2010. See page 404, note 65 for a link to this report.

Duran, Eduardo, in conversation with Laura Calderón de la Barca. "An Indigenous Lens on Psychotherapy as a Soul Healing." *Collective Trauma Summit 2021 / Collective Healing in Action.* Video and transcript. Novato, CA: Inner Science, 2021.

Easwaran, Eknath, trans., *The Dhammapada.* Tomales, CA: Nilgiri Press, 1985.

Emerson, Ralph Waldo. "The American Scholar." *The American Tradition in Literature.* 4th edition. Eds. Sculley Bradley, Richard Croom Beatty, et. al. New York: Grosset & Dunlap, 1974.

Equal Justice Initiative. *Lynching in America: Confronting the Legacy of Racial Terror.* 3rd Edition. Montgomery, AL: Equal Justice Initiative, 2017.

—. *Lynching in America: Targeting Black Veterans.* Online PDF. Montgomery, AL: Equal Justice Initiative, 2017. Accessed April 1, 2021.

—. *Reconstruction in America: Racial Violence after the Civil War, 1865-1876.* Montgomery, AL: Equal Justice Initiative, 2020.

—. *Segregation in America.* Montgomery, AL: Equal Justice Initiative, 2018.

Faludi, Susan. *Backlash: The Undeclared War Against American Women.* New York: Crown, 1991.

—. *Stiffed: The Betrayal of the American Man.* New York: William Morrow, 1999.

The Fog of War. Errol Morris, Director. Sony Picture Classics, 2003.

Forché, Carolyn, ed. *Against Forgetting: Twentieth-Century Poetry of Witness.* New York: W.W. Norton, 1993.

Forché, Carolyn, and Duncan Wu, eds. *Poetry of Witness: The Tradition in English, 1500-2001.* New York: W.W. Norton, 2014.

Foundation for Inner Peace. *A Course in Miracles.* 2nd ed. Glen Ellen CA: Foundation for Inner Peace, 1976.

Fowler. *Stages of Faith: The Psychology of Human Development and the Quest for Meaning.* New York: HarperSanFrancisco, 1981.

Gaspard, Bridgit Dengel. *The Final 8th: Enlist Your Inner Selves to Accomplish Your Goals.* Novato, CA: New World Library, 2020.

Gawande, Atul. *Being Mortal: Medicine and What Matters in the End.* New York: Metropolitan/Henry Holt, 2014.

Gillan, Maria Mazziotti, and Jennifer Gillan, eds. *Unsettling America: An Anthology of Contemporary Multicultural Poetry.* New York: Penguin, 1994.

Gilligan, Carol. *In a Different Voice: Psychological Theory and Women's Development.* Cambridge, MA: Harvard University Press, 1993 (1982).

Halifax, Joan. *Being with Dying. Cultivating Compassion and Fearlessness in the Presence of Death.* Boston: Shambhala, 2008. I first came across this work in 1997 on cassette, now available via digital download at: https://www.soundstrue.com/products/being-with-dying.

Hari, Johann. *Lost Connections: Uncovering the Real Causes of Depression—and the Unexpected Solutions.* New York: Bloomsbury, 2018.

Heidler, David S. and Heidler, Jeanne T. "Manifest Destiny." *Encyclopedia Britannica*, 18 Nov. 2020, https://www.britannica.com/event/Manifest-Destiny. Accessed February 9, 2021.

Hentoff, Nat. *Free Speech for Me—But Not for Thee: How the American Left and Right Relentlessly Censor Each Other.* New York: HarperCollins, 1992.

Hill, Gareth, S. *Masculine and Feminine: The Natural Flow of Opposites in the Psyche.* Boston: Shambhala, 1992.

Hoagland, Tony. "The Cure for Racism Is Cancer." *The Sun.* Issue 513, September 2018, 13-15.

Hoagland, Tony, with Kay Cosgrove. *The Art of Voice.* New York: W.W. Norton, 2019.

Hoffman, Yoel, ed. *Japanese Death Poems: Written by Zen Monks and Haiku Poets on the Verge of Death.* Rutland, VT: Tuttle, 1996.

hooks, bell. *Outlaw Culture: Resisting Representations.* New York: Routledge Classics, 2006/Routledge, 1994.

Housden, Roger, ed. *Risking Everything: 110 Poems of Love and Revelation.* New York: Harmony, 2003.

Hübl, Thomas. *Healing Collective Trauma: A Process for Integrating Our Intergenerational Cultural Wounds.* Boulder, CO: Sounds True, 2020.

Johnson, Robert A. *Owning Your Own Shadow: Understanding the Dark Side of Your Psyche.* New York: HarperOne, 1991.

Johnson, Trebbe. *Radical Joy for Hard Times: Finding Meaning and Making Beauty in Earth's Broken Places.* Berkeley: North Atlantic, 2018.

Joiner, Bill, and Stephen Josephs. *Leadership Agility: Five Levels of Mastery for Anticipating and Initiating Change.* San Francisco: Wiley/Jossey-Bass, 2007.

Kakutani, Michiko, *The Death of Truth: Notes on Falsehood in the Age of Trump.* New York: Tim Duggan/Crown, 2018.

Kegan, Robert. *In Over Our Heads: The Mental Demands of Modern Life.* Cambridge: Harvard University Press, 1994.

Kegan, Robert, and Lisa Laskow Lahey. *How the Way We Talk Can Change the Way We Work: Seven Languages for Transformation.* San Francisco: Jossey-Bass, 2001.

—. *Immunity to Change: How to Overcome It and Unlock the Potential in Yourself and Your Organization.* Boston: Harvard Business Press, 2009.

Kendi, Ibram X. *How to Be an Antiracist.* New York: One World/ Random House, 2019.

—. *Stamped from the Beginning: The Definitive History of Racist Ideas in America.* New York: Bold Type/Hachette, 2016.

Kessler, Glenn, Salvador Rizzo, and Meg Kelly. *Donald Trump and His Assault on Truth: The President's Falsehoods, Misleading Claims and Flat-Out Lies.* New York: Scribner, 2020.

Klein, Ezra. *Why We're Polarized.* New York: Avid Reader-Simon & Schuster, 2020.

Kornfield, Jack. *After the Ecstasy, the Laundry: How the Heart Grows Wise on the Spiritual Path.* New York: Bantam, 2000.

Laloux, Frederic. *Reinventing Organizations: A Guide to Creating Organizations Inspired by the Next Stage of Human Consciousness.* Brussels, Belgium: Nelson Parker, 2014.

Lebron, Christopher J. "The Germantown Petition Against Slavery." *Four Hundred Souls: A Community History of African America, 1619-2019.* Eds. Ibram X. Kendi and Keisha N. Blain. New York: One World/ Random House. 62-64.

Leonnig, Carol, and Philip Rucker. *I Alone Can Fix It: Donald J. Trump's Catastrophic Final Year.* New York: Penguin, 2021.

Levine, Peter, A. *In an Unspoken Voice: How the Body Releases Trauma and Restores Goodness.* Berkeley: North Atlantic Books, 2010.

—. *Trauma and Memory: Brain and Body in a Search for the Living Past – a Practical Guide for Understanding and Working with Traumatic Memory.* Berkeley: North Atlantic Books, 2015.

Levine, Stephen. *A Year to Live: How to Live This Year as if It Were Your Last.* New York: Bell Tower/Harmony, 1997.

Lewis, John, with Brenda Jones. *Across That Bridge: A Vision for Change and the Future of America.* New York: Hachette, 2012.

Lewis, John, with Michael D'Orso. *Walking with the Wind: A Memoir of the Movement.* New York: Simon & Schuster, 1998.

Lorde, Audre. *The Cancer Journals.* New York: Penguin, 2020 (1980).

—. *Sister Outsider.* Berkeley, CA: Crossing/Ten Speed, 1984.

Lukianoff, Greg, and Jonathan Haidt. *The Coddling of the American Mind: How Good Intentions and Bad Ideas Are Setting Up a Generation for Failure.* New York: Penguin, 2018.

Macfarlane, Robert. *Underland: A Deep Time Journey.* New York: Norton, 2019.

Marra, Reggie. *Enough with the… Talking Points: Doing More Good than Harm in Conversation.* Litchfield, CT: From the Heart Press, 2020.

—. *Killing America: Our United States of Ignorance, Fear, Bigotry, Violence & Greed.* Litchfield, CT: From the Heart Press, 2018.

—. *The Quality of Effort: Integrity in Sport and Life for Student-Athletes, Parents, and Coaches.* Revised edition. Naugatuck, CT: From the Heart Press, 2013 (1991).

Maté, Gabor. *In the Realm of Hungry Ghosts: Close Encounters with Addiction.* Berkeley: North Atlantic Books, 2008.

—. *When the Body Says No: Exploring the Stress-Disease Connection.* Hoboken, New Jersey: John Wiley & Sons, 2003.

Matthiessen, Peter. *In the Spirit of Crazy Horse.* New York: Viking/ Penguin, 1991 (1980).

McChrystal, Stanley, and Tantum Collins, et al. *Team of Teams: New Rules of Engagement for a Complex World.* New York: Portfolio/ Penguin, 2015.

McNamara, Robert S., with Brian VanDeMark. *In Retrospect: The Tragedy and Lessons of Vietnam.* New York: Vintage, 1996.

McWhorter, John. *Woke Racism: How a New Religion Has Betrayed Black America.* New York: Portfolio/Penguin, 2021.

Meacham, Jon. *His Truth Is Marching On: John Lewis and the Power of Hope.* New York: Random House, 2020.

—. *The Soul of America: The Battle for Our Better Angels.* New York: Random House, 2019.

Menakem, Resmaa. *My Grandmother's Hands: Racialized Trauma and the Pathway to Mending Our Hearts and Bodies.* Las Vegas: Central Recovery Press, 2017.

Merton, Thomas. "The Inner Experience." *Thomas Merton: Spiritual Master.* Lawrence Cunningham, ed. Mahwah, NJ: Paulist, 1992.

Miller, Jean Baker. *Toward a New Psychology of Women.* Boston: Beacon, 1986 (1976).

Moore, Lt. General Harold G. (Ret.), and Joseph L. Galloway. *We Were Soldiers Once…and Young: Ia Drang—the Battle That Changed the War in Vietnam.* New York: Ballantine, 1992. Citations from 2004 mass market edition.

Muller, Wayne. *How, Then, Shall We Live? Four Simple Questions That Reveal the Beauty and Meaning of Our Lives.* New York: Bantam, 1996.

Nhat Hanh, Thich. *At Home in the World: Stories and Essential Teachings from a Monk's Life.* Berkeley, CA: Parallax, 2019.

—. *Call Me by My True Names.* Berkeley, CA: Parallax, 2005.

—. *Teachings on Love.* Berkeley, CA: Parallax, 1998.

NIV Study Bible. Kenneth Barker, ed. Grand Rapids, MI: Zondervan, 1995 (1973).

Nuland, Sherwin, B. *How We Die: Reflections on Life's Final Chapter.* New York: Knopf, 1993.

—. *The Wisdom of the Body.* New York: Knopf, 1997.

O'Brien, Tim. *The Things They Carried.* New York: Mariner/Houghton Mifflin Harcourt, 2009 (1990).

Oliver, Mary. *New and Selected Poems.* Boston: Beacon, 1992.

The Oxford Companion to English Literature. Margaret Drabble, ed. 5th edition. Oxford: Oxford University Press, 1985.

Palmer, Parker J. *The Courage to Teach: Exploring the Inner Landscape of a Teacher's Life.* San Francisco: Jossey-Bass, 1998.

Patterson, Kerry, Joseph Grenny, et. al. *Crucial Conversations: Tools for Talking When Stakes Are High,* (New York: McGraw-Hill, 2002).

Patten, Terry. *A New Republic of the Heart: An Ethos for Revolutionaries.* Berkeley, CA: North Atlantic Books, 2018.

Pauls, Elizabeth Prine. "Trail of Tears." Encyclopedia Britannica, 11 Nov. 2019. https://www.britannica.com/event/Trail-of-Tears. Accessed February 10, 2021.

Peck, M. Scott. *The Different Drum: Community-Making and Peace.* New York: Touchstone/Simon & Schuster, 1987.

—. *The Road Less Traveled.* New York: Touchstone/Simon & Schuster, 1978.

—. *The Road Less Traveled and Beyond: Spiritual Growth in an Age of Anxiety.* New York: Simon & Schuster, 1997.

Plotkin, Bill. *The Journey of Soul Initiation: A Field Guide for Visionaries, Evolutionaries, and Revolutionaries.* Novato, CA: New World Library, 2021.

—. *Nature and the Human Soul: Cultivating Wholeness and Community in a Fragmented World.* Novato, CA: New World Library, 2008.

—. *Soulcraft: Crossing into the Mysteries of Nature and Psyche.* Novato, CA: New World Library, 2003.

—. *Wild Mind: A Field Guide to the Human Psyche.* Novato, CA: New World Library, 2013.

Pollard, Edward A. *The Lost Cause Regained.* New York: G.W. Carleton & Co., 1868. Kindle edition. Miami: HardPress, 2017.

Rauch, Jonathan. *The Constitution of Knowledge: A Defense of Truth.* Washington, D.C.: Brookings Institution Press, 2021.

Ravitch, Diane, ed. *The American Reader: Words that Moved a Nation.* New York: Harper Perennial, 1991.

Saunt, Claudio. *Unworthy Republic: The Dispossession of Native Americans and the Road to Indian Territory.* New York: W.W. Norton, 2020.

Scharmer, Otto. *Theory U: The Social Technology of Presencing.* San Francisco: Berrett-Koehler, 2009.

Schell, Jonathan. *The Jonathan Schell Reader: On the United States at War, The Long Crisis of the American Republic, and the Fate of the Earth.* New York: Nation/Avalon, 2004.

Schwartz, Tony. *What Really Matters: Searching for Wisdom in America.* New York: Bantam, 1995.

Sheehan, Neil. *A Bright Shining Lie: John Paul Vann and America in Vietnam.* New York: Random House, 1988.

Sheehan, Neil, Hedrick Smith, E.W. Kenworthy, and Fox Butterfield. *The Pentagon Papers: The Secret History of the Vietnam War.* New York: Racehorse, 2017.

Shelley, Mary. *Frankenstein, Or, the Modern Prometheus.* New York: Signet/Penguin, 2013.

Simmons, Philip. *Learning to Fall: The Blessings of an Imperfect Life.* New York: Bantam, 2002.

Sogyal Rinpoche. *The Tibetan Book of Living and Dying.* Patrick Gaffney and Andrew Harvey, eds. New York: HarperSanFrancisco, 1993.

Sopko, John F., et. al. *What We Need to Learn: Lessons from Twenty Years of Afghanistan Reconstruction.* Arlington, VA: Special Inspector General for Afghanistan Reconstruction, August 2021. https://www.sigar.mil/pdf/lessonslearned/SIGAR-21-46-LL.pdf Accessed August 18, 2021.

Steindl-Rast, Brother David. *Gratefulness, the Heart of Prayer: An Approach to Life in Fullness.* New York/Ramsey, NJ: Paulist, 1984.

Stone, Hal, and Sidra L. Stone. *Embracing Our Selves: The Voice Dialogue Manual.* Novato, CA: Navaraj-New World Library, 1989.

Sutcliff, Rosemary. "Gawain and the Loathely Lady." *The Sword and the Circle.* New York: Puffin-Penguin, 1981. 224-42.

Tarrant, John. *Bring Me the Rhinoceros: and Other Zen Koans That Will Save Your Life.* Boston: Shambhala, 2008.

Torbert, Bill, and Associates. *Action Inquiry: The Secret of Timely and Transforming Leadership.* San Francisco: Berrett-Koehler, 2004.

Twenge, Jean. *iGen: Why Today's Super-Connected Kids Are Growing Up Less Rebellious, More Tolerant, Less Happy—and Completely Unprepared for Adulthood and What That Means for the Rest of Us.* New York: Atria, 2017.

Van der Kolk, Bessel. *The Body Keeps the Score: Brain, Mind and Body in the Healing of Trauma.* New York: Penguin, 2014.

Walker, Maureen. *When Getting Along Is Not Enough: Reconstructing Race in Our Lives and Relationships.* New York: Teachers College Press, 2020.

Ward, Larry. *America's Racial Karma: An Invitation to Heal.* Berkeley, CA: Parallax, 2020.

Whitlock, Craig. *The Afghanistan Papers: A Secret History of the War.* New York: Simon & Schuster, 2021.

Whyte, David. *The House of Belonging.* Langley, WA: Many Rivers, 1997.

Wilber, Ken. *Integral Spirituality: A Startling New Role for Religion in the Modern and Postmodern World.* Boston: Integral-Shambhala, 2006.

—. *The Religion of Tomorrow: A Vision for the Future of the Great Traditions.* Boulder: Shambhala, (2017).

Wilkerson, Isabel. *Caste: The Origins of Our Discontents.* New York: Random House, 2020.

—. "The Great Migration." *Four Hundred Souls: A Community History of African America, 1619-2019.* Ibram X. Kendi and Keisha N. Blain, eds. New York: One World/Random House, 2021. 278-82.

Williamson, Marianne. *A Return to Love: Reflections on the Principles of* A Course in Miracles. New York: HarperPaperbacks, 1993.

Wright, Evan. *Generation Kill: Devil Dogs, Captain America, and the New Face of American War.* New York: G. P. Putnam's Sons, 2004.

Zinn, Howard. *A People's History of the United States: 1492-Present.*
New York: Harper Perennial, 1999 (1980).

—. *Declarations of Independence: Cross-Examining American Ideology.*
New York: HarperPerennial, 1990.

—. "Just and Unjust War." *The Zinn Reader: Writings on Disobedience
and Democracy.* New York: Seven Stories Press, 1997.

Zweig, Connie, and Jeremiah Abrams, eds. *Meeting the Shadow: The
Hidden Power of the Dark Side of Human Nature.* New York:
Tarcher/Penguin, 1991.

About the Author

REGGIE MARRA is the author, most recently, of *Enough with the… Talking Points* (nonfiction, 2020), *Killing America* (poetry, 2018), and *And Now, Still* (poetry, 2016). His first work of nonfiction, *The Quality of Effort,* was published in 1991 and released in a second edition in 2013. Reggie is a cofounder, along with Kent Frazier, of Fully Human at Work—a 21st-Century Imperative. In addition to writing, he delivers his gifts to the world as a professional coach, a teaching poet, and a workshop facilitator. In the distant past Reggie spent twenty-one years as a classroom teacher, administrator, and basketball coach in secondary and higher education.

https://reggiemarra.com/
https://fullyhumanatwork.com/
https://healingamericasnarratives.com/